MOBILISING THE MASSES

POPULIST CONSERVATIVE MOVEMENTS
IN AUSTRALIA AND NEW ZEALAND
DURING THE GREAT DEPRESSION

MOBILISING THE MASSES

POPULIST CONSERVATIVE MOVEMENTS IN AUSTRALIA AND NEW ZEALAND DURING THE GREAT DEPRESSION

MATTHEW CUNNINGHAM

Australian
National
University

ANU PRESS

Australian
National
University

ANU PRESS

Published by ANU Press
The Australian National University
Canberra ACT 2600, Australia
Email: anupress@anu.edu.au

Available to download for free at press.anu.edu.au

ISBN (print): 9781760465100
ISBN (online): 9781760465117

WorldCat (print): 1306511323
WorldCat (online): 1306510403

DOI: 110.22459/MM.2022

Cover design and layout by ANU Press

This book is published under the aegis of the Social Sciences Editorial Committee of the ANU Press.

Contents

Abbreviations

ATL	Alexander Turnbull Library (Wellington)
AUL	Auckland University Library (Auckland)
BEU	British Empire Union
CLSA	Citizens' League of South Australia
NLA	National Library of Australia (Canberra)
NSW	New South Wales
NZL	New Zealand Legion
SLNSW	State Library of New South Wales (Sydney)
SLSA	State Library of South Australia (Adelaide)
SLWA	State Library of Western Australia (Perth)

List of figures

List of plates

List of tables

Acknowledgements

I commenced the thesis upon which this book is based in mid-2010. The timing seemed uncanny—the world was still recovering from a financial crisis popularly deemed to be the worst since the Great Depression, and right-wing parties and movements seemed to be on the rise in several countries. I was particularly struck by the similarities between the populist conservative movements that arose in Australia and New Zealand during the Depression and the contemporary Tea Party protests in the United States. Yet by the time I finished in early 2015, the sharp edge of this phenomenon seemed to have worn off—a sign, I hoped, that the passing of the GFC might remove the sense of crisis from our politics.

Then came Brexit, Trump, Bolsonaro. The right-wing backlash against the huge numbers of Middle Eastern asylum seekers seeking refuge in Europe from the Syrian conflict. The rise of the alt-right, of identitarianism. The 'Unite the Right' rally in Charlottesville, the Charleston church attacks. The murder of 51 innocent Muslims in Christchurch by an extreme right terrorist. Suddenly, and tragically, my thesis seemed very relevant again. The populist conservative movements I examined did not commit such atrocities, but they represented a similar period of political radicalisation in our history that few people are aware of.

Transforming my thesis into a manuscript has only increased the number of people I am indebted to. Then, as now, the first and foremost place must be reserved for my partner Helen. You have always supported me in everything I do, even when it's led me to spend too many evenings in front of my computer when I should have been with you. As with all things, this book would not have happened without you. Nor without our daughter Abigail for that matter, who desperately makes me want our generation to do better. Thank you also to my parents and family, who ceaselessly encouraged me and were unfortunate enough to have had a draft chapter or two land in their laps at some point in time.

And to my friends, who have at various points discussed my thesis with me and provided valuable ideas and insights, thank you. Particular thanks must go to Malcolm McKinnon, who is infinitely generous with his time and advice; to Christopher Burke, whose work on James Courage spurred me to come up with my core argument; and to Tristan-Cordelia Egarr, Ross Webb and Shirley Jones, who provided valuable feedback on the introduction to this book. Thank you also to all of those in Australia who let me stay with you during my three-month research trip in 2011— Mum, Dad, Doug, Sonja, Rachael and Mary. You made the time away from Helen bearable.

Thank you to my thesis supervisors as well, who always knew just the right balance between giving me free rein and checking in on me. Jim McAloon, Giacomo Lichtner, Kate Hunter—you each guided me at various points and challenged me to think about things in new ways. To Jim in particular, my primary supervisor, I remain eternally amazed and grateful for your encyclopedic knowledge of New Zealand and Australian history and your extensive familiarity with the historiography. Any time I had a question about secondary literature, you instantly pointed me to the foremost experts. Thank you also to Victoria University of Wellington and the history program itself, which provided me with the resources to complete my thesis. If it hadn't been for your generous scholarship, this book would never have come to be.

I am indebted to the archivists at the various libraries I visited in Australia and New Zealand. You made my research trips that much more productive. I would particularly like to acknowledge the JC Beaglehole Room at Victoria University of Wellington, the State Library of New South Wales, and the National Libraries of Australia and New Zealand for several of the images I have used in this book.

Every effort has been made to determine the copyright status of the images reproduced in this book, to seek permissions where required, and to include the appropriate acknowledgements. While most were out of copyright, it proved impossible to conclusively determine the status of a few of the old and orphaned items. If notified of any errors or omissions I will be pleased to rectify them at the earliest opportunity.

I am also indebted to the descendants of prominent figures in this book who gave me permission—and often invited me into their homes—to view the papers left behind by their tupuna. To Fiona and Joan Begg, Pamela Durrant, Jim Barclay, Bruce Meachen, Jen and Johnny Ormond, Paul Harper, Susan Lucina, Sandy Bathgate, Helen and Angus De Salis, David Treloar, Rosemary Farrow, Mark Alford, Marion Smith, Max Ellis, and Helen Sutch—thank you for placing your trust in me.

I would also like to acknowledge all of the staff and associates of ANU Press who shepherded me through my first (but hopefully not my only) book. Frank Bongiorno, Richard Reid, Emily Tinker, the external peer reviewers, Jan Borrie (copyeditor extraordinaire), and everyone else—thank you for the time and resources you devoted to bringing this book to fruition. The end product is all the better for it.

And finally, thank you to Sooty (our cat) for constantly reminding me that, if I can't eat it, play with it or sleep on it, it's probably not that important.

Introduction

On 30 January 1931, the editor of *The Argus*—a widely circulated, conservative-leaning Melbourne newspaper—issued an editorial titled 'A Call to Citizenship'. It was 15 months after Black Friday, the stock market crash of October 1929 that is generally viewed as the start of the Great Depression. The ripple effects of that crash wreaked havoc on the global economy. For Australia and New Zealand, which depended heavily on the export of primary products, the effects were devastating. With no clear end in sight, the editor of *The Argus* looked to the 'average citizens'—everyday professionals, businesspeople, tradespeople, and wage-earners—for the solution. These average citizens, the editor argued, were the only body of people 'divorced from any strong party affiliations or sectional interests'. The time had come for them to shrug off their political apathy and organise themselves into a body that could act for the nation as a whole:

> The time is ripe for what may be described as a 'Citizens' Movement', with the one definite objective of making articulate this great body of sane opinion, illuminated by a reasonable knowledge of affairs, and not clouded by class antipathy or doctrinaire prepossessions.[1]

The Argus did not have to wait long to see its vision of a 'citizens' movement' realised. In fact, as the editor was likely aware, the first such movement had already been launched. On 3 October 1930, 35 'members and friends' of the South Australian Constitutional Club gathered at Balfour's Café in Adelaide. Their aim was 'to register a strong protest against the criminal procrastination' of the government's response to the Depression. At the height of the meeting, an insurance agent named Edward Daniel Alexander Bagot gave an 'impassionate speech' regarding the causes of the crisis. The problem, he claimed, lay in the very nature of Australia's political system. Party politics were inherently divisive and inefficient,

---

1   *The Argus*, [Melbourne], 30 January 1931, 6.

and only a strong leader with the nation's best interest at heart could reverse the 'political and financial bankruptcy' that gripped the country. The meeting resolved to form a mass movement known as the Citizens' League of South Australia.[2] By the time of *The Argus*'s editorial in January 1931, the league's membership was more than 5,000, which rose to 22,000 by the middle of the year.

More was to come. On 12 February 1931, a large public rally was held in the Killara Memorial Hall on Sydney's North Shore. The hall was so full a loudspeaker was set up outside to broadcast the speakers' messages to the overflow audience. Australia, the gathering was told, was fast approaching 'a crisis in [its] national honour' through reckless state spending, incitement of class warfare, and 'the setting of party and personal power above the interests of the State'. A new movement was needed: a united, classless, non-political body comprising rational, disinterested citizens who would set aside their own personal interests for the sake of the country. The All for Australia League, as the new movement called itself, had sold 137,000 membership badges by the time of its first state executive meeting in June 1931.[3]

One week after the meeting in Killara, a similar meeting was held in the Melbourne Town Hall to launch the Australian Citizens' League. Three thousand attendees filled every nook and cranny of the voluminous hall, with a further thousand turned away at the door. Union Jacks and Australian flags hung from the balconies and draped the podium, and a banner proclaimed that 'all who love Australia are welcome as members'. The speakers were a veritable 'who's who' of Melbourne's high society, including Sir John MacFarland (the Chancellor of Melbourne University), W.H. Taylor (Mayor of Bendigo), and Edwin Lee Neil (Managing Director of Myer Emporium). They stressed that, as the government did not have the courage to adopt the measures needed to restore economic confidence, it behoved everyday citizens to build 'a strong force of public opinion' that could not be ignored.[4] One month later, the Australian Citizens' League adopted the name and objectives of the All for Australia League.[5] By July 1931, its membership exceeded 100,000 people.

---

2   Minutes of Inaugural Meeting, 3 October 1930, box 1, item 1, Citizens' League of South Australia Papers, MS 1186 [hereinafter CLSA Papers], National Library of Australia, Canberra [hereinafter NLA].
3   *Sydney Morning Herald*, 13 February 1931, 11.
4   *The Argus*, [Melbourne], 20 February 1931, 5, 7.
5   I will continue to refer to the Australian Citizens' League by its original name rather than its adopted name, to differentiate it from the All for Australia League in New South Wales.

A strikingly similar group, called the New Zealand Legion, arose across the Tasman two years later. On 8 February 1933, a conference of businessmen and farmers agreed to launch an organisation that would 'obliterate all sectional interests' and 'unite all the people of New Zealand to meet the national crisis'.[6] Robert Campbell Begg, a Wellington urologist, was appointed as national organiser. Over the following month, Begg undertook a whirlwind tour of New Zealand to promote the new movement. He attended 42 meetings and oversaw the formation of 17 divisions. The meetings were by invitation only, increasing the public's curiosity about the new movement. All told, Begg travelled 8,491 kilometres by rail, car, air, and ferry in pursuit of his rigorous campaigning, while other organisers travelled a further 6,647 kilometres. Within several months, the legion boasted more than 20,000 members and had captured the attention of every major newspaper in the country. As the editor of the *New Zealand Herald* saw it, the legion 'should inspire courage by its certainty of touch no less than by its wholesome ideals. It deserves success'.[7]

Plate 0.1 The inaugural meeting of the Australian Citizens' League in the Melbourne Town Hall
Source: *Argus*, 20 February 1931, p. 5.

6   *Manawatu Standard*, [Palmerston North, NZ], 23 February 1933, 7.
7   *New Zealand Herald*, [Auckland], 17 March 1933, 8.

Politics in times of crisis

Crises are often breeding grounds for extremism. When faced with great uncertainty or insecurity, common wisdom suggests, people look eagerly for alternatives to the status quo: ideas, movements, and leaders that promise to provide a way out of the crisis. In some cases, as the long history of fascist and authoritarian movements in the twentieth century suggests, these promises turn out to be a poisoned chalice. In others, the status quo is opened for a time, as politicians and the populace renegotiate the values and beliefs in which they are willing to place their faith. When the crisis passes, the political system resolidifies around a new consensus. This often results in paradigm shifts in global politics, such as the Keynesian consensus in the post–World War Two period and the rise of neoliberalism in the 1980s.[8]

The rise of right-wing populism in recent years may represent a similar paradigm shift. Across the world, right-wing politics are being increasingly shaped by a deep sense of frustration with mainstream politics and politicians, the economic dislocation caused by 40 years of neoliberalism, and the supposedly 'politically correct' culture of the twenty-first century. New forms of political identity such as the alt-right stress by their very name that they derive their legitimacy from alternative sources. Populist leaders such as Donald Trump, Jair Bolsonaro, and Rodrigo Duterte have capitalised on this groundswell of discontent to build large support bases. In addition to challenging the political left, this new generation of populist leaders and their followers seek to coopt or supplant the centre-right parties and the neoliberal values that have guided them for the past 30 years. While we may think ourselves immune to this phenomenon in Australia and New Zealand, one need only look around to see parallels in the One Nation and New Zealand First parties, as well as more extreme examples like the United Patriots Front and Action Zealandia. The horrific attacks perpetrated against two Christchurch mosques in March 2019 represent the sharp end of this international trend.

---

8   Peter Gourevitch, *Politics in Hard Times: Comparative Responses to International Economic Crises* (Ithaca, NY: Cornell University Press, 1986); Manuel Funke, Moritz Schularick, and Christoph Trebesch, 'Going to Extremes: Politics after Financial Crises, 1870–2014', *European Economic Review* 88 (2016): 227–60.

It is now more important than ever to understand similar moments in Australian and New Zealand history. This book concerns one such moment, the Great Depression, and the sudden explosion of large, populist conservative groups that accompanied the crisis. These 'citizens' movements', as they often described themselves, sprang into being virtually overnight and amassed a combined membership in the hundreds of thousands. They staunchly opposed party politicians and political parties for their supposed inaction and infighting. Whether left or right, it did not matter. They wanted to use their vast numbers to pressure their governments into enacting proposals that they believed were in the national interest: a smaller, more streamlined government in which members of parliament (MPs) were free to act according to their conscience rather than their party allegiance. At the same time, the movements prescribed antidotes for their nation's economic ill health that were often radical and occasionally anti-democratic. At the height of their power, they threatened to disrupt or outright replace the centre-right political parties of the time—particularly in Australia. At a time when fascism and right-wing authoritarianism were on the march internationally, the future shape of conservative politics was at stake.

The radicalising effect of the Great Depression

Most Australians and New Zealanders are familiar with the general narrative of the Depression. Then, as now, the wealth of both countries depended on the export of primary products such as wool, wheat, and protein. A downward trend in international prices for these products in early 1929 had already begun to have run-on effects on other parts of the economies of both countries. The Wall Street crash in late 1929 and the resulting economic fallout intensified this decline. Export prices dropped by up to 40 per cent over the next few years. Public debt—already high before the Depression—became increasingly more difficult to service with the reduced tax intake. The London capital market, which had loaned significant sums to the Australian and New Zealand governments in the 1920s to fund the expansion of public infrastructure, was unwilling to extend new loans. Domestic banks, too, were less willing to loan money to new and existing businesses. Household spending dropped, and spending on imported goods fell by up to 50 per cent. Many businesses closed due to the reduction in demand for their goods and services. Unemployment skyrocketed, especially in Australia, where it reached approximately 30 per cent in early 1932, and those who retained employment often did so on reduced wages. New words entered the Australasian vocabulary, like 'susso' (relief payments for the unemployed in Australia) and 'sugarbags' (makeshift swags used to carry one's possessions, particularly when looking for work).[9]

Plate 0.2 New Zealand Legion cartoon lamenting the lack of unity between political parties during the Great Depression
Source: *National Opinion* [Wellington], 1(4) (21 September 1933): 4.

This was fertile soil for the growth of radicalism. Some on the left turned to unemployed workers' movements or the communist parties of Australia and New Zealand. Others found answers in fringe economic theories like Douglas social credit, or conspiracy theories involving sinister cabals of international financiers holding the world's economy to ransom. A small number of people looked to fascism's intense patriotism and fervent anti-communism for answers. Yet for many, the problem did not lie with capitalism or the representative system of government. These were the inheritance of centuries of British tradition, bound to the tried and tested

---

9   David Meredith and Barrie Dyster, *Australia in the Global Economy: Continuity and Change* (Cambridge, UK: Cambridge University Press, 1999); C.B. Schedvin, *Australia and the Great Depression: A Study of Economic Development and Policy in the 1920s and 1930s* (Sydney: University of Sydney Press, 1970); J.B. Condliffe, *New Zealand in the Making: A Study of Economic and Social Development* (London: Allen & Unwin, 1936); Gary Hawke, 'Australian and New Zealand Economic Development from about 1890 to 1940', in *Tasman Relations: New Zealand and Australia, 1788–1988*, ed. Keith Sinclair (Auckland: Auckland University Press, 1987), 104–23; Gary Hawke, *The Making of New Zealand: An Economic History* (Cambridge, UK: Cambridge University Press, 1985); Malcolm McKinnon, *The Broken Decade: Prosperity, Depression and Recovery in New Zealand, 1928–39* (Dunedin, NZ: Otago University Press, 2016).

principles of liberty, democracy, and the rule of law. The blame for the Depression, as they saw it—or at the very least, the failure to quickly recover from it—lay with the petty squabbles of political parties and self-serving politicians. At the time, the political rhythm in both countries had settled into something like the modern two-party system: labour on the left, and an alliance of business, farming, and manufacturing organisations on the right. While these parties had always been popular targets for public ire, the Depression lent this criticism a much stronger, more radical edge—a phenomenon that Peter Loveday termed 'anti-political political thought'.[10] According to this line of thought, the time had come for politicians to sink their differences and form an all-party government, or to abandon their parties altogether and serve as independents free from rigid party platforms. Some even called for a temporary dictatorship or government by commission until the crisis was over.

The citizens' movements built on this powerful populist backlash. They argued that the party system of government was morally bankrupt. It led politicians to put the petty, parochial interests of their party and its supporters—whom today's populists might call 'lobby groups'—above the interests of the nation. The two-party system, they argued, had left in the middle a large body of decent, respectable citizens whose interests were being sacrificed on the altar of party politics. These citizens were animated by a quiet sense of patriotic duty to Britain and their country rather than the antagonisms of those on the left and the right. They were loyal, hardworking, and independent. Many had served in the Great War, and those who had not were nevertheless driven by the same sense of duty and self-sacrifice. By mobilising this large body of people, the citizens' movements hoped to undercut the political parties entirely and secure the election of independent candidates who would legislate in the interests of the whole nation. This populist approach to politics—pitting a virtuous and homogeneous 'people' against political parties and politicians—was a simple yet incredibly appealing vision.

Yet while the citizens' movements portrayed themselves as apolitical, their beliefs drew heavily on traditional conservative views about government and the economy. They called for drastic reductions in public spending to curb what they saw as excessive, 'socialistic' government programs driven by special interest groups. They sought a simpler, more streamlined

---

10   Peter Loveday, 'Anti-Political Political Thought', *Labour History* 17 (1969): 121–35.

government comprising fewer MPs, the consolidation of government functions, and a smaller public service. They vigorously opposed communism, and they implored employers and workers to cooperate rather than resort to industrial action such as strikes and lockouts. They beseeched their followers to emulate the example of their pioneering British ancestors, who, they alleged, had broken in and built their countries without resorting to government handouts. If society could be weaned off the teat of government spending, they argued, the economy would rebound. All these were the standard tropes of the centre-right political parties—something that made the citizens' movements so threatening to the political status quo. If they were willing to sponsor independent candidates for election, or field their own candidates, there was a strong chance they could split the right-wing vote and hand power to federal and state labour parties.

This heady mix of populism and conservatism was complemented by a willingness to explore radical—and occasionally anti-democratic— political alternatives. This was a time when new political experiments were proliferating internationally. Italian fascism was maturing and electoral support for the Nazis was growing exponentially in Germany. Leaders in the Western world were exploring the possibility of increasing public spending to buoy their faltering economies, and Douglas social credit was experiencing a surge in popularity. The new groups that arose in Australia and New Zealand explored ideas such as replacing geographical electorates with vocational (industry-based) electorates or replacing aspects of elected government entirely with non-elected experts and committees. The New Zealand Legion even toyed with the idea of a centrally planned economy—a remarkable political position for a group founded on the principles of classical liberalism.

The citizens' movements were not the only populist conservative response to the Great Depression. In New South Wales, tens of thousands joined a paramilitary organisation known as the New Guard. While its ostensible purpose was to defend constitutional government and uphold loyalty to the British Crown, its members also frequently broke up left-wing meetings, engaged in brawls, and conducted drills and mobilisation exercises in anticipation of a communist uprising. The New Guard leadership, or elements within it, also plotted to kidnap the NSW Premier and launch a coup to take over the state government. A similar number of people also joined more clandestine paramilitary organisations in several Australian states, the objectives of which were to assist police and the armed forces in the event of a communist insurrection or a breakdown in public services.[11] At the same time, several large 'new state' movements across rural New South Wales demanded that their regions be split off and constituted as separate states under the Australian Government. The Riverina and New England new-state movements were the most prominent of these.[12] On the other side of the continent, a group called the Dominion League of Western Australia agitated for complete secession from the rest of Australia. This was endorsed by approximately 66 per cent of registered West Australian voters in a referendum on the subject in April 1933.[13]

The citizens' movements existed alongside these other groups. They shared ideas, objectives, and strategies, and their memberships often overlapped. Eric Campbell, the leader of the New Guard, went so far as to argue in his memoirs that 'the New Guard was the fighting wing and the A.F.A. [All for Australia League] the political wing of the same brand of thought'.[14] These connections are an important part of the story of the citizens' movements and will be explored throughout this book.

Writing about the citizens' movements

The citizens' movements faded rapidly from the political scene—and, indeed, from the collective memory of Australian and New Zealand societies. As a historian whose expertise lies in this area, I have constantly been struck by how surprised people are to learn that such movements existed in our humble Antipodean backwater. Except for the paramilitary New Guard, they have not been the subject of much scholarly research. This understudied aspect of our history raises many questions. Why did

11 Keith Amos, *The New Guard Movement, 1931–1935* (Melbourne: Melbourne University Press, 1976); Michael Cathcart, *Defending the National Tuckshop: Australia's Secret Army Intrigue of 1931* (Melbourne: McPhee Gribble, 1988); Andrew Moore, *The Secret Army and the Premier: Conservative Paramilitary Organisations in New South Wales, 1930–32* (Sydney: UNSW Press, 1989).
12 Ullrich Ellis, *A Pen in Politics (Finished and published by Max Ellis)* (Canberra: Ginninderra Press, 2007); Ulrich Ellis, *The Country Party: A Political and Social History of the Party in New South Wales* (Melbourne: F.W. Cheshire, 1958); Don Aitkin, *The Country Party in New South Wales: A Study of Organisation and Survival* (Canberra: Australian National University Press, 1972); Peter Tuziak, Riverina awake! A history of the Riverina Movement (BA Hons diss., University of Sydney, 1990); W.A. Beveridge, The Riverina Movement and Charles Hardy (BA Hons diss., University of Sydney, 1954).
13 Edward Watt, Western separation: The history of the secession movement in Western Australia, 1918–1935 (MA diss., University of Western Australia, Perth, 1957); Thomas Musgrave, 'The Western Australian Secessionist Movement', *Macquarie Law Journal* 3 (2003): 98–129.
14 Eric Campbell, *The Rallying Point: My Story of the New Guard* (Melbourne: Melbourne University Press, 1965), 43.

these groups arise in the first place, and how did they manage to animate so many people in such a short time? They did not emerge in an ideological vacuum, after all; the ideas that drove them must have had deep roots in the Australasian psyche for so many to respond positively to them. Who supported the citizens' movements, and why? And why did the movements decline so rapidly without having the transformative effect on the political system that sometimes occurs during times of crisis? We like to think that our carefree, laidback Antipodean attitudes make us immune to wild swings in our style of government, but was it really that simple?

This book is the first scholarly work to focus specifically on the citizens' movements. Apart from a smattering of journal articles and theses, the published literature on right-wing groups and ideas in Australia and New Zealand is slim. Andrew Moore's brief history of right-wing politics in Australia remains the standard reference text, despite being published almost 30 years ago.[15] Likewise, Paul Spoonley's history of racism and the extreme right in New Zealand is the only general overview that exists, and it focuses primarily on the period after World War Two.[16] While other authors have commented on the citizens' movements in passing, they have tended to focus on more militaristic groups such as the New Guard or the careers of leading conservative politicians such as Robert Menzies or Joseph and Enid Lyons.[17] The growing body of work examining the history of modern Australian liberalism also provides only brief commentary on the citizens' movements, due to their authors' focus on broader political trends.[18]

---

15   Andrew Moore, *The Right Road: A History of Right-Wing Politics in Australia* (Melbourne: Oxford University Press, 1995).
16   Paul Spoonley, *The Politics of Nostalgia: Racism and the Extreme Right in New Zealand* (Palmerston North, NZ: Dunmore Press, 1987).
17   Key works include Amos, *The New Guard Movement*; Cathcart, *Defending the National Tuckshop*; Moore, *The Secret Army and the Premier*; Anne Henderson, *Enid Lyons: Leading Lady to a Nation* (Melbourne: Pluto Press, 2008); Anne Henderson, *Joseph Lyons: The People's Prime Minister* (Sydney: UNSW Press, 2012); A.W. Martin, *Robert Menzies: A Life. Volume 1, 1894–1943* (Melbourne: Melbourne University Press, 1993).
18   Judith Brett, *Australian Liberals and the Moral Middle Class* (Cambridge, UK: Cambridge University Press, 2003); Greg Melleuish, *Cultural Liberalism in Australia* (Cambridge, UK: Cambridge University Press, 1995); J.R. Nethercote, *Liberalism and the Australian Federation* (Sydney: The Federation Press, 2001).

The reactionary and the radical

The citizens' movements were a complex social and political phenomenon. Simultaneously conservative and populist, they looked both forward and backward for political inspiration. They sought new and occasionally radical alternatives to the problems of their time while expressing nostalgia for an illusory nineteenth-century colonial society epitomised by limited government, independent politicians, and self-sufficient pioneers. Nor is it entirely appropriate to speak of them as monolithic blocks, as unified 'movements' that moved in lock step. Each of the four citizens' movements had its own idiosyncrasies, driven by the time and context within which it arose, the nature of the crises they faced, and the predispositions of their leaders and wider membership. Furthermore, each individual movement comprised people who held a variety of values and were drawn to the movements for different reasons.

While it is accurate to describe the citizens' movements as 'populist conservative movements', it is also accurate to say that this broad ideology concealed a number of often contradictory and competing views. This is unsurprising. Political movements are often an exercise in contradictions: their leaders must balance the competing interests of different factions, all of whom are clamouring to be heard. If they cannot get this juggling act right, they risk being replaced—or, worse yet, splitting the movement. But the inherent contradictions at the core of the citizens' movements were much more fundamental. These contradictions, put simply, lay between the movements' radical aspirations and their more reactionary traditions. They were conservatives, and they were radicals. They supported the status quo, yet they also sought to fundamentally alter it. They supported parliamentary democracy, yet they railed against the political parties who they believed were robbing it of its essence. The contradictions between these viewpoints could be glossed over so long as the movements focused on ideals rather than substance, but this strategy could only serve them for so long. The demands of real-world politics, and their members' desire for substantive policy, exposed these contradictions.

Viewing the citizens' movements as a contradictory blend of reactionary and radical tendencies provides a useful framework for understanding them. It allows us to embrace their contradictions rather than trying to iron them out in favour of a simple, consistent story. I will return to this framework throughout the book to explain various aspects of the movements' history, from their origins to their decline. Before doing that, we must define the core strands of that framework: conservatism and populism.

Definitions

I have described the citizens' movements as 'populist conservative movements'. These two terms—conservatism and populism—are essential to understanding the citizens' movements. They cut to the very core of how their members understood the problems besetting their countries and what motivated them to respond to those problems. But what do they mean? And, equally importantly, what did they mean to the 'average citizen' whom the citizens' movements claimed to represent? I briefly define these terms below, along with another term that became increasingly important on the international stage as the 1930s progressed: fascism.

Conservatism

The term 'conservative' carries a lot of ideological baggage in Australia and New Zealand. Unlike the United Kingdom and the United States, there was no wide-scale self-professed tradition of Antipodean conservatism in the nineteenth or (early) twentieth centuries. Those described as conservative generally identified with other labels such as 'progressive' or 'liberal'; indeed, the rise of neoliberalism in the 1980s has demonstrated just how politicised is the 'liberal' tradition in Australian politics.[19] This is partly because the term 'liberal' was consciously adopted at the end of the nineteenth century by political factions in each country that were willing to increase the role of the state in social and economic matters: Alfred Deakin's Victorian liberals and the New Zealand Liberal Party.[20]

---

19   Paul Kelly, *The End of Certainty: Power, Politics, and Business in Australia* (Sydney: Allen & Unwin, 1994); Melleuish, *Cultural Liberalism in Australia*; Gregory Melleuish, *A Short History of Australian Liberalism* (Sydney: Centre for Independent Studies, 2001), vii; Gregory Melleuish, 'Australian Liberalism', in *Liberalism and the Australian Federation*, ed. J.R. Nethercote (Sydney: The Federation Press, 2001), 28–41.

20   Tim Rowse, *Australian Liberalism and National Character* (Melbourne: Kibble Books, 1978); Stuart Macintyre, *A Colonial Liberalism: The Lost World of Three Victorian Visionaries* (Melbourne: Oxford University Press, 1991); David Hamer, *The New Zealand Liberals: The Years of Power, 1891–1912* (Auckland: Auckland University Press, 1988); Keith Sinclair, 'The Legislation of the Liberal Party, 1891–1898', in *Ends and Means in New Zealand Politics*, ed. Robert Chapman (Auckland: Dobbie Press, 1961), 11–17; Robert Chapman, 'The Decline of the Liberals', in *Ends and Means in New Zealand Politics*, ed. Robert Chapman (Auckland: Dobbie Press, 1961), 18–24; Marion Sawer, *The Ethical State? Social Liberalism in Australia* (Melbourne: Melbourne University Press, 2003), 57; Brett, *Australian Liberals and the Moral Middle Class*, 20–21; A.J. Reitsma, *Trade Protection in Australia* (Brisbane: University of Queensland Press, 1960), 7; W.A. Sinclair, *The Process of Economic Development in Australia* (Melbourne: Cheshire Publishing, 1976), 94–95; Andrew Leigh, 'Trade Liberalisation and the Australian Labor Party', *Australian Journal of Politics and History* 48(4) (2002): 487–508, at pp. 489–90; John Lonie, 'From Liberal to Liberal: The Emergence of the Liberal Party and Australian Capitalism, 1900–45', in *Critical Essays in Australian Politics*, ed. Graeme Duncan (Melbourne: Edward Arnold Ltd, 1978), 54–55.

The 'conservative' label also did not sit well with the aspiration shared by most colonial politicians to build 'better Britains' in the South Seas that were not bound by Britain's rigid hierarchical system.[21] But more prosaically, Australia and New Zealand were new European settlements that lacked a hereditary landed aristocracy seeking to preserve its power. The colonial upper class had generally come from a growing British middle class that sought new entrepreneurial opportunities in the colonies. They had arrived fortuitously early in the settlement process to benefit from the expropriation of indigenous land, or they had provided vital financial and marketing services to burgeoning agricultural enterprises.[22] One exception was New South Wales, which already possessed an ageing generation of landed elites by the 1850s. Epitomised by the redoubtable Macarthur family, these individuals played a key role in the political foundation of the colony.[23]

The new Australasian colonies also lacked the commitment to laissez-faire capitalism shared by British conservatives and liberals. Their governments were heavily involved in economic activity from the outset of European colonisation. This originally served a pragmatic purpose: colonial enterprise was simply too underdeveloped, and the accumulation of private capital was too slow, to provide essential services to the market. As colonial primary industries expanded, state involvement in the economy likewise expanded to incentivise these industries. Railways, roads, postal services, immigration schemes, communication technologies, and port facilities were all developed to service primary industry. Closer settlement of the land was encouraged by public investment in agricultural technologies such as fertilisers, pesticides, and refrigeration, as well as the virtual state monopoly on the expropriation of land from indigenous peoples.[24] Scholars have variously described the state's active involvement in the

---

21   James Belich, *Paradise Reforged: A History of the New Zealanders from the 1880s to the Year 2000* (Auckland: Penguin Press, 2001).

22   Jim McAloon, *No Idle Rich: The Wealthy in Canterbury and Otago, 1840–1914* (Dunedin, NZ: Otago University Press, 2002), 171–82; Ken Buckley, 'Primary Accumulation: The Genesis of Australian Capitalism', in *Essays in the Political Economy of Australian Capitalism*, eds E.L. Wheelwright and Ken Buckley, 2 vols (Sydney: Australia & New Zealand Book Company, 1975).

23   Melleuish, *A Short History of Australian Liberalism*, 1.

24   Noel G. Butlin, *Investment in Australian Economic Development, 1861–1900* (London: Cambridge University Press, 1964); Michael Bassett, *The State in New Zealand* (Auckland: Auckland University Press, 1998). See also Hawke, *The Making of New Zealand*, 103–21; Judith Bassett, 'Sir Harry Atkinson and the Conservative Faction in New Zealand Politics, 1879–1890', *New Zealand Journal of History* 2(2) (1968): 130–47, at pp. 135–36.

early economies of Australia and New Zealand as 'colonial socialism' or 'progressive colonisation'.[25] This national development ethos overrode some of the traditional laissez-faire tensions between public and private enterprise, so long as state involvement could be justified as being in the national interest.

If conservatism was rarely used as a political identifier at the time, why use it in this book? The answer is that conservatism is far more than a political ideology. It is a sentiment, a framework for mediating change through the guidelines of tradition. The English political theorist Michael Oakeshott defined conservatism as a 'disposition' rather than 'a creed or doctrine'. Conservatives

> prefer the familiar to the unknown ... the tried to the untried, fact to mystery, the actual to the possible, the limited to the unbounded, the near to the distant, the sufficient to the superabundant, the convenient to the perfect, present laughter to utopian bliss.[26]

Hayden White suggested that conservatives are 'suspicious of programmatic transformations of the status quo' and 'inclined to imagine historical evolution as a progressive elaboration of the institutional structure that currently prevails, which structure they regard as a "utopia"'. Rather than opposing change entirely, conservatives envision it as occurring via 'plantlike gradualizations' that do not fundamentally alter or challenge the 'structural relationships' on which society is based.[27] Put simply, there are always some who look to the status quo for stability and reassurance, and who use it as a lens through which to consider any proposals for change. This sentiment was central to the citizens' movements and their supporters, whether or not they called it 'conservatism'.

Based on this definition, there was a well-established tradition of conservatism in Australia and New Zealand by the 1920s. It had three key components. The first was a strong patriotic and economic

---

25   Noel G. Butlin, 'Colonial Socialism in Australia, 1860–1900', in *The State and Economic Growth*, ed. Hugh Aitken (New York: Social Science Research Council, 1959), 26–78; James Belich, *Making Peoples: A History of the New Zealanders from Polynesian Settlement to the End of the Nineteenth Century* (Auckland: Penguin Press, 1996), 375.

26   Michael Oakeshott, 'On Being Conservative', in *Rationalism in Politics, and Other Essays*, ed. Michael Oakeshott (London: Methuen, 1962), 168–96.

27   Hayden White, *Metahistory: The Historical Imagination in Nineteenth-Century Europe* (Baltimore: Johns Hopkins University Press, 1973), 22–25; Karl Mannheim, *Ideology and Utopia: An Introduction to the Sociology of Knowledge* (New York: Harcourt, 1946), 104.

orientation towards Britain. Britain was the mother country—the source of liberty, democracy, and the rule of law—and its vast navy was a source of protection against potential or perceived enemies. It was also the destination of the majority of Australia's and New Zealand's primary exports, and hence a vital cog in their economic prosperity. A second, equally important component was a general commitment to free-market capitalism, mediated by the nineteenth-century state developmentalist ethos discussed above. This commitment had a strong moral component: self-reliance, without needing to draw on the state for support, was an important part of good citizenship. This also applied to governments, for if the individual was expected to live within their means, should not the state do so, too? Limited government, a small public sector, and balanced public budgets were seen as essential elements of a strong and resilient society. Third, conservatives staunchly opposed communism and socialism and, while they did not completely oppose trade unionism, they were wary of its more militant tactics. In their view, the interests of employers and workers were conjoined: class antagonisms were a fallacy—a tension stoked by extremists to serve their own nefarious interests. Preserving traditional gender roles and a white majority was also a component of this conservative tradition, although to some extent these were fairly mainstream views at the time.

Populism

Populism has a more unusual political lineage. The term first emerged at the end of the nineteenth century, when it was used to describe two left-wing agrarian political movements: the People's Party in the United States, and the Narodniks in Russia. The People's Party was one of several left-wing responses to the growing power of corporate and financial interests in the United States near the turn of the century. Claiming that 'money power' had too much control over the government and the economy, the People's Party called for stronger collective bargaining, nationalisation of the railroads, and a national banking system. It became more conspiratorial in outlook in the build-up to the 1896 presidential election, with some members embracing the anti-Semitic conspiracy theory that prominent Jewish families in finance were using their power to control the economy and ruin small farmers. Democratic Party presidential candidate William Jennings Bryan also incorporated populist policy and rhetoric into his campaign. The influence of the People's Party rapidly declined after the election, although it managed to limp on into the early twentieth century.[28] The Narodniks, in contrast, were a group of socialist intellectuals who sought to mobilise the peasantry to overthrow the Russian monarchy. They appealed directly to 'the people' to educate them about the need for an economic and political revolution.[29]

So, what did Australian and New Zealand conservatives in the 1930s know about populism? It is unlikely they had heard of the term, given that it was not used to describe movements other than the People's Party and the Narodniks until the 1950s.[30] As such, it is also unlikely the leaders of the citizens' movements thought of themselves as populists. They were, in their view, standing up for the average citizen against the tyranny of party politicians who were holding the nation in thrall to their own sectional interests. But Australian conservatives were familiar with the Labor politicians in their midst who relied on populist-style appeals to 'the people' against the 'money power' that supposedly wielded undue influence over government and the economy. This populist stream in Labor thinking was first mobilised in response to the bank crashes of the early 1890s and was directly influenced by the People's Party. Jack Lang, two-time Labor Premier of New South Wales in the 1920s and 1930s, epitomised this style of politics in Australia, as did the Douglas social credit movement, which siphoned off some Labor supporters who were uncomfortable with the party's ostensible goal of socialisation. The Australian citizens' movements may well have sought to emulate Lang's example—and, likewise, the conservative political establishment's fear that the movements might split the centre-right vote may have been partially influenced by their awareness of Lang's ability to galvanise his supporters through similarly populist rhetoric. While New Zealand lacked such a comprehensive left-wing critique of money power, leading Labour

---

28   Peter H. Argersinger, *Populism and Politics: William Alfred Peffer and the People's Party* (Lexington, KY: University Press of Kentucky, 2015); Robert Franklin Durden, *The Climax of Populism: The Election of 1896* (Lexington, KY: University Press of Kentucky, 2015); Matthew Hild, *Greenbackers, Knights of Labor, and Populists: Farmer–Labor Insurgency in the Late-Nineteenth-Century South* (Athens, GA: University of Georgia Press, 2007).

29   Franco Venturi, *Roots of Revolution: A History of the Populist and Socialist Movements in 19th Century Russia* (New York: Phoenix Press, 2001).

30   J.B. Allcock, 'Populism: A Brief Biography', *Sociology* 5(3) (1971): 371–87, at pp. 372–73.

Party figure John A. Lee did exhibit some populist characteristics.[31] So, conservatives in the 1930s would have had some familiarity with the style of populist politics, even if the word 'populism' likely did not have wide parlance.

The term 'populism' has been used to describe a wide variety of parties, movements, and individuals since the 1950s. As a result, the literature on the subject has increased substantially, particularly concerning Europe and Latin America. Academic and popular interest in the subject have accelerated even further in the past two decades, as populist leaders, parties, and movements have achieved greater degrees of power and influence in many countries. This research has focused predominantly on the growth of what Cas Mudde called the 'populist radical right', which had become 'the dominant ideology within the European far right' by the turn of the century.[32] Despite this plethora of research, an agreed definition of populism remains elusive. Rovira Kaltwasser and Benjamin Moffitt have identified three broad schools of thought in the literature: the ideational, politico-strategic, and sociocultural (which Moffitt describes as 'discursive-performative') approaches. The ideational approach defines populism as an ideology, albeit a 'thin' one that cannot stand alone; it is always combined with other ideologies, such as liberalism, conservatism, and nationalism. The strategic approach views populism as a form of political strategy employed by a 'leader' who has a direct connection to 'the people' they claim to represent. The sociocultural approach stresses that populism is, above all, a form of language. Not only is language used to describe the conflict between 'the people' and their enemies, it also is used to construct who in fact are the people and their enemies.[33]

31 Peter Love, *Labour and the Money Power: Australian Labour Populism, 1890–1950* (Melbourne: Melbourne University Press, 1984); Robin Gollan, 'American Populism and Australian Utopianism', *Labour History* 9 (1965): 15–21; Marinus La Rooij, Political antisemitism in New Zealand during the Great Depression: A case study in the myth of the Jewish world conspiracy (MA diss., Victoria University of Wellington, 1998), 165–66; Ben Thomas McLachlan, In search of a New Zealand populism: Heresthetics, character and populist political leadership (MA diss., Victoria University of Wellington, 2013), 37–60; Barry Gustafson, 'Populist Roots of Political Leadership in New Zealand', in *Political Leadership in New Zealand*, eds Raymond Miller and Michael Mintrom (Auckland: Auckland University Press, 2006), 51–69.
32 Cas Mudde, *The Far Right Today* (Cambridge, UK: Polity Press, 2019), 18.
33 Benjamin Moffitt, *Populism: Key Concepts in Political Theory* (Oxford, UK: Polity Press, 2020), 10–29; Rovira Kaltwasser, Paul Taggart, Paulina Ochoa Espejo, and Pierre Ostiguy, 'Populism: An Overview of the Concept and the State of the Art', in *The Oxford Handbook of Populism*, eds Rovira Kaltwasser, Paul Taggart, Paulina Ochoa Espejo, and Pierre Ostiguy (New York: Oxford University Press, 2017), 10–29.

The different approaches to populism are not mutually exclusive and multiple approaches can be employed in a particular context. There are also certain characteristics that are common across all approaches. For example, it is universally accepted that the core struggle uniting all populists is between 'the people' and a corrupt and uncaring 'elite' whose self-serving political tactics have alienated them from the people and brought traditional community values under threat. Some other commonly agreed features of populism include a personality-driven form of leadership, focusing on a current or impending crisis, and a call to exclude an 'other' of some kind that is seen as dangerous or divisive.[34] Daniele Albertazzi and Duncan McDonnell have suggested the following succinct definition:

> [Populism] pits a virtuous and homogeneous people against a set of elites and dangerous 'others' who were together depicted as depriving (or attempting to deprive) the sovereign people of their rights, values, prosperity, identity, and voice.[35]

Whether populism is an ideology, a political strategy, or a form of political performance or discourse is ultimately beyond the scope of this book to answer. What is more important are the key facets of populism described above, which were all core components of the citizens' movements. I will also draw on Moffitt's concept of populism as a 'political style' in which 'the leader is seen as *the performer*, "the people" as *the audience*, and crisis and media as *the stage* on which populism plays out'.[36] While Moffitt developed this approach to describe twenty-first-century populism, it also has some relevance to what I describe as the 'populist culture' of mass conservative mobilisation during the Depression. The relationship between the citizens' movements' leaders and their followers played out through semi-ritualised mass meetings, where speeches and resolutions were used to construct who 'the people' and 'the elite' were: average citizens and party politicians. And while the citizens' movements did not have access to social media or the internet, they made excellent use

---

34 See, for example, Margaret Canovan, 'Trust the People! Populism and the Two Faces of Democracy', *Political Studies* 47(1) (1999): 2–16; Paul Taggart, *Populism* (Buckingham, UK: Open University Press, 2000), 95; Mudde, *The Far Right Today*, 7–8; Moffitt, *Populism*, 10.

35 Daniele Albertazzi and Duncan McDonnell, 'Introduction: The Sceptre and the Spectre', in *Twenty-First Century Populism: The Spectre of Western European Democracy*, eds Daniele Albertazzi and Duncan McDonnell (New York: Palgrave Macmillan, 2008), 3.

36 Emphasis in original; Benjamin Moffitt, *The Global Rise of Populism: Performance, Political Style, and Representation* (Palo Alto, CA: Stanford University Press, 2017), 2.

of the media of their age. Books, pamphlets, dodgers, posters, and the burgeoning technology of radio were all used to disseminate their message to 'the people'.

Fascism

As with populism, there is no single agreed definition of fascism. The history of the scholarly quest to define fascism can be broadly understood as an ongoing, and often highly controversial, debate between ideological and material approaches.[37] In simple terms, the ideological approach involves the attempt to identify a common set of ideas that all fascist movements (or at least the major ones) shared. This is often referred to as a 'fascist minimum'. It has resulted in a wide range of definitions, ranging from Stanley G. Payne's long list of fascist ideas, goals, styles, and 'negations' (anti-liberalism, anti-communism, and anti-conservatism) to Roger Griffin's more succinct definition of fascism as a 'palingenetic form of populist ultra-nationalism' based on the myth of national rebirth.[38] The material approach, in contrast, explores the conditions from which fascism arose. It suggests that fascism was a response to economic crisis—often (but not exclusively) described as a stage of capitalist development where the propertied class backs a brutally repressive regime to protect their interests.[39]

Both the ideological and the material approaches to fascism have drawbacks. The former overlooks the historical causes of fascist movements and their relationship with those who hold economic and political power, while the latter risks overextending the definition of fascism by neglecting to engage with the common factors that distinguish it from other forms of right-wing mobilisation. Nor are the approaches mutually exclusive. I draw on aspects of both approaches in this book to understand how the origins and the ideology of the citizens' movements compare with fascism. I also explore whether the citizens' movements attracted the same cross-class support as was common with the fascist movements in Europe.

37 Daniel Woodley, *Fascism and Political Theory: Critical Perspectives on Fascist Ideology* (New York: Routledge, 2010), 1.
38 Roger Griffin, *The Nature of Fascism* (London: Routledge, 1993); Stanley G. Payne, *A History of Fascism 1914–1945* (Madison: University of Wisconsin Press, 1995); Zeev Sternhell, *The Birth of Fascist Ideology* (Princeton, NJ: Princeton University Press, 1994).
39 See, for example, Nicos Poulantzas, *Fascism and Dictatorship: The Third International and the Problem of Fascism* (London: NLB, 1974); David Renton, *Fascism: Theory and Practice* (London: Pluto Press, 1999).

It is also important to understand what Australasian conservatives knew of fascism in the 1930s. While there is a robust literature on the influence of fascism in Australia, much less has been written on the subject in New Zealand. Nevertheless, some tentative extrapolations can be drawn between the two countries. For instance, the observation of several scholars that many Australian conservatives admired fascism's anti-communism and its intense patriotism, and viewed it as a potential solution to class conflict, is likely to have also been the case among some New Zealand conservatives.[40] Political figures such as Robert Menzies and Joseph Lyons, for example, expressed a quiet admiration for fascism's apparent unity of purpose, and literary figures such as Percy Reginald 'Inky' Stephensen became so enamoured with fascism that he drifted rightwards to the far-right Australia First Movement and was interned during World War Two as a potential subversive.[41] However, Australasian conservatives' knowledge of fascism was limited by their lack of understanding of its opposition to liberal and conservative values, and their (sometimes deliberate) willingness to overlook fascist violence and abuses of power.[42] Wilfrid Kent Hughes, the Australian MP who proudly declared himself a fascist in 1933, exemplified this misunderstanding of fascism.[43] For the most part, fascism was largely contained within Italian and German diaspora communities in Australia and New Zealand, due mainly to the insistence of consular officials that fascism should act as a shield against cultural integration.[44] However, as this book will show, this did not stop some individuals within the citizens' movements from toying with aspects

---

40   John McCarthy, '"All for Australia": Some Right Wing Responses to the Depression in New South Wales, 1929–1932', *Journal of the Royal Australian Historical Society* 57(2) (1971): 160–71, at pp. 162–64; Moore, *The Right Road*, 46–48; Roslyn Pesman Cooper, '"We Want a Mussolini": Views of Fascist Italy in Australia', *Australian Journal of Politics and History* 39(3) (1993): 348–66.

41   David Bird, *Nazi Dreamtime: Australian Enthusiasts for Hitler's Germany* (Melbourne: Australian Scholarly Publishing, 2012). For more information on 'Inky' Stephensen and the Australia First Movement, see Barbara Winter, *The Australia-First Movement: Dreaming of a National Socialist Australia* (Brisbane: Interactive Publications, 2005); Bruce Muirden, *The Puzzled Patriots: The Story of the Australia First Movement* (Melbourne: Melbourne University Press, 1968).

42   Carolyn Rasmussen, *The Lesser Evil? Opposition to War and Fascism in Australia 1920–1941* (Melbourne: Melbourne University Press, 1992).

43   See Frederick Howard, *Kent Hughes: A Biography of Colonel the Hon. Sir Wilfred Kent Hughes* (Melbourne: Macmillan, 1972); Geoff Spenceley, '"The Minister for Starvation": Wilfrid Kent Hughes, Fascism and the Unemployment Relief (Administration) Act of 1933', *Labour History* 81 (2001): 135–54.

44   Gianfranco Cresciani, *Fascism, Anti-Fascism and Italians in Australia, 1922–1945* (Canberra: Australian National University Press, 1980); Paul Elenio, *'Alla Fine Del Mondo': To the Ends of the Earth* (Wellington: Petone Settlers Museum & the Club Garibaldi, 1995), 58–59; John Perkins, 'The Swastika Down Under: Nazi Activities in Australia, 1933–39', *Journal of Contemporary History* 26(1) (1991): 111–29.

of fascist ideology. It also did not prevent the paramilitary New Guard movement from overtly adopting the trappings of fascism from the end of 1932.[45]

International comparisons, influences, and connections

This book approaches the four citizens' movements from a comparative, and occasionally a cross-national, perspective. Deborah Cohen and Maura O'Connor described the distinction between these two approaches as follows:

> Comparative history is seemingly concerned with similarities and differences; in explaining a given phenomenon, it asks which conditions, or factors, were broadly shared, and which were distinctive … [C]ross-national histories follow topics beyond national boundaries. They seek to understand reciprocal influences, as well as the ways in which the act of transplantation itself changes the topic under study.[46]

The two are 'complementary rather than competing methods of writing multinational history'.[47] Comparative history allows similar phenomena in different countries to be assessed against each other to better determine what is unique about each, while cross-national history traces the links between these phenomena. This book primarily adopts a comparative approach, in that it compares the three Australian citizens' movements with their sole New Zealand counterpart. The similar European history of these two settler societies provides an ideal 'laboratory' in which to identify and explain the key differences between the movements. Two key differences this book explores are the different times the groups arose—in late 1930 and early 1931 in Australia and early 1933 in New Zealand—

---

45 Matthew Cunningham, 'Australian Fascism? A Revisionist Analysis of the Ideology of the New Guard', *Politics, Religion & Ideology* 13(3) (2012): 375–93; Stephen Reid, The New Guard in decline: Eric Campbell and the Centre Party, 1933–1935' (BA Hons diss., Macquarie University, Sydney, 1980); Keith Richmond, 'The New Road to Salvation: Eric Campbell and the Centre Party', *Journal of the Royal Australian Historical Society* 66(3) (1980): 184–98; Andrew Moore, 'Discredited Fascism: The New Guard after 1932', *Australian Journal of Politics and History* 57(2) (2011): 188–206.
46 Deborah Cohen and Maura O'Connor, *Comparison and History: Europe in Cross-National Perspective* (New York: Routledge, 2004), xi–xii.
47 Michael Miller, 'Comparative and Cross-National History: Approaches, Differences, Problems', in *Comparison and History: Europe in Cross-National Perspective*, eds Deborah Cohen and Maura O'Connor (New York: Routledge, 2004), 126–27.

and the unique ideological debates that played a key role in exposing contradictions within the Australian and New Zealand movements. This book also compares the citizens' movements with other conservative, right-wing, and fascist groups that arose internationally during the interwar years, as well as more contemporary far-right groups.

The three Australian citizens' movements were intimately connected to each other and to the broader network of paramilitary, new-state, and secessionist movements that arose at the same time. However, despite the striking similarities between the Australian and the New Zealand citizens' movements, this book has not uncovered any direct connections between the two. Yet the New Zealand Legion's founders were aware of the paramilitary New Guard and of the rise of fascism. From the legion's inception in early 1933, its leaders went to great lengths to stress that it was 'not a New Guard' or a 'Fascist group'.[48] They reiterated this assurance at every opportunity—at public meetings, in their booklets and pamphlets, and in internal correspondence. The legion's concern exemplifies the idea that adopting a comparative approach alone is insufficient. To understand the citizens' movements, we must also understand how they were shaped by international influences, including any direct connections they and their predecessors had with similar groups overseas. This distinction between influences and connections is important for two key reasons and is reflected in the way this book is structured. First, while this book reveals that the citizens' movements had few direct connections or alliances with overseas groups, they were significantly influenced by a variety of international ideas and trends. The legion, for example, did not have any formal connections to the New Guard or fascist groups (although this book reveals some informal connections with the former), yet its leaders felt compelled to explicitly disavow them nonetheless. Its platform was shaped from the outset in opposition to groups with which it had no formal relationship—a sort of anti-influence, perhaps. Second, the various groups that preceded the citizens' movements (which are discussed in Chapter One) very deliberately sought out connections with groups overseas. The New Zealand Welfare League, one of the groups that influenced the birth of the legion, actively participated in an international network of anti-communist groups from the 1920s:

---

48 *Light on the Legion* (Wellington: Commercial Printing Company Ltd, 1933), 1.

> We have always ... maintained our connection with similar
> organisation[s] in several other countries, notably Great Britain,
> America, Australia, China, and an International body with
> headquarters at Geneva ... Applications for information on
> Socialism, Communism, and other subjects are frequent and our
> world wide connections enable us to provide reliable information
> on these subjects.[49]

These connections were forged for a variety of reasons, including a pan-British sentiment, a desire to connect with like-minded individuals across the world, and a belief that the 'enemies' they were fighting were international in nature. Chapter One, unlike the other chapters, is written in a cross-national fashion. However, targeted use of cross-national history is also made throughout the other chapters where there are international influences and connections that are important to highlight.

I have benefited considerably from the growing body of historical work that places Australia and New Zealand in a broader global context. Then, as now, people, money, and ideas were constantly on the move, pushed and pulled by countless political, economic, social, and cultural factors. This movement knitted together disparate locations across the world into shared spaces. In the nineteenth and early twentieth centuries, three shared spaces were particularly relevant for Australia and New Zealand: the 'Tasman world', which is discussed further below; the 'British world', comprising the United Kingdom and its colonies; and the broader 'Anglo world', which also incorporated British settler communities in the United States, South America, Africa, and Asia. Historians in recent decades have begun to use terms such as 'webs' and 'networks' to describe this dynamic and ever-changing set of international connections.[50] They occurred in the state sphere, such as the sharing of ideas between government offices across the British Empire and the migration of public officials between colonies.[51] They occurred in the private sphere, such as the mass movement

---

49 New Zealand Welfare League—General Report for year ending 31 December 1932, 3, 73-148-089, Arthur Nelson Field Papers, MS-Group-1534 [hereinafter Field Papers], Alexander Turnbull Library, Wellington [hereinafter ATL].
50 For example, Tony Ballantyne, *Webs of Empire: Locating New Zealand's Colonial Past* (Wellington: Bridget Williams Books, 2012); Alan Lester, *Imperial Networks: Creating Identities in Nineteenth-Century South Africa and Britain* (London: Routledge, 2001).
51 C.A. Bayly, *Empire and Information: Intelligence Gathering and Social Communication in India, 1780–1870* (Cambridge, UK: Cambridge University Press, 1996); Zoë Laidlaw, *Colonial Connections, 1815–45: Patronage, the Information Revolution and Colonial Government* (Manchester, UK: Manchester University Press, 2005); John Griffiths, 'Were there Municipal Networks in the British World c. 1890–1939?', *Journal of Imperial and Commonwealth History* 37(4) (2009): 575–97.

of people driven by the gold rushes in the United States, Australia, and New Zealand.[52] They occurred through international business ventures, through written correspondence, and through the vast amount of printed reading material—including newspapers, books, journals, and magazines—that attracted an international readership.[53] From the late nineteenth century, Australia and New Zealand were incorporated into a growing 'imperial press system' centred on London. Comprising a number of private press enterprises and facilitated by a growing network of undersea cables and telegraphs, it allowed news items from the Metropole to be circulated and reproduced in newspapers across the empire.[54]

Connections between Australia and New Zealand were particularly strong, given their proximity and their shared heritage as British colonial states. This 'Tasman world', which dominated political, cultural, and economic exchanges between the Australian and New Zealand colonies in the nineteenth century, has witnessed a resurgence in scholarly interest in recent years.[55] These ties did not end with the Federation of the six Australian colonies in 1901. They continued to grow and develop in less recognised ways, including in trade relations, defence policy, travel, immigration, print culture, trade union activities, and a reciprocal interest in the policy experiments carried out by both governments in areas such

---

52   David Goodman, *Gold Seeking: Victoria and California in the 1850s* (Stanford, CA: Stanford University Press, 1994); Eli Daniel Potts and Annette Potts, *Young America and Australian Gold: Americans and the Gold Rush of the 1850s* (Brisbane: University of Queensland Press, 1974).

53   Alexis Weedon, *Victorian Publishing: The Economics of Book Production for a Mass Market, 1836–1916* (Aldershot, UK: Ashgate, 2003); Martyn Lyons, 'Britain's Largest Export Market', in *A History of the Book in Australia, 1891–1945*, eds Martyn Lyons and John Arnold (Brisbane: University of Queensland Press, 2001), 19–26; Susann Liebich, *The Transported Imagination: Australian Interwar Magazines and the Geographical Imaginaries of Colonial Modernity* (New York: Cambria Press, 2018).

54   Simon J. Potter, *News and the British World: The Emergence of an Imperial Press System, 1876–1922* (Oxford, UK: Clarendon Press, 2003); John Arnold, 'Newspapers and Daily Reading', in *A History of the Book in Australia, 1891–1945*, eds Martyn Lyons and John Arnold (Brisbane: University of Queensland Press, 2001), 255–68; Ross Harvey, 'Newspapers', in *Book and Print in New Zealand: A Guide to Print Culture in Aotearoa*, eds Penny Griffith, Ross Harvey, and Keith Maslen (Wellington: Victoria University Press, 1997), 128–35.

55   See Philippa Mein Smith, 'The Tasman World', in *The New Oxford History of New Zealand*, ed. Giselle Byrnes (Melbourne: Oxford University Press, 2009), 299. Mein Smith argued that earlier historians such as Keith Sinclair had sidelined the notion of 'Australasia' in favour of more nationalist narratives; however, the fact that Sinclair devoted an entire edited collection to trans-Tasman connections in the 1980s suggests that 'Australasian' history did not fall out of favour as much as recent historians assume. See Keith Sinclair, ed., *Tasman Relations: New Zealand and Australia, 1788–1988* (Auckland: Auckland University Press, 1987).

as industrial arbitration and social welfare.[56] This led Philippa Mein Smith to conclude that, in both a global and a regional context, 'New Zealand's most important relationship is with Australia'.[57] This reinforces the value of comparing such similar movements on both sides of the Tasman.

Chapter outline

As noted earlier, the citizens' movements present a contradiction between their often-radical aspirations and their more reactionary traditions. To fully comprehend the latter, one must understand the conservative language that underpinned their world view. The citizens' movements did not simply emerge, fully formed, in the midst of a largely unparalleled economic crisis; they drew on a long tradition of conservative political parties, pressure groups, educational associations, and protest movements. This tradition is the subject of Chapter One. Chapter Two explores how this conservative tradition then became radicalised by the Great Depression. It also explains how the citizens' movements came into being at the height of this process.

The citizens' movements expressed a contradictory mix of reactionary and radical ideas that I have described as populist conservatism. Chapter Three explores this mix of ideas in depth. In particular, it outlines how the leaders of the citizens' movements used written and spoken language

---

56   Donald Denoon, 'Re-Membering Australasia: A Repressed Memory', *Australian Historical Studies* 34(122) (2003): 290–304; Peter Hempenstall, ed., *Remaking the Tasman World* (Christchurch, NZ: Canterbury University Press, 2008); Philippa Mein Smith and Peter Hempenstall, 'Australia and New Zealand: Turning Shared Pasts into a Shared History', *History Compass* 1(1) (2003): 1–8; Philippa Mein Smith, Donald Denoon, and Marivic Wyndham, *A History of Australia, New Zealand and the Pacific: The Formation of Identities* (Oxford, UK: Blackwell Publishers, 2000); Ian McGibbon, 'Australia–New Zealand Defence Relations to 1939', in *Tasman Relations: New Zealand and Australia, 1788–1988*, ed. Keith Sinclair (Auckland: Auckland University Press, 1987), 164–82; Miles Fairburn, 'Is There a Good Case for New Zealand Exceptionalism?', in *Disputed Histories: Imagining New Zealand's Pasts*, eds Tony Ballantyne and Brian Moloughney (Dunedin, NZ: Otago University Press, 2006); Hawke, 'Australian and New Zealand Economic Development from about 1890 to 1940', 104–5; Keith Sinclair, 'The Great Anzac Plant War: Australia–New Zealand Trade Relations, 1919–39', in *Tasman Relations: New Zealand and Australia, 1788–1988*, ed. Keith Sinclair (Auckland: Auckland University Press, 1987), 124–41; P.J. Lloyd, 'Australia–New Zealand Trade Relations: NAFTA to CER', in *Tasman Relations: New Zealand and Australia, 1788–1988*, ed. Keith Sinclair (Auckland: Auckland University Press, 1987), 142–63; Erik Olssen and Bruce Scates, 'Class Formation and Political Change: A Trans-Tasman Dialogue', *Labour History* 95 (2008): 3–24; Shelley Harford, 'A Trans-Tasman Union Community: Growing Global Solidarity', *Labour History* 95 (2008): 133–49.
57   Philippa Mein Smith, *A Concise History of New Zealand* (New York: Cambridge University Press, 2005), 91, 249.

to construct a picture of the average citizen and the party politicians they sought to counter. The ideology that was constructed around this populist struggle was high level and somewhat platitudinal, which initially allowed the citizens' movements to gloss over the contradictions between their radical and reactionary components. But ideology was only one of the ways in which the leaders of the citizens' movements used populism to build a mass following. Chapter Four explores what I have described as the 'populist culture' of the citizens' movements. Virtually the entirety of their operations, from the way they promoted themselves to their organisational structure, was designed to build an enthusiastic and committed mass following. Through semi-ritualistic mass meetings and the shrewd use of traditional and modern media—such as pamphlets and journals, but also the burgeoning technology of radio—the movements' leaders deliberately, and successfully, connected with a wide audience and cultivated an image of size and importance. This chapter explores these organisational techniques.

The citizens' movements could only navigate the contradictions between their reactionary and radical ideas for so long. Chapter Five explores the relationship between the three Australian citizens' movements and a revitalised mainstream conservative opposition party called the United Australia Party. This relationship exposed the divide between those who valued the movements' anti-party purity and those who wanted to cooperate with mainstream conservatives to present a united electoral front against Labor. The New Zealand Legion faced a different situation, but one no less threatening to its unity. Chapter Six outlines how some within the legion began experimenting with unorthodox economic theories, ranging from economic planning to monetary reform. These radical alternatives caused friction with the movement's more traditionally conservative members, who favoured limited government and reduced public spending.

Finally, the Conclusion reflects on the significance of the citizens' movements to the understudied history of the right in Australia and New Zealand. It suggests they played an important role in many aspects of Australasian political history, including the emergence of new centre-right parties in the late 1930s and early 1940s. It also compares the movements with other conservative, right-wing, and fascist groups, both at home and abroad, and identifies their position in the broader tradition of the far right in the Antipodes. But before we can appreciate the significance of the citizens' movements, we must first explore their origins. It is to the wider conservative milieu that preceded them that we now turn in Chapter One.

1

Constructing the citizen: The evolution of conservatism in Australia and New Zealand

When the Constitutional Association of New South Wales published its membership rules in March 1931, it prefaced them with the following overarching statement of purpose:

> The Constitutional Association aims at setting up in Australia the highest standards of citizenship. It appeals particularly to younger men to interest themselves in public affairs and thereby to fit themselves for the responsibilities of citizenship in a democratic community.

> It is a political but not a partisan body. Its members are encouraged to join and work for political organisations. They retain complete political independence, and may work for what party they choose … It is searching for men who will subordinate their own personal interests or inclinations to the common welfare, the 'Commonwealth'.[1]

Such words could just as easily have come from any number of organisations. Taken at face value, there was nothing inherently partisan about them. They promised a collegial atmosphere in which individuals of all political persuasions could learn about the duties of being a good

---

1   *The Constitutional Association of New South Wales* (Sydney: W.C. Penfold & Co., March 1931), 1.

citizen. Guest lectures allowed members to learn from some of the leading thinkers in the state, and public speaking classes provided them with the experience and the confidence to present their own views. More dedicated members could run for the executive committee or one of its subcommittees, where they could learn the language of motions, resolutions, and decisions.

Yet beneath this veneer of nonpartisanship, the Constitutional Association was decidedly conservative. It was formed shortly after the Labor Party won a majority in the 1925 NSW state election, which its leaders found intolerable:

> [T]his Association in view of the continuous violation of its principles by the present State Government decides, while maintaining its non-party character, to work for the defeat of the present Government until and during the next General Election … there is a stark necessity for harmony and co-operation between the forces opposed to Labour if success is to be attained at the next election.[2]

How could an organisation that was ostensibly apolitical resolve to oust a Labor government—and claim, in the same breath, that this did not conflict with its 'non-party character'? Was it being deliberately disingenuous or simply naive? The answer is much more complicated. The Constitutional Association was a product of a conservative tradition wherein certain values were viewed not as political or partisan; they were simply common sense. The pillars of that tradition—a strong patriotic and economic orientation towards Britain, a general commitment to free-market capitalism, and staunch opposition to communism and socialism—were tried and tested values akin to natural laws. They represented the national interest, unlike the values of their opponents. By definition, supporting these values could not be partisan.

The roots of this conservative tradition lay in the dramatic political changes that occurred in the late nineteenth and early twentieth centuries. The franchise was expanding to include men and women who had never voted before. This was accompanied by the growth of new forms of political expression, such as trade unionism, political labourism, and

---

2   Letter from the Constitutional Association to T.R. Bavin, 15 November 1926, box 1, item 2, Constitutional Association of New South Wales Papers, 1925–61, MLMSS 7646C [hereinafter CANSW Papers], State Library of New South Wales, Sydney [hereinafter SLNSW].

feminism. At the same time, the liberal political factions in each country were challenging the conservative status quo; they were using the power of the state to promote social welfare and break up the large tracts of land held by prominent families for closer settlement by small landowners. Nineteenth-century conservatism needed to evolve if it was to meet these challenges and remain relevant to the growing number of enfranchised men and women. But how could it do that without abandoning its core pillars?

Consolidation of the two-party system

In the late nineteenth century, conservatism and liberalism were the dominant political factions in Australasian politics. Conservatism was generally represented in Australia by the Free Trade Party, and in New Zealand by a loose coalition of independent MPs. By the first decade of the twentieth century, these conservative factions had been relegated to the opposition benches. The New Zealand Liberal Party had held power since 1891, and Alfred Deakin's Liberal Protectionist Party led the first two Australian ministries after Federation in 1901. These 'social liberals' believed the state should play a more active role in improving social welfare and, particularly in Australia, protecting fledgling domestic industries by imposing tariffs on imported manufactured goods. Their willingness to use the state apparatus to intervene in the economy occasionally led them to align with labour representatives, although this was often a fractious relationship.

The emergence of an independent political labour faction changed this dynamic. Broadly speaking, the labour movement sought the redistribution of political and economic power between the bourgeoisie and the working class. It had already demonstrated its power in the field of industrial action during the empire-wide maritime strikes of 1890, and again in New Zealand during the 1913 Great Strike. The turn of the century saw many within the labour movement begin redirecting their energy towards the parliamentary process, in part because of the failure of large-scale industrial action. Labour and socialist political parties began to proliferate, culminating in the formation of the Australian Labor Party in 1901 and the New Zealand Labour Party in 1916. To conservatives and, to some extent, liberals as well, the collectivist ideology of labour seemed to threaten the foundations of society and the economy. Rather than being a new contender in the arena of politics, labour was an existential threat to the very system of politics. The editor of the Brisbane *Telegraph* penned the following concerned editorial in May 1893 after the formation of the Queensland Labour Party:

> The political life of the colony has reached a graver crisis … than it ever passed through before. A general election is not now a contest between two political parties, each seeking its ends through constitutional methods, but a great struggle between a party of constitutional conservatism and a party of irrational revolutionism.
>
> … The labour party seek their ends by political weapons and fire stick, not by Winchesters and bayonets. But the objects are the same as though they took the field with armed companies. Those objects must be resisted with all the moral force of the country, and all who aid and abet the aims and objects of that party must be resisted also.[3]

Political conservatism needed to adapt to survive. One of the ways it did so was by consolidating with liberalism to present a united centre-right front against the growing power of political labour. This process has been described by one New Zealand historian as a shift from 'patrician' to 'popular' conservatism.[4] In Australia, this process of political consolidation commenced with the fusion in 1909 of the Liberal Protectionist Party and the Free Trade Party (which had intuitively renamed itself the Anti-Socialist Party). The resulting organisation was named the Commonwealth Liberal Party, which subsequently merged with a splinter labour group in 1917 to become the Nationalist Party.[5]

3   *Telegraph*, [Brisbane], 1 May 1893, 4.
4   David Orwin, Conservatism in New Zealand (PhD diss., University of Auckland, 1999), 93–131.
5   Brett, *Australian Liberals and the Moral Middle Class*, 19–25; Judith Brett, 'Class, Party and the Foundations of the Australian Party System: A Revisionist Interpretation', *Australian Journal of Political Science* 37(1) (2002): 39–56; Judith Brett, '"The Fortunes of My Own Little Band": The Dilemma of Deakin and the Liberal Protectionists', in *Confusion: The Making of the Australian Two-Party System*, eds Paul Strangio and Nick Dyrenfurth (Melbourne: Melbourne University Press, 2009), 23–44; Ian Marsh, 'The Federation Decade', in *Liberalism and the Australian Federation*, ed. J.R. Nethercote (Sydney: The Federation Press, 2001), 93–97; Peter Loveday, 'The Federal Parties', in *The Emergence of the Australian Party System*, eds Peter Loveday, A.W. Martin, and R.S. Parker (Sydney: Hale & Iremonger, 1977), 449–52; Paul Strangio, 'Introduction: From Confusion to Stability', in *Confusion: The Making of the Australian Two-Party System*, eds Paul Strangio and Nick Dyrenfurth (Melbourne: Melbourne University Press, 2009), 8; Margaret Fitzherbert, 'Alfred Deakin and the Australian Women's National League', in *Liberalism and the Australian Federation*, ed. J.R. Nethercote (Sydney: The Federation Press, 2001), 98–112.

The chief vessel of popular conservatism in New Zealand was the Reform Party. It began as a loose coalition of individualist and anti-socialist groups in the 1890s, including the Farmers' Union, the Political Reform League, and the National Association. By 1909, this coalition had formally arranged itself behind William Massey as a unified opposition party. The Reform Party positioned itself as a defender of property, the rule of law, and the free market, as opposed to the 'socialistic' policies of the Liberal Party, although Massey was quite comfortable with the developmentalist ethos of the nineteenth century. At the same time, the Liberals were entering a period of protracted decline, due in part to their working-class supporters shifting their allegiance to the growing number of political labour parties. The Reform Party won a majority of seats in the 1911 election and formed a government in 1912.[6] The 1913 Great Strike furthered the consolidation of conservative forces in New Zealand through the cooperation of the state and private employers and farmers in combating the strikers.[7] This cemented Reform's position as the dominant party in New Zealand and discredited the Liberals' concessions to labour. It also hardened the lines between the propertied classes and organised labour, the latter of whom began to increasingly redirect their energies towards the nascent Labour Party.[8] Nevertheless, the Liberal Party would

6   For an account of the rise of the Reform Party, see Liz Ward, 'For light and liberty': The origins and early development of the Reform Party, 1887–1915 (PhD diss., Massey University, Palmerston North, NZ, 2018); L.C. Webb, Rise of the Reform Party: A history of party politics in New Zealand between 1910 and 1920 (MA diss., Victoria University of Wellington, 1928); W.J. Gardner, 'The Reform Party', in Ends and Means in New Zealand Politics, ed. Robert Chapman (Auckland: Dobbie Press, 1961), 25–33; Michael Bassett, Three Party Politics in New Zealand, 1911–1931 (Auckland: Historical Publications, 1982), 3–14. On the decline of the Liberal Party, see Chapman, 'The Decline of the Liberals'; Hamer, The New Zealand Liberals, 309–60.

7   For a good introduction to the 1913 Strike, see Melanie Nolan, ed., Revolution: The 1913 Great Strike in New Zealand (Christchurch, NZ: Canterbury University Press, 2005); Erik Olssen, The Red Feds: Revolutionary Industrial Unionism and the New Zealand Federation of Labour, 1908–14 (New York: Oxford University Press, 1988). See also V. Hughes, Massey's Cossacks: The farmers and the 1913 Strike (MA diss., University of Auckland, 1977). The literature on employers' organisations in New Zealand is sparse, but there are a few good overviews: see Selwyn Parker, Wealthmakers: A History of the Northern Employers' and Manufacturers' Associations (Auckland: Employers' & Manufacturers' Association [Northern] Inc., 2005); J.H. Millar, The Merchants Paved the Way: The First Hundred Years of the Wellington Chamber of Commerce (Wellington: Reed, 1956); Kynan Gentry, Raising the Capital: An Illustrated History of 100 Years of the Wellington Regional Chambers of Commerce (Wellington: Raupo Publishing, 2006).

8   Jim McAloon, 'The Making of the New Zealand Ruling Class', in Revolution: The 1913 Great Strike in New Zealand, ed. Melanie Nolan (Christchurch, NZ: Canterbury University Press, 2005), 234; Olssen, The Red Feds, 210–23.

limp on in the background, and it was only in 1936 that the conservative and liberal parties in New Zealand finally merged to form a single centre-right party.

The consolidation of the conservative political machine could not prevent divisions arising between different economic factions within the centre-right. Manufacturers, primary producers, and professionals and businesspeople were united in their opposition to labour; however, their economic interests differed in some crucial respects. Manufacturers, for instance, broadly believed in individualism and market principles; however, as their industries were largely in their infancy, their primary concern was to secure tariff protection against foreign competitors. This led them to clash with primary producers over the higher costs associated with buying domestic farming equipment and machinery. But primary producers could hardly claim independence of state assistance; many of the nineteenth-century 'colonial socialist' interventions had been directed towards furthering their interests, and small farmers were not averse to demanding compulsory pooling and guaranteed prices from the state when it suited them. In contrast, the professional and business fraction, which lacked the kind of tangible goods for which the other two fractions sought state protection, found it easier to adhere to the tenets of the free market and limited government.

In Australia, where a long history of protectionism had been absorbed into the centre-right Nationalist Party, these divisions resulted in the formation of a separate Country Party in 1920.[9] The Country Party drew on an agrarian yeoman ideology that exalted the economic and cultural supremacy of rural life over the supposedly nasty and parasitic life of the cities.[10] Although the Country Party entered into a coalition agreement with the Nationalist Party in 1922, it failed to prevent the average tariff rate

---

9   Ulrich Ellis, *A History of the Australian Country Party* (Melbourne: Melbourne University Press, 1963), 1–60; B.D. Graham, *The Formation of the Australian Country Parties* (Canberra: Australian National University Press, 1966), 31–142; Meredith and Dyster, *Australia in the Global Economy*, 103–5. The origins of the Australian Country Party lay in groups such as the Farmers' and Settlers' Association and the Graziers' Association; see William A. Bayley, *History of the Farmers and Settlers' Association of N.S.W.* (Sydney: Farmers and Settlers' Association, 1957).
10   Don Aitkin, '"Countrymindedness": The Spread of an Idea', in *Australian Cultural History*, eds S.L. Goldberg and F.B. Smith (Melbourne: Cambridge University Press, 1988), 51. While Aitkin spoke only of the Australian context, John Martin used a similar concept to describe rural communities in New Zealand. He argued that the small populations and personal working relationships associated with the country acted as dampeners of class differences. See John Martin, 'Development from Above: God Made the Country and Man the Town', in *Development Tracks: The Theory and Practice of Community Development*, ed. Ian Shirley (Palmerston North, NZ: Dunmore Press, 1982), 90–116.

from doubling by the end of the decade.[11] In New Zealand, the division between rural and urban conservatives was exposed by the policies of the Reform Party. A Country Party was formed by the Auckland branch of the Farmers' Union in the mid-1920s due to a belief that the Reform Party was beginning to favour urban business interests over those of primary producers, although it never enjoyed anything approaching the success of its Australian counterpart.[12] On the other side of the divide, a backlash from businesspeople and professionals arose against the increasingly interventionist policies of the Reform Party in the agricultural sector. This led several prominent Reformers to form a new political party in 1927 with what remained of the Liberals.[13] The new conservative party, which named itself the United Party, organised urban business interests against the 'socialistic' policies of the Reform Party while calling for reductions in the size and scope of government.[14]

Citizenship, conservative political language, and 'non-party' organisation

But the conservative world view did not simply evolve through its official party organs. It emerged from the words and actions of a diverse array of conservative pressure groups, educational associations, and protest movements that arose across the British and Anglo worlds from the late nineteenth century. These included pro-empire societies, defence and naval leagues, anti-communist and anti-socialist organisations, conservative feminist groups, paramilitary organisations, xenophobic and sectarian groups, and populist movements. These myriad organisations consciously positioned themselves within an international context. They saw themselves as part of a wider community: the British Empire, or white settler societies, or capitalist countries that were under threat from

---

11   Leigh, 'Trade Liberalisation and the Australian Labor Party', 490; Meredith and Dyster, *Australia in the Global Economy*, 106; Leon Glezer, *Tariff Politics: Australian Policy-Making 1960–1980* (Melbourne: Melbourne University Press, 1982), 11.
12   B.D. Graham, 'The Country Party Idea in New Zealand Politics, 1901–1935', in *Studies of a Small Democracy*, eds Robert Chapman and Keith Sinclair (Auckland: Auckland University Press, 1963), 175–200.
13   Michael C. Pugh, The New Zealand Legion and conservative protest in the Great Depression (MA diss., University of Auckland, 1969), 11–16; Graham, 'The Country Party Idea in New Zealand Politics', 183; Michael Bassett, *Coates of Kaipara* (Auckland: Auckland University Press, 1995), 91–129.
14   Pugh, The New Zealand Legion and conservative protest in the Great Depression, 16–27; Bassett, *Coates of Kaipara*, 138–53.

a growing socialist menace. Their leaders specifically built international connections and alliances to spread their message and were in turn influenced by the informal spread of people, money, and ideas through immigration, travel, business, and print culture.

The growth of these non-party conservative organisations can be broken into three broadly chronological periods, each of which is discussed below. The first, which ran from the late nineteenth century until the onset of the Great War, was characterised primarily by a wave of pro-Empire organisations that desired to promote greater imperial unity. Almost all of them originated overseas (primarily in Britain) before spreading to Australia, New Zealand, and other British settler societies. The foreign and domestic tensions of the Great War heralded the second period, during which a considerable number of patriotic, xenophobic, sectarian, and populist groups emerged on the Australian and New Zealand home fronts. Their energy was directed against several perceived enemies, including Germans, striking workers, Catholics, and supporters of the Easter Rising; however, the Russian Revolution in November 1917 provided a unifying trope, the Bolshevik, under which the various forces of disloyalty could be grouped. The third period, from the beginning of the 1920s, was one in which a network of organisations emerged across the Anglo world in response to the perceived threat of international communism. These organisations explicitly linked the defence of the British Empire with the defence of capitalism, both of which they believed were being undermined from within by an insidious communist fifth column.

Before discussing these various organisations, it is important to highlight the role language played in constructing the conservative world view. This wider conservative milieu utilised language to build a broader, more inclusive vision of what it meant to be a conservative based on certain key words and phrases, such as 'empire', 'liberty', 'democracy', 'the rule of law', 'constitutional', 'loyalist', 'sane', 'decent', 'honourable', and 'respectable'. While the meaning of these terms varied slightly between different conservative groups, the similarities far outweighed the differences. They carried implied meaning to those who understood them, while providing the justification to ostracise or delegitimise those who appeared to threaten them. They formed part of a political language used by conservatives to present an image of objective reality—a natural order of things, built on tried and tested tradition. This language was negotiated through countless manifestos and platforms, pamphlets and letters to the editor, public meetings and speaking tours, newspaper articles and correspondence networks. Two crucial components of this language for the emergence of the citizens' movements were the 'citizen' and 'non-party'.

The 'citizen'

The 'citizen' was the staple figure in the language of conservatism in the late nineteenth and early twentieth centuries. He or she (most typically codified by the patriarchal *he*) was a figure heavily steeped in the values and traditions of British society. He was respectable, genteel, and God-fearing, and he possessed a healthy respect for British political and religious institutions, particularly the monarchy and the church. He was economically self-reliant, and he exercised his political franchise with care and consideration. Charitable and good-natured, he was always willing to help those less fortunate than himself—provided they were worthy of that help. In that vein, while he may have begrudgingly accepted some forms of state pension or unemployment insurance—especially in the colonies, where a certain degree of developmental pragmatism was part of the status quo—he shuddered at the thought that the state might provide succour to those who were unwilling to help themselves. He believed that the *rights* he enjoyed as a citizen came with a *responsibility* to protect and uphold those rights, whether at a community, national, or imperial level. It was only by fulfilling this unwritten contract that he could assume the mantle of good citizenship.

The importance of the 'citizen' to the evolution of conservatism in Australasia cannot be overstated. The notion of 'good citizenship' was elucidated by conservatives as a means of addressing the potentially transformative powers of the broadening electorate. By extolling the 'values of good citizenship'—in particular, the sense of reciprocal responsibilities with the state—conservatives hoped to dampen the electoral demands of the newly enfranchised and undercut popular support for radical reforms.[15] But defining 'good citizenship' was not a top-down process enforced by an elite tier of conservative politicians and the bourgeoisie. It was an organic response by various agents and agencies to the dramatic transformations of the turn of the century, including churches and religious associations,

---

15   Keith McClelland and Sonya Rose, 'Citizenship and Empire, 1867–1928', in *At Home with the Empire: Metropolitan Culture and the Imperial World*, eds Catherine Hall and Sonya Rose (Cambridge, UK: Cambridge University Press, 2006), 284–85.

educationalists, imperialists, and youth organisations.[16] Judith Brett argued that the term 'citizenship' was largely captured by non-labour forces in Australia during the twentieth century and imbued with moral as well as political dimensions. A true citizen served the national interest first and foremost, rather than the sectional interests of a particular class or creed.[17]

'Non-party'

The various conservative organisations that arose from the late nineteenth century provided an environment in which a good citizen could exercise his political judgement outside the party system. By positioning themselves as 'non-party', these conservative organisations established a dichotomic language between themselves and the world of politics. Their motives were clean and pure, whereas politics was full of the selfish and the greedy. Their methods were voluntaristic and rational, while politicians squabbled and bickered among themselves. Their ideals were classless and nationally focused, unlike the sectional and parochial policies of political parties. This protected participants from the 'taint' of politics, replete as it was with the connotations of backroom deals, self-serving motives, questionable alliances, and nepotism. These organisations also allowed conservatives to exercise their political judgement without challenging the status quo. They were not political parties fielding their own candidates, but merely bodies that presented their ideas to MPs for consideration. However, given their values largely aligned with mainstream conservative parties, they acted like an unofficial extra-parliamentary arm of the centre-right. In short, 'non-party' organisations could claim to be apolitical while being fluent in the language of conservatism.

The 'non-party' language used by these conservative organisations was also a reaction against the emergence of the first political parties at the end of the nineteenth century. While party governments proved more stable and long-lived than the revolving door of independent premiers and ministries that preceded them, they were also believed to have reduced the freedom that MPs had once enjoyed. In Australia, this criticism was directed primarily against labour parties, given the energy

---

16   For a good discussion of the *fin de siècle*, see Mikuláš Teich and Roy Porter, eds, *Fin de Siècle and its Legacy* (Cambridge, UK: Cambridge University Press, 1990).

17   Judith Brett, 'Retrieving the Partisan History of Australian Citizenship', *Australian Journal of Political Science* 36(3) (2001): 423–37.

they devoted to building organisational unity. Official platforms were agreed on by members at party conventions and a list of candidates preselected who were willing to uphold the platform. This process may seem uncontroversial today—indeed, it is the norm in most Western countries—but it was a novelty in late nineteenth and early twentieth-century Australasian politics. For Australian conservatives, this unwanted intrusion was described as 'machine politics'—a term first used in the United States to describe the clientelism of political organisations such as Tammany Hall.[18] These labour 'machines', according to their conservative opponents, were dominated by sectional interests—trade unions, socialists, and others who were only interested in stoking class tensions. Any labour politician who dared to step out of line was quickly called to order by the party whip. As a united Labour Party was not formed in New Zealand until 1916, anti-party ire was originally directed at the Liberal Party—the country's first official political party, which governed from 1891 until 1912. However, the rhetoric was the same: party government robbed MPs of their independence and made them shills of their party masters.[19] It was this criticism of 'machine politics', and the exaltation of the 'non-party' label, that would eventually metastasise into the anti-party populism of the citizens' movements.

Building imperial networks, 1860s – 1913

Pro-empire organisations

The Royal Colonial Institute was the first major pro-empire society. Founded in 1869 in London as a centre for imperial and colonial studies, its aim was to foster closer imperial unity through the production of educational material such as leaflets, pamphlets, posters, school textbooks, and imperial exhibitions. Its facilities—in particular, its extensive library—became a haven for prominent colonial citizens when visiting Britain. It was a place to share ideas, to forge business connections, and to rub shoulders with the elite. As a resident of Hobart described it on returning from a trip to London:

---

18   M. Craig Brown and Charles N. Halaby, 'Machine Politics in America, 1870–1945', *Journal of Interdisciplinary History* 17(3) (1987): 587–612; Rodney K. Smith, *Against the Machines: Minor Parties and Independents in New South Wales, 1910–2006* (Sydney: The Federation Press, 2006).

19   *Otago Daily Times*, [Dunedin, NZ], 8 May 1895, 2.

> Nearly all the colonists during their sojourn in London, and especially public men, are glad to avail themselves of the facilities that the Institute affords. They find it to be a convenient rendezvous, a place where they ascertain who is in London from their own or neighbouring colonies, often have pleasant surprises in unexpectedly meeting friends and acquaintances, and obtain information from the energetic and courteous secretary (Mr J.S. O'Halloran, C.M.G.) on many subjects, and who is always anxious to get visitors from the colonies to read papers and promote discussion at the Institute's periodical meetings on colonial subjects.[20]

A similar organisation named the Imperial Institute was established by royal charter in 1888. Its planners had unsuccessfully tried to convince the Royal Colonial Institute and other bodies to unite into a single institution for empire study and propaganda. Instead, a plethora of pro-empire organisations sprouted across the British world between the 1880s and the beginning of the Great War.[21] This reflected the importance of voluntary participation in the conservative world view; coercion into a single pro-empire organisation was contrary to the individualism that good citizens were meant to display.

The Primrose League was another early pro-empire organisation. Founded in 1883 in honour of the late Benjamin Disraeli, the Primrose League sought to generate widespread popular support for 'the maintenance of Religion, the Estates of the Realm and the unity of the British Empire'.[22] In practice, it was little more than an appendage of the British Conservative Party; its leading members were almost always Conservative MPs, and its 'Grand Chancellor' was usually also the leader of the Conservative Party. The Primrose League also acted as an unpaid canvasser for the Conservatives during elections, allowing the party to circumvent legislation passed in 1883 limiting expenditure on elections.[23] Nevertheless, its generic principles and its claim to be apolitical generated widespread cross-class support. By 1891, it claimed more than a million

---

20   *Mercury*, [Hobart], 29 July 1899, 2.

21   John Mackenzie, *Propaganda and Empire: The Manipulation of British Public Opinion, 1880–1960* (Manchester, UK: Manchester University Press, 1984), 148.

22   ibid., 149–50; Matthew Hendley, 'Constructing the Citizen: The Primrose League and the Definition of Citizenship in the Age of Mass Democracy in Britain, 1918–1928', *Journal of the Canadian Historical Association* 7(1) (1996): 3–297, at p. 128. See also Martin Pugh, *The Tories and the People, 1880–1935* (Oxford, UK: Basil Blackwell Publishing, 1985).

23   Hendley, 'Constructing the Citizen', 128–29; Martin Pugh, 'Popular Conservatism in Britain: Continuity and Change, 1880–1987', *Journal of British Studies* 27(3) (1988): 254–82, at p. 257.

members, including a strong working-class cohort in industrial strongholds such as Newcastle and Sheffield.[24] It gathered this high level of support through leaflets, lantern displays, lectures, and imperial exhibitions, but also social functions such as fetes and garden parties.[25] New Zealand conservatives were inspired by the Primrose League to form a National Association to combat the electoral dominance of the Liberal Party. Several leading members of the National Association were also members of the Primrose League, including Sir John Hall and F.D.H. Bell.[26] The National Association later contributed to the formation of the Reform Party.

The Liberty and Property Defence League was more specifically focused on defending laissez-faire capitalism. Founded in July 1882, it sought to counter what its founders perceived to be a 'socialistic' trend in British government and legislation.[27] It considered capitalism to be apolitical in nature; in the report of its fifth annual meeting, the league described its desire 'to get men, irrespective of party differences, to combine for the defence of liberty and the protection and security of property'.[28] It also sought to spread its ideas to the colonies through correspondence, newspapers, and the dissemination of its literature. The Australian Club, a Sydney gentlemen's group frequented by the colonial elite, maintained an ongoing correspondence with the league.[29] In January 1892, W.C. Crofts, the league's secretary, wrote to New Zealand conservative politician John Hall suggesting the formation of a New Zealand Liberty and Property Defence League to counter the 'socialistic' legislation of the Liberal Party.[30] League publications such as *A Plea for Liberty* were distributed by booksellers in major cities across the Tasman world, and one such

---

24   Hendley, 'Constructing the Citizen', 130–31. On the phenomenon of British working-class deference to conservative principles, see Pugh, 'Popular Conservatism in Britain', 273; Frank Parkin, 'Working-Class Conservatives: A Theory of Political Deviance', *The British Journal of Sociology* 18 (1967): 278–90.

25   Mackenzie, *Propaganda and Empire*, 150–51; Hendley, 'Constructing the Citizen', 131–32; Pugh, 'Popular Conservatism in Britain', 269.

26   Orwin, Conservatism in New Zealand, 96–98.

27   David Nicholls, 'Positive Liberty, 1880–1914', *The American Political Science Review* 56(1) (1962): 114–28, at pp. 119–20; Edward Bristow, 'The Liberty and Property Defence League and Individualism', *The Historical Journal* 18(4) (1975): 761–89, at p. 761; Norbert Soldon, '*Laissez-Faire* as Dogma: The Liberty and Property Defence League, 1882–1914', in *Essays in Anti-Labour History: Responses to the Rise of Labour in Britain*, ed. K.D. Brown (London: Macmillan, 1974).

28   *Report of the Fifth Annual Meeting of the Liberty and Property Defence League* (London: Liberty and Property Defence League, 1887), 37.

29   ibid., 47.

30   Letter from W.C. Crofts to John Hall, 18 January 1892, Sir John Hall Papers, MS-Papers-1784-183 [hereinafter Hall Papers], ATL.

publication, Frederick Millar's *Socialism: Its Fallacies and Dangers*, had a circulation of 25,000 within Australia.[31] The speeches or press releases of the league's leaders appeared occasionally in the major Australasian newspapers, usually in the form of 'Home Letters' from correspondents in London. While this did not result in the widespread formation of local branches of the Liberty and Property Defence League, it contributed to the express linking of the British Empire with capitalism in the conservative world view.[32]

The height of imperial fervour at the turn of the century witnessed the birth of a significant number of pro-empire organisations. These organisations—which included the Imperial Federation Defence Committee, the British Empire League, the League of the Empire, and the Overseas Club—spread quickly across the British world. The League of the Empire, for example, established branches in Tasmania, South Australia, and New Zealand by 1904.[33] Its main aim was to foster imperial sentiment through education, which it did through a series of colonial education conferences in London from 1907. It also produced a series of textbooks and atlases for use in elementary and secondary schools, and established the Comrades Correspondence Branch in schools, which at its height facilitated connections between 30,000 students across the British Empire.[34] In 1910, it entered into a partnership with the Overseas Club, which brought with it more than 100,000 empire loyalists from across the dominions.[35] The NSW branch of the British Empire League was instrumental in making Empire Day an official national holiday in 1905.[36]

---

31 Moore, *The Right Road*, 16–17.

32 The Victorian Liberty and Property Defence League, founded in 1884, and the Liberty League, founded in Christchurch in 1896, were focused primarily on combating prohibition. See *The Argus*, [Melbourne], 17 July 1884, 6; *Otago Daily Times*, [Dunedin, NZ], 18 July 1896, 7.

33 *The Colonist*, [Sydney], 21 July 1903, 3; *Australian Town and Country Journal*, [Sydney], 25 May 1904, 43; *The Advertiser*, [Adelaide], 9 July 1904, 10; Helen Jones, 'Rees George, Madeline (1851–1931)', *Australian Dictionary of Biography* (National Centre of Biography, The Australian National University, published first in hardcopy 1981), available from: adb.anu.edu.au/biography/george-madeline-rees-6296.

34 Mackenzie, *Propaganda and Empire*, 155–56.

35 ibid, 158.

36 Maurice French, '"One People, One Destiny": A Question of Loyalty—The Origins of Empire Day in New South Wales, 1900–1905', *Journal of the Royal Australian Historical Society* 61(4) (1975): 236–48, at p. 242. For a summary of its parent league in Britain, see Mackenzie, *Propaganda and Empire*, 151–52.

Female imperialism and conservative feminism

Women's pro-empire organisations played an important part in the propagation of imperial sentiment. The Imperial Order Daughters of the Empire was founded in Canada in January 1900 in response to a telegram circulated by Margaret Clark Murray, the wife of an influential professor, to the mayors of every provincial capital. Clark Murray had recently returned from Britain, where she had been at the outbreak of the Boer War, and was keen to harness the pro-war sentiment she had witnessed.[37] Around the same time, the Guild of Loyal Women was founded in South Africa by a group of Dutch and English women.[38] The two groups began cooperating with each other shortly after their formation, and the guild added 'Daughters of the Empire' to its official title.[39]

The Victoria League, which was founded in London in April 1901, was the most prominent women's pro-empire organisation in Australia and New Zealand. As with its sister societies in South Africa and Canada, the Victoria League was formed in response to the Boer War. Many of its founding members had accompanied their officer husbands to South Africa during the war and had participated in the formative discussions of the Guild of Loyal Women. This provided them with both a model for their own organisation and a series of colonial contacts.[40] A Tasmanian branch of the Victoria League was established in 1903, followed by one in Otago in 1905 and, by the end of the Great War, there were branches in most Australian states and major New Zealand cities.[41] The process of branch formation was given a boost by a tour of the dominions by London League Secretary Meriel Talbot between 1909 and 1911.[42] This imperial network was important for fostering mutual hospitality; headquarters in London regularly entertained visitors from the colonies and introduced

---

37   Katie Pickles, *Female Imperialism and National Identity: Imperial Order Daughters of the Empire* (Manchester, UK: Manchester University Press, 2002), 15–17.

38   Elizabeth van Heyningen and Pat Merrett, '"The Healing Touch": The Guild of Loyal Women of South Africa 1900–1912', *South African Historical Journal* 47(1) (2003): 24–50, at pp. 24–27; Julia Bush, *Edwardian Ladies and Imperial Power* (London: Leicester University Press, 2000), 90–91.

39   van Heyningen and Merrett, '"The Healing Touch"', 29–30.

40   Eliza Riedi, 'Women, Gender, and the Promotion of Empire: The Victoria League, 1901–1914', *The Historical Journal* 45(3)(2002): 569–99, at pp. 573–75; Bush, *Edwardian Ladies and Imperial Power*, 47–49; van Heyningen and Merrett, '"The Healing Touch"', 30–38.

41   Katie Pickles, 'A Link in "the Great Chain of Empire Friendship": The Victoria League in New Zealand', *Journal of Imperial and Commonwealth History* 33(1) (2005): 29–50, at pp. 36–37; Sarah Dowling, Female imperialism: The Victoria League in Canterbury, New Zealand, 1910–2003 (MA diss., University of Canterbury, Christchurch, NZ, 2004), 20–21.

42   Riedi, 'Women, Gender, and the Promotion of Empire', 593.

them to respectable society, while the Antipodean branches welcomed immigrants from Britain and assisted their transition to colonial life.[43] Lantern-slide lectures and British literature were also distributed to the colonies, and a pen-pal scheme between British and colonial children was established.[44]

The women's pro-empire organisations practised what Katie Pickles called 'female imperialism', which stressed that women had a unique role to play in promoting the British Empire through 'hospitality and socialising in the "private" female world, to the support of immigration and education'.[45] Apart from being an example of 'acceptable' public activity for women, pro-empire organisations provided an outlet for the political and moral aspirations of newly enfranchised women that had previously been limited to temperance movements:

> The [Boer] war … offered loyalist women the first real opportunity to engage themselves politically and to speak out on public platforms without incurring male hostility. Not only was an expression of loyalism acceptable; women could argue that they brought special womanly gifts to reinforcing the bonds of Empire and healing the wounds of war. They were the peacemakers who could 'calm the troubled spirits and heal the broken hearts'.[46]

This focus on moral authority also allowed women's leagues to maintain a nonpartisan stance while implicitly reinforcing conservative political and cultural ideals. Women's pro-empire leagues avoided any overt association with political parties and contentious political issues. Instead, they focused their efforts on activities that could be considered extensions of the 'domestic sphere', including a war fund for widows, orphans, and soldiers' graves in South Africa, and affiliations with schools to encourage the adoption of an empire-centric curriculum.[47]

The spread of women's empire leagues to Australasia intersected with the rise of domestic women's non-party organisations. In Australia, such organisations first began appearing in the 1880s, but increased substantially

---

43 ibid., 582–84; Dowling, Female imperialism, 55–78.
44 Riedi, 'Women, Gender, and the Promotion of Empire', 585–88.
45 Pickles, *Female Imperialism and National Identity*, 16; Pickles, 'A Link in "the Great Chain of Empire Friendship"', 26.
46 van Heyningen and Merrett, '"The Healing Touch"', 27; Bush, *Edwardian Ladies and Imperial Power*, 90–91.
47 Riedi, 'Women, Gender, and the Promotion of Empire', 576–79, 585–86; Mackenzie, *Propaganda and Empire*, 49, 90–91.

after white women achieved Commonwealth suffrage in 1902. Once enfranchised, some Australian suffragists directed their energies into harnessing women's voting power towards furthering the position of women and the family in society and politics. This led to the formation of non-party political groups such as the Women's Non-Party Association of South Australia, the Australian Federation of Women's Societies for Equal Citizenship, and the National Council of Women.[48] Some more explicitly conservative women's political lobby groups practised what Marian Simms termed 'conservative feminism', and shared many features with second-wave feminism.[49] The Australian Women's National League, which became a significant force in Australian conservative politics, had four key objectives: '[t]o support loyalty to the throne and Empire', 'to combat state socialism', 'to educate women in politics', and 'to protect the purity of home life'.[50] In New Zealand, the local wing of the Women's Christian Temperance Union worked with local Franchise Leagues on the suffrage campaign, and remained a prominent political lobby group into the twentieth century. The proliferation of women's groups after suffrage was achieved in 1893 led to a successful proposal to consolidate under the National Council of Women, which likewise continued to exercise its influence throughout the twentieth century (apart from a brief recess in the early 1900s).[51] I will return to some of the Australian non-party women's groups in subsequent chapters, as they collaborated with the citizens' movements in several cases.

---

48   Judith Smart, 'Women's Non-Party Political Organisations', *The Encyclopedia of Women and Leadership in Twentieth-Century Australia* (Australian Women's Archives Project, 2014), available from: www.womenaustralia.info/leaders/biogs/WLE0693b.htm.

49   Marian Simms, 'Conservative Feminism in Australia: A Case Study of Feminist Ideology', *Women's Studies International Quarterly* 2(3) (1979): 305–18.

50   See, for example, Margaret Fitzherbert, *Liberal Women: Federation to 1949* (Sydney: The Federation Press, 2004), Ch. 3; Fitzherbert, 'Alfred Deakin and the Australian Women's National League'; Marian Quartly, 'Defending "the Purity of Home Life" against Socialism: The Founding Years of the Australian Women's National League', *Australian Journal of Politics and History* 50(2) (2004): 178–93; Judith Smart, '"Principles Do Not Alter, but the Means by Which We Attain Them Change": The Australian Women's National League and Political Citizenship, 1921–1945', *Women's History Review* 15(1) (2006): 51–68.

51   Jeanne Wood, *A Challenge Not a Truce: A History of the New Zealand Women's Christian Temperance Union, 1885–1985* (Nelson, NZ: New Zealand Women's Christian Temperance Union Inc., 1985); Sarah Dalton, The pure in heart: The New Zealand Women's Christian Temperance Union and social purity, 1885–1930 (MA diss., Victoria University of Wellington, 1993). On the Women's National Council, see Roberta Nicholls, 'The Collapse of the Early National Council of the Women of New Zealand, 1896–1906', *New Zealand Journal of History* 27(2) (1993): 157–72; 'Women and the Vote: The National Council of Women', *New Zealand History* (Wellington: Ministry for Culture and Heritage, updated 13 March 2018), available from: www.nzhistory.net.nz/politics/womens-suffrage/national-council-of-women.

Defending the empire

One strand of the pro-empire groups directed their attention towards imperial defence. The earliest of these, the Navy League, was the product of the 'naval revival' between 1889 and 1914 that stressed the importance of maintaining a strong British Navy as both a symbol of national honour and a guarantor of imperial security.[52] Established at a conference of prominent businessmen, naval officers, and Conservative MPs in December 1894, it quickly spread to the colonies. Letters were sent out in July 1895 from Navy League headquarters in London to colonial governors, mayors, and prominent businessmen throughout the British world urging the formation of local branches. The content of the letters, which were signed by Admiral Richard Vesey Hamilton, stressed the personal significance of empire defence:

> The purpose of the League is to fix public attention in all lands under the British flag, inhabited by English-speaking people, to the inexpressible and fundamental importance to them all of increasing the strength of the British Navy.[53]

Within a few years, branches appeared in Australia and New Zealand. While many soon lapsed into inactivity, they were reinvigorated by a tour of the dominions by Harold Fraser Wyatt, a member of the London Navy League's executive, in 1903–04. Wyatt was especially impressed with the 'diligence' of the South Australian and New Zealand branches, and told a meeting of the former that, apart from championing the need for a stronger navy, the league was 'a political instrument to bring about … that effective, live organized union of all the scattered members of our race'.[54] More pragmatically, the leading proponents of the Navy League in Australasia were also driven by economic concerns; as leading businessmen, farmers, and shipping company owners, their financial interest lay in the preservation of the imperial waterways and the British export market.[55]

---

52 W. Mark Hamilton, 'The "New Navalism" and the British Navy League, 1895–1914', *The Mariner's Mirror* 64(1) (1978): 37–44, at pp. 37–38; Anne Summers, 'The Character of Edwardian Nationalism: Three Popular Leagues', in *Nationalist and Racialist Movements in Britain and Germany before 1914*, eds Paul Kennedy and Anthony Nicholls (London: Macmillan, 1981), 68–69.
53 Hamilton, 'The "New Navalism" and the British Navy League', 39.
54 ibid., 39; Jim McAloon, Militarist campaigns in New Zealand c. 1899–1914: Trade and imperialism, Paper presented at the New Zealand Historical Association Conference, Wellington, 1996.
55 McAloon, Militarist campaigns in New Zealand', 2–4, 8, 12.

While the Navy League looked to the sea, the National Service League championed the defence of the land. It was formed in 1901 in response to the length and expense of the Boer War, combined with the fact that a large percentage of British men were deemed medically unfit for combat. Its first organising secretary summarised these arguments in a well-circulated pamphlet titled *The Briton's First Duty*, wherein he claimed that only compulsory military training would ensure Britain's readiness for the next great conflict.[56] The National Service League inspired the formation of similar groups in Australia and New Zealand. The Australian National Defence League was founded in September 1905 by William Morris Hughes, a leading Labor parliamentarian and future prime minister, and Lieutenant-Colonel Gerald R. Campbell, on the basis of securing universal military training along the lines of the Swiss system.[57] It regularly traded correspondence and printed material with its 'parent' organisation in Britain.[58] Despite never achieving a large membership, the league was highly influential among Labor and Protectionist politicians, including Prime Minister Alfred Deakin.[59] The National Defence League of New Zealand was formed in August 1906.[60] It achieved widespread success, gathering more than 6,600 members as well as the support of

---

56 Summers, 'The Character of Edwardian Nationalism', 69–70, 74–75.

57 *Sydney Morning Herald*, 6 September 1905, 6; John Barrett, 'Campbell, Gerald Ross (1858–1942)', *Australian Dictionary of Biography* (National Centre of Biography, The Australian National University, published first in hardcopy 1979), available from: adb.anu.edu.au/biography/campbell-gerald-ross-5489. An unrelated organisation with the same name had existed in Adelaide since 1891. Its aims were '[t]o oppose all undue class influence in Parliament' and '[t]o help candidates at elections who are in favor of the preservation of law, order, and property'. See *The Advertiser*, [Adelaide], 24 July 1891, 4.

58 Letters from Shee to Campbell, 3 May and 10 October 1906, and Letter from Field-Marshal Earl Roberts to Campbell, 27 October 1906, series 3, wallet 1; Letter from Campbell to Elliott E. Mills, 17 June 1907, and Letter from Shee to Campbell, 16 February 1909, series 4, wallet 2, Australian National Defence League NSW Division Papers, 1905–38, 2DRL/1098, Australian War Memorial, Canberra. The two main booklets written by Campbell on the Swiss military system were G.R. Campbell, *Summary of Swiss Military System, and Suggestions as to How a Similar System Might Be Applied in Australia* (Sydney: Australian National Defence League, 1905) and *The Swiss Military System Including Proposed Changes* (Sydney: Australian National Defence League, 1907).

59 The NSW branch reached its peak of 1,500 members in 1909; see Barrett, 'Campbell, Gerald Ross'. Deakin chaired the inaugural meeting of the Victorian branch in 1906 and addressed a 'magnificent meeting' of the British National Service League in London during the 1907 imperial conference. Later that year, he introduced the first compulsory military training bill, which was scuttled when his government was defeated in 1908. See R. Norris, 'Deakin, Alfred (1856–1919)', *Australian Dictionary of Biography* (National Centre of Biography, The Australian National University, published first in hardcopy 1981), available from: adb.anu.edu.au/biography/deakin-alfred-5927; *The Advertiser*, [Adelaide], 2 December 1905, 11; Letter from George F. Shee to Campbell, 22 May 1907, series 4, wallet 2, Australian National Defence League NSW Division Papers, 1905–38, 2DRL/1098, Australian War Memorial, Canberra.

60 *The Evening Post*, [Wellington], 25 August 1906, 5.

leading politicians and major press outlets.[61] Its members may also have assisted in the Australian league's campaign to establish a royal military college for Australian and New Zealand cadets, as well as contributing to its publication, the *Australasian Military and Naval Annual*, from 1912.[62]

This cornucopia of pro-empire organisations provided one of the key channels for the dispersion of conservative ideals. They formed a space where conservatives of like minds could meet and share ideas, both domestically and internationally. They were also a means by which those ideas could then be communicated to political representatives and the public in the hopes of effecting change. In addition, their predominantly middle and upper-class memberships frequently overlapped. The inaugural executive of the Canterbury Victoria League, for example, contained several current and previous members of the local Navy League executive, including prominent lawyer A.E.G. Rhodes.[63] The leagues also cooperated with each other wherever possible: the Australian British Empire League was recognised as the representative of the Victoria League in New South Wales, and Lady Dixson held prominent positions in both organisations.[64] The techniques these organisations developed to spread their message became standard practice for future conservative organisations. Their memberships were usually based on a small coterie of dedicated activists, supported by a paid secretariat, and surrounded by a larger circle of members, affiliates, sympathisers, and financial contributors. They accomplished their goals through a combination of social functions, lobbying the government and MPs, and public education—which ranged from circulating printed and visual propaganda to public lectures and

61 Paul Goldstone, 'Lane, William' (*New Zealand Dictionary of Biography*, first published in 1996), *Te Ara: The Encyclopedia of New Zealand*, available from: www.teara.govt.nz/en/biographies/3l3/1.
62 See the sixth, seventh and eighth annual reports of the *Executive Committee of the Australian National Defence League, N.S.W. Division* (Sydney: Australian National Defence League, 1911–13). The *Australasian Naval and Military Annual* contained detailed information on the strengths of the various defence forces across the British Empire, as well as the dispositions of the different dominion parliaments towards compulsory military training. For the sections on New Zealand, see *The Australasian Naval and Military Annual, 1911–1912* (Sydney: Angus & Robertson, 1912), 68–73; *The Australasian Naval and Military Annual, 1912–1913* (Sydney: Angus & Robertson, 1913), Part I, 83–86, Part II, 41–45.
63 *The Press*, [Christchurch, NZ], 22 March 1910, 7, and 5 May 1910, 8; McAloon, Militarist campaigns in New Zealand, 8. The Victoria and Navy leagues in Canterbury cooperated on several ventures over the following decades, including a long-running essay competition for primary and secondary schools; see Dowling, Female imperialism, 72–73.
64 Bush, *Edwardian Ladies and Imperial Power*, 92; *Sydney Morning Herald*, 26 August 1911, 13; B. Cook, 'Dixson, Sir Hugh (1841–1926)', *Australian Dictionary of Biography* (National Centre of Biography, The Australian National University, published first in hardcopy 1981), available from: adb.anu.edu.au/biography/dixson-sir-hugh-5983.

classes. This combination of organisation, activism, and networking provided the ideological foundation on which subsequent conservative non-party organisations built.

The Kyabram Reform Movement

One other important organisation of this period, which was not part of the pro-empire phenomenon, was the Kyabram Reform Movement. It arose in Victoria in 1901 on a wave of middle-class discontent with the state government's expenditure—specifically, its failure to reduce the number of Victorian politicians after Federation. When the state premier refused to accede to their demands, the Kyabram Reform Movement embarked on a massive membership drive in the hope that its sheer voting power could elect a government more inclined to its ideals. By late 1902, it had more than 10,000 members and 200 branches across Victoria, as well as the support of the state opposition leader. In October 1902, the opposition won a sweeping victory on the back of this mass support and immediately began reducing the numbers in parliament and the salaries of public sector employees.[65] The dramatic success of the Kyabram Reform Movement had a lasting impact on the conservative world view and would be remembered by the citizens' movements on both sides of the Tasman 30 years later.

Mobilising against organised labour

While these pro-empire leagues were flourishing, employers and the state were developing new means to respond to organised labour, particularly the threat of strike action. This included the introduction of national industrial arbitration legislation (in 1894 in New Zealand, and 1904 in Australia) to foster better relations between employers and trade unions, regulate the negotiation of wages and other working conditions, and prevent (or outlaw) strikes. Moments of industrial tension sometimes generated more extreme responses from conservatives. In New Zealand, employers' attempts to encourage non-union employees to form moderate unions to undercut their more militant counterparts contributed to

---

65 Brett, *Australian Liberals and the Moral Middle Class*, 21–22; Frank Bongiorno, *The People's Party: Victorian Labor and the Radical Tradition, 1875–1915* (Melbourne: Melbourne University Press, 1996), 55–57; John Rickard, *Class and Politics: New South Wales, Victoria and the Early Commonwealth, 1890–1910* (Canberra: Australian National University Press, 1976), 177; William Henry Bossence, *Kyabram* (Melbourne: Hawthorn Press, 1963); Don Anderson, *The Kyabram Reform Movement of 1902* (Kyabram, Vic.: Kyabram Free Press, 1989).

a goldminers' strike in Waihī in 1912. The newly elected conservative government under Massey used police and strikebreakers to end the strike, and a violent attack on the local union hall by strikebreakers resulted in the death of one striker.

However, it was the 1913 Great Strike in New Zealand that generated the most extreme response by conservative employers and primary producers. Two local disputes, in Huntly and Wellington, quickly spread to other mines and ports and, by October 1913, between 14,000 and 16,000 workers across the country had shut down most of the nation's major ports. A decision to use the military to support the police was quickly reversed after a protest by the acting commandant of New Zealand's armed forces. Instead, the government recruited considerable mounted and foot special constables under military supervision to reopen the wharves. At the same time, employers and farmers organised themselves into united Defence Committees in major centres to coordinate the recruitment of 'free' labour, establish communal funds to assist employers, pressure the government into reopening the wharves by force, and ensure that no individual employers broke ranks.[66] Some of the leading figures in the Defence Committees and the special constabulary went on to join other anti-communist movements after the Great War. The 1917 General Strike in Australia, which shortly preceded the second of two highly divisive conscription referendums in December, had a similarly radicalising effect on conservatives. This is discussed in the next section.

The Great War and the great 'other', 1913–1919

Patriotic societies

The Great War helped to solidify the position of popular conservatism. One of the ways in which this occurred was the emergence of thousands of new patriotic societies and fundraising clubs on both sides of the Tasman. In Australia, these included the Adelaide Mayor's Patriotic Fund, the St Kilda Patriotic Society, and the Young Workers' Patriotic Guild, the last of which boasted more than 80,000 members. Patriotic societies

---

66   Matthew Cunningham, 'Massey's Cossacks Reborn? Public and Private Counterrevolutionary Preparations in New Zealand, 1920–1921' (currently seeking publication).

in New Zealand included the Wellington War Relief Association, the Canterbury Patriotic Fund, and the Otago and Southland Women's Patriotic Association. The last was one of more than 900 women's patriotic societies that raised money and provided knitted goods for soldiers fighting at the front.[67] Their efforts often overlapped with those of the pre-war empire leagues—for example, the Canterbury branch of the Victoria League sent care packages to the front and raised money for the purchase of ambulances and machine guns. They also directed their resources into soldier rehabilitation and remembrance.[68]

Coordinating the efforts of hundreds of patriotic societies gave New Zealand conservatives an opportunity to come together to share ideas. One of the earliest coordination proposals was put forth by C.P. Skerrett, a prominent Wellington lawyer (and later a chief justice), at a conference in September 1915. His proposal was ultimately rejected because of a clause that required solvent societies to contribute to the funding of insolvent ones.[69] A subsequent conference called by the Minister for Internal Affairs in February 1916 proved more successful, and the Federation of New Zealand Patriotic War Relief Societies was created to provide uniformity in the granting of relief funds. Each of its constituent patriotic societies nominated a representative to a central advisory board. These included L.O.H. Tripp, partner of the law firm Chapman and Tripp; J.J. Dougall, Commandant of the Canterbury Citizens' Defence Corps and a member of the Navy League; and J.T. Paul, a right-wing Labour politician and former commander of the National Defence League.[70] The society worked solidly throughout the war and continued to dispense its considerable funds on soldier rehabilitation after the armistice.[71]

---

67 'Women Fundraising for Belgium, First World War', *New Zealand History* (Wellington: Ministry for Culture and Heritage, updated 17 May 2017), available from: www.nzhistory.net.nz/media/photo/womens-fundraising. See also Sarah Jane Piesse, Patriotic welfare in Otago: A history of the Otago Patriotic and General Welfare Association 1914–1950 and the Otago Provincial Patriotic Council 1939– (MA diss., University of Otago, Dunedin, NZ, 1981).

68 Dowling, Female imperialism, 40–54.

69 L.O.H. Tripp, *The War Effort of New Zealand* (Auckland: Whitcombe & Tombs, 1923), 177. Skerrett's proposal is detailed in *Wanganui Chronicle*, 22 September 1915, 6.

70 Tripp, *The War Effort of New Zealand*, 180–82; *The Colonist*, [Sydney], 19 February 1916, 4; *Marlborough Express*, [Blenheim, NZ], 4 March 1916, 2; *The Evening Post*, [Wellington], 4 May 1916, 8; Letter from J.J. Dougall to Minister of Defence, 19 November 1914, Rifle Clubs—Christchurch Citizens Defence Corps, 1914–1919, AAYS 8638 AD1/1035, Archives New Zealand, Wellington; *The Press*, [Christchurch, NZ], 24 May 1915, 9; Erik Olssen, 'Paul, John Thomas' (*Dictionary of New Zealand Biography*, first published in 1996), *Te Ara: The Encyclopedia of New Zealand*, available from: www.teara.govt.nz/en/biographies/3p16/1.

71 *The Evening Post*, [Wellington], 9 October 1919, 6.

The campaign for national efficiency in New Zealand also brought together like-minded conservatives. This campaign arose because of the unprecedented demands the Great War placed on New Zealand's human and material resources. In February 1917, the government appointed a National Efficiency Board to consider the means for organising the nation's industries and regulating competing demands for military and industrial manpower.[72] Its chairman, William Ferguson, was a prominent Wellington engineer who had played a leading role in the development of the capital's harbour facilities.[73] He was also a member of the Wellington War Relief Association executive alongside the Federation of New Zealand Patriotic War Relief Societies delegate Tripp.[74] Ferguson's colleagues on the National Efficiency Board included prominent businessmen and politicians such as Thomas Moss and J.H. Gunson, as well as Dunedin sheepfarmer and longstanding member of the Victorian and Navy leagues, James Begg.[75] By June 1917, the board had produced a detailed list of recommendations to the government based on its ranking of New Zealand's industries in terms of their 'essentiality'.[76] However, apart from implementing restrictions on the import, manufacture, and sale of liquor, the government dismissed the board's recommendations, and it dissolved shortly after the war ended.[77]

Despite its lack of impact on government, the National Efficiency Board provided valuable experience to its members. It gave them a national stage on which to develop and hone their ideas on the operation and management of New Zealand industries. These ideas in turn contributed to a wider conservative dialogue on cultivating a harmonious relationship between employers and employees in the interests of national development. Unlike the employers' and farmers' associations, of which many of the board's members were a part, the National Efficiency Board required at

72   John Martin, 'Blueprint for the Future? "National Efficiency" and the First World War', in *New Zealand's Great War: New Zealand, the Allies and the First World War*, eds John Crawford and Ian McGibbon (Auckland: Exisle Publishing, 2007), 520.

73   ibid., 521; F. Nigel Stace, 'Ferguson, William' (*Dictionary of New Zealand Biography*, first published in 1996), *Te Ara: The Encyclopedia of New Zealand*, available from: www.teara.govt.nz/en/biographies/3f4/1.

74   *The Evening Post*, [Wellington], 4 March 1916, 9. Ferguson resigned from this position on commencing work with the board; see *The Evening Post*, [Wellington], 7 February 1917, 6.

75   Martin, 'Blueprint for the Future?', 520, 526; Letter from Marjorie Macandrew to Mrs Begg, 26 May 1960, and Obituary in the *Otago Daily Times*, date not mentioned, James Begg Papers [hereinafter Begg Papers], privately held.

76   David Littlewood, 'Should he serve?' The Military Service Boards' operations in the Wellington Provincial District, 1916–1918' (MA diss., Massey University, Palmerston North, NZ, 2010), 32–33.

77   Martin, 'Blueprint for the Future?', 521–30.

least a token effort to balance the interests of capital and labour to achieve a perceived 'common good'.[78] Linking such recommendations to the war effort allowed the board to disguise them under the smokescreen of the 'public interest'.[79] Together, the National Efficiency Board and the Federation of New Zealand Patriotic War Relief Societies provided New Zealand conservatives with the experience, the contacts, and the ideological repository to form a number of important anti-communist organisations after the war.

In addition to the plethora of patriotic societies, the tensions of the Great War spurred the growth of several xenophobic, sectarian, and populist organisations. Rising patriotic and imperial fervour, combined with growing anxieties about the war's progress and its massive toll on human life, led people to look for an 'other' on the home front that might be subverting the war effort. They found one such 'other' in the 'German menace': German immigrants, or people of German descent, whom they feared might be secretly in league with the Kaiser. Anti-German leagues in Australia and New Zealand called for a boycott of German shops and goods, the removal of government officials and educators of German heritage, and the confiscation of German property.[80] The rhetoric expressed at their public meetings was often heated and vitriolic:

> I have no patience ... with the public man who sympathises with a German because his window has been broken (Wild applause). When I hear of a man doing a thing like that my mind runs back to the murderous fumes of France and the diabolical outrages of Belgium ... The Germans don't fight fairly; It's not war they are waging—it's just an instrument of hell to ruin the civilised world (Cheers).[81]

Such xenophobia was not new—immigrants from China, Russia, and other countries had been similarly demonised before the war—but the war gave anti-Germanism added fervour.

---

78   ibid., 524–25.
79   ibid., 526.
80   For sample literature, see Alexander Trapeznik, 'New Zealand's Perceptions of the Russian Revolution of 1917', *Revolutionary Russia* 19(1) (2006): 63–77; Andrew Francis, 'To be truly British we must be anti-German': Patriotism, citizenship and anti-alienism in New Zealand during the Great War (PhD diss., Victoria University of Wellington, 2009), 42–52; Frank Cain, 'Some Aspects of Australian–Soviet Relations from 1800 to 1960', *Journal of Communist Studies* 7(4) (1991): 501–21.
81   *Sydney Morning Herald*, 6 September 1915, 10.

The emergence of wartime anti-German societies in Australasia mirrored what was happening in Britain. The most important and long-lasting group was the British Empire Union. Founded by Sir George Makgill in 1915 as the Anti-German Union, it aimed to uproot the supposed German fifth column from all aspects of British life.[82] Makgill had previously been a member of the Anti-Socialist Union, a laissez-faire organisation with links to the Liberty and Property Defence League, and many of its leading figures were prominent in other pro-empire leagues.[83] The Anti-German Union was renamed the British Empire Union in 1916 to emphasise its constructive rather than negative side, in the hopes of encouraging people to shift 'from the old habit of merely working for one party or another' to cooperate in 'the welfare of the Empire'. In pursuing its imperial ideals, the union specifically sought to expand overseas:

> [We seek] a Union of men and women not only in Great Britain but in every portion of the Empire; to foster actively and pursue Imperial ideals; to promote a closer Union, a freer intercourse between all parts of the Empire; to initiate, encourage, and support measures calculated to solidify and strengthen the Empire, and to oppose vigorously all measures antagonistic to these principles.[84]

However, the British Empire Union had limited success in attempting to form Australian and New Zealand branches. The Australian Anti-German League was aware of the union's activities, noting its successes as early as December 1915.[85] The All-British League in Adelaide corresponded in 1916 with Makgill, who replied with an offer for cooperation and copies of several of the union's circulars.[86] A Victorian branch of the British Empire Union was supposedly founded by Colonel C.E. Merrett in 1915, although the first press mention of the union in Australia did

---

82   Ian Thomas, Confronting the challenge of socialism: The British Empire Union and the National Citizens' Union, 1917–1927 (MA diss., University of Wolverhampton, 2010), 18–19; Panikos Panayi, 'The British Empire Union in the First World War', in *The Politics of Marginality*, eds Tony Kushner and Kenneth Lunn (London: Frank Cass, 1990), 113–19.

83   One of the Liberty and Property Defence League's leading thinkers, W.H. Mallock, worked for the Anti-Socialist Union after its founding in 1908. See Bristow, 'The Liberty and Property Defence League and Individualism', 774; Mackenzie, *Propaganda and Empire*, 156–57.

84   Thomas, Confronting the challenge of socialism, 5–6; British Empire Union Leaflet No. 15, quoted in Panayi, 'The British Empire Union in the First World War', 124.

85   *Record*, 25 December 1915, 2.

86   *The Advertiser*, [Adelaide], 26 June 1916, 5.

not appear until December 1917.[87] Around that time, the Anti-German League merged with the British Empire Union in Melbourne, perhaps as a means to escape a defamation suit from a local book publisher.[88] It must have disbanded over the next two years, for in November 1919, the British Empire Union in Australia, founded in Sydney, claimed to be 'a new organisation'.[89] In contrast, the only branch of the British Empire Union in New Zealand was in the small town of Akaroa.[90] When other branches did not eventuate, the Akaroa branch redirected its efforts towards influencing popular opinion via a consistent stream of propaganda produced by a small but dedicated coterie of faithful members. It produced several anti-German pamphlets, one of which was sent to the Taranaki Education Board in the hopes it might be circulated to schoolchildren in the region.[91] Another of its pamphlets, titled 'The Bolshevist Lie', secured a wide enough distribution to be quoted in parliament by Reform MP Thomas Field.[92]

Populist conservative organisations: The Loyalist League and the Protestant Political Association

Domestic and international tensions also created the conditions for larger populist conservative responses. Two organisations bore many similarities to the citizens' movements that arose during the Great Depression: the Loyalist League of Victoria and the New Zealand Protestant Political Association. The Easter Rising—an armed insurrection by Irish republicans in April 1916 aimed at ending British rule in Ireland—was a key factor

87   British Empire Union [London], *Annual Report*, 1924, 24, quoted in Thomas, Confronting the challenge of socialism, 51; *Western Argus*, [Kalgoorlie, WA], 25 December 1917, 5. The Kalgoorlie branch had emerged from a local group calling itself the All-British Association, which had decided only the week before the deputation to transform itself into a branch of the British Empire Union. See *Western Argus*, [Kalgoorlie, WA], 25 December 1917, 19.
88   *Essendon Gazette and Keilor, Bulla and Broadmeadows Reporter*, 28 March 1918, 2. It is possible the Victorian branch of the British Empire Union was simply the Anti-German League under a new name; the lawyer pursuing damages claimed they were 'identical', although this may have been a legal tactic to make the recovery of damages more feasible.
89   *Sydney Morning Herald*, 4 November 1919, 7.
90   It appears the founding of the branch was due in large part to the efforts of a Mr W.K. Virtue, who collected subscriptions from 28 residents of Akaroa for the British Empire Union's *Monthly Review*. When sending the subscriptions to London, Virtue included an offer to form a branch in Akaroa, which was heartily accepted. See *Akaroa Mail and Banks Peninsula Advertiser*, 23 March 1917, 3.
91   The level-headed chairman of the board refused, saying: 'I don't think we ought to try to keep up a spirit of hatred towards the Germans or any other people.' See *The Colonist*, [Sydney], 18 February 1919, 2.
92   *The Colonist*, [Sydney], 17 October 1919, 3.

in raising tensions among Australasian conservatives, who viewed the insurrection as an outrageous and opportunistic act of defiance. It also heightened sectarian tensions between Protestants and Catholics. Given the majority of Catholics in Australia and New Zealand were of Irish heritage, many Protestants questioned whether their loyalties lay with the British Crown, Irish republicans, or the Roman Papacy.

However, it took crises closer to home to lead to the formation of the two organisations. In Australia, two bitterly divisive failed referendums to introduce conscription, in 1916 and 1917, provided the necessary fuel for populist mobilisation. Those opposing conscription included trade unions, socialist minorities such as the Industrial Workers of the World, most of the Labor Party, and Catholics—led by the redoubtable Melbourne Archbishop Daniel Mannix. Supporters of conscription included Labor Prime Minister William Hughes and a small coterie within the Labor Party, urban businessmen, newspaper proprietors, and the Commonwealth Liberal Party.[93] The referendums were punctuated by the General Strike in 1917, which involved up to 100,000 workers across Australia.[94] Herbert Brookes, a prominent manufacturer who had worked closely with Prime Minister Hughes on the two failed referendums, began in early 1918 to look for alternative means to combat those who had successfully opposed them.[95] He found fertile ground for his ideas in Melbourne and, in March 1918, several patriotic leagues, including the British Empire Union and the Australian Women's National League, appointed representatives to a combined Citizens' Loyalist Committee. One of its members, a prominent educationalist named L.A. Adamson, had also attended the last two imperial teaching conferences of the League of the Empire in London.[96] This demonstrated both the novelty and the continuity of the burgeoning populist movement; while it was

93   Brett, *Australian Liberals and the Moral Middle Class*, 48; Dan Coward, The impact of war on New South Wales: Some aspects of social and political history, 1914–1917 (PhD diss., The Australian National University, Canberra, 1974), 367; Moore, *The Secret Army and the Premier*, 17–18; Amos, *The New Guard Movement*, 5–7. By this time, the Commonwealth Liberal Party had been renamed the People's Liberal Party.
94   For a detailed analysis of the strikes, see Robert Bollard, 'The active chorus': The mass strike of 1917 in eastern Australia (PhD thesis, Victoria University, Melbourne, 2007).
95   Alison Patrick, 'Brookes, Herbert Robinson (1867–1963)', *Australian Dictionary of Biography* (National Centre of Biography, The Australian National University, published first in hardcopy 1979), available from: adb.anu.edu.au/biography/brookes-herbert-robinson-5372; Rohan Rivett, *Australian Citizen: Herbert Brookes, 1867–1963* (Melbourne: Melbourne University Press, 1965).
96   *West Australian*, [Perth], 31 May 1907, 5, and 7 November 1912, 9. For a full list of members of the Citizens' Loyalist Committee, see Citizens' Loyalist Committee members, undated, series 21, item 109, Herbert and Ivy Brookes Papers, MS 1924 [hereinafter Brookes Papers], NLA.

a new organisation facing a contemporary threat, some of its chief backers came from existing pro-empire organisations and carried with them their existing ideas and experiences.

The Citizens' Loyalist Committee used populist language to distinguish itself from its enemies. Those who had supported their country with their bodies, their finances, and their votes were loyal, honest, and trustworthy patriots; in contrast, those who opposed the war or conscription, or who had dared to strike in favour of better conditions when the men at the front needed the fruits of Australian industry so badly, were traitorous and disloyal. 'Loyalism' and 'disloyalism' became staples of the conservative world view thereafter.[97] That there were 'disloyalists' in Australia at all was a source of great consternation for conservatives such as Brookes. Surely Australians, who had time and again proved themselves of good British stock, were clever enough to see through the ruses of militant socialists and Archbishop Mannix? The answer, which likewise become a staple tool for conservative scapegoating in the future, could only be that a small, insidious group was exploiting the fears and insecurities of their fellow men with their false doctrines. The Citizens' Loyalist Committee contrasted 'the growing disloyalty exhibited by Archbishop Mannix and his followers' with 'the loyal attitude of large numbers of Catholics who have nobly shouldered their responsibilities to the Empire'.[98] This approach deliberately separated the disloyal minority from the 'noble' majority and expressed hope that those persuaded by the likes of Mannix would certainly be as loyal and decent as their fellow countrymen if the traitorous influences were expunged from Australia.

The centrality of public ceremony and populist rhetoric distinguished the Citizens' Loyalist Committee from previous pro-empire organisations. For example, a 'loyalist demonstration' held on 9 April in the Melbourne Exhibition Hall attracted an audience of 40,000 people. The demonstration was so large it had three separate platforms for speakers and the singing of patriotic songs.[99] The two resolutions passed at the demonstration

---

97   This rhetorical dichotomy between 'loyalists' and 'disloyalists' is explored in Ray Evans, '"Some Furious Outbursts of Riot": Returned Soldiers and Queensland's "Red Flag" Disturbances, 1918–1919', *War and Society* 3(2) (1985): 75–98, at pp. 78–80, 90–92; Raymond Evans, *The Red Flag Riots: A Study of Intolerance* (Brisbane: University of Queensland Press, 1988), 187–90.

98   *The Advertiser*, [Adelaide], 23 March 1918, 17.

99   Circular from Herbert Brookes, 25 March 1918, series 21, item 1, Loyalist Demonstration, 9 April 1918, series 21, item 13, Loyalist Demonstration Programme, 9 April 1918, series 21, item 16, Brookes Papers, NLA; *The Argus*, [Melbourne], 18 April 1918, 8.

were redolent with the new language of loyalism, under which a militant minority of socialists, Irish Republicans, and Catholics were undermining the war effort by sowing discord among otherwise loyal Australians:

> That at this moment, when the men of our race are dying for freedom by the thousands in the most stupendous battle known to history, this meeting affirms its passionate loyalty to the ideal for which their sacrifice has been made, and to that Empire which, throughout Australia's existence, has secured her in liberty, honour, and prosperity, and which now stands before the world as the champion of civilization and of all that makes it precious to mankind.

> That this meeting records its keen gratification that the Commonwealth Government has created fresh powers for the suppression of disloyal utterances, demonstrations, and emblems, and hopes that in the highest interests of Australia there will be swift and drastic action should the offences be repeated. The meeting also affirms its conviction that the vast majority of Australians are loyal to their country and to the Motherland, and would eagerly support the Government in any measures taken against traitors, who are striving for the disruption of the Empire on which Australia's life and liberty depend.[100]

The committee decided to follow up on the success of the demonstration by establishing a permanent Loyalist League, which was launched at a second demonstration on 11 October 1918.[101] However, being bound to a particular domestic crisis made the appeal of the new movement short-lived. By the beginning of 1919, it had only 255 members, which was a far cry from the thousands who turned up to the first loyalist demonstration.[102] It may have encouraged or contributed to the formation of the Australian Loyalty League in New South Wales, although this appears to have been influenced more by an American group named the Guardians of Liberty.[103] The Loyalist League also had several subscribers to its pamphlets in New Zealand, including the *New Zealand Sentinel* and J.P. Shand, a member of the Wellington Education Board.[104] It managed

---

100 Loyalist Demonstration Programme, 9 April 1918, series 21, item 16, Brookes Papers, NLA.
101 Circular from E.D. Patterson, 2 October 1918, series 21, item 24; Letter from T.W. Lyttleton to Brookes, 10 October 1918, series 21, item 27, Brookes Papers, NLA.
102 Brief History of the Loyalist League, c. 1919, series 21, item 107, Brookes Papers, NLA.
103 Australian League of Loyalty flyer, c. 1919, series 21, item 528, Brookes Papers, NLA.
104 Accounts Outstanding on 1 October 1920, series 21, item 534, Brookes Papers, NLA.

to limp on until 1921, when its last publicised action was a joint cabled message with the British Empire League to Lloyd George opposing Irish independence.[105]

While conscription was successfully introduced in New Zealand in 1916, there were still polarising sectarian debates about who should be exempt. New Zealand Catholics opposed the conscription of their priests, theological students, and members of the Marist Brothers, other than to provide chaplaincy services. While the *Military Service Act 1916* did not exempt these groups from being conscripted, Catholic bishops reached an agreement with several government ministers that, if any individuals from these groups were called up in one of the random conscription ballots, the government would certify it was not in the public interest for them to be conscripted. However, discrepancies in how this was applied led some regional military boards—which were legally empowered to decide whether there was sufficient reason to exempt men who had been balloted in their region—to reject the government's certificates in early 1917. This led Catholic bishops to publicly accuse the government of being duplicitous and underhanded.[106]

The acrimonious public exchange between Catholics and the government over conscription amplified existing sectarian tensions, which had already been raised by the Easter Rising the previous year and a debate about the use of the Bible in public schools shortly before the war. One of the most prominent Protestant agitators was Baptist minister Howard Leslie Elliott, a longstanding critic of Catholicism. From early 1916, Elliott began working with the Orange Lodge and a group called the Vigilance Committee to hold public meetings and spread anti-Catholic propaganda. One of the committee's pamphlets, titled 'Rome's Hideous Guilt in the European Carnage', sold more than 20,000 copies.[107] Elliott's meetings were well attended (a meeting in Hamilton in February 1917 attracted more than 900 people) and occasionally descended into chaos as Catholic protestors arrived to condemn his fiery rhetoric.

105 *The Argus*, [Melbourne], 15 October 1921, 19.
106 P.S. O'Connor, 'Storm Over the Clergy: New Zealand 1917', *Journal of Religious History* 4(2) (1966–67): 129–48.
107 Brad Patterson, '"We Stand for the Protestant Religion, the (Protestant) King and the Empire": The Rise of the Protestant Political Association in World War One', in *New Zealand Society at War 1914–1918*, ed. Steven Loveridge (Wellington: Victoria University Press, 2016), 241–42.

All this was a prelude to the formation of the Protestant Political Association, which was formally launched by Elliott at the Auckland Town Hall on 11 July 1917.[108] Like the Victorian Loyalty League, the Protestant Political Association utilised populist rhetoric and public ceremony to build awareness. Some 3,500 people attended the inaugural meeting, with more crowding outside to listen. Elliott told the audience that a Catholic conspiracy was at work to undermine the nation's war effort, infiltrate the public sector, and gain special treatment for Catholics. They hoped to force an early election, he claimed, so the fledgling Labour Party—which he believed was dominated by Catholics—could sneak into power while so many loyal Protestant men were fighting overseas.[109] Elliott went on to give hundreds of speeches around the country to packed venues. The association tried to curry favour with the Reform Party and actively campaigned against several Liberal and Labour political candidates in the 1919 election in the belief that they favoured Catholic interests. At the association's peak in 1920, Elliott claimed its membership had reached 250,000, although this was likely an exaggeration. Elliott was invited to give a speech to the Victorian Loyalty League in October 1921, which they reprinted in pamphlet form under the title 'How New Zealand Defeated the Roman Menace'.[110] The Protestant Political Association rapidly declined in the early 1920s as sectarian tensions eased, although it managed to survive in a much-diminished form until the early 1930s.

The Bolshevik menace

In October 1917, a new 'other' arose that overshadowed all that had come before it. The Bolshevik revolution in Russia, which would later result in the creation of the Soviet Union, became a unifying trope that

---

108 The main piece of work on the Protestant Political Association and its origins is Harold Moores, The rise of the Protestant Political Association: Sectarianism in New Zealand during World War I (MA diss., University of Auckland, 1966). Other sources include Max Satchell, Pulpit politics: The Protestant Political Association in Dunedin from 1917 to 1922 (BA Hons diss., University of Otago, Dunedin, NZ, 1983); P.S. O'Connor, 'Sectarian Conflict in New Zealand, 1911–1920', *Political Science* 19(1) (July 1967): 3–16; P.S. O'Connor, 'Mr Massey and the PPA: A Suspicion Confirmed', *New Zealand Journal of Public Administration* 28(2) (March 1966): 69–74; Christopher John van der Krogt, More a part than apart: The Catholic community in New Zealand Society, 1918–1940 (PhD diss., Massey University, Palmerston North, NZ, 1994); Dickon John Milnes, The church militant: Dunedin churches and society during WWI (PhD diss., University of Otago, Dunedin, NZ, 2015), Ch. 5; Rory M. Sweetman, New Zealand Catholicism, war, politics and the Irish issue 1912–1922 (PhD diss., University of Cambridge, 1990).
109 *New Zealand Herald*, [Auckland], 12 July 1917, 6.
110 *Daily Telegraph*, [Sydney], 4 October 1921, 6, series 21, item 79, 1869–70, Brookes Papers, NLA.

brought together all the 'others' that had emerged during the war. Some conservatives believed Bolshevism, Germanism, Irish Republicanism, and militant trade unionism were all part of a single grand conspiracy against the British Empire; others simply lumped them together under the category of 'disloyalism' for rhetorical convenience. The distinctions between them were often consciously blurred, as was demonstrated in a speech by T.E. Ruth, a leading speaker for the Victorian Loyalist League, in 1919:

> [N]o Australian obsessed by Sinn Fein spite or anti-British hate should be allowed to befoul the Australian nest with Bolshevik corruption … Sinn Feinism or Bolshevism or Prussianism or Suffragetism can only be regarded as a stupid excrescence on our Australian life.[111]

Reverend Elliott used similar words to describe the attitude of the Protestant Political Association (PPA):

> The P.P.A. [is] absolutely opposed to Sinn Feinism, Bolshevism, and Red Fedism, for people of these persuasions would deny equal rights to all, and claimed special privileges for one class in the community, which they called the proletariat.[112]

Fear of Bolshevism was exacerbated by the economic uncertainty of the postwar years. The wartime demands that had buoyed primary industries declined and the end of guaranteed markets and prices for Australian and New Zealand primary produce cast farmers back on to the open market. Rising unemployment and declining wages caused renewed industrial turmoil: Australia lost more days to strikes in 1919 than in any other year until the 1970s.[113] To Australasian employers, working-class radicalism at home appeared to have been emboldened by the success of the Bolshevik revolution and was threatening the very basis of industrial relations. This appeared to be confirmed by the formation of the Australian and New Zealand communist parties, the adoption of socialisation planks by the labour parties, and the renewed campaigns of the Industrial Workers of

---

111 *Revolution or Evolution?* (Melbourne: The Loyalist League of Victoria, 1919), 8, 10. The Loyalist League was a prolific publisher of pamphlets; some of its other titles included *Sinn Fein and Germany* (1919), *The True Story of Sinn Fein* (1919), *Industrial Sectarianism versus Industrial Democracy* (1920), and *The Menace of an Irish Republic* (1920).
112 *The Evening Post*, [Wellington], 16 June 1919, 7.
113 Humphrey McQueen, 'Shoot the Bolshevik! Hang the Profiteer! Reconstructing Australian Capitalism 1918–1921', in *Essays in the Political Economy of Australian Capitalism*, eds E.L. Wheelwright and Ken Buckley (Sydney: ANZ Book Company, 1978), 193.

the World (IWW) and the One Big Union movement.[114] The conservative press reflected this increasing paranoia through the use of buzzwords like 'class war', 'bourgeoisie', and 'proletariat'.[115] As one anxious business organisation in New Zealand wrote: 'There is no question that there exists in this Dominion a small minority of persons, supporters of and agitators for, Bolshevik and I.W.W. principles and propaganda.'[116]

The Bolshevist threat spurred the formation of another mass right-wing organisation in Australia that bore many similarities to the citizens' movements. The King and Empire Alliance arose through a coalition of loyalist leagues and patriotic societies in Queensland termed the United Loyalist Executive, which participated in a series of xenophobic riots across Brisbane in March 1919.[117] Inspired by the Queensland example, a group of prominent businessmen, politicians, and military officers organised a public meeting in the Sydney Town Hall on 19 July 1920 to form the King and Empire Alliance in New South Wales. They explained their rationale as follows:

> During the currency of the war, and since the date of the Armistice, particularly during the months of May, June and July of this year, many instances occurred of a small but organised section of the community taking up an attitude distinctly hostile to constituted authority, distinctly anti-British, and disloyal in the extreme.
>
> A few citizens of Sydney, feeling that such exhibitions of disloyalty were and are a menace to our Empire, and calculated to cause bitterness and strife in our midst, decided to take steps to organise the Loyal Strength of the Community.[118]

---

114 Moore, *The Secret Army and the Premier*, 36; Brett, *Australian Liberals and the Moral Middle Class*, 51–52, 73–74; Trapeznik, 'New Zealand's Perceptions of the Russian Revolution of 1917'.

115 Amanda Gordon, 'The Conservative Press and the Russian Revolution', in *Australian Conservatism: Essays in Twentieth Century Political History*, ed. Cameron Hazlehurst (Canberra: Australian National University Press, 1979), 45–46.

116 *New Zealand Employers' Federation: Seventeenth Annual Report*, 27 September 1919, Minute book 30 November 1917 – 30 September 1925, New Zealand Employers' Federation Papers, 2001-129-01/3, ATL.

117 Evans, '"Some Furious Outbursts of Riot"', 87–89; Moore, *The Secret Army and the Premier*, 24–33; Evans, *The Red Flag Riots*, 44–46, 64–65, 70–72, 186.

118 *Reports of Inaugural Meetings* (Sydney: King and Empire Alliance, 1920), 3.

Plate 1.1 The conjoining of 'Bolshevist savagery' with 'German kultur' in the late 1910s

Source: *Western Mail*, [Perth], 20 September 1918, 26.

Plate 1.2 Linking anti-Catholic and anti-Bolshevik prejudices in the late 1910s

Source: *New Zealand Truth*, [Wellington], 27 December 1919, 5.

Like the Loyalist League, the King and Empire Alliance believed its enemy was a 'small but organised section of the community' that was stirring up disloyal sentiment among a wider group of people. The solution was for loyal citizens to unite in a broad, classless bulwark against this seditious minority. Such a bulwark would represent all sections of the community and express the true national interest. This sizeable demonstration would easily counter the dangerous revolutionary propaganda of its enemy.[119] By February 1921, the King and Empire Alliance claimed a membership of 5,300, with an additional 10,000 members in affiliated groups.[120] Its influence proved far greater during a 'loyalist rally' it organised in the Sydney Town Hall in response to the shredding of a Union Jack on May Day 1921 in the Sydney Domain. Attendance was so great that more than 15,000 individuals had to stand outside the hall.[121] The following morning, a crowd of more than 100,000 assembled in the Domain and stormed the platforms of the Socialist Labor Party, the Communist Party, and the returned soldiers' section of the Labor Party.[122]

The King and Empire Alliance was influenced by several existing pro-empire leagues. Several of its councillors—including Colonel Gerald Campbell, Brigadier-General James Macarthur Onslow, and Professor Mungo MacCallum—were leading figures in the National Defence League.[123] Old habits evidently died hard, for Campbell wrote several articles for the alliance's journal, *King and Empire*, supporting the retention of compulsory military training.[124] The alliance's closest ally—after its fellow branches in Queensland, South Australia, and Tasmania—was the British Empire Union in Australia, which was reborn in New South Wales in November 1919 from a nucleus of disgruntled former British Empire League members.[125] The alliance and the union shared the same president, John Stinson, and many union members were present at the inaugural meeting of the alliance, two of whom subsequently served on the first

---

119 ibid., 12–13.
120 *Sydney Morning Herald*, 26 February 1921, 14.
121 ibid., 7 May 1921, 13.
122 Moore, *The Secret Army and the Premier*, 39–41.
123 *The Australasian Naval and Military Annual, 1911–1912*, iv.
124 See, for example, *King and Empire*, 25 February 1922, 17–18.
125 *Sydney Morning Herald*, 4 November 1919, 7. The organiser, Sir William McMillan, would not go into detail regarding the nature of their disagreement with the British Empire League, merely noting that 'as far as we, whom I have called together, are concerned, we have all ceased to belong to that organisation'.

alliance council.[126] This exposed the alliance to the ideas of the British Empire Union and its parent in Britain, with which the Australian Union was in frequent contact.[127] The two cooperated on several endeavours, including a committee of patriotic societies responsible for coordinating annual Empire Day celebrations that also included representatives of the Victoria and Navy leagues.[128] At its height in 1922, the King and Empire Alliance unsuccessfully sought a formal amalgamation with the British Empire Union.[129] Its influence rapidly fell away after this, although its stronghold in the Sydney suburb of Petersham survived until 1926.[130]

A similar Australian organisation, the League of Good Citizenship, adopted a less populist approach. It emerged from the merger of a group called the King's Men, which was led by former prime minister Edmund Barton and several veterans from the National Defence League, the British Empire Union, and the short-lived Directorate of War Propaganda founded by the Australian Federal Government in August 1918.[131] The League of Good Citizenship combined many conservative tropes and strategies into a single platform, including classlessness, the

---

126 *Sydney Morning Herald*, 11 August 1920, 10; Minutes of General Meeting, 27 May 1920, box 1, British Empire Union in Australia Records, MLMSS 1532 [hereinafter BEU in Australia Records], SLNSW. For a list of those present at the inaugural meeting of the King and Empire Alliance, see *Reports of Inaugural Meetings*, 4–5. For a list of new members of the British Empire Union in the first half of 1920, see Minutes of Committee Meeting, 24 June 1920, and Minutes of Committee Meeting, 8 July 1920, box 1, BEU in Australia Records, SLNSW. The two union members on the first alliance council were J. Harrison and A.F. Gay.

127 The constitution of the British Empire Union of Australia was explicitly modelled on that of its British parent; see Minutes of Meeting of Members, 19 August 1919, box 1, BEU in Australia Records, SLNSW. Apart from receiving regular correspondence from London, speakers from the Australian union also visited Britain and met with members of its parent; see Minutes of Special Meeting of Provisional Committee, 25 February 1920; Minutes of Annual General Meeting of Members, 22 February 1922; Minutes of Committee Meeting, 28 February 1922; Minutes of Committee Meeting, 15 March 1922; Minutes of Committee Meeting, 26 January 1924, box 1, BEU in Australia Records, SLNSW.

128 See the annual reports of the British Empire Union for 1923–26, box 1, BEU in Australia Records, SLNSW. See also *Sydney Morning Herald*, 10 April 1923, 5.

129 Minutes of Committee Meeting, 29 June 1922; Minutes of a Special Meeting of Executive Council, 10 July 1922; Second Conference between delegates of the King and Empire Alliance and the British Empire Union, 15 July 1922, box 1, BEU in Australia Records, SLNSW.

130 The last recorded meeting of the Petersham branch of the King and Empire Alliance was held in May 1926; see *Sydney Morning Herald*, 25 May 1926, 10.

131 Directorate of War Propaganda: General Scheme of Work, 1918, Letter from M.M. Threlfall to I. Maclean, Chief Archivist at the Commonwealth Archives Office, 8 March 1962, Directorate of War Propaganda Papers, MS 897 [hereinafter War Directorate Papers], NLA; *Sydney Morning Herald*, 21 December 1918, 13.

national interest, non-partyism, and educating the public. As such, its objects—which could easily be interchanged for those of the four citizens' movements that emerged during the Depression—bear repeating in full:

> To show that the interests of the community as a whole must precede those of any individual, party or class, and that this common interest is at the present time jeopardised by forces making for disintegration and anarchy.
>
> To create and foster a spirit of national unity.
>
> To work by educational methods towards the realisation of a constructive policy based on an orderly progress and repudiating revolutionary excess.
>
> To show the necessity for increased production and to discuss the problems of private and public ownership; the relations between capital and labour, producers and consumers, and social problems generally in such a spirit as to promote a clear, accurate, and sympathetic understanding of the nature and value of the services of each section of the community.
>
> To pursue these objects on strictly non-party and non-sectarian lines.[132]

The league also released a series of pamphlets directed at a working-class audience that contrasted 'common sense' and 'proved methods' with the 'destructive' and 'revolutionary' tactics of 'fanatics and dreamers'.[133]

Anti-communist organisations, 1919–1929

Building an international network against communism

Conservative 'non-party' organisations continued to evolve after the Great War. One emerging strand of thought in the postwar period focused on defending capitalism against the forces of Bolshevism and organised labour. Unlike most of the conservative organisations that preceded them,

---

132 *Objects, League of Good Citizenship: A Collection of Policy Statements and Speeches of the League* (Sydney: League of Good Citizenship, 1919).
133 *Parliament vs Soviet; To Working Men and Women, League of Good Citizenship: A Collection of Policy Statements and Speeches of the League* (Sydney: League of Good Citizenship, 1919).

these new groups explicitly linked the defence of empire, liberty, and British traditions with laissez-faire capitalism. To these new organisations, collectivism represented a very real and genuine threat; its proponents were active and motivated, and its doctrines were dangerously pervasive among the population. Educating the public in the merits of capitalism was the only means of combating this insidious threat. However, despite their focus on anti-communism, these groups displayed a marked continuity with their predecessors: they drew on existing notions of the national interest and the 'other', they utilised similar organisational and propagandist techniques, and they often included the same individuals who had been involved in previous conservative organisations. By the mid-1920s, these anti-communist organisations had appeared across most of the Anglo world and had begun to coordinate their efforts in a transnational network of anti-communist propaganda.

Three of the more prominent organisations in this international network were the Economic League in Britain, the Sane Democracy League of Australia, and the New Zealand Welfare League. The Economic League was originally established under the title National Propaganda in early 1919 as an offshoot of an industrialist pressure group the British Commonwealth Union.[134] It soon became the foremost anti-communist group in Britain, coordinating the efforts of other right-wing organisations such as the British Empire Union, the National Citizens' Union, and various economic study clubs.[135] The Economic League also drew influence from several of its predecessors. It shared its office space with Frederick Millar, president of the all-but-defunct Liberty and Property Defence League, and several members of its executive also served on the executive of the Anti-Socialist Union.[136]

The New Zealand Welfare League was also founded in early 1919.[137] Most of its leading figures had worked together through the Federation of New Zealand Patriotic War Relief Societies, including league founder and first

134 Mike Hughes, *Spies at Work* (Bradford, UK: 1 in 12 Publications, 1994), Ch. 1. For a history of the British Commonwealth Union, see J.A. Turner, 'The British Commonwealth Union and the General Election of 1918', *English Historical Review* 93(368) (1978): 528–59.
135 Hughes, *Spies at Work*, Ch. 1; Arthur McIvor, '"A Crusade for Capitalism": The Economic League, 1919–1939', *Journal of Contemporary History* 23(4) (1988): 631–55, at p. 634.
136 Hughes, *Spies at Work*, Ch. 1. Millar had always effectively run the Liberty and Property Defence League, including editing its journal, *Liberty Review*. He continued to do so until his death in 1929. See Bristow, 'The Liberty and Property Defence League and Individualism', 768, 788.
137 *The Colonist*, [Sydney], 15 March 1919, 6. See also M.A. Noonan, 'The Aims of the New Zealand Welfare League, 1919–1922', *Historical Society Annual* (1969): 28–46.

president, C.P. Skerrett, L.O.H. Tripp, and D. McLaren from Wellington; Hope Gibbons from Wanganui; and E.H. Williams from Hastings.[138] National Efficiency Board member James Begg was a vice-president of the league, and his board colleague J.H. Gunson was an 'honoured protégé'. Begg's and Gunson's connections with the league probably came through National Efficiency Board chairman William Ferguson, who worked with Tripp and McLaren on the Wellington War Relief Association.[139] Other members included Major D.H. Lusk, commander of the mounted special constabulary in Auckland during the 1913 Great Strike and founder of the short-lived Anti-Party Political League, and C.M. Olliver, President of the Canterbury Progress League.[140]

The Sane Democracy League was founded in 1920 as the Commercial and Industrial Publicity Bureau, but was renamed in 1925 when the league was revitalised under new leadership.[141] Unlike the Economic and Welfare leagues, the Sane Democracy League's founders do not appear to have been part of any of the prewar and wartime conservative organisations in Australia. However, this league overlapped with several organisations in the immediate postwar period, including the King and Empire Alliance and the League of Good Citizenship. One of the leading propagandists of the Sane Democracy League, George Waite, was praised by the League of Good Citizenship for his 'courageous stand against the enemies of our Empire' and invited to join their movement in 'combating all disloyal propaganda'.[142]

138 *Wanganui Chronicle*, 25 March 1916, 6; *The Colonist*, [Sydney], 10 July 1919, 5. Hope Gibbons was the Welfare League's sole member in Wanganui; see *Wanganui Chronicle*, 8 December 1919, 4. Tripp and McLaren seem to have been the league's unofficial envoys to the New Zealand Employers' Federation whenever the two groups sought to cooperate on an issue; see, for example, Minutes of meeting of New Zealand Employers' Federation: Industrial Peace Conference, 9 June 1920, Minute book, 30 November 1917 – 30 September 1925, New Zealand Employers' Federation Papers, 2001-129-01/3, ATL.

139 *New Zealand Observer*, [Auckland], 20 December 1919, 9.

140 *Marlborough Express*, [Blenheim, NZ], 26 May 1919, 5; John Crawford, 'A Tale of Two Cities: Military Involvement in the 1913 Strike', in *Revolution: The 1913 Great Strike in New Zealand*, ed. Melanie Nolan (Christchurch, NZ: Canterbury University Press, 2005), 130; *The Northern Advocate*, [Whangarei, NZ], 5 September 1918, 4; *The Evening Post*, [Wellington], 13 December 1918, 7. The Anti-Party Political League was formed early in 1919 by members of the Marlborough and Auckland farmers' unions (the latter of which Luck was an executive member of). Its aim—reminiscent of the rhetoric of the future citizens' movements—was 'to abolish party Government and to support only those who pledge themselves to vote for measures and not for men'.

141 Keith Richmond, 'Reaction to Radicalism: Non-Labour Movements, 1920–9', *Journal of Australian Studies* (5) (1979): 50–63, at p. 54; Richmond, 'Response to the Threat of Communism: The Sane Democracy League and the People's Union of New South Wales', *Journal of Australian Studies* (1) (1977): 70–84, at p. 70.

142 Letter from the President of the League of Good Citizenship to George Waite, 9 May 1921, box 2, item 6, George Waite Papers, 1885–1926, MLMSS 208 [hereinafter Waite Papers], SLNSW.

Building on the model of the 'other' used by wartime right-wing groups, the leagues directed their efforts against what they believed was a small but dedicated band of communist agitators seeking to undermine constitutional authority. The Sane Democracy and Welfare leagues were convinced that communists were working tirelessly to 'white-ant' social democratic parties, trade unions, and working men's associations to extend their influence beyond their small circle of supporters. This distinction between communist agitators and the wider body of the working class provided a convenient device with which the leagues could reconcile the industrial turmoil of the postwar period with their image of a classless society in which the interests of employer and employee were conjoined. The working class was, under typical circumstances, loyal and patriotic, and negotiations for modest improvements in pay and working conditions were 'just' and 'reasonable'. Communist agitators had disrupted this natural order by exploiting class hatred and social tension with their insidious propaganda.[143] To reinforce this dichotomy, the anti-communist leagues developed a thorough language of opposites: 'loyalism' and 'disloyalism' were complemented with 'sane' and 'insane', 'moral' and 'immoral', and 'clean' and 'dirty'. This further delegitimised the politics of those who lay outside the range of naturalised conservative dictum.

The anti-communist leagues imagined their enemy and, by extension, their own struggle as transnational in nature. The international communist network they sought to combat was supposedly centred on, and rigidly regimented by, Bolshevik forces in Moscow using the Third International as their vehicle.[144] In contrast, the anti-communist leagues described themselves as an organic phenomenon that had arisen independently across multiple countries before deciding to coordinate their efforts. As the New Zealand Welfare League put it in May 1921:

> [I]t is significant that conditions obtaining in this country and which called for a strong non-party, national and educative movement, also existed in other parts of the Empire, and were met in the same way—by the formation of organisations, so like our own that, in all cases, we could exchange constitutions without

---

143 *Sane Democracy*, [Sydney], No. 14, 21 May 1925, 1, and No. 31, 18 September 1925, 1; Chris Priday, Sane Democracy in New South Wales 1920–1940 (BA Hons diss., Macquarie University, Sydney, 1975), 10, 12–13; Arthur P. Harper, *The Revolutionary Campaign: Facts Which Everyone Should Know* (Wellington: New Zealand Welfare League, 1921). See also Noonan, 'The Aims of the New Zealand Welfare League', 31–40.
144 *Sane Democracy*, [Sydney], No. 15, 21 March 1930, 2; Harper, *The Revolutionary Campaign*.

losing our original objectives. This proves that the movement which the Welfare League has originated in New Zealand— its fight against the forces of disorder—its attempt to place the community and national interests before party or section—is the natural outcome of an Empire-wide condition of affairs.[145]

By the mid-1920s, the Economic League was regularly corresponding with the Welfare League, the Sane Democracy League, and several other anti-communist organisations around the world, including the American Vigilant Intelligence Federation and the Constitutional Defence League in Shanghai. The Economic League also introduced the Australasian leagues to the International Entente against the Third International, a Swiss organisation that coordinated the activities of more than two dozen anti-communist organisations throughout Europe.[146]

Educating the public

The anti-communist leagues filled both a combative and an educative function. In addition to identifying and combating the supposed threat posed by international communism, they sought to enlighten the public about the merits of capitalism. Drawing on the established tradition that conservative values were 'natural', the leagues presented capitalism as an inextricable, and therefore apolitical, part of the human condition. Capitalism, as these organisations saw it, was based on certain natural laws that existed outside any political ideology, and any attempts to replace it—or even curb its excesses through legislation aimed at improving social welfare—were doomed to fail. As the Sane Democracy League stated in the first volume of its journal:

> Our system of industry is built upon the constancy of certain conditions of human existence, upon the certainty of economic forces which thence arise, and upon the fact that these forces act with perfect regularity under changeless laws. We can try to

---

145 New Zealand Welfare League, Interim report for Period Ending 31 May 1921, 1, MHE 14:114, NLA; *The Evening Post*, [Wellington], 5 February 1921, 9.

146 McIvor, "'A Crusade for Capitalism'", 641–42; Beatrice Penati, Anticommunism and empire in China (1924–1939): A transnational network among Shanghailanders and Russian emigres (Final research note, research internship, Hokkaido University, Sapporo, 2008), 1, 13–15. References to overseas connections are peppered throughout the material of the Antipodean leagues, most prominently in the journal *Sane Democracy* and the annual reports of the Welfare League (only some of which have survived). The privately held papers of Aubrey Colville Henri de Rune Barclay also contain several references to the Economic League and the International Entente, especially within the pages of his long-time correspondence with the Chicago anti-Semite Harry Curran Wilbur.

redirect these laws against one group or another through bad legislation but in the end we [can] never destroy an economic force any more than we [can] destroy a physical force.[147]

Capitalism represented the 'national interest'—a phrase commonly used by conservatives by this time, and which the anti-communist leagues happily reproduced. The Welfare League, for example, claimed that it sought to 'place the National or Community interests before those of any Party, Section, or Individual'.[148]

To combat the efforts of the communist 'other', the anti-communist leagues employed the same low-level propagandist methods utilised by many of the conservative organisations that preceded them. Since this only required the services of a small number of dedicated members, the leagues proved much more long-lasting than the large populist movements that arose in Australia and New Zealand at the end of the war.[149] Between 1923 and 1926, the Economic League held more than 22,000 public meetings and 4,000 study circles, drawing a total audience of more than four million, and distributed countless books and pamphlets.[150] It also began secretly compiling dossiers on supposed communists and other working-class agitators, which it passed on to businesses and government intelligence agencies.[151] The Sane Democracy League conducted public speaking campaigns, wrote countless letters to newspapers, and produced dozens of pamphlets. It also presented a radio series in 1926, which included topics such as 'How to Raise Wages in Australia', 'Communism & Capitalism—A Contrast in Methods', and 'Production for Profit is Production for Use'.[152] The Welfare League relied heavily on newspaper contributions: its longstanding secretary, the mountaineer A.P. Harper, claimed the league perused a package of newspaper clippings from Illot & Co. every morning for 'dangerous propaganda' and issued responses to any it found. The league also sent weekly articles to about 60 newspapers

---

147 *Sane Democracy*, [Sydney], No. 9, 17 April 1925, 1.
148 *The Colonist*, [Sydney], 15 March 1919, 6.
149 Both the Sane Democracy and Welfare leagues appear to have survived until at least the late 1930s, due in large part to the lifelong efforts of their secretaries, Aubrey de Rune Barclay and Arthur Paul Harper, respectively. The Economic League survived until the end of the Cold War.
150 McIvor, '"A Crusade for Capitalism"', 639.
151 Hughes, *Spies at Work*, Ch. 2; McIvor, '"A Crusade for Capitalism"', 650–51; Mark Hollingsworth and Charles Tremayne, *The Economic League: The Silent McCarthyism* (London: National Council for Civil Liberties, 1989), 3–4.
152 *Sane Democracy: Some Radio Lectures on 2KY* (Sydney: Sane Democracy League, 1926).

and claimed a publication rate of '60 to 70 per cent'.[153] These methods placed a steady stream of anti-communist material before the public consciousness, which reinforced the value of free-market capitalism.

Educating the public was also the goal of several other conservative organisations that arose in the 1920s. The Constitutional Association (which was discussed at the start of this chapter) was established in Sydney in May 1925 to promote discussions on the economic, political, and constitutional questions of the day. The empire-wide waterside strike in August of that year gave the association added impetus, and constitutional 'clubs' soon emerged in Brisbane, Melbourne, and Adelaide.[154] In Western Australia, the Argonauts Civic and Political Club was founded in May 1925 on the principles of 'imperial unity', 'the development of the state upon constitutional lines', 'the counter-acting of the growth of socialism', and the 'freedom and development of the individual'.[155] By July 1926, the argonauts were running several study groups, a model parliament, an Information and Employment Bureau, as well as several 'industrial groups' designed to convince workers of the dangers of communism.[156] The Welfare League actively encouraged the formation of other conservative organisations in New Zealand. In 1921, it collaborated with the Wellington Progress League and Town-Planning Association to form the Wellington Civic League.[157] While the Civic League was nominally 'independent of all party or sectional control', its activities served political goals: it supported conservative candidates at municipal elections and its secretary, David McLaren, was the national organiser of the Welfare League.[158] These various groups would play a crucial role in the emergence of the citizens' movements during the Depression.

---

153 New Zealand Welfare League—General Report for year ending 31 December 1931, 3, Alphabetical correspondence—Nacker-Norton, 1929–62, 73-148-089, Field Papers, ATL. The Welfare League also began publishing its own broadsheet in 1919 called *Freedom*, but this appears to have been short-lived. Only one issue survives: see *Freedom* [Wellington] 1(1) (12 December 1919).
154 Richmond, 'Reaction to Radicalism', 56–57; Moore, *The Secret Army and the Premier*, 51–52; *Sydney Morning Herald*, 26 February 1926, 10.
155 *Argonaut* [Perth] 1(2) (September 1925): 2–3.
156 F.G. Clarke, 'The Argonauts Civic and Political Club: An Early Attempt at Industrial Group Organisation in W.A., 1925–1930', *Labour History* (18) (1970): 32–39, at p. 35.
157 New Zealand Welfare League, Interim report for Period Ending 31 May 1921, MHE 14:114, NLA, 4; *The Dominion*, [Wellington], 18 June 1921, 4.
158 Civic Organisation: Proposed Constitution, Wellington Civic League Papers, 1921, MS-Papers-0158-300D, ATL; Kerry Taylor, 'McLaren, David' (*Dictionary of New Zealand Biography*, first published in 1996), *Te Ara: The Encyclopedia of New Zealand*, available from: www.teara.govt.nz/en/biographies/3m22/1; *The Evening Post*, [Wellington], 4 April 1925, 7.

By the end of the 1920s, there was a well-established conservative tradition in Australia and New Zealand. This tradition had evolved since the late nineteenth century through two key mechanisms: the consolidation of the conservative and liberal political factions into a single centre-right party, and the proliferation of conservative pressure groups, educational associations, and protest movements across the British and Anglo worlds from the late nineteenth century. While the centre-right political parties constructed a unified conservatism within the political process, the 'non-party' organisations reinforced it from outside. The construction of a shared language, with the notion of the 'good citizen' at its centre, ensured that conservatism remained relevant to a new generation of enfranchised voters in the late nineteenth and early twentieth centuries. It was transnational in scope, built on a variety of formal and informal connections across the British and Anglo worlds.

The various conservative organisations that emerged in Australia and New Zealand between the late nineteenth century and 1929 were, for the most part, reactionary rather than radical. While the occasionally extreme and populist rhetoric of the wartime movements may have been on the fringes of respectable opinion, it was still part of the milieu of mainstream conservatism. The Victorian Loyalty League and the New Zealand Protestant Political Association were, to some extent, exceptions. Their populist rhetoric and use of public ceremony occasionally drew the opprobrium of conservative politicians and the press, especially in the case of the Protestant Political Association, which was often denounced as fanatical.[159] Overall, however, the 'non-party' nature of these organisations made it possible for them to espouse political values without being part of the political machinery itself. This reinforced rather than challenged the hegemony of the centre-right conservative political parties of the time. However, the Depression would lead to a radicalisation of this tradition as conservatives attempted to find new solutions to the political, social, and economic troubles they faced. As the next chapter will show, the metastasising of the non-party label into a populist form of anti-partyism laid the foundations for a direct challenge to the conservative political establishment.

---

159 Patterson, '"We Stand for the Protestant Religion, the (Protestant) King and the Empire"', 242–43; Milnes, The church militant, 292–93.

2

From reactionary to radical: The Great Depression and the origins of the citizens' movements

On 31 March 1931, the *Sydney Morning Herald* published a letter from a concerned citizen titled 'Save us from our politicians'. By that time, the Great Depression was well and truly being felt in the Antipodes, particularly in Australia. Plummeting export receipts were having a run-on effect across the rest of the economy, causing mass unemployment and social dislocation, reduced business confidence, and increased exposure of government indebtedness. The letter's author wrote:

> Here we have one of the grandest countries in the world, and if only given a fair chance, it would be more prosperous thany [sic] any of them. However, politicians—and we have armies of them—are so busily engaged in snapping and snarling at one another, like so many demented dingoes, that they will not allow prosperity to come. A commission of a dozen good business men—such as were appointed to 'clean up' Sydney City Council affairs some time back—would accomplish more towards re-establishing confidence in Australia, and putting business matters on a fair footing than all these place-seeking politicians.
>
> What we want in Australia is unity. We want friendship and co-operation between employer and employee. We want the fact recognised that labour cannot get along without capital—any more than capital can get along without labour. All parties—in

> both State and Federal—have borrowed till they have pretty well
> caused the country to 'burst'. The only pity is that they did not
> 'burst' themselves—instead of the country.[1]

The author deployed many of the standard tropes of the conservative tradition. He abhorred excessive public spending. He lauded the business confidence that supposedly came with limited government. He conjoined the interests of employers and employees, arguing that they could not get along without each other. In presenting these values as apolitical, he also demonstrated the 'non-party' conservative language discussed in the previous chapter. At the same time, the author specifically attacked politicians from 'all parties' for their alleged petty squabbling.

Like many conservatives in Australia and New Zealand at the time, the author was experiencing a crisis of confidence. An economic calamity unprecedented in most people's lifetimes was wreaking havoc on the global economy, and representative democracy seemed incapable of addressing it. This led many conservatives to dramatically reappraise the kind of political and economic systems in which they were prepared to place their faith. A small number looked for inspiration to the rise of fascist and authoritarian movements overseas. Others, particularly in New Zealand, turned to fringe economic theories like Douglas social credit, or conspiracies about international financiers. But most conservatives did not so easily part with their traditions. A strong patriotic and economic orientation towards Britain, a general commitment to free-market capitalism, and staunch opposition to communism and socialism—these were a priceless inheritance, tried and tested to such an extent that they were akin to natural laws. The fault, they deduced, must therefore lie in the political machinery of government: political parties and self-serving politicians who were incapable of putting the nation's interests above their own.

This mistrust of party politics was not new. As the previous chapter demonstrated, low-level dissatisfaction with 'machine politics' had existed virtually since the first political parties were formed, particularly labour parties. But the Depression drove this mistrust to new, often radical, heights. The conservative tradition in Australasia, which had evolved since the late nineteenth century, became the basis for a populist revolt against the party system of government. 'Non-party' metastasised into

---

1   *Sydney Morning Herald*, 31 March 1931, 5.

'anti-party'; a distrust of machine politics became an outright desire to smash all political machines, or at least render them irrelevant. In some cases, this condemnation of political parties extended to the questioning of democracy itself. As the author of the letter to the *Sydney Morning Herald* suggested, a temporary hiatus in representative government might be required where politics had veered too far away from conservative traditions. In this instance, the author referred positively to the three unelected commissioners who had been appointed to run the Sydney City Council from 1928 to 1930 after alleged corruption in the management of public contracts.[2] For some conservatives, a similar commission at a national level seemed the best way to steer the ship of state to safer waters.

The onset of the Great Depression in Australia

Labor triumphant

The Labor Party won a landslide victory in the October 1929 election for the Federal House of Representatives, ending 13 years in opposition. In a remarkable case of bad timing, the stock market crash occurred two weeks after the new Prime Minister, James Scullin, took office. Australia's economic situation had already been far from ideal before the crash, having entered a steep recession in 1928–29. Export prices had dropped by 30 per cent by the middle of 1929, and the combined overseas debt of the federal and state governments totalled £631 million. Servicing the interest on this debt alone required 40 per cent of export receipts.[3] Unemployment was at its highest point in a decade at 11.1 per cent, and the nation's trade deficit in 1929–30 was two-thirds greater than the average deficit of the previous four years.[4] The Depression accelerated this downward spiral. Export prices continued to plummet, and creditors in Britain and the United States—so essential to the expansion of public

---

2   Susan Wright, *A Short Electoral History of the Sydney City Council, 1842–1992* (Sydney: City of Sydney, n.d.), 18, accessed from www.cityofsydney.nsw.gov.au/__data/assets/pdf_file/0011/65549/ hs_chos_electoral_history.pdf [page discontinued].

3   Alex Millmow, *The Power of Economic Ideas: The Origins of Keynesian Macroeconomic Management in Interwar Australia 1929–39* (Canberra: ANU E Press, 2010), Ch. 3.

4   *Year Book Australia* (Canberra: Australian Bureau of Statistics, 2001), 243; Meredith and Dyster, *Australia in the Global Economy*, 120.

infrastructure in the 1920s—were unwilling to extend new loans.[5] Registered male unemployment skyrocketed to more than 30 per cent in 1932.[6]

The Federal Labor Government's response to the Depression was handicapped by the Senate, which remained controlled by the Nationalist Party, and the private banking sector. At the onset of the crisis, the government's ability to regulate the supply and distribution of money was limited by the lack of a modern central bank. The Commonwealth Bank possessed some of the features of a central bank, including the authority to issue bank notes, but its independence from government made it difficult for the government to enact monetary policy in times of crisis. Labor Treasurer E.G. 'Ted' Theodore attempted to resolve this problem in April 1930 by introducing the Central Reserve Bank Bill, which proposed splitting the Commonwealth Bank into a fully fledged central bank and a private commercial trading bank.[7] The Commonwealth Bank and several other private banks opposed the Bill as an unnecessary interference in the banking sector. In a highly unprecedented move, Commonwealth Bank Chairman Robert Gibson spoke against the Bill before the Nationalist-controlled Senate, which ultimately rejected it.[8] The Senate also blocked the government's Wheat Bill, which was introduced to establish a compulsory wheat pool that would offer farmers a guaranteed price per bushel of wheat. Many farmers were encouraged by the Bill and the government's broader 'Grow More Wheat' campaign, and wheat acreage increased by 21 per cent over the sowing season. After the Wheat Bill failed, farmers received less than half what the guaranteed price had envisioned, which drove many farmers and country businesses into bankruptcy.[9] The only economic measure the government successfully managed to pass during this period was a substantial increase in the tariff in April 1930.[10]

---

5   Stuart Macintyre, *A Concise History of Australia* (Melbourne: Cambridge University Press, 2004), 177–81; National Archives of Australia, 'James Scullin', *Australia's Prime Ministers* (Canberra: National Archives of Australia), available from: www.naa.gov.au/explore-collection/australias-prime-ministers/james-scullin; Meredith and Dyster, *Australia in the Global Economy*, 123.

6   *Year Book Australia*, 243; Meredith and Dyster, *Australia in the Global Economy*, 131.

7   Ross Fitzgerald, *'Red Ted': The Life of E.G. Theodore* (Brisbane: University of Queensland Press, 1994), 238.

8   Schedvin, *Australia and the Great Depression*, 172–76.

9   Macintyre, *A Concise History of Australia*, 124; Schedvin, *Australia and the Great Depression*, 146–53; Edgars Dunsdorfs, *The Australian Wheat-Growing Industry, 1788–1948* (Melbourne: Melbourne University Press, 1956), 267–75.

10 Meredith, *Australia in the Global Economy*, 122; Leigh, 'Trade Liberalisation and the Australian Labor Party', 490; Ann Capling and Brian Galligan, *Beyond the Protective State: The Political Economy of Australia's Manufacturing Industry Policy* (Cambridge, UK: Cambridge University Press, 1992), 95–101; Meredith and Dyster, *Australia in the Global Economy*, 122–23.

As a result of this opposition, the government's policy vacillated between economic orthodoxy—cutting spending and balancing budgets—and attempts to stimulate the economy through additional spending. In 1930, the Commonwealth Bank, in agreement with Prime Minister Scullin, invited Sir Otto Niemeyer from the Bank of England to visit Australia and advise the government on its finances. Niemeyer's visit was controversial, as was the long list of austerity measures he recommended to ensure Australia's loan commitments were met, including drastic cuts in expenditure and public sector wages. Nevertheless, his proposals were adopted at a conference of state premiers in Melbourne in August 1930, and Scullin spent the next several months in Britain negotiating reduced interest payments on Australian debts. The New Zealand Government also invited Niemeyer to provide advice on banking and currency, and his key recommendation that New Zealand establish a central bank was subsequently realised in 1934.

One of the chief supporters of the 'Melbourne Agreement' within Cabinet was Joseph Lyons, who was appointed Acting Treasurer in July 1930 when Theodore stepped down to deal with a corruption charge. He was joined by Acting Prime Minister James Fenton in his support for the agreement.[11] Lyons was a relative newcomer to federal politics. He had served as Premier of Tasmania from 1923, before winning a seat in the House of Representatives in 1929. Nicknamed 'Honest Joe', Lyons was one of the more economically centrist members of Scullin's Cabinet.[12] As Acting Treasurer, he proposed to balance the budget, cut public sector wages, and lower interest rates. This approach was described by conservatives as 'deflation'. It was premised on the notion that, as private businesses and individual incomes contracted, the public sector likewise needed to 'deflate' to live within its means, and interest rates on both public and private loans needed to be lowered. This would ensure an 'equality of sacrifice' among all sections of the community.

In the closing months of 1930, Lyons demonstrated his commitment to lowering interest rates by running a highly publicised 'loan conversion' campaign with the assistance of several prominent conservative businesspeople. When it became apparent that the government might be

---

11   Meredith and Dyster, *Australia in the Global Economy*, 128–31; National Archives of Australia, 'James Scullin'.
12   The most thorough account of Lyons' life and political achievements is contained in Henderson, *Joseph Lyons*.

unable to meet a combined federal and state loan of £27 million that expired on 15 December 1930, Lyons launched a campaign to renew the loan without resorting to legislative intervention. Existing bondholders were encouraged to voluntarily renew their holdings at a lower interest rate or, if they preferred to cash out their holdings, they were asked to encourage other citizens to subscribe at the lower interest rate so the government could buy out the existing bondholders. The new loan was oversubscribed in a significant wave of publicity and patriotic fanfare, and Lyons became a nationally recognised figure.[13]

Inflation and repudiation

Theodore was one of the main opponents of the deflationary approach epitomised in the Melbourne Agreement. He believed the government needed to adopt a 'reflationary' policy: an expansion of public credit to finance an extensive public works program. Theodore was influenced by economists such as R.F. Irvine, and was familiar with some of the early works of John Maynard Keynes, the architect of the postwar Keynesian consensus when a stronger government role in the economy became the norm.[14] Scullin was persuaded by Theodore's ideas on returning to Australia at the beginning of 1931, and he reinstated him as Treasurer on 26 January.[15] Lyons and Fenton immediately resigned from Cabinet in protest, although they remained part of the Labor caucus. In March 1931, Lyons and a small group of supporters resigned from the Labor Party and crossed the floor to the opposition benches after Cabinet approved Theodore's fiduciary notes proposal, which would involve the issuing of £18 million in fiduciary notes for an extensive public works program.[16]

---

13   P.R. Hart, 'Lyons: Labor Minister—Leader of the U.A.P.', *Labour History* 17 (1969): 37–51, at pp. 41–42.

14   Bruce McFarlane, *Professor Irvine's Economics in Australian Labour History: 1913–1933* (Canberra: Australian Society for the Study of Labour History, 1966), 19.

15   Neville Cain, 'Theodore, Edward Granville (1884–1950)', *Australian Dictionary of Biography* (National Centre of Biography, The Australian National University, published first in hardcopy 1990), available from: adb.anu.edu.au/biography/theodore-edward-granville-8776.

16   P.R. Hart and C.J. Lloyd, 'Lyons, Joseph Aloysius (Joe) (1879–1939)', *Australian Dictionary of Biography* (National Centre of Biography, The Australian National University, published first in hardcopy 1986), available from: adb.anu.edu.au/biography/lyons-joseph-aloysius-joe-7278; National Archives of Australia, 'Joseph Lyons', *Australia's Prime Ministers* (Canberra: National Archives of Australia), available from: www.naa.gov.au/explore-collection/australias-prime-ministers/joseph-lyons.

Conservatives responded to Theodore's proposals with alarm. They feared that any expansion of the money supply would cause runaway inflation, destroying the value of the currency and wiping out savings. In January 1931, the Anti-Inflation League was founded in Sydney 'to combat the iniquitous and suicidal doctrine of inflation'.[17] Economists and bankers were especially critical of Theodore's proposals. 'Australia is financially sick', wrote Sir Ernest Wreford of the National Bank, 'and will not get well by drinking the financial champagne of further borrowing or note inflation.'[18] A publication titled *The Menace of Inflation*, written by South Australian educator and historian Archibald Grenfell Price and sponsored by several economists, sold 30,000 copies in its first print run in March 1931.[19] Price laid the blame for the Depression on the 'orgy of borrowing and extravagance' in the 1920s, and claimed that 'immediate action and grave sacrifices' were required 'to avoid the ruin which inflation nearly always brings in its train'.[20] Embedded in his criticism of inflation were the moral imperatives of thrift and self-reliance. Australians had been 'spoon-fed by arbitration, by pensions, and by a dozen socialistic policies, which had temporarily sapped the foundations of individualism'.[21] Labor's Fiduciary Notes Bill was subsequently blocked by the Senate in April 1931.[22]

Conservative fears of inflation were equalled by their fear of 'repudiation'. From the middle of 1930, it became a very real possibility that the Australian federal and state governments might be unable—or unwilling—to meet their public debt repayments. Repudiation of debt struck at the very core of what it meant to be a conservative. When individuals or groups entered willingly into financial agreements with each other, they were honour bound to meet the terms of those agreements. Governments were no exception: if individuals' ability to meet their debts was a matter of personal honour, the government's ability to meet its debts was a matter of national honour. More pragmatically, it was also a signal to international

---

17 *Sydney Morning Herald*, 14 January 1931, 12.
18 Quoted in Millmow, *The Power of Economic Ideas*, Ch. 5.
19 Archibald G. Price, 'The Emergency Committee of South Australia and the Origin of the Premiers' Plan, 1931–2', *South Australiana* 17(1) (1978): 5–55, at pp. 11–12. This piece was originally written by Price in 1932 but was not published until the year after his death. See also Millmow, *The Power of Economic Ideas*, Ch. 5.
20 A.G. Price, *The Menace of Inflation* (Adelaide: F.W. Preece & Sons, 1931), 6–10.
21 Price, 'The Emergency Committee of South Australia and the Origin of the Premiers' Plan', 40.
22 Millmow, *The Power of Economic Ideas*, Ch. 5; Meredith and Dyster, *Australia in the Global Economy*, 131–33; National Archives of Australia, 'James Scullin'.

creditors of the nation's economic stability. This was what drove Lyons to launch the successful loan conversion campaign in the closing months of 1930.

The biggest threat of repudiation came from Jack Lang, the leader of the Labor Party in New South Wales. Lang had a long history of stirring up conservative ire. In his first term as NSW Premier between 1925 and 1927, he enacted several reforms deemed radical by conservatives, including mandatory workers' compensation insurance and a 44-hour working week. In October 1930, Lang was returned to office on a campaign of restoring public servant salaries, increasing child welfare payments, and an extensive public works program. To pay for this, he suggested at a second conference of state premiers in February 1931 that Australia should halt interest payments to British bondholders until the crisis passed.[23] At the same conference, Scullin and Theodore presented their proposal to inflate the public supply of money to fund an extensive public works program. The conference generated an explosive reaction from conservatives. Two ideas that were anathema to the conservative tradition had been espoused in a single forum: inflation and repudiation. More than any other event, the premiers' conference in February 1931 was the trigger for the rise of populist conservatism in Australia.

The onset of the Great Depression in New Zealand

United and Reform

New Zealand's economy was affected by the Depression in the same general fashion as Australia, albeit not as severely in some measures. Farming formed the backbone of both economies; almost one-third of New Zealanders were employed in primary production in the 1920s, and agricultural goods made up the majority of the country's exports.[24] Like Australia, New Zealand's economy had already been weakened in 1929

---

23   Bede Nairn, *The 'Big Fella': Jack Lang and the Australian Labor Party, 1891–1949* (Melbourne: Melbourne University Press, 1986), 223.

24   Brian Easton, 'Economy: Agricultural Production', *Te Ara: The Encyclopedia of New Zealand* (updated 16 September 2016), available from: www.TeAra.govt.nz/en/diagram/4236/percentage-of-employment-in-different-sectors-1841-2001. This figure includes those employed in the mining sector.

by an international fall in export prices, especially in the wool market.[25] The Depression exacerbated the drop and, by 1933, export prices had declined by 45 per cent from their 1929 level. From 1930, businesspeople and professionals began to feel the flow-on effects: the volume of imports had decreased by 40 per cent by 1933, and prices for domestic goods fell by as much as 12 per cent. Public sector wages were cut by between 10 and 20 per cent, and the average private sector wage fell by 10 per cent. The economy reached its nadir in mid-1933 when the unemployment rate reached 12 per cent of the registered workforce.[26]

Unlike Australia, New Zealand was governed almost solely by conservative and liberal political parties throughout the Depression. In 1929, it was governed by the United Party with the support of Labour. As conditions worsened, Prime Minister Joseph Ward found himself unable to fully meet his election promise of a £70 million spending program—which had attracted the Labour Party—or to cut public spending, as United supporters demanded. Ward's deteriorating health further immobilised his government, and he resigned in May 1930 in favour of Finance Minister George Forbes.[27] The United government spent the following year juggling deflationary policy and its agreement with Labour, which it honoured through the *Unemployment Act*, which provided relief payments for the unemployed. When Forbes announced his plan to reduce public servant salaries in February 1931, Labour withdrew its support for the government. United turned to Reform for support, and the two parties agreed to form a coalition government in September 1931, which was returned to power in the December general election.[28]

The Coalition responded to the Depression in two ways: traditional deflationary methods designed to lower wages and expenditure, and state intervention to address unemployment and insolvency. The key supporter of deflation was Finance Minister William Downie Stewart, the only urban business representative in Cabinet. These methods were epitomised by the *1932 National Expenditure Adjustment Act*, which introduced

25 Condliffe, *New Zealand in the Making*, 45.
26 These figures were drawn from Hawke, *The Making of New Zealand*, 124, 127, 134, 148, 155.
27 Michael Bassett, 'Ward, Joseph George' (*Dictionary of New Zealand Biography*, first published in 1993), *Te Ara: The Encyclopedia of New Zealand*, available from: www.teara.govt.nz/en/biographies/2w9/1.
28 Pugh, The New Zealand Legion and conservative protest in the Great Depression, 32–37; W.J. Gardner, 'Forbes, George William' (*Dictionary of New Zealand Biography*, first published in 1996), *Te Ara: The Encyclopedia of New Zealand*, available from: www.teara.govt.nz/en/biographies/3f9/1; McKinnon, *The Broken Decade*.

rigorous public spending cuts, decreased pension payments, increased reductions in public service salaries, and removed compulsory arbitration from the *Industrial Conciliation and Arbitration Act*.[29] However, despite the Coalition's desire to effect greater government economies, public debt grew as the national income continued to decline. In April 1932, Downie Stewart alarmed conservatives when he announced a projected budget deficit of £8.3 million for the next financial year. The specially appointed Economists' Committee called the budget situation 'critical' and recommended further budget cuts and the introduction of new taxation.[30] Some of these measures made their way into the *National Expenditure Adjustment Act* and, by October, the Coalition claimed the deficit would be reduced to £1 million by the end of the year.[31] Despite this reassurance, projected deficit figures continued to float over the following months and were not fully settled until a small surplus was announced with the release of the following year's budget in May 1933.[32]

Deflationary methods contributed to a series of riots in the first half of 1932. The most serious riots occurred in Auckland in April during a march of the Unemployed Workers Movement and public servants protesting the second round of salary cuts. When the leader of the march was struck with a baton by a policeman, the crowd reacted by attacking the police cordon and looting several shopfronts along Queen Street.[33] Some conservatives reacted with alarm to the events in Auckland and other centres. The Wellington Chamber of Commerce, for example, urged the immediate imprisonment of the leaders of the Communist Party, and the *Auckland Star* called for the formation of a 'widespread official organisation of citizens … free from any suggestion of party politics'.[34] But no New Guard or citizens' movement arose in response. This was partially because a conservative government was in power at the time, which responded quickly. Special constables were rapidly sworn in to help quell the riots, and the Coalition passed the Public Safety Conservation Bill within days of the Auckland riots, which granted it comprehensive

---

29   Hawke, *The Making of New Zealand*, 150, 152–53, 155; Pugh, The New Zealand Legion and conservative protest in the Great Depression, 46–48.

30   *The Evening Post*, [Wellington], 8 April 1932, 7; Hawke, *The Making of New Zealand*, 150.

31   *The Evening Post*, [Wellington], 5 October 1932, 4.

32   ibid., 25 January 1933, 8; 17 February 1933, 6; 1 May 1933, 10.

33   'The Depression Riots, 1932' (*An Encyclopedia of New Zealand*, ed. A.H. McLintock, originally published in 1966), *Te Ara: The Encyclopedia of New Zealand*, available from: www.teara.govt.nz/en/1966/riots/6.

34   Quoted in Pugh, The New Zealand Legion and conservative protest in the Great Depression, 51–53.

powers to deal with future emergencies.[35] Responses to the riots were also mixed—for example, some thought retrenchment had gone too far and contributed to the riots.[36]

The second, more interventionist government response tested the boundaries of conservative tradition. The *Unemployment Act* of 1930 had introduced tax-financed (rather than loan-financed) unemployment assistance. The Coalition significantly increased this taxation for unemployment relief, under the rubric of sharing the burden equally across all classes. Other policies, such as the 20 per cent reduction in interest rates and rents provided by the *National Expenditure Adjustment Act*, were similarly able to appeal to a perceived equality of sacrifice, although the challenge to the sanctity of the contract led Downie Stewart to threaten resignation. Rural relief in the form of the *Mortgages and Tenants Relief Act* aroused greater concern among conservatives, but it was grudgingly accepted as necessary to alleviate the growing insolvency of the farming community.[37] State intervention in the economy to alleviate the distress of farmers and the unemployed was acceptable, provided it fell within the bounds of the Australasian developmentalist ethos.

Devaluing the currency

Without a labour bogeyman, it took an unorthodox economic act of the Coalition—devaluing the currency in January 1933—to stir disconcerted conservatives into action. The chief supporter of the move, Reform leader Gordon Coates, hoped that by devaluing the currency from NZ£110:UK£100 to NZ£125:UK£100, the resulting boost in farmers' incomes would flow through to the rest of the economy.[38] However, the benefits accrued to farmers by a devalued currency had the opposite effect on import-dependent businesspeople, who would have to pay more for the products on which their enterprises were based. This cleavage between rural and urban interests fractured the relative unity that conservatives had enjoyed until that point. A strong urban backlash arose against the

---

35   *The Evening Post*, [Wellington], 19 April 1932, 8.
36   Pugh, The New Zealand Legion and conservative protest in the Great Depression, 50–53.
37   Hawke, *The Making of New Zealand*, 145–49, 152, 154; Pugh, The New Zealand Legion and conservative protest in the Great Depression, 48–49.
38   Hawke, *The Making of New Zealand*, 153–55; Pugh, The New Zealand Legion and conservative protest in the Great Depression, 59–61; Michael Bassett, 'Coates, Joseph Gordon' (*Dictionary of New Zealand Biography*, first published in 1996), *Te Ara: The Encyclopedia of New Zealand*, available from: www.teara.govt.nz/en/biographies/3c24/1.

raised exchange rate, which was seen as benefiting the interests of primary producers above all others. The Wellington Chamber of Commerce condemned the measure as a violation of basic economic principles:

> [T]he Council of the Wellington Chamber of Commerce emphatically condemns the action of the Government in violating established banking practice and universally recognised economic principles by causing the rate of exchange to be artificially pegged; this action must inevitably create greater evils than the present action is calculated to overcome and in the meantime the majority must suffer for the benefit of a minority.[39]

The move also compounded fears of a budget crisis, with rumours circulating that a devalued currency would swell the deficit by an additional £3 million.[40] But it was the shock that a conservative government would unilaterally intervene in favour of one section of the population that caused the most outrage. Downie Stewart resigned as Finance Minister in protest—mere days away from the anniversary of Lyons' similar action in Australia two years earlier.

Conservative responses to the Great Depression in Australia

Mobilising against Labor

Australian conservatives responded to the growing perception of crisis in several ways. Many focused their frustrations on the triumvirate of Labor bogeymen in Scullin, Theodore, and Lang. The release of Labor's first budget in July 1930, which included a tax increase to fund an additional £1 million in public spending, prompted urban business organisations to hold protest meetings in several state capitals.[41] The Sydney Chamber of Commerce sent a delegation to Canberra claiming to represent 'all classes of taxpayers' to convince Scullin to reduce taxes and balance the budget.[42]

---

39 Meeting of Council, 24 January 1933, Minute book August 1932 – December 1935, Wellington Chamber of Commerce Papers, MS-Group-0018, ATL.
40 *The Evening Post*, [Wellington], 25 January 1933, 8.
41 *The Advertiser*, [Adelaide], 12 July 1930, 15; *Sydney Morning Herald*, 12 July 1930, 15.
42 *The Argus*, [Melbourne], 12 July 1930, 21; *The Advertiser*, [Adelaide], 15 July 1930, 16.

Similar distaste was reserved for compulsory wheat pooling, which groups like the Town and Country Union condemned as 'socialistic' interference with individual liberty and private enterprise.[43]

Plate 2.1 A 'starvation debenture' lampooning Jack Lang's 'repudiationist' policies during the Depression
Source: Item 50, Mutch Papers, SLNSW.

Many conservatives drew on the memory of the Kyabram Reform Movement, the turn-of-the-century Victorian conservative organisation discussed in Chapter One, for inspiration. In July, the Wheat Producers' Freedom Association decided to launch a 'new Kyabram' at a meeting in the South Australian country town of Moonta.[44] Their enthusiasm quickly waned, due in part to the deflationary nature of the Melbourne Agreement in August, and the promise of a new Kyabram was not met.[45] A meeting of businesspeople in the Adelaide Town Hall on 16 July 1930 was similarly inspired to send a deputation to Canberra to convince Prime Minister Scullin to create an advisory body of financial and commercial

43   *The Advertiser*, [Adelaide], 30 April 1930, 16; *Burra Record*, 4 June 1930, 3.
44   *The Advertiser*, [Adelaide], 12 July 1930, 15; 15 July 1930, 15; 19 July 1930, 15.
45   Michael J. Thompson, Government and depression in South Australia, 1927 to 1934 (MEc diss., Flinders University, Adelaide, 1972), 167–68; John Lonie, Conservatism and class in South Australia during the Depression years, 1929–34' (MA diss., University of Adelaide, 1973), 207–8.

experts. Scullin refused, and no further deputations were sent.[46] However, the memory of Kyabram would remain an important influence on the citizens' movements in both Australia and New Zealand.

"Revolution comes by stages."

Plate 2.2 Cartoon implying that Lang's policies presaged communism 'by stages'

Source: *A Recipe for Revolution* (Sydney: Constitutional Association of New South Wales, 1932), 12.

Existing conservative non-party organisations such as the Constitutional Association and the Sane Democracy League also mobilised against Labor. Indeed, one of the chief consequences of the Depression was that it tore away the thin nonpartisan shield these organisations used to disguise their world view. Lang's victory in the October 1930 NSW elections led the Constitutional Association of New South Wales to abandon its nominally

---

46   Thompson, *Government and depression in South Australia*, 165–66.

nonpartisan stance in favour of an 'immediate policy' to combat Lang.[47]
This policy called for balanced budgets, reduced costs of production
and distribution, greater industrial cooperation, and firm opposition to
inflation and repudiation. Its purpose was to bring attention to 'the urgent
necessity for immediate public action' to combat 'party strife and vacillating
government'.[48] Several months later, the association released *Lang, Lunacy,
Loot*, a pamphlet condemning Lang's policies as an attempt to '[k]ill private
enterprise' and foist socialism on the state.[49] A follow-up pamphlet in 1932
claimed that Lang Labor had been infiltrated by communists who were
plotting 'a revolutionary conspiracy against constitutional government'.[50]

The Sane Democracy League was also boosted by its opposition to Lang.
The league had castigated Lang as a demagogue and a communist puppet
since the mid-1920s, and had produced anti-Lang posters during his
failed re-election bid in 1927.[51] At the time, they argued that

> the whole community has been split into groups continually kept
> in a state of hostility by the yapping of the politicians and the
> operation of the machinery that the politicians have created.[52]

However, the league's criticism of Lang reached unprecedented vitriolic
heights in 1930, with two entire issues of their journal, *Sane Democracy*,
devoted against his campaign.[53] When Lang won the election in
a landslide, the league foretold dire results. The Nationalists' platform
'was not a party policy nor even a state policy, but an Australian policy',
wrote *Sane Democracy* of Lang's opponent.[54] This language reinforced
the naturalisation of conservative values as being in the 'national interest'
in contrast to the values of Labor. It also demonstrated that, while the
league was willing to channel popular discontent with the status quo,
it did not wish to challenge the position of mainstream conservative
parties. As Chapter Five will show, this fear of splitting the centre-right
vote by criticising or campaigning against the Nationalists was a powerful
undercurrent within the Australian citizens' movements.

---

47 Minutes of Committee Meeting, 28 October 1930, box 2, item 1, CANSW Papers, SLNSW.
48 Minutes of Special Committee Meeting, 2 February 1931, box 2, item 1, CANSW Papers, SLNSW.
49 *Lang, Lunacy, Loot* (Sydney: Constitutional Association of New South Wales, 1931), 50.
50 *A Recipe for Revolution* (Sydney: Constitutional Association of New South Wales, 1932), 1.
51 *Sane Democracy*, [Sydney], No. 8, 9 April 1925, 1; No. 16, 5 June 1925, 1; No. 134, 7 October 1927, 1.
52 ibid., No. 106, 25 March 1927, 1.
53 See *Sane Democracy*, [Sydney], [NS], No. 29, 3 October 1930, and [NS], No. 30, 17 October 1930.
54 ibid., [NS], No. 31, 31 October 1930, 1.

Anti-political political thought

While many conservatives retained their faith in the existing political system, others began to look for alternatives. The economic prosperity of the previous decade appeared to be crumbling around them. People were losing their jobs, their businesses, their homes. The government seemed incapable of adopting the measures required to address the crisis, or—even worse—had proposed measures that conservatives feared would cause rampant inflation or damage Australia's financial honour. They felt a pressing need to do *something* about it, both as good citizens and out of fear for their own economic interests. The internal dilemma that many of these frustrated conservatives faced was that, while they wanted to do something dramatic to address the crisis, they remained fundamentally committed to the core values of conservatism. They shared these values with the centre-right Nationalist Party, which had been in power from 1917 until 1929 (in coalition with the Country Party from 1922). Conservatism had been in the ascendant throughout the roaring Twenties, despite the occasional rifts between urban and rural conservatives over matters such as the tariff. Yet something had clearly gone horribly wrong. Where did the blame lie, and what could frustrated conservatives do about it?

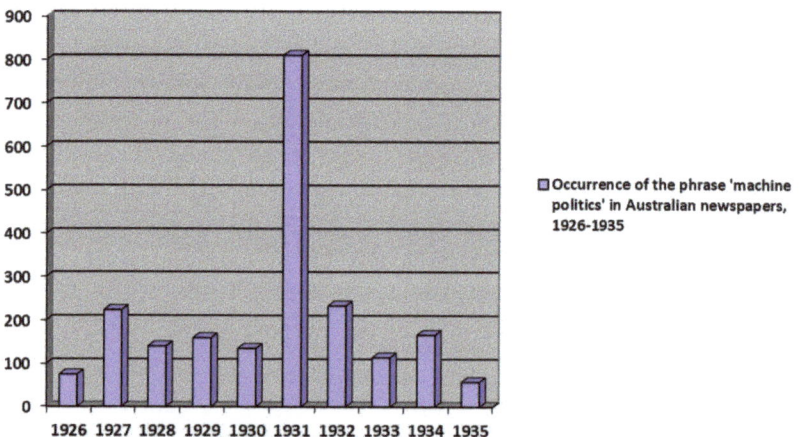

Figure 2.1 Occurrence of the phrase 'machine politics' in Australian newspapers, 1926–1935

Source: Compiled by the author from Trove, searched 15 October 2020 (www.trove. nla.gov.au).

One solution to this dilemma was to criticise the political system itself. If the values of conservatism were not to blame, it must be the politicians and political parties the public had trusted to implement them. Political machines, with their rigid party platforms and their sycophantic lists of preselected candidates, must have stacked parliament with self-serving politicians who were devoted to protecting the special interests that backed them. This had, in turn, resulted in governments that were in thrall to their political parties, bound to legislate in favour of minorities rather than the interests of the nation. The extravagant public borrowing of the 1920s proved that. According to this line of thought, the entire party system of government made it impossible for politicians to exercise their own political judgement. If they had, Australia would be able to deal with the crisis at hand and emerge from the doldrums of the Depression. Loveday aptly defined this phenomenon as 'anti-political political thought'.[55] It provided a scapegoat for conservative anxieties while allowing them to hold on to their traditional conservative values.

Print culture was one means by which anti-partyism was spread. The use of the phrase 'machine politics' (the background to which is discussed in Chapter One) increased significantly during the Depression. Figure 2.1 demonstrates the occurrence of the phrase 'machine politics' in Australian newspapers between 1926 and 1935. The year in which the phrase occurred the most, 1931, was also the year in which the citizens' movements were at their height. Anti-party sentiment was also spread in the editorials of popular journals and weeklies and was given a semi-academic gloss by publications such as the *Australian Quarterly*. Founded in 1929 by the Constitutional Association, the *Australian Quarterly* regularly published articles on arbitration, tariff and parliamentary reform, and the need for greater financial stringency and decreased production costs.[56] An article in September 1929 by Mildred Muscio on the growing popularity of non-party movements argued that party politics meant 'government

55 Loveday, 'Anti-Political Political Thought'.
56 F.A.A. Russell, 'Should Industrial Arbitration Go? The Evolution of Industrial Arbitration', *Australian Quarterly* [Sydney] 1(2) (June 1929): 38–49; L.G. Melville, 'The Australian Tariff: A Review on the Report of the Committee Appointed by the Prime Minister', *Australian Quarterly* [Sydney] 1(3) (September 1929): 54–63; Norman Cowper, 'Reform of the Upper House of New South Wales', *Australian Quarterly* [Sydney] 1(4) (December 1929): 107–18; B.S.B. Stevens, 'Financial and Economical Outlook', *Australian Quarterly* [Sydney] 2(1) (March 1930): 16–27; Hal Colebatch, 'Inflation, Deflation, or Common Sense', *Australian Quarterly* [Sydney] 2(4) (December 1930): 31–43. Regular contributors included Nationalist politician and future state premier B.S.B. Stevens, senator and former Agent-General for Western Australia Sir Hal Colebatch, and general manager of the Graziers' Cooperative Shearing Company R.C. Wilson.

by warfare' under which '[s]incerity and constructive thought vanish'.[57] The reason for this, wrote William Harrison Moore in December 1930, was the increasing extension of government to areas about which its members were ignorant. Both Muscio and Moore advocated for a greater reliance on experts in economics, business, and history in government affairs.[58] Luminaries of previous conservative non-party organisations also contributed to the anti-party fervour. Reverend T.E. Ruth, a leading member and speaker for the Loyalty League of Victoria (discussed in Chapter One), released a booklet titled *Australia at the Crossroads* that was heavily critical of Lang's proposed repudiation. It also railed against several other perceived enemies, including party politicians and communists. Ruth addressed the volume 'to the newly-awakened members of the All for Australia League'.[59]

Anti-partyism was also spread by the birth of several new conservative organisations. One of these, the 'Who's for Australia?' League, was something of a prototype for the Australian citizens' movements. The origins of this unusual organisation lay in the Australian branch of the International Theosophical Society, a spiritual and esoteric organisation founded in the United States in the late nineteenth century. Theosophists believe they are the inheritors of an ancient religion that will one day come to eclipse all other world religions. One of the goals of theosophy is to forge a 'universal brotherhood of humanity' in which all distinctions— including class, creed, and nationality—are set aside.[60] At first glance, this goal would appear to be at odds with early twentieth-century conservative values. However, a leading figure in the global theosophist movement named George Arundale thought otherwise. During the 1920s, Arundale concluded that the seed of a universal brotherhood lay in the spirit of patriotism, which he believed could drive individuals to sacrifice their self-interests for a higher cause. The imperial patriotism of Britain and its colonies—in particular, Australia and New Zealand—spanned multiple

---

57   Mildred Muscio, 'Reflections on Party Politics', *Australian Quarterly* [Sydney] 1(3) (September 1929): 91.

58   ibid., 100; William Harrison Moore, 'Experts in Government', *Australian Quarterly* [Sydney] 2(4) (December 1930): 29–30.

59   T.E. Ruth, *Australia at the Crossroads* (Sydney: Robert Dey & Co., 1931).

60   The principles of theosophy are drawn from H.P. Blavatsky, *The Key to Theosophy* (Pasadena, CA: Theosophical University Press Online Edition), available from: www.theosociety.org/pasadena/key/key-3.htm.

countries. If this patriotism could be sharpened in one colony first, Arundale imagined that it might then be extended in stages across the British Empire, and eventually across the world.[61]

Arundale chose Australia as the laboratory for what he later called his 'Australian experiment'.[62] He relocated to Australia in 1926 and became the general secretary of the Australian section of the Theosophical Society. Using new and existing technologies, he broadcast his message of unwavering patriotism to a wide audience. Arundale founded 2GB, one of the most widely listened-to radio stations in Sydney today, in 1926 as a 'Theosophical Broadcasting Station'.[63] He also founded a new Australian theosophical journal, *Advance! Australia*, which was aimed at a wider audience than the more traditional *Australian Theosophist*. The new journal drew heavily on conservative tropes regarding good citizenship and applied them to the goal of a universal brotherhood:

> 'Advance! Australia' will stand for the promotion of a noble type of Australian citizenship, vitally Australian, eagerly conscious of Australia's specific place and part in the building of the future, no less eagerly conscious of the wider and equally vital citizenship involved in Australia's membership of the British Commonwealth, and recognising, too, that beyond even this Commonwealth-citizenship there is a World-citizenship, the obligations of which may no longer be ignored.[64]

Advance! Australia invoked several important ideas in its defence of good citizenship. Drawing on the Anzac ethos, it argued that 'the supreme sacrifice of more than a million of our comrades in that Great Adventure' would have been for nothing 'if we have not learned that Peace must continue and perfect the virtues war called forth'.[65] This same sense of 'brotherhood' and 'sacrifice' was needed to overcome the problems contemporary society faced, including class conflict, religious tensions,

61 Josephine Ransom, *A Short History of the Theosophical Society* (Madras: Vasanta Press, 1938), 476; G.S. Arundale, 'The Australian Experiment', *World Theosophy* (February 1931): 103–6; *Australian Theosophist* [Sydney] 1(1) (1926): 9–13; *Advance! Australia* [Sydney] 1(1) (July 1926): 9.
62 Arundale, 'The Australian Experiment'. For a general history of theosophy in Australia, see Jill Roe, *Beyond Belief: Theosophy in Australia 1879–1939* (Sydney: UNSW Press, 1986).
63 *Australian Theosophist* [Sydney] 1(2) (15 August 1926): 43–44; *Sydney Morning Herald*, 24 August 1926, 10.
64 *Advance! Australia* [Sydney] 1(1) (July 1926): 9.
65 ibid.

international strife, and party politics.[66] *Advance! Australia* urged these warring groups to set aside their parochial concerns in favour of 'the welfare of the community as a whole'.[67]

The 'Who's for Australia?' League was founded in November 1929 to transform Arundale's experiment into a mass movement.[68] Its use of populist rhetoric and its focus on building a mass organisation were reminiscent of the Loyalist League and the King and Empire Alliance, which had arisen 10 years earlier and presaged the formation of the citizens' movements. Its co-founder and general secretary, A.E. Bennett, was a fellow theosophist, the manager of 2GB, and an ardent admirer of Benito Mussolini.[69] The league boomed under his leadership, and several dozen business and metropolitan branches were established by June 1930.[70] This included several branches in Queensland, South Australia, Victoria, and Western Australia, the last of which included Harold Boas, leader of the defunct Argonauts Civic and Constitutional Club.[71] It also produced a journal and several pamphlets.[72]

The ideology of the 'Who's for Australia?' League was an inchoate mixture of fervent patriotism, populism, and economic nationalism. The league also sought a strong leader who would put Australia before all other interests. On the first page of the inaugural volume of its journal, the league's ambitions were explained thus:

> We do not need a Mussolini; but we do need an Australian-hearted Australian, man or woman, an Australian who puts Australia first, who loves Australia with passion, who knows no interests above Australian interests, who knows no fear nor favour. Such a man or woman Australia needs to arouse her citizens to the active service of their great Motherland—prostituted today to selfishness and class interest.

---

66   ibid., 2–3, 9.

67   ibid., 2.

68   The name seems to have come from an old theosophist question, 'Who is for Us?', which was often raised during times of crisis; see Ransom, *A Short History of the Theosophical Society*, 508.

69   *Australian Theosophist* [Sydney] 1(2) (15 August 1926): 35–36; Philip Geeves, 'Bennett, Alfred Edward (1889–1963)', *Australian Dictionary of Biography* (National Centre of Biography, The Australian National University, published first in hardcopy 1979), available from: adb.anu.edu.au/biography/bennett-alfred-edward-5207.

70   *Who's for Australia?* [Sydney] 2(2) (25 June 1930): 11.

71   *Who's for Australia?* [Sydney] 1(8) (23 April 1930): 3; 2(1) (11 June 1930): 5; 2(2) (25 June 1930): 11; 2(4) (23 July 1930): 3; 2(5) (6 August 1930): 12.

72   See, for example, *Who's for Australia? League* (Sydney: 'Who's for Australia?' League, 1929); *Who's for Australia? Four Songs in Her Praise* (Sydney: 'Who's for Australia?' League, 1930).

... Australia needs a leader. Australia needs a statesman. Australia needs a patriot. She has had enough of politicians, and of all who serve party or class or sect before Australia, who are content to subordinate the welfare of Australia to the interests of a movement, who make Australia a stepping-stone to personal prestige and power.[73]

By the end of 1930, when the Depression had truly taken hold in Australia, the journal was calling on everyday citizens to tear down political parties and replace them with 'a government composed of free men who will be slaves to no juntas'.[74]

At its height in November 1930, the 'Who's for Australia?' League boasted 9,000 members.[75] However, it petered out rapidly in early 1931. Its failure may have been due to its inability—or unwillingness—to tap into the discontent with the proposed economic policies of Scullin, Theodore, and Lang. Instead, its primary contribution to economics was to encourage Australians to 'be patriotic' and buy Australian-made and manufactured goods. It shared this objective with several other groups with which it was in contact, including the Advance Australia League in Adelaide.[76] It organised two well-publicised exhibitions of Australian-manufactured goods in early 1930.[77] While economic nationalism was not necessarily incompatible with conservative dictum—especially given its internal divisions regarding the use of the tariff—the 'Who's for Australia?' League missed the opportunity to capitalise on conservative discontent with Labor's 'inflationary' and 'repudiationist' proposals. As a result, it was quickly superseded by the citizens' movements. Nevertheless, its populism and its focus on building a mass organisation would become important tools in the arsenal of the citizens' movements.

The South Australian Political Reform League was another conservative organisation that espoused the populist language of anti-partyism. It was formed in January 1929 by a young solicitor named Keith Wilson to provide a voice for young conservatives in the South Australian Liberal

---

73   *Who's for Australia?* [Sydney] 1(1) (15 January 1930): 1.
74   ibid., 2(12) (12 November 1930): 2.
75   The peak of 9,000 members was reached in November 1930; see *Who's for Australia?* [Sydney] 2(13) (26 November 1930): 4.
76   ibid., 1(5) (12 March 1930): 3.
77   ibid., 1(4) (26 February 1930): 4, and 2(2) (25 June 1930): 12; *Exhibition of all Australian Manufactures at Drummoyne* (Sydney: 'Who's for Australia?' League, 1930).

Federation.[78] It was partially intended to be a successor to the Essential Service Maintenance Volunteers, a strikebreaking force formed in September 1928 by a group of prominent Adelaide businesspeople and professionals in response to a labour dispute on the waterfront.[79] After the strike dissipated, the volunteers' chairman, Captain A.S. Blackburn, recommended the group's leaders 'consider what further action might be taken' to 'weld into one social mass the whole of the anti-social[ist] element in South Australia'.[80] He subsequently served on the Political Reform League's first executive.[81]

While dedicated to supporting the Liberal Federation, the Political Reform League expressed deep dissatisfaction with the existing form of government. It sought a parliament in which members could 'legislate for the good of the State as a whole' rather than being 'restricted by Caucus or party platform'. To accomplish this, it proposed simplifying the platform of the Liberal Federation to allow candidates to vote according to their conscience.[82] While this was in part a response to the Liberal Federation's method of caucus control, the relative youth of the movement and its inexperienced president also suggest an idealistic impatience with the status quo. Indeed, Wilson's first public statement as president was full of phrases such as 'new blood', 'latent zeal', and 'broad vision', which he contrasted with the 'fetter[s]' and 'restrictions' of the Liberal Federation.[83] After the Depression hit, the league proposed to alleviate the crisis by reducing the size of parliament, curbing government interference in private enterprise, rationalising government administration 'by seeking the advice of experts', and encouraging those 'skilled in commerce, science, [and]

---

78 *Register News-Pictorial*, [Adelaide], 9 January 1929, 13. In many ways, the Political Reform League might be considered the interwar equivalent of the 'youth wings' of today's political parties. In fact, it renamed itself the Young Liberal League in March 1932. See Interview with Sir Keith Wilson [sound recording], Interviewer: Susan Marsden, 1983, SRG 660/1/147 [hereinafter Wilson Interview], State Library of South Australia, Adelaide [hereinafter SLSA].

79 Moore, *The Secret Army and the Premier*, 64; C.J. Lloyd, The formation and development of the U.A.P., 1929–1937 (PhD diss., The Australian National University, Canberra, 1984), 57; Stephen A. James, 'The big hand of service': The Citizens' League of South Australia, 1930–1934—Origins, ideology and policy (BA Hons diss., University of Melbourne, 1986), 21; Ray Broomhill, 'Political Consciousness and Dissent: The Unemployed in Adelaide during the Depression', *Labour History* 34 (1978): 58–67.

80 *The Advertiser*, [Adelaide], 8 March 1929, 19.

81 For the 1929 executive, see *The Advertiser*, [Adelaide], 16 January 1929, 12. For the 1930 executive, see *Policy and Aims of [Political Reform] League* (Adelaide: Commercial Printing House, 1930).

82 *Policy and Aims of [Political Reform] League*.

83 *Register News-Pictorial*, [Adelaide], 14 January 1929, 8.

industry' to run for parliament.[84] Much like the various conservative non-party organisations that preceded it, the league attempted to naturalise these values as apolitical by claiming they were 'for the good of the State as a whole'.[85]

Conservative responses to the Great Depression in New Zealand

Protests against the Coalition government

Before the devaluation of the currency in January 1933, there was no widespread conservative revolt in New Zealand. However, the Coalition's willingness to experiment with interventionist policies before 1933 caused some frustration among a small section of the Reform Party. These typically younger members of the party were disappointed that its leaders had opted to align with the United Party rather than develop a bolder deflationary policy. They were also frustrated with the Coalition's decision to support sitting members in the 1931 general election, which curtailed their ability to stand for parliament with the party's backing. They were led by J.D. Ormond, a 27-year-old sheep farmer who had stood as an independent for the Waipawa seat in 1931 in defiance of the Coalition's decision to support sitting members. After their delegation to the Reform executive in April 1932 failed to convince the party to adopt a firmer policy, Ormond and his colleagues resolved to 'reform the Reform Party or form a new party' and that 'an organisation should be started to support such a move'. A tour of the South Island found widespread support for such an organisation, so the New Zealand National Movement was formed at an inaugural meeting of 30 businesspeople and farmers on 23 July 1932.[86]

The New Zealand National Movement expressed a mixture of laissez-faire economics and opposition to party politics. It condemned the 'extravagant and socialistic policy' of past governments and called for 'strict economy in Gov[ernmen]t expenditure', 'curtailment of external borrowing', and

84 *Policy and Aims of [Political Reform] League.*
85 ibid.
86 Pugh, The New Zealand Legion and conservative protest in the Great Depression, 53–55; P.S. Tait, *In the Chair: The Public Life of Sir John Ormond* (Waipukurau, NZ: CHB Print, 1989), 12–17.

the 'encouragement of Private enterprise, personal initiative and thrift'.[87] It also sought the 'eradication of the petty Party spirit' and the introduction of fresh talent into national politics. Ormond told Coates that the Reform Party executive was 'as much out of touch with the public as the moon is from the earth'. While the new movement was not opposed to the Reform Party, Ormond claimed that its motives were purer than party politics:

> I set this new political movement going, my idea being to get the moderate minded people in the Dominion backed up by the youth of the Country to take a more active interest in politics and support men who would go into Parliament with an intelligent and unselfish outlook and with the interest of the Country at heart—Party politics do not concern me nor do individuals.[88]

The riots that had taken place a few months earlier do not appear to have been a significant factor in the movement's formation. While one of the speakers at the inaugural meeting gave an update on the '[c]ommunistic activities over the past period', this did not have a significant influence on the movement's objectives.[89] One of its founding members later recalled that 'fear of rioting did not arise'.[90] Without an event that would galvanise widespread conservative support, the New Zealand National Movement had made little headway by the end of 1932.

New Zealand conservatives and monetary reform

A distinctive feature of the Depression in New Zealand was the growing popularity of 'unorthodox' economic theories. With conservative and liberal governments in power throughout the Depression, individuals of all political persuasions—not just conservatives—became more willing to look for alternatives to, or modifications of, the general commitment to free-market capitalism. Indeed, in a sense, the dramatic rise of the New Zealand Labour Party, cemented by its landslide election victory in 1935, could be seen as an example of this. Supporters of unorthodox economics subscribed to a multitude of ideas, ranging from revolutionary socialists to those who simply sought to 'finetune' the capitalist economic

---

87 *New Zealand National Movement Circular*, No. 2, October 1932, reproduced in Pugh, The New Zealand Legion and conservative protest in the Great Depression, 200–2.
88 Letter from Ormond to Coates, 20 September 1932, Ormond Family Papers, privately held.
89 Notes of a meeting of the movement held in the Grand Hotel Palmerston North, 23 July 1932, Ormond Family Papers, privately held.
90 Pugh, The New Zealand Legion and conservative protest in the Great Depression, 54.

system. The latter included an astounding number of organisations that were founded with the aim of reforming the monetary system. These 'monetary reformists' believed that capitalism, as it was currently conceived, had failed due to structural deficiencies in the way resources were allocated rather than a fundamental flaw in capitalism itself. Put simply, they believed the amount of wealth employees received in the form of wages was insufficient to purchase the goods and services they produced as workers. This imbalance resulted in an overproduction of goods and services, which the majority of the population did not have the resources to consume. Some monetary reformers believed this imbalance was the result of deliberate action by a small coterie of conspirators who controlled international finance, and who had engineered the Depression to gain more control over the world economy. This conspiratorial world view was heavily imbued with anti-Semitism.

The earliest monetary reform organisation in New Zealand was Douglas social credit. Founded by Major C.H. Douglas in Britain after World War One, it quickly spread to Canada, Australia, and New Zealand. However, while Douglas social credit study circles were first established in New Zealand in the 1920s, it was not until the publication of Arthur Nelson Field's *The Truth about the Slump* in 1931 that monetary reform achieved wider attention. Field's work, which laid the blame for the Depression on a small clique of prominent Jewish financiers and their families, was well received by the New Zealand public and was discussed in parliament by Harry Atmore and Bob Semple.[91] The number of monetary reform groups in New Zealand—termed 'funny money' by their opponents— multiplied exponentially. In October 1932, an attempt was made by one such group, the Stable Money League, to unite these various monetary reformers. The resulting Federation of Monetary Reform Associations included representatives from 33 different organisations as well as the Auckland and Hawke's Bay provincial districts of the Farmers' Union.[92]

91   Marinus La Rooij, 'From Colonial Conservative to International Antisemite: The Life and Work of Arthur Nelson Field', *Journal of Contemporary History* 37(2) (2002): 223–39, at pp. 229–33; Robin Clifton, Douglas credit and the Labour Party, 1930–1935 (MA diss., Victoria University of Wellington, 1961), 65.
92   Minutes of Special Meeting of Hawke's Bay Provincial District, 15 October 1932, Hawke's Bay branch minute book 1928–1936, MSY-0288, New Zealand Farmers' Union Papers, MS-Papers-1159, ATL; Circular from Wynford O. Beere, c. October 1932, printed matter associated with the Federation of Monetary Reform Associations 1932, MS-Papers-8615-052, Field Papers, ATL.

The federation was overshadowed by the formation of a united Douglas social credit movement in New Zealand the following January. By 1935, there were social credit branches throughout rural New Zealand and in several major cities with a total membership of around 4,000 people.[93] These various monetary reform movements were able to bring a considerable force of public opinion to bear: in 1932–33, 48 separate petitions calling for 'an enquiry into the present monetary system and alternatives thereto' made their way to parliament, one of which had 2,700 signatories.[94] Bowing to popular pressure, the government established the Monetary Commission in 1934, although its mandate did not extend to an evaluation of the existing capitalist economic system. The commission's most distinguished witness was Major C.H. Douglas himself, who was then touring New Zealand as a guest of the Douglas social credit movement.[95]

Monetary reformists—in particular, social creditors—were keen to forge transnational connections. The Melbourne social credit journal, *New Economics*, included regular reports and correspondence from the burgeoning social credit movement in New Zealand.[96] Field's *The Truth* had also attracted significant attention overseas and, by the end of 1932, he had received orders from hundreds of foreign publishers and individuals.[97] It was particularly popular among Australian monetary reformists, as was his release of a local edition of *The Protocols of the Elders of Zion* with added commentary from himself. One of his most fervent disciples was a young Eric Butler, who would play a leading role in the Australian far-right in the post–World War Two period.[98]

The popularity of monetary reformism in New Zealand during the Depression can be understood as a form of protest against orthodox economics. In Australia, conservatives could direct their frustrations against either the federal or the state Labor governments since deflationary economic policy had not been consistently applied by either. Unlike Australia, however, New Zealand was governed almost entirely

---

93 Clifton, Douglas credit and the Labour Party, 71–76, 128–29, 150–52.
94 Malcolm McKinnon, Funny about money?, Paper presented at the Reserve Bank of New Zealand Museum, Wellington, 24 July 2012.
95 ibid.; Clifton, Douglas credit and the Labour Party, 90–91, 210–16.
96 See, for example, *New Economics*, [Melbourne], 1 June 1931, 12; 1 October 1931, 11; 2 November 1931, 8; 1 August 1932, 12–13.
97 Marinus La Rooij, 'Arthur Nelson Field: Kiwi Theoretician of the Australian Radical Right?', *Labour History* 89 (2005): 37–54.
98 ibid.

by conservatives throughout the Depression, and power was held by a coalition of the two conservative parties during its nadir. Conservative frustration had few other targets except orthodox economics, at least until the currency devaluation in January 1933. As New Zealand psychologist T.A. Hunter argued in 1934, economics had usurped the role of the church as the people's new religion, with '[b]uying price, selling price and profit constitut[ing] the new trinity'. The simple solutions offered by monetary reform, which suggested a minor tweak or alteration in the capitalist system would restore prosperity, acted as an emotional salve for these disenchanted conservatives.[99] It allowed them to remain loyal to the tenets of private property and individualism while seeking to alter elements of the economic system such as the control and distribution of currency.

Monetary reform was also popular among New Zealand theosophists—so much so that it curtailed an attempt to replicate Arundale's 'Australian experiment' in New Zealand. Tom Naylor, the president of the New Zealand section of the World Federation of Young Theosophists, was so inspired by Arundale's example, he aspired to 'awaken the patriotic spirit' of New Zealanders through patriotic folklore. He produced an intermittent journal in the late 1920s titled *Advance! Zealandia*, although it proved far less successful than its Australian counterpart.[100] Even less successful was his plan to form a 'Who's for Zealandia?' League modelled on the 'Who's for Australia?' League after Arundale gave a speaking tour of New Zealand in 1930. Naylor noted that his ideas had been given the 'cold shoulder' from the New Zealand section of the Theosophical Society and their journal, *Theosophy in New Zealand*.[101]

---

99 T.A. Hunter, 'Some Aspects of Depression Psychology in New Zealand', *Economic Record* 10(1) (1934): 31–45, at pp. 38–39.

100 No copies of this journal appear to have survived, but it is discussed in the World Federation of Young Theosophists correspondence; see Letter from Tom Naylor to Raymond Ernest Hansen, 3 April 1930, Letter from Naylor to Hansen, Empire Day 1930, Inward correspondence 1930–58, Raymond Ernest Hansen Papers, 84-204-74 [hereinafter Hansen Papers], ATL. The journal is also mentioned in the Australian Theosophical Society's list of periodicals; see 'Theosophy in New Zealand, 1908–2006' (The Theosophical Society in Australia, last modified on 16 March 2012), available from: www.austheos.org.au/indices/TINNZ_.HTM.

101 Letter from Naylor to Hansen [c. 1930], Hansen Papers, ATL.

The birth of the Australian citizens' movements

The Citizens' League of South Australia

The process of conservative radicalisation is epitomised by Edward Daniel Alexander Bagot, founder of the first citizens' movement, known as the Citizens' League of South Australia. Born on 25 December 1893 at Henley Beach in South Australia to a middle-class Protestant family, Bagot was educated in England at Framlingham and Lowestoft. He served as a lieutenant in the 1st Australian Wireless Signal Squadron during the Great War and ran a series of semi-successful transport services in Mesopotamia and Australia during the 1920s.[102] His travels made him a popular figure and, in 1929, while working as an insurance agent in Adelaide, he was invited to give a speech to the Constitutional Club on emerging markets in the Middle East. At the time, his knowledge of politics was limited to an appreciation of sound business practice; his speech criticised the high labour costs that made Australian exports prohibitively expensive in emerging markets.[103] His words evidently inspired the club, for they coopted him on to the executive committee in June 1929.[104]

Like many other conservative non-party organisations of its kind, the Constitutional Club served as an incubator for a younger and more radical generation of conservatives during the Depression. It began to host public speakers who called for the 'rationalisation of industry' and an end to the government's 'orgy of expenditure'.[105] One guest speaker, leader of the state Country Party and MP A.G. Cameron, claimed that party politics had caused the Depression and warned that the country was headed for a military dictatorship 'unless there was a cleaning up of the present Parliamentary system'.[106] It was within this environment that Bagot, like many of his fellow small businesspeople and professionals of a conservative

---

102 Stephen A. James, 'God, Mammon and Mussolini: The Ideology and Policy of the Citizens' League of South Australia, 1930–1934', *Australian Journal of Politics and History* 37(1) (1991): 39–60, at p. 40; John Lonie, 'Bagot, Edward Daniel (1893–1968)', *Australian Dictionary of Biography* (National Centre of Biography, The Australian National University, published first in hardcopy 1979), available from: adb.anu.edu.au/biography/bagot-edward-daniel-5091.
103 *The Advertiser*, [Adelaide], 28 March 1929, 14; *Register News-Pictorial*, [Adelaide], 28 March 1929, 8.
104 *Register News-Pictorial*, [Adelaide], 21 June 1929, 5.
105 *The Advertiser*, [Adelaide], 31 July 1930, 12; 2 October 1930, 10.
106 ibid., 24 July 1930, 8.

mindset, anxiously sought a solution to the Great Depression. In April 1930, he wrote to an associate in Melbourne criticising Scullin's proposed wheat pool as an 'attempt at sovietism'. He suggested that if simultaneous protest meetings were organised by the forces of capital in every city, Scullin would be compelled to establish a 'supreme economic council' to deal with the Depression.[107] Shortly after Cameron's foreboding speech to the Constitutional Club, Bagot wrote to *The Advertiser* openly calling for a dictatorship:

> Surely through the length and breadth of this country, which produced such outstanding personalities in time of war, the individual exists who is able and willing to take command in time of peace, one strong enough to cut the shackles of party politics, to displace those useless politicians both Liberal and Labour who have allowed the country to drift into insolvency by their sheer ineptitude[.]

Such a dictator, Bagot continued, would need to be 'a big man in business leadership', who would remove the government from all forms of enterprise, abolish arbitration, revise tariffs and bounties, and replace state parliaments with 'small Councils of efficient operatives well paid for their services'.[108]

As the Depression worsened, Bagot was driven by a sense of urgency. In a September 1930 address to the Political Reform League, he stressed the need to 'act and to act immediately if we are to avert one of the biggest crashes that Australia has ever seen'. The crisis, he stated, was twofold: political, in that democracy had become subservient to 'party politics' and 'partisan platforms'; and financial, due to the 'insidious onslaught of political power on commercial fields':

> It is not an uncommon occurrence for a country to be faced with a serious political crisis or a financial panic independently of each other, but when both happen together the blow is so staggering that for a while we are numbed by its strength and thus dazed, are inclined to let others find a remedy while we do nothing. In other words we are inclined to say 'Isn't it appalling? Something will have to be done soon' instead of saying 'Isn't it appalling; *something must be done now*'. [Emphasis in original]

---

107 Letter from Bagot to Harold Darling, 14 May 1930, box 7, item 36, CLSA Papers, NLA.
108 Bagot, 'A Dictator Needed', submitted to the Editor of *The Advertiser*, 5 September 1930, box 3, item 25D, CLSA Papers, NLA.

The urgent need to do something to avoid a pending crisis was reinforced by the failure of earlier responses. The meeting of businesspeople in July 1930, Bagot noted, had 'passed resolutions and sent a few gentlemen to Canberra who achieved little', and the revived Kyabram Reform Movement founded at Moonta earlier that year 'no longer moves'. The time had come, he concluded, to 'show our politicians ... that there is a section of the public—a long suffering section indeed—that has nearly reached the limit of its endurance—that now cries halt!'.[109]

Bagot decided to follow through on his pledge to do something by forming a new protest movement. He drew on the knowledge and expertise of existing conservative non-party organisations. During September 1930, he utilised the connections of the South Australian Constitutional Club to approach several such organisations with a view to organising a combined demonstration against 'the criminal procrastination of the Federal Government'.[110] His proposal was well received, and a meeting was held at Balfour's Café on 3 October 1930 to organise the demonstration. Present at the meeting were 35 'members and friends' of the Constitutional Club, including Keith Wilson and C.L. Abbott from the Political Reform League and A.L. Langsford from the Wheat Producers' Freedom Association. Those present resolved to hold the demonstration in the Adelaide Town Hall on 14 October 1930.[111]

Crucially, the attendees also agreed that the demonstration would be complemented by 'a permanent body of citizens to follow up this protest with further concerted action'. This resolution gave birth to the Citizens' League of South Australia, the first of the citizens' movements, which would eventually amass a membership of around 22,000 individuals across the state. An executive committee of 10 was appointed for the new movement, including Bagot as leader and general organiser, Langsford as country organiser, Abbott as town hall meeting planner, and several members of the Constitutional Club.[112] The newly formed Citizens' League also absorbed an existing right-wing organisation known as the Empire Loyalty League, and agreed to cooperate with the South Australian

109 Bagot, Speech given to the Political Reform League, September 1930, box 3, item 25A, CLSA Papers, NLA.
110 Address by L.V. Pellew, 14 October 1930; Minutes of inaugural meeting, 3 October 1930, box 1, item 1, CLSA Papers, NLA.
111 Minutes of inaugural meeting, 3 October 1930, box 1, item 1, CLSA Papers, NLA.
112 Minutes of General Meeting of the Citizens' League, 7 October 1930, box 1, item 1, CLSA Papers, NLA; *The Advertiser*, [Adelaide], 13 November 1930, 11.

Proportional Representation Group, the Advance Australia League, and the South Australian branch of the Women's Non-Party Association.[113] These organisations solidified the connections between the Citizens' League and the conservative non-party tradition that preceded it.

The Australian Citizens' League

From its inception, Bagot envisioned the Citizens' League of South Australia as the nucleus of a nationwide movement. His attempts to influence the formation of branches in other states are discussed more generally in Chapter Four. However, Bagot played a more direct role in the formation of the Australian Citizens' League in Victoria. As he was scheduled to visit Melbourne in January 1931 on other business, the Citizens' League executive resolved that he should attempt to establish a branch of the league while he was there. His first stop in Melbourne was the local branch of the Constitutional Club, given the role that organisation had played in forming the league in Adelaide. He was well received by the Constitutional Club, which resolved to form a branch of the Citizens' League in Victoria.

Bagot then attended the 'winding up meeting' of the Citizens' Committee, a group of influential Melbourne businessmen that had formed in December 1930 to assist Acting Treasurer Lyons with the loan conversion campaign. The Citizens' Committee included prominent members of Victoria's conservative elite such as H.D. Luxton (Mayor of Melbourne), R.W. Knox (Chairman of the National Union), and Kingsley Henderson (partner at the architectural firm A.&K. Henderson).[114] The committee was also associated with 'the Group of Six', a small clique of conservative politicians and professionals including Robert Menzies (President of the

113 Minutes of Special Joint Sub-Committee meeting of the Citizens' League and the Empire Loyalty League, 22 October 1930; Report of Executive Committee presented at First Convention of Delegates of Branch Committees, 1 December 1930; Minutes of Executive Committee Meeting, 12 January 1931, box 1, item 1; Minutes of Executive Committee Meeting, 7 July 1931, box 1, item 2, CLSA Papers, NLA.
114 D.H. Borchardt, 'Knox, Sir Robert Wilson (1890–1973)', *Australian Dictionary of Biography* (National Centre of Biography, The Australian National University, published first in hardcopy 1983), available from: adb.anu.edu.au/biography/knox-sir-robert-wilson-6993; Susan M. Balderstone, 'Henderson, Kingsley Anketell (1883–1942)', *Australian Dictionary of Biography* (National Centre of Biography, The Australian National University, published first in hardcopy 1983), available from: adb.anu.edu.au/biography/henderson-kingsley-anketell-6634.

Victorian Young Nationalists Organisation) and Staniforth Ricketson (stockbroker at J.B. Were & Sons), who encouraged Lyons and his followers to split from the Labor Party in March 1931.[115]

Bagot viewed the Citizens' Committee as a potential ally in forming a Victorian Citizens' League. He gave a brief presentation on the work that had been done so far in South Australia, which led the Citizens' Committee to agree in principle to work with the Melbourne Constitutional Club to form a citizens' movement in Victoria. There were, however, two potentially divisive matters that remained to be resolved. First, the Citizens' Committee was too associated with conservative party politics for Bagot's liking. He recommended that the committee support Constitutional Club secretary P.W. Powell for leadership of the new movement rather than nominate one of their own members.[116] The committee agreed with Bagot about the need for political 'neutrality' but was disinclined to serve under Powell. In his place, they recommended E. Lee Neil, managing director of Myer Emporium and a lay canon of St Paul's Cathedral. Before he left Melbourne, Bagot had 'a long interview' with Lee Neil in which he stressed 'the absolute necessity for bringing in from the outset all classes of the community and making it a real Citizens' movement'. Lee Neil heartily agreed. The two also debated the idea of leaving the matter of leadership to the central committee of the proposed movement, which could appoint a chair each time they met.[117]

A second and ultimately more divisive issue was whether the Victorian or South Australian citizens' movements would take the lead on the national stage. Bagot envisioned the new Victorian movement as a mirror of his own, and requested that it adopt the name and badge of the Citizens' League of South Australia.[118] While the Melbourne Constitutional Club was happy with this plan, the Citizens' Committee wanted to form an entirely new movement named the Australian Citizens' League, which would then spread to Sydney and Brisbane, rather than accepting 'the extension of a League already formed'.[119] The committee won the argument, and Bagot

---

115 Hart, 'Lyons', 44; Frank Strahan, 'Ricketson, Staniforth (1891–1967)', *Australian Dictionary of Biography* (National Centre of Biography, The Australian National University, published first in hardcopy 2002), available from: adb.anu.edu.au/biography/ricketson-staniforth-11521.
116 Letter from Bagot to Knox, 17 January 1931, box 13, item 12, CLSA Papers, NLA.
117 Letter from Bagot to H.E.A. McCarthy, 17 January 1931, box 13, item 16, CLSA Papers, NLA.
118 Letter from Bagot to Knox, 17 January 1931, box 13, item 12, CLSA Papers, NLA.
119 Letter from Bagot to H.E.A. McCarthy, 17 January 1931, box 13, item 16, CLSA Papers, NLA.

left Melbourne with little beyond a vague promise of cooperation.[120] Even this was not forthcoming, as the Citizens' Committee was keen to demonstrate its independence from the South Australian movement. In a public statement released to the media on 31 January 1931, Henderson said the new Victorian citizens' movement would be a continuation of the work of the Citizens' Committee rather than a partnership with the Citizens' League of South Australia.[121] The announcement took Bagot by surprise; he had been trying unsuccessfully to contact Knox for an update on the movement's progress.[122] When Knox finally replied to Bagot in early February, his tone was patronising:

> Apparently you do not get copies of the Melbourne 'Argus'; otherwise, you would have seen, almost daily, accounts of the Citizens' Movement which was brought before the notice of the public last week very forcibly by a strong 'leader' … The movement is making in every way satisfactory progress.[123]

The league was subsequently launched at a meeting at Melbourne Town Hall on 19 February 1931.

Why was the Citizens' Committee so reluctant to cooperate with Bagot, or to follow his lead? The answer may lie in the cleavage between middle and upper-class conservatives. Members of the Citizens' Committee came from the upper echelons of Melbourne society and had close ties to the National Federation of Victoria. Bagot, in contrast, was a political newcomer from the professional middle class. While the Citizens' Committee shared Bagot's desire to uphold orthodox economic values, his fiery rhetoric and populist anti-partyism made him a wild card with the potential to split the conservative vote. The reluctance of the Citizens' Committee to follow Bagot or the Melbourne Constitutional Club may have also stemmed from the role they had played in securing the conversion loan. Citizens' Committee members had, in their eyes, defended the nation's honour from the stain of repudiation through their 'patriotic and painstaking efforts'.[124] It is possible their vision of themselves made it difficult for them to imagine falling in behind the bombastic novice from South Australia.

120 Minutes of Executive Committee Meeting, 21 January 1931, box 1, item 2, CLSA Papers, NLA; *Horsham Times*, 23 January 1931, 6.
121 *The Argus*, [Melbourne], 31 January 1931, 19.
122 Letter from Bagot to R.W. Knox, 31 January 1931; Letter from Bagot to Knox, 2 February 1931, box 13, item 12, CLSA Papers, NLA.
123 Letter from Knox to Bagot, 6 February 1931, box 13, item 12, CLSA Papers, NLA.
124 Or so the note of thanks from Lyons said; see *The Argus*, [Melbourne], 27 December 1930, 8.

The All for Australia League

Unlike the Australian Citizens' League, the All for Australia League arose independently of the Citizens' League of South Australia.[125] One of its early influences was a rural protest movement, the Producers' Advisory Council, which emerged from the 'financial panic' that followed Lang's electoral victory in October 1930. The council's key instigators were Graziers' Association President F.H. Tout and former Member for Gwydir C.L.A. Abbott, who met several times to discuss 'what could be done to prevent a smash'. Abbott suggested the Country Party Central Council set up a meeting of various primary producer, business, and manufacturing organisations. This widely attended meeting on 4 December 1930 agreed to form a pressure group that would organise protest meetings throughout the NSW countryside calling for lowered costs of production through drastic government economies, tariff reductions, and the abolition of arbitration.[126] Its early activities gathered significant public attention: in January 1931 alone, it addressed a total of 40,000 people at 40 meetings.[127]

Abbott's efforts impressed several Sydney businessmen, who wondered whether a similar organisation could be formed in the city. These included R.A. Malloch of farming equipment manufacturer Dangar, Gedye & Malloch, and deputy chairman of Associated Newspapers, Sydney Snow. Abbott explained to the two men what the Producers' Advisory Council had done in the country and 'suggested they should try to do the same in Sydney'.[128] At the same time, a group of Sydney Rotarians including Alex J. Gibson (consulting engineer with Julius Gibson & Poole) and Norman Keysor (managing director of General Industries) held separate discussions on the deteriorating economic situation. After meeting with the leaders of several business and manufacturers' organisations, they convened a conference in the Sydney Chamber of Commerce on 28 January 1931. As was the case with the Citizens' League of South Australia, the attendees at this inaugural conference were associated with several current and

---

125 However, Bagot regularly corresponded with the Constitutional Association of New South Wales, which participated in the formative meetings of the All for Australia League. See Report of Sub-Committee, 21 October 1930, box 1, item 1, and Minutes of Executive Committee Meeting, 21 October 1930, box 1, item 2, CLSA Papers, NLA; Minutes of Committee Meeting, 28 October 1930, box 2, item 1, 1925–61, CANSW Papers, SLNSW.
126 C.L.A. Abbott, Family Background: The Upper Hunter Abbotts, folder 5, 335–38, Hilda and C.L.A. Abbott Papers, MS 4744 [hereinafter Abbott Papers], NLA; *Primary Producers' Problems: The Way Out* (Sydney: Land Newspaper Ltd, 1931).
127 *Sydney Morning Herald*, 27 February 1931, 7.
128 Abbott, Family Background: The Upper Hunter Abbotts, 339, Abbott Papers, NLA.

former conservative non-party organisations. These included A.E. Heath from the Constitutional Association and the Producers' Advisory Council; Sir Henry Braddon, whose long list of organisational affiliations included the Sane Democracy League and the King and Empire Alliance; Malloch and Snow, who had recently spoken with Abbott about the Producers' Advisory Council; and Major-General H.G. Bennett, brother of 'Who's for Australia?' League president A.E. Bennett.[129] These individuals later formed the nucleus of the first State Council of the All for Australia League. They also coopted Bennett from the 'Who's for Australia?' League and O.D.A. Oberg from the Sane Democracy League and Constitutional Association.[130] The new movement was launched at a public meeting in the Killara Memorial Hall on 12 February 1931.

Paramilitary and new-state movements in New South Wales

The three Australian citizens' movements were not the only populist conservative responses to the Depression. The actions of the Lang Government—in particular, Lang's proposal at the February 1931 state premiers' conference to repudiate interest payments to British bondholders until the crisis passed—stirred up a wide variety of responses. In New South Wales, tens of thousands of individuals joined the New Guard, a paramilitary organisation whose objectives were to uphold loyalty to the British Crown and individual liberty, to suppress disloyal elements in government, industry, and society, and to abolish 'machine politics'. The New Guard originated from the secretive 'Old Guard', a clandestine paramilitary organisation formed by several prominent Sydney businessmen in the weeks after Lang's election victory. The Old Guard's aim was to form a statewide organisation that would assist the police to maintain essential services and act as a special constabulary force in the event of a communist uprising or the disintegration of the Lang Government.[131] It shared these objectives with similar secret organisations

---

129 Trevor Matthews, 'The All for Australia League', in *The Great Depression in Australia*, ed. Robert Cooksey (Canberra: Australian Society for the Study of Labour History, 1970), 138–39; *Sydney Morning Herald*, 20 May 1931, 11; Family Background: The Upper Hunter Abbotts, 339, Abbott Papers, NLA; *Reports of Inaugural Meetings*, 4–6; *Singleton Argus*, 21 January 1931, 4.
130 *Sydney Morning Herald*, 20 May 1931, 11; Minutes of Committee Meeting, 26 May 1931, box 2, item 1, CANSW Papers, SLNSW.
131 Moore, *The Secret Army and the Premier*, 86–88.

in other states, including the Victorian League of National Security.[132] Eric Campbell, a Sydney solicitor appointed as one of the Old Guard's recruiters, became dissatisfied with the movement's secrecy and its unwillingness to openly challenge the Lang Government. He acceded to a polite request to resign in February 1931—but not without taking a small nucleus of young officers with him. This group officially formed the New Guard on 18 February 1931, nine days after the premiers' conference.[133] After months of organising and recruiting, the New Guard was publicly launched at a packed rally in the Sydney Town Hall on 22 July 1931.

The Depression also gave added impetus to rural protest organisations— in particular, 'new state' movements. The Riverina and New England regions of New South Wales had a long tradition of agitating for separation as discrete states under the Commonwealth of Australia. Lang's proposal at the premiers' conference galvanised support for separation. The New England Movement, which had existed since the 1920s, was joined by new or revitalised movements in the Riverina, the Monaro–South Coast, and the western region of New South Wales. The Riverina Movement, however, was by far the largest and most populist of the new-state movements. Led by Charles Hardy, a fiery orator described as the 'Cromwell of the Riverina', the Riverina Movement soon amassed tens of thousands of members. Hardy called for separation from New South Wales—unilaterally, if necessary—along with a reduction in government expenditure, immediate assistance to primary producers, and an end to the machine politics of the city.[134] While the new-state movements agitated

---

132 Cathcart, *Defending the National Tuckshop*; John Schauble, Right-wing militancy in Australia: The rise of the League of National Security (BA Hons diss., University of Melbourne, 1979); Paul James, 'Armies of the Right: In Defence of Empire and Nation', *Melbourne Journal of Politics* 16 (1984–85): 78–101, at pp. 87–90; Paul James, Militarism and loyalty: Civilian paramilitary movements in Melbourne during the interwar period (BA Hons diss., University of Melbourne, 1980).

133 Amos, *The New Guard Movement*, 24–28.

134 Ellis, *The Country Party*, 79–165; Ellis, *A Pen in Politics*, 172–203; Aitkin, *The Country Party in New South Wales*, 31–34; R.G. Neale, 'New States Movement', *Australian Quarterly* [Sydney] 22(3) (1950): 9–23; Grant Harman, 'New State Agitation in Northern New South Wales, 1920–1929', *Journal of the Royal Australian Historical Society* 63(1) (1977): 26–39; E.R. Woolmington, The geographical scope of support for the new state movement in northern N.S.W. (PhD diss., University of New England, Armidale, NSW, 1963); Nancy Blacklow, '"Riverina Roused": Representative Support for the Riverina New State Movements of the 1920s and 1930s', *Journal of the Royal Australian Historical Society: Special Riverina Issue* 80(3–4) (1994): 176–94; Nancy Blacklow, Regional support for Riverina new state movements in the 1920s and 1930s (BA Hons diss., Charles Sturt University, Wagga Wagga, NSW, 1992); Sherry Morris, *Wagga Wagga: A History* (Wagga Wagga, NSW: Council of the City of Wagga Wagga, 1999), 178–84; James Logan, 'Re-Examining Senator Charles Hardy's Role in Coordinating the Country Protest Movements in NSW in the 1930s', *The Page Review* 1(2) (2005): 19–27; Tuziak, Riverina awake!; Beveridge, The Riverina Movement and Charles Hardy.

for separation from New South Wales, the Dominion League of Western Australia—established in July 1930—sought complete secession from Australia as an independent dominion within the British Empire.[135] I will return to the New Guard, the Riverina Movement, and the Dominion League in later chapters.

The birth of the New Zealand Legion

Trans-Tasman influences and connections

New Zealanders were well informed of the political and economic turmoil unfolding in Australia in the early years of the Depression. Correspondents in Sydney provided a steady flow of news coverage. Businesspeople anxiously swapped stories about the deteriorating economic situation. Individuals and organisations in both countries corresponded with each other, keen to swap ideas and experiences or to forge alliances. Many prominent figures in the Australian citizens' movements had business and professional interests on both sides of the Tasman. The Melbourne architectural firm of Australian Citizens' League Secretary Kingsley Henderson, for example, designed several New Zealand buildings throughout the interwar years, including the Bank of Australasia in Whangarei and the T&G Building in Wellington.[136] It was also a consultant to the Commercial Bank of Australia in New Zealand, where it worked with local architectural firms such as Clere & Clere.[137] All for Australia League State Council member F.J. Walker ran an international meat exporting firm with offices in Auckland, Wellington, and Christchurch, and he negotiated several shipments of beef during the Depression on behalf of the Australian and New Zealand Land Company.[138]

---

135 Musgrave, 'The Western Australian Secessionist Movement'; Harry H. Hiller, 'Secession in Western Australia: A Continuing Phenomenon?', *Australian Quarterly* [Sydney] 59(2) (1987): 222–33; F.R. Beasley, 'The Secession Movement in Western Australia', *The Australian Quarterly* [Sydney] 8 (1936): 31–36; Edward Watt, 'Secession in Western Australia', *University Studies in Western Australian History* (3) (1958): 43–86; Watt, Western separation; Geoffrey Bolton, *A Fine Country to Starve In* (Perth: University of Western Australia Press, 1994).

136 Now called the Harcourts Building. For some of A.&K. Henderson's New Zealand projects, see box 70A, folder 186; box 99, folders 187, 131, 242; box 129, folders 3c, 204c, 64, 103; box 161, folders 60, 60b, 111, A.&K. Henderson Records, 1878–1960, MS9317, State Library of Victoria, Melbourne.

137 Box 176, folders 133D, 151, A.&K. Henderson Records, 1878–1960, MS9317, State Library of Victoria, Melbourne.

138 *Sydney Morning Herald*, 4 January 1934, 9.

New Zealand employers' and farmers' organisations were certainly aware of the deteriorating financial situation in Australia in 1931, and they stressed the need for drastic government action to prevent the same thing happening in New Zealand. In his speech to the annual dominion conference of the Farmers' Union in July 1931, President W.J. Polson stated that New Zealand would 'be faced with the precise financial problems which confront New South Wales' unless rural and urban interests cooperated in cutting production costs. One attendee at the conference suggested New Zealand should follow the example of Lyons' loan conversion campaign and reduce interest rates on government bonds.[139] When New Zealand was at its lowest economic point in 1933, members of the Associated Chambers of Commerce claimed the Australian economy had begun to improve since the new conservative government had started implementing policies that incentivised private industry.[140]

Print culture kept New Zealanders abreast of events transpiring in Australia during the Depression. The entire June 1931 issue of the *New Zealand Financial Times* was devoted to the economic situation in Australia, paying particular attention to the Commonwealth Bank's attempt to scuttle the Scullin Government's proposal to establish a central bank. It also noted with approval the formation of 'citizen groups' such as the All for Australia League, whose badge was reproduced on the front cover with the slogan 'Loyal Australians Prepare to Uphold Australia's Honour'.[141] Newspapers were a particularly vital channel of information: the trans-Tasman cables from Auckland and Wellington both originated in Sydney, which allowed news items from Australia and the wider British Empire to be rapidly reprinted in New Zealand. The growth of the citizens' movements in Australia was covered throughout 1931, with newspapers noting favourably their call for national unity in the face of party strife. One reporter expressed incredulity that party politicians might prevent a similar unity from being achieved in New Zealand:

139 Report of Thirtieth Dominion Conference, 7 July 1931, 19, Dominion meetings and conferences—Minutes 1931, MSY-0248, New Zealand Farmers' Union Papers, MS-Papers-1159, ATL.
140 Report of Proceedings at the Annual Conference of the Associated Chambers of Commerce of New Zealand, 26–27 October 1933, 49, Wellington Chamber of Commerce Papers, ATL.
141 *New Zealand Financial Times*, [Wellington], June 1931, 1.

Can it be that just as the friends of good government in Australia are uniting, regardless of party, to save the country, our own leaders will resist the call to national unity and aggravate the common danger by maintaining the artificial division of the party system[?][142]

The All for Australia League attracted most of this press attention, due perhaps to the geographical proximity of New South Wales and the historical ties it shared with New Zealand. New South Wales was also the site of the most heated divisions during the Depression: Jack Lang's Labor faction held power there until May 1932, which provided the press with a convenient rhetorical opposite to the values the citizens' movements espoused.[143] At the very least, this suggests that many New Zealanders were aware of the Australian citizens' movements.

It is somewhat surprising, therefore, that there do not appear to have been any direct connections between the Australian citizens' movements and the founders of the New Zealand Legion. The formation of the New Zealand Legion received passing mention in the Australian press, but it otherwise attracted little attention in Australia.[144] There was one Australian subscriber to the legion's journal, A.N. Ekman of Kew, Victoria, but it is unclear whether he had been a member of the Australian Citizens' League.[145] This may have been a matter of timing; by the time the New Zealand Legion was established in 1933, the Australian movements were either moribund or had ceased to exist.

The paramilitary New Guard, however, did have a direct influence on the emergence of the New Zealand Legion. This was even though the leaders of the legion went to great lengths to disavow any connections to the New Guard, as is discussed in Chapter Three. The combative rhetoric of its leader, Eric Campbell, combined with its violent clashes with unemployed and communist gatherings across Sydney in the summer of 1931–32, was regularly covered by the New Zealand press. However, the antics of a mounted New Guardsman at the Sydney Harbour Bridge opening ceremony in March 1932 were what attracted the most attention.[146] Francis de Groot, a zealous member of the New

---

142 *The Evening Post*, [Wellington], 17 April 1931, 6.
143 ibid., 23 February 1931, 9.
144 *The Argus*, [Melbourne], 24 February 1933, 9.
145 *National Opinion* [Wellington] 2(23) (5 July 1934): 14–15.
146 *The Evening Post*, [Wellington], 19 March 1932, 12.

Guard, was tasked by Campbell with upstaging Lang at the opening ceremony. Riding up to the ceremonial ribbon on horseback in his World War One uniform, de Groot sliced the ribbon in half in an act of public defiance against Lang's government. He became a trans-Tasman celebrity virtually overnight; several New Zealanders sent him fan mail, including a schoolboy in Canterbury who attended a fancy dress ball in a de Groot costume.[147] A promotional film containing statements from de Groot and Eric Campbell was screened before feature films at the St James Theatre in Wellington and was met with applause.[148] The opening of the Haupiri Bridge in Kopara was disrupted by an 'amateur "De Groot"', who 'galloped up on a horse and, with a dramatic sweep of a stick, severed the ribbon across the bridge'.[149] This positive reception soured after May 1932 when a police investigation revealed the New Guard's secret plans to launch a coup against the state government.[150] By the end of 1932, the movement had begun adopting the trappings of fascism, which further tarnished its reputation in New Zealand.[151]

The declining popularity of the New Guard coincided with the birth of the New Zealand Legion. As with the Australian citizens' movements, the legion emerged from the tradition of conservative non-party organisation that preceded it. By November 1932, the New Zealand National Movement was all but defunct and its organiser, J.R.V. Sherston, began canvassing leading conservative figures across the country about forming a new movement. The first individual he approached was Arthur Nelson Field, the prominent monetary reformer from Nelson. Apart from being knowledgeable about monetary reform, Field was also well placed to inform Sherston of developments overseas. He had received orders from hundreds of foreign publishers and individuals for his work, and his Australian correspondents kept him well informed of events across the Tasman, including those involving the New Guard.[152] However, Field and Sherston held different views on what a new movement would look like,

---

147 See Letters from Cecil Sweet Allen, D.A. Blackman, Oswald Cotterell, and Henry G. Ford, volume 4, CY3091; and from A.H. MacKay, H.T. Morton, and Unknown, volume 5, CY3092, Francis Edward de Groot Papers [hereinafter de Groot Papers], SLNSW. Cotterell was the schoolboy.

148 *The Evening Post*, [Wellington], 9 April 1932, 8; Letter from Mr M.V. Nelson [undated], volume 5, CY3092, de Groot Papers, SLNSW.

149 *The Evening Post*, [Wellington], 21 November 1932, 8.

150 ibid., 11 May 1932, 7; 17 June 1932, 7.

151 Cunningham, 'Australian Fascism?', 388–89.

152 La Rooij, 'Arthur Nelson Field'; Letter from Arthur James Vogan, 28 March 1932, Scrapbook of correspondence enclosing some clippings, 1930–38, MS-Papers-8615-083, Field Papers, ATL.

so the two men agreed to part ways.[153] Sherston then met with Sir Andrew Russell, a long-time acquaintance who had served as a general during the Great War. Russell was associated with several conservative organisations, including the National Defence League and the Returned Services Association, and he had a particular interest in monetary reform.[154] The two men met in January 1933, and Russell agreed wholeheartedly with Sherston's ideas. '[W]e need a fresh start', Russell recorded in his diary, 'doing away with party government, not quite socialism nor yet fascism, rather a combination.'[155] Russell later became chairman of the Hawke's Bay Division of the New Zealand Legion.

Sherston also met with several Wellington businessmen and professionals in January 1933. One of these was a urologist, Robert Campbell Begg, who had recently become renowned for his election to the Wellington Hospital Board as a candidate for the Wellington Civic League, the body formed by the anti-communist Welfare League in 1921. Begg's campaign was based on his belief that hospital administration was heavily politicised, haphazard, and inefficient, and required self-sacrificing and nonpartisan leadership if it were to become more economic and sustainable.[156] Begg's views on public service were influenced by his involvement with the Wellington Rotary Club, where he had served in a leadership or committee member role since 1929.[157] He was also the younger brother of Dunedin sheep farmer James Begg, who was a longstanding member of the Victoria and Navy leagues and a founding member of the Welfare League. When Begg met with Sherston, he had already been considering how his successful rationalisation of the Wellington Hospital Board might be extended to local and central government across New Zealand.[158]

It was around this time that tenuous links appear to have been established between the New Guard and the founders of the New Zealand Legion. During a stopover in Fremantle, Western Australia, on 19 January 1933 on his way to Europe for business, Campbell told the press that the New

---

153 Letter from Field to Sherston, 16 January 1933; Letter from Sherston to Field, 20 January 1933, Alphabetical correspondence, 73-148-108, Field Papers, ATL.

154 Jock Vennell, *The Forgotten General: New Zealand's World War I Commander Major-General Sir Andrew Russell* (Auckland: Allen & Unwin, 2011), 219–20, 224–25, 252–56.

155 Quoted in ibid., 253.

156 *The Evening Post*, [Wellington], 3 March 1931, 4.

157 Minutes of Annual General Meeting, 25 June 1929, Wellington Rotary Club Papers, MSY-3661, ATL.

158 Robert Campbell Begg, *The Secret of the Knife* (Norwich, UK: Jarrold & Sons, 1966), 84.

Guard had established ties with a 'strong body in New Zealand'.[159] This may have been hyperbole considering Campbell boasted in the same breath that the New Guard had 250,000 members and active branches in every Australian state, when in fact its support had dwindled to a few thousand members. Nevertheless, it is interesting that his claim coincided with the formative discussions of the New Zealand Legion in January 1933. His announcement led a New Zealand Labour MP to ask the Minister for Justice in February whether he had any information regarding a local branch of the New Guard, and 'what steps he proposed to take to suppress it'. The minister replied that he no information that such an organisation existed.[160]

In 1968, Campbell recalled that someone in New Zealand had contacted him during the Depression seeking advice on setting up a large conservative organisation. While he could not remember who made the inquiry, he recalled that '[t]here was no discussion of policy … [as] there was a similarity between our objectives that made comment unnecessary'.[161] Since the New Guard was well and truly dead by the 1960s and Campbell was no longer in the public spotlight, there was far less reason for him to exaggerate his international connections than there had been in 1933. One historian has suggested it was Hugh McLean Campbell, the Reform Party MP for Hawke's Bay, who contacted the New Guard leader. This assumption appears to have been based on the author's mistaken belief that Hugh was Eric Campbell's uncle, which he seems to have gathered from an article in the *New Zealand Observer*.[162] However, Eric Campbell's first cousin (once removed) was Sir Andrew Russell, and it was possible the Hawke's Bay sheep farmer contacted Campbell after being canvassed by Sherston in January 1933.[163] It may also have been Sherston himself: if he had discussed his proposed organisation with prominent New Zealand personalities such as Russell, Field, and Begg, he may also have sought the advice of conservative luminaries in Australia.

---

159 *West Australian*, [Perth], 19 January 1933, 4.
160 *The Evening Post*, [Wellington], 7 February 1933, 9.
161 Pugh, The New Zealand Legion and conservative protest in the Great Depression, 54.
162 *New Zealand Observer*, [Auckland], 21 April 1932, 4. Eric Campbell's daughter informed me that she 'doubt[ed] that Hugh McLean Campbell was a relative (definitely not an uncle) of EC'.
163 The information on Campbell's relationship to Russell is drawn from the Eric Campbell Memoirs, privately held.

Information about the New Guard was also carried to the New Zealand Legion by an author and journalist named Will Lawson. Born in Durham, England, in 1876, Lawson and his family migrated to New Zealand in 1880 and settled in Brisbane four years later. After working for several years as a clerk, he embarked on a lifelong career as a writer, which saw him travel back and forth across the Tasman almost 30 times throughout his life.[164] He was working for the *Evening News* in Sydney when the Depression hit, and his fellow reporters wrote several approving articles about the formation of the All for Australia League in February 1931.[165] After the *News* merged with the *Sun* in March, Lawson commenced full-time work in the Sydney office of the New Zealand–based Mount Cook Tourist Company, until it closed in April and requested that he relocate to the head office in Wellington. When the company folded at the end of 1931, Lawson moved to Auckland, where he worked as a publicity man for a flax company and wrote occasional pieces for local newspapers.[166] Lawson was working as a freelance writer for the *New Zealand Observer* in Auckland during the riots of April 1932. His experiences led him to write fondly about the way the New Guard had dealt with the unemployed in Sydney:

> From a mere handful of carefully picked men, whose loyalty to high Australian ideals was undoubted, it has grown into a body composed of many thousands of patriots of the highest calibre. By its silent work, as well as its spectacular posing, it undoubtedly saved Australian cities from disturbances such as those which have occurred in Auckland.

While Lawson incorrectly claimed that the New Guard had been formed by the All for Australia League, he argued that a similar body should be formed in New Zealand 'while the Soviet propaganda is stirring the people in one direction or another'.[167] When the legion was formed in 1933, Lawson was working in Wellington on a booklet for the centenary

---

164 Biographical information drawn from the three drafts of his autobiography; see Will Lawson, The Golden horseman, Will Lawson Papers, MS-Papers-1679-5 [hereinafter Lawson Papers], ATL; Will Lawson, Baa' baa' Black Sheep: An autobiography, MLMSS 356, and Baa' baa' Black Sheep: An autobiography of an Australian author, MLMSS 3129, in Will Lawson Papers, SLNSW. See also Elizabeth Webby, 'Lawson, William (Will) (1876–1957)', *Australian Dictionary of Biography* (National Centre of Biography, The Australian National University, published first in hardcopy 1986), available from: adb.anu.edu.au/biography/lawson-william-will-7122.

165 *The Evening News*, [Wellington], 13 February 1931, 4.

166 Baa' baa' Black Sheep: An autobiography of an Australian author, 259–66, MLMSS 3129, Will Lawson Papers, SLNSW.

167 *New Zealand Observer*, [Auckland], 21 April 1932, 4.

celebrations.[168] He was hired as the editor for the movement's new journal, *National Opinion*, where he worked alongside Begg in the legion's head office in Kelvin Chambers, Wellington. It is possible that, in the close confines of the legion's office, Lawson and Begg held many conversations about policy.[169] Lawson's editorials were among some of the fieriest articles published in *National Opinion*.[170]

The trigger for the legion's birth

There was plenty of ideological material and conservative discontent available to draw on by the beginning of 1933. While conservatives had begrudgingly accepted the government's measures to help the unemployed, reduce interest rates and wages, and alleviate farmers' indebtedness, they did so with some concern. An increasing number were being drawn to unorthodox monetary theories such as Douglas social credit. However, in the absence of a galvanising event like the Australian premiers' conference in February 1931, there had been no large populist conservative response in New Zealand. New Zealanders were certainly familiar with the movements that had arisen in Australia, particularly the New Guard, and there had been some calls to form a similar organisation in the wake of the riots in April and May 1932. But the Coalition government's swift and decisive response to the riots forestalled any sense of lingering crisis.

Devaluing the New Zealand currency was the trigger for a more extreme form of conservative response. New conservative parties and protest groups sprung up like mushrooms, including the short-lived All New Zealand Party and the Seddon Liberal Party. Begg and Sherston, who had already been discussing the formation of a new movement that would place national interests above those of party or class, doubled their efforts. The New Zealand Legion was established at a conference of businessmen and farmers organised by the Wellington Civic League on 8 February 1933. Begg was chosen to lead the new movement and a committee was

---

168 *Baa' baa' Black Sheep: An autobiography*, 206, MLMSS 356, Will Lawson Papers, SLNSW.
169 As an example of the proximity of Begg and the journal's editor, W.R. Kingston-Smith (Lawson's successor) noted that he often left material on Begg's desk in Kelvin Chambers for his perusal; see Letter from W.R. Kingston Smith to J.F. Nelson, 11 May 1934, file 4, folder 1, Hawke's Bay Division of the New Zealand Legion Papers, A38 [hereinafter NZL Papers], Auckland University Library [hereinafter AUL].
170 *National Opinion* [Wellington] 1(33) (7 September 1933): 3.

empowered to establish branches across the country.[171] The committee included two of Begg's associates from the Civic League, a fellow member of the Wellington Rotary Club, and Sherston from the New Zealand National Movement.[172] Many of the founders of the National Movement also became prominent members of the legion.[173]

The citizens' movements arose at the crest of a wave of conservative discontent on both sides of the Tasman. The ingredients for a widespread populist response were all there: an economic crisis, a large body of concerned conservatives, and an unpopular 'other' in the form of politicians and party politics. The question was, how would the leaders of the four citizens' movements capitalise on this situation to build an enthusiastic and committed mass following that would be able to achieve the transformative changes they so desired? One of the ways they did this was by deploying a populist form of conservatism that combined both reactionary and radical ideas. This contradictory ideological blend is explored in the next chapter.

171 Letter from Sherston to Field, 22 May 1933, Alphabetical correspondence—Sherston, J.R.V., 1932–36, 73-148-108, Field Papers, ATL; No. N.Z.L. 2, 11 March 1933—To Every Member of the Legion, file 1, folder 2, NZL Papers, AUL; *The Dominion*, [Wellington], 11 March 1933, 11; *The Evening Post*, [Wellington], 20 March 1933, 8. The role of the Civic League is mentioned in an earlier draft of Begg's autobiography; see Early draft of 'The Secret of the Knife' [undated], Begg Papers, privately held.
172 The Civic League associates were W. Appleton and W.J. McEldowney (both of whom stood alongside Begg in the 1931 Wellington municipal elections). F. Vosseler was the fellow Rotarian. See Minutes of Meeting of the Provisional National Council, 4–5 April 1933, file 1, folder 1, NZL Papers, AUL; *The Evening Post*, [Wellington], 18 March 1931, 10; Meeting of Directors, 3 March 1932, Minute book July 1930 – December 1937, Wellington Rotary Club Papers, MSY-3662, MS-Group-0286, ATL.
173 These were J.D. Ormond, M. Smith, J.W. Harding, and J.F. Nelson from Hawke's Bay; W.G. Black from Palmerston North; and A. St Clare Brown from Auckland; see Notes of a meeting of the movement held in the Grand Hotel Palmerston North, 23 July 1932, Ormond Family Papers, privately held; Minutes of Meeting of the Provisional National Council, 4–5 April 1933, file 1, folder 1, NZL Papers, AUL.

3

Give us a creed: The ideology of the citizens' movements

What are ideologies? According to Michael Freeden, they are patterns of thinking that help us understand the political and social worlds that surround us. They are the deeply held values and assumptions that govern how we interpret political facts, events, occurrences, and actions, and are commonly (but not exclusively) identified by the suffix of 'ism': liberalism, conservatism, socialism, anarchism, and fascism, to name a few. We all have one, whether or not we express it consciously. They allow us to interpret the otherwise random bits of information that we receive every day and come to (often competing) conclusions. In short, ideologies help us to make sense of the world.[1]

The citizens' movements' claims to be purely apolitical should therefore be taken with a grain of salt. As the previous two chapters have shown, there was a well-established tradition of conservatism in Australia and New Zealand by the 1920s with three main components: a strong patriotic and economic orientation towards Britain, a general commitment to free-market capitalism, and staunch opposition to communism and socialism. This was clearly an ideology, despite the claims of its adherents that such values represented the national interest and were apolitical, or 'non-party', in nature. The citizens' movements inherited this conservative tradition. At the same time, they also harnessed the radical sentiments expressed by a growing swathe of conservatives dismayed by the worsening economic

---

1   Michael Freeden, *Ideology: A Very Short Introduction* (New York: Oxford University Press, 2003), 2–3.

situation. This primarily took the form of a populist revolt against the party system of government. The movements claimed to represent 'the citizens'—an apolitical and homogeneous group between the extremes of left and right—against the petty, parochial interests of party politicians and the political parties that served them. But the leaders of the citizens' movements were not content to simply criticise politicians. They also developed various proposals to reform government to make it more efficient and better able to deal with the complexities of a modern industrial economy. While the ostensible purpose of these reforms was to eliminate the supposedly nefarious influence of political parties, they occasionally veered in an alarmingly anti-democratic direction.

The result was an ideology comprising reactionary and radical elements that I have termed 'populist conservatism'. The citizens' movements simultaneously sought new and occasionally radical alternatives to the problems of their time while expressing nostalgia for an illusory nineteenth-century colonial society epitomised by limited government, independent politicians, and self-sufficient pioneers. At its core was a populist struggle between the virtuous citizenry and a political elite who were portrayed as selling out the nation for their own petty gains. This struggle, however, was not something neutral that the citizens' movements picked up and ran with; it was something they constructed, both consciously and unconsciously, through language. In other words, the citizens and party politicians were not objective categories, but concepts that the citizens' movements built in relation and opposition to each other.

The struggle between 'the citizens' and 'party politicians'

Idealism over policy

At the highest level of abstraction, the citizens' movements saw themselves as forces of political and moral rejuvenation. Their mission was just as much a spiritual one as it was an ideological one, for they aimed at nothing less than the awakening of the civic spirit of the citizenry and the transformation of the nation's moribund political apparatus. This awakening, they believed, had already begun. As the Citizens' League of South Australia put it:

We are not a political party and have no desire to become one, but we are a conscience, a sentiment, a force, the force of public opinion, public sentiment, public conscience, which, awakened at last by the crisis that confronts us, demands to make itself both heard and felt.[2]

The All for Australia League termed this 'a spontaneous rising of the public conscience', possessing 'something almost of a spiritual nature'; in Victoria, Australian Citizens' League President Ernest Turnbull wrote that he 'might as well be leading a whirlwind'.[3] This demonstrates the supply and demand aspects of populist conservatism. While widespread frustration already existed among 'the citizens' (demand), it required individuals with the nous to channel this frustration into a mass movement (supply). The citizens' movements saw themselves as the focal point of a wider grassroots wave of righteous frustration with the status quo. At the same time, the legitimacy of the movements themselves was based on the existence of this nebulous sense of frustration; without it, they would not exist.

The citizens' movements viewed concrete policy as secondary to the need to focus on high ideals and principles. While there may have been an element of pragmatism in this, the movements were primarily motivated by their belief that theirs was a much more transformative, and therefore a more fundamental, agenda than the shallow and parochial platforms of political parties. Indeed, the citizens' movements believed their aims transcended politics entirely. It was their job to rebuild the tattered and fragmented political system and ensure that the right kind of individuals were elected to keep it that way:

That is the problem—to call up a crusading spirit, to sound a rallying cry, not to elaborate details of policy. Details divide, we need to unite. Give us a common basis on which we can agree—first principles, fundamentals. In short, give us a creed, a confession of faith, high in its ideals, daring in its demands ... Let us leave the details to those whose job it is to work them out. Ours be the job of putting into expression the hopes and fears and dreams of the common man.[4]

2   Address by E.D.A. Bagot at a Citizens' Public Meeting in Adelaide Town Hal, 14 October 1930, box 1, item 1, CLSA Papers, NLA.
3   *All for Australia League: Its Real Significance* (Sydney: All for Australia League, 1931), 2, 3; R.W. Kenderdine, 'The Demand for Honest Government', *Life* (1 May 1931): 400.
4   *National Opinion* [Wellington] 1(3) (7 September 1933): 3.

The New Zealand Legion called this 'a more definite, concrete and daring objective than any political party has had the courage to formulate'.[5] This did not prevent the citizens' movements from developing policy, as this chapter will show; it simply meant that policy was secondary to principle. 'There must be a practical side to any movement the purpose of which is to shape public policy', stated the All for Australia League, 'but the husk must not be mistaken for the kernel, the visible machinery must not dominate the underlying purpose.'[6] As Chapters Five and Six demonstrate, this tension between the desire to preserve ideological unity and the need to translate idealism into policy was a central problem of the movements, and it ultimately contributed to their downfall.

The populist struggle between the citizens and party politicians sat at the core of the citizens' movements' ideology. It was the rationale for their existence and the reason the economies of Australia and New Zealand were in such a parlous state. It was woven throughout the corpus of the movements' communications, from their leaders' speeches before large town hall–style gatherings to the multitude of booklets, journals, pamphlets, posters, and flyers they produced. They drew on it in internal circulars, in letters to the editor, and in radio broadcasts. This core message was complemented by reinforcing a sense of crisis and a sense of urgency that something needed to be done. But neither 'the citizens' nor the 'party politicians' were objective categories that existed outside human perception. They, along with a sense of crisis, were carefully constructed devices. As the sociocultural approach to populist studies suggests, the citizens' movements used language to define who the citizens and party politicians were just as much as it pitted them against each other. This was as much an unconscious process as it was a conscious one. The previous two chapters have shown how a political language of conservatism evolved in Australia and New Zealand over time that carried implied meaning for those who understood it. The citizens' movements built on this language to construct the populist struggle that underpinned their ideology. The following sections explain how they did this.

---

5   No. NZL 3, 11 March 1933, file 1, folder 2, NZL Papers, AUL.
6   All for Australia League: A Call to Citizenship, item 70, Thomas D. Mutch Papers, MLMSS 426 [hereinafter Mutch Papers], SLNSW.

The citizens

The citizens were the good, honest people whom the citizens' movements claimed to represent. They were the voice of reason and moderation in a world of extremes. Steeped in the values and traditions of British society, the citizen occupied an ideological 'middle ground'. He (once again, described most often using the masculine pronoun) was stoic, hardworking, and willing to put the interests of the nation above his own parochial concerns. As E. Lee Neil, a founding member of the Australian Citizens' League, put it:

> I believe myself to be typical of thousands of serious-minded citizens who, over and above all party preferences or convictions, are as jealous as they are determined that our country shall be wisely led through the present stress … it is of the highest importance that we as a people should be judged not upon extremist or factional opinions, but upon the considered views and determinations of the great body of sane, sober-minded citizens properly organised to express what they stand for in the life of the nation.[7]

A crucial aspect of the citizen's character was that he was not beholden to the world of politics. While aware of his patriotic duty to vote, he did so dispassionately, without aligning himself with the extreme factions on the right and left. This, however, left him unrepresented—a 'long suffering section of the public', which, according to the Citizens' League of South Australia, had gone without adequate political representation while the political extremists on either side developed sophisticated political machinery to represent themselves. The citizens' movements intended to change that:

> Although all other interests appear to be represented by strong and influential organisations, John Citizen alone remains without any machinery through which his voice can be effectively sounded. He is sick and tired of being the shuttlecock of party politics. The time has come, therefore, and he intends to rouse himself and show the party-bound politicians what a powerful force of public opinion can become.[8]

---

7 E. Lee Neil, *Why We Need a Citizens' League* (Melbourne: Australian Citizens' League, 1931), 3.
8 *Citizens' League: Its Formation, Aims, and Objects* (Adelaide: Citizens' League of South Australia, 1931), 4.

Class played a role in the citizens' movements' descriptions of the loyal citizenry. Positioned as they were between two political poles, it was necessary for the movements to describe what those poles were. They used a variety of terms, including 'Reactionary Tories' and 'Red Labour' or 'Diehards' and 'Reds'.[9] This analysis of class, however, had less to do with the relationship to the means of production than it did with the dominant position these poles supposedly held within the political system. As the All for Australia League put it:

> [C]lass-consciousness has found expression in the political sphere through organisations of employers and employees whose respective political and industrial activities, pursued without regard to the interests of the community as a whole induce a state of mutual antagonism rather than co-operation for the common weal.[10]

The shallowness of this class analysis was demonstrated by the appeal of the citizens' movements to a form of class collaborationism. Like many of the conservative non-party organisations that preceded them, they rejected the validity of class difference in favour of a broad horizontal kinship based on ideological rather than material interests. As the New Zealand Legion argued:

> New Zealanders of all walks of life—labourers, farmers, merchants, artisans, clerks, professional men—share this belief with us and, given a common ground on which to meet, will gladly work together for its attainment, instead of importer against exporter, farmer against townsman, and employee against employer.[11]

The movements even suggested that class consciousness had been artificially engineered by a minority of 'extremists' on either side of the political spectrum. They believed the loyal citizenry comprised moderate employers and employees who recognised that their interests were complementary rather than contradictory:

> The A.F.A. [All for Australia] League aims at excluding the extremists on both sides and reconstructing the body politic ... [around] Sane Labour and the business and producing interests [who] constitute the great majority of the citizens in this country. Freed from the domination of extremists, the Australian people

---

9 The Financial Record of Party Politics, undated, item 68, Mutch Papers, SLNSW; E.D.A. Bagot, 'Principles in Politic: What the Citizens' League Hopes to Achieve', *Progress*, 31 October 1930, 11.
10 *All for Australia League: Draft Policy* (Sydney: All for Australia League, 1931), 1.
11 *National Opinion* [Wellington] 1(5) (5 October 1933): 2.

have energy, initiative, courage, and ability sufficient to frame a policy and carry it into effect by legislation designed to promote the welfare of the whole community and not of any particular class or section.[12]

The citizens' movements aimed to provide a 'common ground' on which these groups could come together free from the corrupting influence of party politics.[13]

Despite their glorification of the loyal citizenry, the citizens' movements also chastised them for their political apathy. During times of plenty, they had been willing to ignore the welfare of their country in favour of material concerns, leaving matters of state in the hands of 'party hacks'.[14] The movements thus perceived themselves as fulfilling a vital educative function by encouraging their members to 'think nationally instead of individually' and 'be prepared to render service as the price of citizenship'.[15] This followed the pattern of previous conservative non-party organisations such as the constitutional associations, which considered their primary function to be educating the public on matters of public affairs. The New Zealand Legion was particularly concerned with providing a 'space' for honest political discussion that was free from sectional influences. It encouraged its centres to consider questions of national importance, and it formed central committees to produce and disseminate reading material on a wide range of subjects including central government, local government, economics, unemployment, and land.[16] By reminding their members of the duties of citizenship, the movements hoped to encourage the values of 'frankness, altruism and insight' in place of 'hypocrisy, selfishness, and superficial thought'.[17]

Party politicians and machine politics

Had the citizens' movements simply sought to educate a large body of individuals in their duties as citizens, they may have amounted to little more than a larger version of the conservative non-party organisations that

---

12 The Financial Record of Party Politics, undated, item 68, Mutch Papers, SLNSW.
13 *All for Australia League: Its Real Significance*, 3.
14 *National Unity in Crisis: The Story of the N.Z. Legion* (Wellington: New Zealand Legion, 1933), 2–3; *Citizens' League: Its Formation, Aims, and Objects*, 9–10.
15 *Citizens' League: Its Formation, Aims, and Objects*, 5.
16 Minutes of Meeting of the Provisional National Council, 4–5 April 1933; Minutes of Meeting of the National Council, 19–21 July 1933, file 1, folder 1, NZL Papers, AUL.
17 *National Opinion* [Wellington] 1(4) (21 September 1933): 3.

preceded them. However, the citizens whom they claimed to represent were uncompromisingly pitted against a sinister and powerful elite: party politicians and the extra-parliamentary structures that supported them. Chapter One demonstrated how, at the turn of the century, conservative politicians had distinguished themselves from the 'machine politics' of their labour counterparts by highlighting their independence. However, conservatives had to adapt to this political challenge and, by the 1920s, they had largely replicated the organisational unity and extra-parliamentary support structures of labour. This was most apparent in New South Wales, where political figures such as Archdale Parkhill had devoted their careers to establishing a party structure to rival Labor's—often to the extreme criticism of their contemporaries.[18]

The citizens' movements defined party politicians in the same way they did the citizenry: by drawing on the existing tropes in the conservative world view. They focused on two elements of 'machine politics' in particular: party platforms and the preselection of candidates. Both were partially defined in opposition to the values that were associated with the citizen. Party platforms, which were enforced through candidate pledges and block voting in parliament, were believed to undermine the reasoned and independent thought that was so central to the conservative world view:

> The present political parties form 'platforms' with numbers of 'planks' to which their candidates must adhere absolutely. Any display of individuality is severely 'disciplined.' By a system of pre-selection, electors must vote for candidates who may have no other qualifications than their obedience to their party 'bosses.' Thus, individuality is destroyed and Governments, instead of governing, are dictated to by cliques and caucus.[19]

This hearkened back to the conservative ideal of voluntary political participation. The citizens' movements believed the key to good citizenship lay in complete independence from any organisational structure that sought to impose collective rules, behaviours, or ideas. Party platforms robbed candidates of the ability to exercise their own judgement on political matters, resulting in a form of 'party dictatorship'.[20] The citizens'

---

18 Peter Loveday, 'Emergence: Realignment and Consolidation', in *The Emergence of the Australian Party System*, eds Peter Loveday, A.W. Martin, and R.S. Parker (Sydney: Hale & Iremonger, 1977), 453–87; Smith, *Against the Machines*, 23–50.
19 Bagot, 'Principles in Politic', 11.
20 *National Opinion* [Wellington] 1(1) (10 August 1933): 2.

movements considered this to be anti-democratic and immoral: it had caused 'the degradation of the political conscience of the people'.[21] In a particularly vitriolic turn of phase, the New Zealand Legion termed party politics an 'abrogation of democracy' that had 'led to the substance of the State being poured out as a bloody sacrifice to the Moloch of party'.[22]

The citizens' movements also considered preselection to be anti-democratic. They argued that by only selecting candidates who were willing to follow the party line, party machines limited the electoral choice available to everyday citizens and actively prevented alternative political candidates from emerging:

> Such pre-selected persons are then submitted as the candidates of the respective parties, and the only franchise the individual elector can exercise is to support the candidate, whoever he might be, of one or other of the contending parties. Thus the electors no longer vote for responsible representatives in Parliament, but vote for a party, and, by the strength of their machines, the major parties endeavour to defeat any effort to bring new political aspirations of the people into existence.[23]

This robbed individuals of the chance to fully exercise their democratic responsibilities as informed and reasoned citizens. As the All for Australia League put it, preselection 'deprived the people of their freedom in the choice of their Parliamentary representatives' and 'defeated the freedom of adult franchise'.[24] Instead of promoting the kind of deliberative and democratic parliament the citizens' movements envisioned, preselection encouraged mediocrity and cronyism. Only 'incompetent men' could be elected under such a 'treacherous electoral system', and only 'blind adherence' and 'ready acquiescence' could guarantee them a continued seat.[25] As a result, it was 'practically impossible for a citizen to secure election to Parliament against the will of the party machines and the powerful sectional interests that dominate them'.[26]

---

21   *All for Australia League: Its Real Significance*, 2.

22   *National Opinion* [Wellington] 1(1) (10 August 1933): 2.

23   *Policy as Adopted by Convention of the League* (Sydney: All for Australia League, 1931), 9.

24   ibid., 8; *All for Australia League: Its Real Significance*, 1–2.

25   Minutes of Inaugural Meeting, 3 October 1930, box 1, item 1, CLSA Papers, NLA; *National Opinion* [Wellington] 1(1) (10 August 1933), 2.

26   *Policy as Adopted by Convention of the League*, 9.

The citizens' movements portrayed party politicians and their supporting machines as a small but powerful political minority whose interests lay solely in retaining and enhancing their power at the expense of the national interest. They were the 'elite' recognised by all theories of populism, imposing their will over the citizenry, and robbing them of their rights. As the All for Australia League put it:

> By the caucus machine control, a minority in Parliament can impose its will on a Parliamentary party, and, because party solidarity demands that members shall place their party before their conscience or their country, such minority can dominate Parliament and the Country.[27]

In contrast to these party politicians, the citizens' movements stressed their supposedly apolitical and national credentials. As non-party movements, their members were governed by purer motives than self-serving and parochially minded party politicians. They were willing to put the nation ahead of their own personal desires by facing the Depression crisis with disinterested determination. They represented the true voice of democracy, the nation's 'noblest, truest interests', devoid of class or sectional prejudices.[28] The following passage from a speech by Bagot demonstrates how the concepts of the citizen and party politicians were constructed in relation to each other:

> We can do nothing until we can convince the political leaders that we are sick to death of party politics, that we will not consent any longer to remain passive while they bicker and quarrel and play for their own ends instead of sinking their differences and uniting for the good of the country as a whole.
>
> … We must take the lead ourselves. We must organise and unite until we are such a huge power that our wishes can no longer be ignored. We must show these politicians, who are so prone to listen to arguments of force, that there is a force which can make itself felt above all others, the force of public opinion directed towards a common objective, and that object the cleansing of our political stables, which we intend to secure by every constitutional means within our power.[29]

---

27 ibid., 8.
28 Lee Neil, *Why We Need a Citizens' League*, 3.
29 Address by E.D.A. Bagot at a Citizens' Public Meeting in Adelaide Town Hall, 14 October 1930, box 1, item 1, CLSA Papers, NLA.

In this, the loyal citizens were portrayed as the inheritors of the Anzac tradition: stoic, hardworking, self-sacrificing, and united in a common purpose. The citizens' movements drew parallels between the Great War and the Depression: both were crises on a national scale, and both required the concerted efforts of the entire nation to address. However, rather than being invoked on a militaristic basis, the Anzac tradition was used to reinforce the values of unity and self-sacrifice that the citizens' movements claimed to represent.[30] Otherwise, the Anzacs did not feature heavily in citizens' movement rhetoric.[31]

The citizens' movements sought to overcome the dominance of party machines and self-serving politicians through the directed voting power of their membership. In place of party lists, they would support individual candidates 'who by their past records merit our confidence as fit and proper persons to represent us'. It did not matter whether they were independents or members of existing parties: the chief criterion that the citizens' movements would require of them was that they were prepared to serve their country before their party.[32] Such a 'loose grouping of Independents' was one of the strategies commonly utilised by minor parties and independents in New South Wales to combat the dominance of the major parties.[33] Instead of being bound by restrictive party preselection lists and pledges, candidates would be free to campaign on their own merits and to exercise their own judgement. This would eventually raise 'the average personal standard of those who enter public life' by encouraging the 'right type of men' to run for parliament.[34] It might also ultimately lead to the abolition of political parties entirely, or at the very least relegate them to irrelevance.

30 Circular Ref. 6/2/34, 6 June 1933, file 1, folder 2; No. NZL 15, file 1, folder 1, NZL Papers, AUL.
31 For examples of the Anzac tradition being invoked, see address by L.V. Pellew at a Citizens' Public Meeting in Adelaide Town Hall, 14 October 1930, box 1, item 1, CLSA Papers, NLA; Citizens' League: Its Formation, Aims, and Objects, 2; Light on the Legion, 5–6, 13; All for Australia League Shows the Way to Prosperity (Melbourne: All for Australia League, 1931), 20, 22; Sydney Morning Herald, 26 February 1931, 10.
32 Report of Executive Committee presented at First Convention of Delegates of Branch Committees of the CLSA, 1 December 1930, box 1, item 1, CLSA Papers, NLA.
33 Smith, Against the Machines, 3–4.
34 All for Australia League: All for Australia, item 70, Mutch Papers, SLNSW; Citizens' League: Its Formation, Aims, and Objects, 14.

Countering the communist menace

While party politicians and their political machines were the main enemy of the citizens' movements, there was another 'other' with which they were concerned. All four movements believed to some extent that communist forces in league with the Soviet Union were secretly fomenting revolution throughout the British Empire. The Citizens' League was the most open about its suspicions, and the most extreme in its suggested solutions. It called on the government to declare communism illegal, ban the distribution of 'dangerous propaganda', and deport all 'agitators' who refused to swear loyalty to the Crown and constitution.[35] This was partially the result of Bagot's personal distaste for communism, which he had been nurturing for several years. He had been particularly affected by the 1928 Adelaide waterfront strikes, which he believed had been 'engineered' by the Militant Minority Movement as part of an ongoing Soviet plan to create 'a ring of socialised States' around 'the Commonwealth of British nations'.[36]

Given their shared belief in a communist conspiracy, the four citizens' movements each considered the possibility of forming paramilitary wings to combat perceived threats to law and order. The extent of their preparations varied according to where, and when, the movements arose. For example, it appears that neither the All for Australia League nor the Australian Citizens' League felt it necessary to assume a paramilitary function. This is probably because highly secretive and semi-official paramilitary movements already existed in New South Wales and Victoria. The Old Guard, in New South Wales, and the League of National Security, in Victoria, were closely tied to the political, economic, and military elite in their state, and it is almost certain the leaders of the All for Australia League and the Australian Citizens' League were aware of their existence. It is also possible that there was a degree of cross-membership between the movements. This does not mean the All for Australia League and the Australian Citizens' League were 'front' organisations for their

---

35   Minutes of Executive Committee Meeting, 27 October 1931, box 1, item 3; Minutes of First Convention of Delegates from District and Branch Committees, 1 December 1930, box 1, item 1; Leaflet No. 6, c. 1931, box 14, item 23; The 'Reds' Revolution, c. December 1931, box 3, item 24, CLSA Papers, NLA.
36   Address given by Bagot at a public rally in Adelaide, 21 July 1931, box 3, item 24, CLSA Papers, NLA.

paramilitary counterparts, as has been suggested by some historians.[37] The ideas they promulgated held wide social traction and did not require paramilitary backing to lend them legitimacy. It is more likely that paramilitarism and populist conservatism were complementary and occasionally overlapping manifestations of the widespread conservative discontent with the Depression.

The Citizens' League specifically sought to build a reserve special constabulary in case of industrial strife. This was intended as a follow-on from the Essential Service Maintenance Volunteers, which had been established in Adelaide in September 1928 in response to a labour dispute on the waterfront. On 1 December 1930, the Citizens' League's Executive Committee recommended the 'formation of committees of loyal citizens able and willing to help maintain essential services in case of industrial unrest'.[38] Bagot discussed this with Colonel G.W. Shaw, an acquaintance in the police commissioner's office, who reported that Police Commissioner R.L. Leane—the man responsible for swearing in the special constables in 1928—'would welcome the formation of a further Essential Service Body'. Bagot was authorised to offer the services of the league to Leane, with the understanding that their discussions 'be kept strictly secret'.[39] By March 1931, several Citizens' League members had been enrolled as special constables 'for the purpose of taking the place of police who are withdrawn from their districts in cases of emergency'. In such an emergency, a smaller force of dedicated specials would also serve alongside regular police under the command of Captain A.S. Blackburn and Lieutenant Colonel W.C.N. Waite—the men who had led the special constabulary in 1928.[40] Bagot was also inspired by the success of the Organisation for the Maintenance of Supplies, a British strikebreaking outfit that had assisted their government with the provision of 'essential services' during the 1926 General Strike. If a similar strike occurred in

---

37 Moore, *The Secret Army and the Premier*, 92, 99; Cathcart, *Defending the National Tuckshop*, 155.
38 Report of Executive Committee presented at First Convention of Delegates of Branch Committees, 1 December 1930, box 1, item 1, CLSA Papers, NLA.
39 Minutes of Executive Committee Meeting, 15 December 1930, box 1, item 2, CLSA Papers, NLA.
40 Minutes of Executive Committee Meeting, 12 January 1931, box 1, item 2, Letter from Bagot to Colonel G.W. Shaw, 24 January 1931, box 13, item 11, CLSA Papers, NLA; The formation of secret bodies in the Commonwealth for the protection of the State against BOLSHEVISM, c. March 1931, D series, Commonwealth Investigation Branch Correspondence Files, A369, National Archives of Australia, Canberra.

Australia, Bagot stated that the Citizens' League would 'carry on and assist in the maintenance of the essential services of the country, just the same as people of England did in 1926'.[41]

In contrast, the discrediting of the New Guard in 1932 made the New Zealand Legion keen to disavow any paramilitary activity. As Chapter Two showed, there were several direct and indirect influences and connections between the New Guard and the New Zealand Legion, ranging from a phone conversation between Eric Campbell and one of the legion's founders to widespread media coverage of the New Guard's troubling antics in New Zealand. It was because of these antics that the New Zealand Legion went to great lengths to dissociate itself from the New Guard. It began its very first pamphlet by stressing that it was 'not a New Guard' or 'a Fascist body', and the same reassurance was sent out in a circular to division and branch chairmen.[42] The same point was presented during public appearances and in press releases.[43] But public comparisons proved difficult to shake. In April, the secretary of the Gisborne centre of the legion reported that the main criticism he had faced during his recruitment campaign was that the legion was a 'New Guard' or 'Fascist' group.[44] When Sherston was asked by a heckler whether the legion was a New Guard movement and what was 'the colour of its shirt'—in reference to the fascist 'blackshirts' and the Nazi 'brownshirts'—he replied that he preferred to wear a coat.[45]

It did not help that Campbell continued to claim that the two movements were connected. In July 1933, he met with British Union of Fascists leader Oswald Mosley while visiting Europe for business. The two established the New Empire Union in July 1933, and Campbell was empowered to speak for the New Guard in Australia and South Africa as well as an unnamed organisation in New Zealand.[46] Members of the legion professed no knowledge of Mosley's New Empire Union, despite Campbell's claim. John MacGibbon, chair of the Canterbury provincial executive, noted in July 1933 that the unnamed organisation 'could not refer to the New

---

41 Address by Bagot at public meeting held in the Exhibition Building, 11 December 1930, box 3, item 25D; The Menace of Communism—Shall Russia Rule Australia?, Address given by Bagot at a public rally in Adelaide, 21 July 1931, box 3, item 24, CLSA Papers, NLA.
42 *Light on the Legion*, 1; No. NZL 6, 11 March 1933, file 1, folder 2, NZL Papers, AUL.
43 For example, *The Evening Post*, [Wellington], 4 March 1933, 11; 11 March 1933, 5.
44 Letter to A.S. Tonkin, 19 April 1933, file 2, folder 2, NZL Papers, AUL.
45 *The Evening Post*, [Wellington], 1 September 1933, 6.
46 *Blackshirt* [London] 11 (8–14 July 1933): 1.

Zealand Legion, for that was not a Fascist organisation'.[47] Yet when Campbell launched the Centre Party—the New Guard's political wing—in December 1933, he mentioned the New Zealand Legion by name:

> Out of our economic chaos is evolving a determination to force ordered existence. Towards this the disciplined will of youth is moving. Across the Tasman Sea the new-born Centre Party calls itself the New Zealand Legion. Here it is the New Guard, and we are exchanging ideas and following closely what is happening in every country where action outside discredited party politics is being effectively directed to repairing the economic system.[48]

What are we to make of Campbell's claims? Was he really empowered by the New Zealand Legion to speak on its behalf? This seems highly unlikely. For one thing, the legion's leadership disavowed any connection with the New Guard both publicly and in internal correspondence. If they were truly interested in an alliance with the New Guard, why would they need to disavow this internally? And what value would an alliance have provided in 1933, when the New Guard had been reduced to a few thousand members and had been increasingly ostracised because of its extreme actions and flirtation with fascism? It seems more likely that Campbell was trying to counter his increasingly marginal position by exaggerating his connections with the legion. There is no reason to doubt that the legion's attempts to distance itself from the New Guard were anything but genuine.

The legion's leadership decided that it would be in the best interests of the movement to entirely avoid making any paramilitary preparations. In April 1933, Begg stated boldly that the legion did not need to commit to strikebreaking because its ideals would render strikes unnecessary.[49] When the Hawke's Bay chairman asked the national executive in June what action the legion should take in the event of civil commotion, their response was blunt:

> [T]he Legion is a society for propagation of political thought and action, and is not concerned with taking upon itself any such function as suggested. The actual control or dealing with Civil commotion is in the hands of the Government and Police and

47 *The Press*, [Christchurch, NZ], 13 July 1933, 15.
48 *Smith's Weekly*, [Sydney], 23 December 1933, 7.
49 *The Evening Post*, [Wellington], 20 April 1933, 12.

> any members of the Legion must act according to their conscience in their private capacity. *This is one of the points that has been very firmly stressed in regard to the movement.* [Emphasis added][50]

The italicised sentence demonstrates the legion's keen desire to dissociate itself from the negative connotations of paramilitarism. The fact that this was internal correspondence reinforces the likelihood that it was genuine. This may have been what Begg was referring to when he told the Provisional National Council in April 1933: 'We must fearlessly analyse the weaknesses in similar movements that caused them to fail.'[51] While he was most likely referring to the failure of the legion's predecessors, such as the New Zealand National Movement, he may also have been hinting at the negative publicity that had befallen the New Guard.

Traditional conservative values

A contract with the past

While the citizens' movements were launching their populist campaign against the political system, they also drew heavily on traditional conservative values. The citizens' movements' ideal society was based on the myth of the rugged and hardy individuals who had broken in the land and brought British civilisation to the colonies. It was to them that they suggested Australia and New Zealand should look for a model of how to reconstruct society:

> [W]hat is essential to-day is a spirit akin to that of our pioneers, who deliberately and willingly faced the dangers, hardships, and privations of the pathway that led to prosperity, progress, and the making of a nation. To-day those hundreds of thousands of sturdy Australians in whom breathes the spirit of their forebears, are looking for a lead, and hoping for the emergence of an organisation that will link them together in a common ideal and a common purpose, so that their desire to re-adjust community life on sound foundations may be crystallised[.][52]

---

50 Letter from E. Littlejohn to A.S. Tonkin, 29 June 1933, file 2, folder 3, NZL Papers, AUL.
51 *National Opinion* [Wellington] 1(4) (21 September 1933): 12.
52 *Manifesto of Provisional Committee of the Australian Citizens' League* (Melbourne: Australian Citizens' League, 1931). 4.

This myth brought together several conservative tropes regarding good citizenship. The pioneer was hardworking, self-sacrificing, and willing to get on with the day-to-day business of carving a nation out of the Antipodean wilderness without fuss or ceremony. Furthermore, he had done all of this without having to resort to the kind of 'State paternalism' and '[s]ervile dependence on the Government' that had supposedly eroded the foundations of individualism since the turn of the century.[53] This provided an ideal archetype for the citizenry of the Depression to aspire to while conveniently ignoring the fact that the nineteenth-century developmentalist ethos of the colonies involved the considerable investment of public funds in the spread of colonisation. There was also an element of implicit racism in this pioneer myth in that it ignored the wholesale appropriation of land from indigenous populations that had enabled an economy based on primary production.

The myth of the pioneer represented an unspoken contract with the past and the conservative values that the citizens' movements projected on to it. As the Citizens' League of South Australia put it:

> Fellow Citizens, we have received from the past a priceless inheritance—a trust that must not be betrayed—and that trust is the fair name of Australia. It remains for each of us to see that we shall pass on to posterity that name unblemished.[54]

Michael Cathcart termed this contract an 'unwritten constitution'— 'a body of principle and tradition which can never be fully known or articulated, but which defines the grounds upon which political activity may legitimately be undertaken'.[55] Anything that lay outside the bounds of this unwritten constitution could thus be delegitimised as sectional, disloyal, or seditious:

> We recognise that differences of political opinion must exist … but when the differences involve a distinction between honesty and dishonesty, integrity and default, honour and dishonour, we rise in our wrath—and I think I can say to-day in our MIGHT— and denounce as traitors to their country those who put forward such views.[56]

53　*Light on the Legion*, 2, 6–7; *National Unity in Crisis*, 3.
54　Address given by Bagot, 11 February 1931, box 3, item 25C, CLSA Papers, NLA.
55　Cathcart, *Defending the National Tuckshop*, 165.
56　*All for Australia League Shows the Way to Prosperity*, 13.

This was reflected in the movements' use of common conservative phrases such as the 'national interest', which framed their values as sacred and inviolable rather than one world view among many. A strong patriotic and economic orientation towards Britain, a general commitment to free-market capitalism, and staunch opposition to communism and socialism—these were part of the natural order, a set of 'fundamental laws' that could not be changed 'any more than we can alter the laws of gravity'.[57]

Individualism

The citizens' movements believed in individualism, which exalted private enterprise and self-reliance over the interference of the state in economic matters. As 'non-party' movements, however, the citizens' movements were able to extol the ideals of individualism without being bound by the practicalities of economic policy or the desires of the electorate for increased state activity. Unhampered by these encumbrances, they levelled criticism at the perceived 'economic interference' displayed by both ends of the political spectrum:

> [The crisis] has been brought about by the ever-increasing inroads made in recent years by the various Governments of Australia— both Federal and State—Liberal and Labour—into the fields of legitimate trade and commerce; inroads so aggressive and unwarranted that we now find every phase of our commercial and financial life subjugated either directly or indirectly to political interference.[58]

Public economic activity, according to this line of thought, was inherently political in that it brought 'legitimate' private enterprise under the control of party politicians. This criticism did not generally extend to the developmental pragmatism of the nineteenth century, although some of the citizens' movements were willing to challenge this. The Citizens' League of South Australia, for example, called for the privatisation of public assets such as railways and waterworks.[59]

---

57 *Citizens' League: Its Formation, Aims, and Objects*, 8–10.
58 Bagot, speech given to the Political Reform League, September 1930, box 3, item 25A, CLSA Papers, NLA.
59 Minutes of Executive Committee Meeting, 29 September 1931, box 1, item 3, and Leaflet No. 8, c. 1931, box 14, item 23, CLSA Papers, NLA; *Citizens' League: Its Formation, Aims, and Objects*, 6–7, 11.

The citizens' movements believed the functions the government retained should be performed in a business-like fashion. They argued that government departments and enterprises should be small, efficient, and free of unnecessary 'trammels' on the growth of private enterprise. They often used the phrase popularised by Warren G. Harding that there should be 'more business in government and less government in business'.[60] They believed government was essentially just another form of business, and should therefore be run in the same fashion:

> [M]achine politics must give way to Government on sound business lines, in which the economic structure of the country is viewed as a gigantic business enterprise, with every member of the community as a shareholder. Overhead charges, represented by Governmental expenses must be kept down so that national dividends may be paid. In this way only can prosperity return.[61]

The central concern of this business-like approach was government debt. The citizens' movements believed that public borrowing had spiralled out of control during the 1920s, resulting in a 'false prosperity' that showed 'a callous disregard of the impossible burdens being prepared for the rising generation'. The movements called on governments to curb such 'reckless' and 'extravagant' borrowing and learn to live within their means.[62] Some, such as the New Zealand Legion, sought to remove the dependence on foreign borrowing altogether; others, like the Australian Citizens' League, recognised its necessity and aimed to reassure British investors of the 'sincerity' of the average citizen by forcing government to honour its debt commitments.[63]

Beyond economics, the citizens' movements believed that individualism provided a framework for the entire ordering of society, from the role of government and the responsibilities of elected officials to the relationships between individuals, associations, and businesses. This was summed up by the All for Australia League as follows:

60   Address given by Bagot at public meeting held in the Exhibition Building, 11 December 1930, box 3, item 25D, CLSA Papers, NLA; *Light on the Legion*, 12.
61   *All for Australia League* (Sydney: All for Australia League, 1931), 5. The New Zealand Legion was also fond of the shareholder analogy; see *Light on the Legion*, 9–10.
62   Address by Bagot to Young People's Employment Conference, 30 May 1931, box 3, item 25C, CLSA Papers, NLA; *Citizens' League: Its Formation, Aims, and Objects*, 9, 11; *Light on the Legion*, 6–7; *National Unity in Crisis*, 3; *All for Australia League: Its Real Significance*, 3; Lee Neil, *Why We Need a Citizens' League*, 4.
63   *National Opinion* [Wellington] 2(14) (1 March 1934): 1, 5; Lee Neil, *Why We Need a Citizens' League*, 5–7; *All for Australia League Shows the Way to Prosperity*, 12–17.

> [We] desire above all things to see Australia's finances restored
> and the country once more on the way to prosperity; to see the
> man on the land, the office-worker and the wage-earner receiving
> the rewards of their efforts untrammelled by those crippling
> experiments in Government—existing and proposed—which
> withhold from a man the full fruits of his labour, and would deny
> him the freedom to work out his destiny in accordance with his
> own inclinations and ability.[64]

Individualism was thus concerned with both the material and the spiritual. Private enterprise and self-reliance were not only the most efficient means of delivering services to the public, but also the most moral. They demonstrated the ability to stand on one's own two feet without having to rely on the charity of others, whether through private donations or the coffers of the state. As such, the movements generally favoured lower taxes, reduced public spending, and a more efficient government whose functions were limited as much as possible to the business of everyday governance.[65] This formed part of a general belief in deflationary economic methods across the board, which they justified as being about 'equality of sacrifice'.[66]

The citizens' movements attempted to incorporate the working class into their individualist world view. The premise of their appeal was that moderate or 'sane' labour had more in common with the middle class than with the 'revolutionaries … masquerading under the honourable title of Labour'.[67] They believed that government borrowing, combined with trade union agitation and arbitration, had led to unrealistically high wages and standards of living. In accordance with their preference for deflationary methods, the movements believed that wages should be allowed to fall in line with the reduced national income to ensure that the 'available wage pool' was 'divided equitably among all workers'.[68] Trade union activity, while not overtly condemned, was suspiciously regarded as a vehicle for extremism:

---

64   *All for Australia League*, 4.
65   *Citizens' League: Its Formation, Aims, and Objects*, 6–7; *Manifesto of Provisional Committee of the Australian Citizens' League*, 6; *Light on the Legion*, 8–12.
66   *All for Australia League: Its Real Significance*, 3; Letter from Norman Keysor to T.D. Mutch, 29 May 1931, item 79, Mutch Papers, SLNSW. 'Equality of sacrifice' was one of the five principles in the 'Big Hand of Service' (see Plate 4.3).
67   The Menace of Communism—Shall Russia Rule Australia?, Address by Bagot at a public rally in Adelaide, 21 July 1931, box 3, item 24, CLSA Papers, NLA.
68   *All for Australia League: Its Real Significance*, 3.

> Trades unionism is recognised as representing one of the most
> beneficent movements of the past century ... In recent times,
> however, trades unionism has been so managed as to become
> a menace to the worker, whom it was designed to protect ...
> Unions cannot claim that they recognise the true worth and
> dignity of the worker when he is used merely as a pawn in political
> strategy or industrial conflict.[69]

This language attempted to restrict the range of legitimate trade union
activity. Honest negotiation in the spirit of cooperation was acceptable,
whereas strikes were selfish and sectional. And while the 'sane' worker
possessed full agency in the former, in the latter, they were unwilling
dupes of a sinister agenda beyond their control.

Imperial patriotism

Imperial patriotism played an important part in the conservative world
view to which the citizens' movements ascribed. Britain and the empire
were the guarantors of the individual liberties that the citizens' movements
claimed to champion. As the legion put it:

> The New Zealand Legion is sturdily loyal to the Crown and
> Constitution. In the whole of the world, citizens of British
> countries have the greatest measure of liberty, the widest scope
> for individual development, the best system of justice. Loyalty to
> the Crown and Constitution is not a blind fetish; it is not old-
> fashioned sentiment; it is robust common-sense; it is the individual
> citizen's insurance policy for personal freedom and justice. There is
> more liberty, equality and fraternity under the British Crown than
> under any republican flag.[70]

The protection offered by belonging to the British Empire was twofold.
In a physical sense, the might of the British Navy was believed to offer
protection against foreign threats, particularly those in the Pacific.[71] In a
moral sense, however, the Crown was a potent symbol of 'those great
ideals of liberty, justice and national righteousness'.[72] At the same time,
the citizens' movements stressed that Australia and New Zealand should

69 *Policy as Adopted by Convention of the League*, 2–3.
70 *Light on the Legion*, 13.
71 Speech given by Bagot to the Political Reform League, September 1930, box 3, item 25, CLSA Papers, NLA.
72 *Light on the Legion*, 13; *All for Australia League: Draft Policy*, 5.

offer more to Britain than mere colonial dependence. The Antipodean colonies were no longer 'the suckling child always at liberty to ask for protection and sustenance'; it was time to become 'grown-up son[s]' and do 'something to assist and support the Mother Country'.[73]

Reforming the system

The rationalisation of government

The combination of traditional conservative values with a populist revolt against the political establishment led the citizens' movements to develop a diverse array of proposals for reform. These typically focused on two areas: the size and scope of government, and the way the economy was managed. Regarding the former, the movements claimed that reform was needed to achieve greater efficiency and decentralisation. In this, they were heavily influenced by standard conservative views about the importance of limited and more efficient government.

Reforming government was of particular importance to the New Zealand Legion and remained one of its most consistent policies throughout its life. From its first press release in February 1933, the legion stressed its devotion to 'more efficient government, [both] central and local'.[74] Local bodies were of particular concern for the legion; their sheer number and overlapping responsibilities made them 'troublesome excrescences on the body politic' in desperate need of rationalisation.[75] To combat the proliferation of local government bodies, the legion proposed dividing New Zealand into a series of autonomous shires along lines of 'communit[ies] of interest' and 'convenience of communication'.[76] Shire councils would be given authority on all matters of local government, including harbours, rivers, highways, power, and health care, leaving national matters such as justice, police, defence, railways, and external affairs in the hands of parliament.[77]

---

73 *National Opinion* [Wellington] 1(7) (2 November 1933): 3.
74 *Auckland Star*, 23 February 1933, 8.
75 *Light on the Legion*, 9.
76 *National Opinion* [Wellington] 1(4) (21 September 1933): 8–10. The legion's policies on governmental reform were largely developed by the Dunedin executive, although the term 'shire' was introduced by the National Council; see Gerard Campbell, The New Zealand Legion in Otago, 1933–1935 (BA Hons diss., University of Otago, Dunedin, NZ, 1987), 27–31.
77 *National Opinion* [Wellington] 2(13) (15 February 1934): 5; 2(14) (1 March 1934): 1, 5–6.

The New Zealand Legion's fixation on governmental reform was due to several factors. In part, the legion was merely rehashing the mainstream conservative stance on the inefficiencies of local government, which had been the subject of criticism in New Zealand since the Depression began.[78] It was also influenced by the prior experiences of its president, who had campaigned to rationalise the Wellington Hospital Board in 1931 and believed the legion could achieve similar economies on a national scale. However, the legion primarily viewed these reforms as a practical fulfilment of its opposition to party politics. It believed that the abolition of the provincial system of government by Julius Vogel in 1876 had created an ever-increasing demand for local government bodies, which exerted a 'tyrannical influence' on their MPs.[79] By strictly delineating the responsibilities of local and central government, the legion intended to free parliament from electoral concerns and allow it to focus solely on national affairs.[80]

The Citizens' League of South Australia took a more extreme view on reforming the size and scope of government. It called for the standardisation of Commonwealth laws and services across all states and territories and the amalgamation of every Australian parliament into a single body comprising '60 honest representatives'. In addition, it called for the salaries of civil servants to be halved because Australia could not 'afford the luxury of supporting a huge army of social parasites'.[81] This was partially a reflection of the league's particularly strong espousal of laissez-faire economics.[82] However, the league was also influenced by the idea of 'economic rationalisation'. Two days before the league's inaugural meeting on 3 October 1930, the Constitutional Club hosted a speaker on the topic of economic rationalisation in Germany and the United States, which he defined as 'a combination of the scientific organisation of materials and products, simplification of processes, and improvement in transport and marketing'.[83] This had a profound impact on Bagot, who was already an admirer of Henry Ford's innovations in management and

78   Pugh, The New Zealand Legion and conservative protest in the Great Depression, 124.
79   National Opinion [Wellington] 1(2) (24 August 1933): 1–2; Light on the Legion, 8.
80   National Opinion [Wellington] 2(13) (15 February 1934): 5.
81   Bagot, Address at Public Meeting, 14 October 1930, box 1, item 1, CLSA Papers, NLA.
82   Meeting of a Special Sub-Committee appointed to draft proposed policy, 18 January 1932, box 1, item 3, CLSA Papers, NLA.
83   Register News-Pictorial, [Adelaide], 2 October 1930, 4.

the division of labour, and during the inaugural Citizens' League meeting, he proclaimed that politics needed to be 'rationalised' in the same fashion as commerce and industry.[84]

The citizens' movements shared a common interest in redistributing power between political parties and voters at a national level. They favoured elective cabinets and proportional voting systems to ensure that no one party could dominate parliament or the executive, and the introduction of the powers of referendum, initiative, and recall to give the electorate greater power in national decision-making.[85] This reflected the movements' desire to transform parliament into a more deliberative body and to elevate the political-mindedness of the citizenry. It also reflected their desire to sideline or eliminate political parties. Voting along party lines would be abolished by these reforms, leaving members free to vote 'according to their conscience' on all proposed legislation. In addition, the people would have the power to ensure that government respected the 'wishes and desires of the people'.[86] By introducing these reforms, the legion even hoped that '[p]arty Government as we know it will cease to exist'.[87]

The Citizens' League of South Australia was willing to support more extreme measures to combat party politics. As with its policies on the 'rationalisation' of politics, this was largely due to Bagot's influence on the movement's ideology. During his process of political radicalisation in 1930, Bagot had become increasingly drawn to the idea of a dictatorship led by a 'big man in business leadership' backed by a 'small strong Committee of Management'.[88] He carried this rhetoric across into the Citizens' League, where he called for the kind of leader who could '"cleave through Party Politics" and establish Law and Order in our Social System'.[89] Bagot favoured a top-down style of governance that favoured personalities over democratic process—providing, of course, that the 'right' kind of personality could be found. Such a leader would be 'of the real

---

84 Minutes of Inaugural Meeting, 3 October 1930, box 1, item 1, CLSA Papers, NLA.
85 *National Opinion* [Wellington] 1(4) (21 September 1933): 8–10; Minutes of Executive Committee Meeting, 2 May 1933, box 1, item 3, Citizens' League Policy for 1934, 6 March 1934, box 1, item 4, Letter from Bagot to W.A. Burns, 2 June 1931, box 12, item 1, CLSA Papers, NLA; *Policy as Adopted by Convention of the League*, 11–12.
86 *Policy as Adopted by Convention of the League*, 11–12.
87 *National Opinion* [Wellington] 2(13) (15 February 1934): 5.
88 Bagot, 'A Dictator Needed', submitted to the Editor of *The Advertiser*, 5 September 1930, box 3, item 25D, CLSA Papers, NLA.
89 Minutes of Inaugural Meeting, 3 October 1930, box 1, item 1, CLSA Papers, NLA.

bull dog breed'—a man willing to take control of the floundering affairs of the state, to place the national interest above all personal or sectional demands, and with the personal gravitas to inspire his fellow citizens:

> Instead of the captain, the whole crew is trying to steer the ship of State. Let us get back the control, select our leader, and say to him: 'In the name of humanity, take charge. We will gladly serve to the best of our ability, so long as you continue to justify our confidence. You shall swear to serve us, fearless and unfaltering, to one end—the welfare of the nation as a whole.' Who will pledge to serve?[90]

Bagot believed Sir John Monash, commander of the Australian corps during the Great War, fitted the bill, and he made it clear he would gladly support a dictatorship led by Monash if it was the only way to abolish party politics.[91] He was even willing to countenance unconstitutional methods, such as the withholding of taxation or a 'show of force', if the government failed to take action.[92] The quest of the Australian citizens' movements to find a suitable leader is discussed further in Chapter Five.

Managing the economy

The citizens' movements also developed various proposals to reform the way the economy was managed. The general thrust of these reforms was that the industrial and technological growth that had occurred since the founding of most Western democracies had outpaced the ability of their political institutions to comprehend them:

> Economic matters to-day are so complex, so diversified, so badly understood as to their general laws, that the people acting blunderingly through their representative institutions, and incapable of calculating and foreseeing the results of the measures adopted, generally have acted so as to injure the very interests which they were trying to defend.[93]

To cement the immunity of government from 'sectional' interests, the movements supported, to varying degrees, devolving authority on economic matters to independent 'experts'. The Citizens' League of

90 *Citizens' League: Its Formation, Aims, and Objects*, 14.
91 *The Advertiser*, [Adelaide], 12 February 1931, 7.
92 Minutes of Inaugural Meeting, 3 October 1930, box 1, item 1, CLSA Papers, NLA.
93 *Policy as Adopted by Convention of the League*, 16–17.

South Australia advocated for 'an independent and qualified Board, free from political influence' to control public expenditure, revise tariffs and bounties, and manage unprofitable assets in preparation for their ultimate privatisation.[94] The All for Australia League advocated a similar policy, although its proposed economic advisory council was, as its name suggests, an advisory body only. Comprising 'the highest experts obtainable in finance, economics and industry', it would 'disinterestedly examine' questions of taxation, wages, and the tariff and provide recommendations to the government on economic policy. This would 'decisively check governmental extravagances or any tendency to the placation of sectional interests'.[95] The New Zealand Legion also proposed an economic advisory council, but it went much further: it supported a centrally planned economy with aspects of monetary reform. This contradictory mix of ideas is discussed in Chapter Six.

The Citizens' League and the All for Australia League complemented these proposed 'expert' bodies with policies on industrial relations. The Citizens' League suggested the creation of industrial boards comprising trade union and employers' association representatives who would determine wages for each industry and impose penalties on 'sweating, profiteering … [and] malingering'.[96] This was envisaged not as an equal partnership, but as a redefinition of industrial relations in favour of employers, who possessed the 'brains' to labour's 'muscle'.[97] To emphasise the point, the league called for the abolition of the existing wage arbitration courts and their 'pernicious awards' that denied men the 'right to work'.[98] With wages subsequently lowered to their 'natural' level, they believed that unemployment would naturally decrease. To ensure that employment was found for all, the league advocated the rationalisation of various local unemployment relief schemes and bureaus under a single state council to avoid duplication of effort. The South Australian Government adopted this recommendation in 1933 in one of the few occasions where a citizens' movement directly affected government policy.[99]

---

94 Address by Bagot at a Citizens' Public Meeting in Adelaide Town Hall, 14 October 1930; Report of Executive Committee presented at First Convention of Delegates of Branch Committees of the CLSA, 1 December 1930, box 1, item 1; Minutes of Executive Committee Meeting, 29 September 1931, box 1, item 3, CLSA Papers, NLA.
95 *Policy as Adopted by Convention of the League*, 8 August 1931, 16–18.
96 Bagot, The Problem of Unemployment, 6 August 1931, box 3, item 25B, CLSA Papers, NLA.
97 James, 'God, Mammon and Mussolini', 52.
98 *Citizens' League: Its Formation, Aims, and Objects*, 9; Bagot, 'A Dictator Needed', submitted to the Editor of *The Advertiser*, 5 September 1930, box 3, item 25D, CLSA Papers, NLA.
99 James, 'God, Mammon and Mussolini', 45.

The All for Australia League's approach to industrial relations was much more ambitious. Like the Citizens' League, it called for the establishment of a federal tribunal to arbitrate wages and working hours based on the advice of the economic advisory council. It, too, opposed the arbitration courts, but not for their 'pernicious awards'; the league believed that state control of arbitration pitted states against each other, which was disruptive of national unity. A federal tribunal would eliminate this disunity by standardising industrial conditions across the Commonwealth.[100] To eliminate the class antagonism that had supposedly been fostered by party politics, the league also proposed an 'industrial parliament' called the 'Bureaux of Industrial Co-operation' that would adjudicate issues between employers and employees and promote a spirit of 'mutual understanding'.[101] In the long term, however, it hoped to encourage the formation of voluntary cooperatives in each industry comprising 'labour, management, capital and consumption' that would plan the production and distribution of goods and services, standardise products and methods, and equitably distribute profits between employers and employees.[102]

The citizens' movements arose at a time of pronounced crisis and uncertainty when there was substantial and prolonged public discontent. They were able to take advantage of this discontent by tapping into long-held public sentiments and prejudices that, in ordinary times, did not animate people to the extent they did during the crisis. But ideology was only one of the ways they channelled this discontent. The movements also practised a 'populist culture' that was predicated on building an enthusiastic and committed mass following, from the way they promoted themselves right down to their organisational structures. This populist culture is explored in the next chapter.

---

100 *Policy as Adopted by Convention of the League*, 19–20.
101 ibid., 20–21.
102 ibid., 22–25.

Box 3.1 The leaders of the citizens' movements

Edward Daniel Alexander Bagot's background before founding the Citizens' League of South Australia is discussed in Chapter Two. The youngest of the four leaders at age 37, Bagot was an imposing, somewhat authoritarian individual with an excellent speaking voice and a flair for organisation. One of his associates described him thus:

> [H]e possesses quite a good presence to which he adds an excellent manner, and a good voice ... He also possesses great courage and individuality, and he had made himself a very fair speaker. Of his organising abilities there is little doubt. His main faults are an extraordinary self-assurance, a domineering attitude (I christened him the 'democratic dictator'), an utter inability to work with anyone on an equal or subordinate footing, and great rashness ... [I]t was always evident to those who worked with him that E.D.A. Bagot and his interests came first[.][103]

Plate 3.1 Portrait of Robert Campbell Begg, c. 1931

Source: Robert Campbell Begg, *The Secret of the Knife* (Norwich, UK: Jarrold & Sons, 1965), 20–21.

Plate 3.2 Portrait of Alexander J. Gibson, c. 1920s

Source: Alexander Gibson Papers, privately held.

103 Archibald Grenfell Price, quoted in James, 'God, Mammon and Mussolini', 40.

Plate 3.3 Portrait of Ernest Turnbull, 1931

Source: *All for Australia League Shows the Way to Prosperity* (Melbourne: All for Australia League, 1931), 8.

Plate 3.4 Portrait of Edward Daniel Alexander Bagot, 1938

Source: *Laura Standard and Crystal Brook Courier*, 24 June 1938, 96.

This negative assessment was due in part to Bagot's political naivety; he was, as one historian argued, a 'maverick in a maverick's movement'.[104] Such naivety proved worrisome to mainstream conservatives in South Australia, with whom Bagot was initially 'dead against cooperation'.[105] Those with whom he did seek to cooperate, such as the leaders of the other citizens' movements, were often alienated by his attempts to corral them behind his vision of a nationwide movement. This domineering attitude extended to his own movement as well, with one initially enthusiastic member resigning because there was 'too much Bagot about it'.[106]

104 John Lonie, '"Good Labor Men" and "Non-Labor" during the Great Depression in South Australia', *Journal of the Historical Society of South Australia* 2(1) (1976): 30–45, at p. 32.
105 Minutes of meeting of representatives to the Emergency Committee, 1 April 1931, series 4, item 1, Archibald Grenfell Price Papers, PRG7 [hereinafter Price Papers], SLSA.
106 Letter from W.A. Blackler to the Secretary of the Citizens' League, 23 October 1931, box 12, item 1, CLSA Papers, NLA.

Robert Campbell Begg was the opposite of Bagot in many ways. An older gentleman at age 47, he was a sombre, hardworking leader who lacked a taste for theatrics. His contemporaries described him as 'a big tall raw-boned Scot' with a 'commanding presence & personality'.[107] As a speaker, however, he was 'placid' and 'undemonstrative'; he preferred audience questions to be collated beforehand, and became easily frustrated when dealing with hecklers.[108] Fellow legion member H.L. Paterson described his oratory at one of the inaugural meetings in Otago:

> I was the Otago branch chairman so I took the chair. Knowing so little of what Begg had in his mind, my introduction was very brief and I handed over to him … He wandered on interminably and his audience became restless. He leaned down to me and asked if he had said enough and I replied quite bluntly. 'Too much.' He had spoken for one and a half hours and told us nothing.[109]

In Begg's defence, his schedule in the legion's first few months was incredibly taxing and the quality of the loud-speaking equipment at some venues was poor.[110] His sincerity and devotion were what appealed to most members; he regularly worked 15-hour days during the legion's heyday, and it was not unusual for him to fly into Wellington early in the morning after giving an address the previous night and head straight to the hospital for his shift.[111] This devotion often bordered on humourlessness, with one member remarking that 'in all the time I knew him, I don't think I ever heard him laugh'.[112]

---

107 Letter from Sir Douglas Robb, 29 September 1972; Letter from W. Bright, 26 August 1972, Transcripts of taped interviews with various people for Tony Simpson, 'The Sugar Bag Years', MS-Papers-9902 [hereinafter Simpson Papers], ATL.
108 Pugh, The New Zealand Legion and conservative protest in the Great Depression, 75; Letter from Peter Hall, 24 August 1972, Simpson Papers, ATL.
109 Tony Simpson, The Sugarbag Years: An Oral History of the 1930s Depression in New Zealand (Auckland: Hodder & Stoughton, 1984), 169.
110 Letter from H. Scott Gilkinson, 29 August 1972, Simpson Papers, ATL.
111 Simpson, The Sugarbag Years, 168; Letter from S.R. McCallum, 26 August 1972, Letter from R.F. Gambrill, 24 August 1972, Letter from Peter Hall, 24 August 1972, Simpson Papers, ATL; Pugh, The New Zealand Legion and conservative protest in the Great Depression, 75; Begg, The Secret of the Knife, 84–85.
112 Letter from Peter Hall, 24 August 1972, Simpson Papers, ATL.

Less information has survived regarding Alex J. Gibson and Ernest Turnbull. Gibson was the oldest of the four at 54, while Turnbull, at 39, was only slightly older than Bagot. The few firsthand accounts of Gibson's leadership of the All for Australia League suggest he was a fiery, strong-willed individual who staunchly opposed cooperation with mainstream conservative parties. However, given these accounts were written by stalwarts of those parties, their reliability is questionable. While A.G. Price may have only been slightly exaggerating in saying that Gibson and his colleagues disliked 'the Nationalists even more than they did the Lang crowd', Producers' Advisory Council Secretary C.L.A. Abbott's claim that 'the tremendous number of members they enrolled went to their heads' smells of sour grapes.[113] Jack Lang himself described Gibson as a 'sinister figure', although his belief that Gibson 'sold out' for the position of consulting engineer to Lang's successor may have sharpened his distaste for the man.[114] The sheer size and, in Victoria at least, the statewide scope of the movements attest to the organisational abilities of the two men, although Turnbull was assisted by Kingsley Henderson, the Victorian league's active and well-spoken secretary, who had proven himself through his role in the league's predecessor, the Citizens' Committee.[115]

---

113 Price, 'The Emergency Committee of South Australia and the Origin of the Premiers' Plan', 18–19; Family Background: The Upper Hunter Abbotts, Abbott Papers, NLA.

114 J.M. Antill, 'Gibson, Alexander James (1876–1960)', *Australian Dictionary of Biography* (National Centre of Biography, The Australian National University, first published in hardcopy 1981), available from: adb.anu.edu.au/biography/gibson-alexander-james-6306.

115 Price described Henderson as far more eloquent than Gibson; see Price, 'The Emergency Committee of South Australia and the Origin of the Premiers' Plan', 18–19.

4

A call to arms: The populist culture of mass conservative mobilisation

Many years after the Depression, a Sydneysider recalled the following about the rise of the All for Australia League:

> [I]n no time a dissident body sprung up, calling itself the All For Australia movement. Members wore a disc in their lapels inscribed 'A.F.A.' One morning on the crowded Mosman ferry a dozen or so of these appeared, not even provoking curiousity [sic]. The following morning there were twenty or thirty. They began to proliferate. By the end of the week a majority of the passengers were wearing them. The same thing was going on in every middle class suburb in Sydney.[1]

In a single week, according to this anecdote, the league's badge became an identifying symbol. In fact, wearing a badge became so common that, by the end of that week, more people were wearing badges than not. Equally important, however, was the fact this practice did not even provoke curiosity among bystanders. The badge held implicit meanings that were widely known and accepted by wearers and non-wearers alike— so widely they did not require comment. Everyone simply knew what they represented.

---

1   Exercise book titled 'Politics; UAP [United Australia Party]; AFA [All for Australia League]', folder 4, 25, H.M. Storey Papers, MS 8539 [hereinafter Storey Papers], NLA.

This rapid proliferation of understanding did not occur by accident. It was the result of a deliberate strategy pursued by the citizens' movements' leaders to connect with a wide audience and cultivate a public image of size—that is, of being a mass movement with significant and widespread support. Virtually the entirety of their operations, from the way they promoted themselves to their organisational structure, was designed to build an enthusiastic and committed mass following. They held large, semi-ritualised meetings and rallies at which speeches were given and resolutions passed to convey the titanic nature of the challenges they claimed to face. They made shrewd use of traditional and modern media, such as books, pamphlets, dodgers, posters, and the burgeoning technology of radio. They courted media publicity, and they submitted countless letters to newspapers to convey their message and to challenge countering opinions. And they brought their considerable organisational skills to bear by forming robust, hierarchical structures that encouraged individuals to join and participate. Combined with their ability to tap into conservatives' ideological dissatisfaction (which was discussed in the previous chapter), this populist culture of mass conservative mobilisation enabled the citizens' movements to recruit considerable membership in a remarkably short period. It represented what Moffatt described as a 'populist political style' in which the leaders and their audience performed their respective roles on a stage of crisis and mass media.[2]

Attaining mass memberships

The previous chapter demonstrated how Edward Daniel Alexander Bagot, the leading figure in the Citizens' League of South Australia, epitomised the process of conservative radicalisation during the Depression. Through his position at the head of the Citizens' League, Bagot also became one of the key influences on the spread of the citizens' movement phenomenon throughout Australia. His primary concern was to avoid the loss of momentum that had crippled previous protests, such as the abortive Kyabram-inspired movement at Moonta earlier in 1930. At the inaugural meeting of the Citizens' League on 3 October 1930, Bagot introduced a successful resolution that the attendees should 'form a permanent body of citizens to follow up this protest with further concerted action'.[3] This resolution embodied the style of protest that Bagot had been increasingly

---

2   Moffitt, *The Global Rise of Populism*, 2.
3   Minutes of Inaugural Meeting, 3 October 1930, box 1, item 1, CLSA Papers, NLA.

drawn towards during his political radicalisation. It was pervasive, in that it would unite a large body of decent, right-minded citizens; and it was sustained, in that it would maintain its enthusiasm through a dedicated body committed to continued action. Such a body would pressure government not through delegations or low-level propaganda, as had often been the case with previous conservative non-party movements, but through the sheer weight of mass public opinion and, if necessary, directed voting power. This method of protest became the standard modus operandi of the citizens' movements and of other forms of mass conservative mobilisation during the Depression.

The leaders of the citizens' movements used several tools in their drive to attain mass memberships. Key among these were their use of public ceremony, their recruitment methods, their organisational skills, their reliance on symbolism, and their deployment of mass media.

Public ceremony

Public ceremony in the form of mass meetings played an important role in attracting new recruits and maintaining enthusiasm among existing members. These meetings built on the ceremony of the 'public meeting' that had been a staple of colonial politics since the nineteenth century.[4] What distinguished the citizens' movements' meetings—poignantly described as 'monster rallies' by the Citizens' League—was their sheer and deliberate size. This was not uncommon on the left (Jack Lang's populist oratory was renowned for attracting large audiences) but was relatively novel on the right. Attendees typically numbered in the thousands, which often required many to stand or queue outside the venue. The inaugural meeting of the Citizens' League of South Australia packed out the Adelaide Town Hall, with those unable to obtain a seat lining the walls, aisles, and 'even the organ galleries'. The inaugural Australian Citizens' League meeting at the Melbourne Town Hall attracted more than 3,000 people, with a similar number turned away at the door.[5] Attendance was so high

---

4   The tradition of public meetings was an inheritance from Britain. They followed a standard protocol that began with speeches, followed by resolutions (often prewritten) put to a popular vote, and the election of a subgroup or 'deputation' to convey the meeting's resolutions to elected officials. See Damen Ward, 'Colonial Communication: Creating Settler Public Opinion in Crown Colony South Australia and New Zealand', in *Imperial Communication: Australia, Britain, and the British Empire c. 1830–50*, ed. Simon J. Potter (London: Menzies Centre for Australian Studies, 2004), 12–21.
5   *Register News-Pictorial*, [Adelaide], 15 October 1930, 3; *The Advertiser*, [Adelaide], 20 February 1931, 14.

at the inaugural All for Australia League meeting at Killara Memorial Hall in Sydney that loudspeakers were set up outside the venue to cater for the overflow.[6] These mass meetings were more than an opportunity to communicate the movements' ideas to a large audience. They were a deliberate attempt to convey an image of overwhelming size and support. Since the movements viewed themselves as the voice of the silent majority—the average citizen—public meetings provided an opportunity to display the weight of numbers they claimed to represent.

The mass meeting also provided a means for the citizens' movements to engage directly with their membership. Advertisements for meetings, which were published and distributed as widely as possible, used emotive and personal language to appeal directly to the reader's sense of duty. In its advertisement for a 'monster meeting' on 11 December 1930 (displayed in Plate 4.1), the Citizens' League of South Australia linked the fate of the nation with that of the individual. Australia's future, it proclaimed, rested with the reader, and it was only by taking action—by joining the Citizens' League—that ruin would be averted. General platitudes and a lack of specific or controversial policies ensured the advertisements appealed to a wide audience. Once at the meeting, attendees listened to speakers who were familiar with the nature of their grievances and understood their desire for urgent action. Bagot urged the crowd at the inaugural Citizens' League of South Australia meeting to bring about 'the cleansing of our political stables', while other speakers warned that 'a crisis is approaching' that required 'immediate action'.[7] Gibson gave a rousing speech to the inaugural All for Australia League meeting that listed a plethora of grievances with the government, including its 'reckless borrowing and expenditure', the 'deliberate alignment of class against class', and 'the setting of party and personal power above the interests of the State'. Speakers often involved the audience in their speeches by asking questions that appealed to their sense of duty:

> [The Depression] had been referred to as a financial crisis: but they were approaching a crisis in their national honour. Were they going to stand by and see the fair name of Australia dragged in the dust of infamy? (Cries of 'No' and 'Never'.)[8]

---

6   *Sydney Morning Herald*, 13 February 1931, 11.
7   Addresses by E.D.A. Bagot, L.V. Pellew, and T.R.H. Griffiths at a Citizens' Public Meeting in Adelaide Town Hall, 14 October 1930, box 1, item 1, CLSA Papers, NLA.
8   *Sydney Morning Herald*, 13 February 1931, 11.

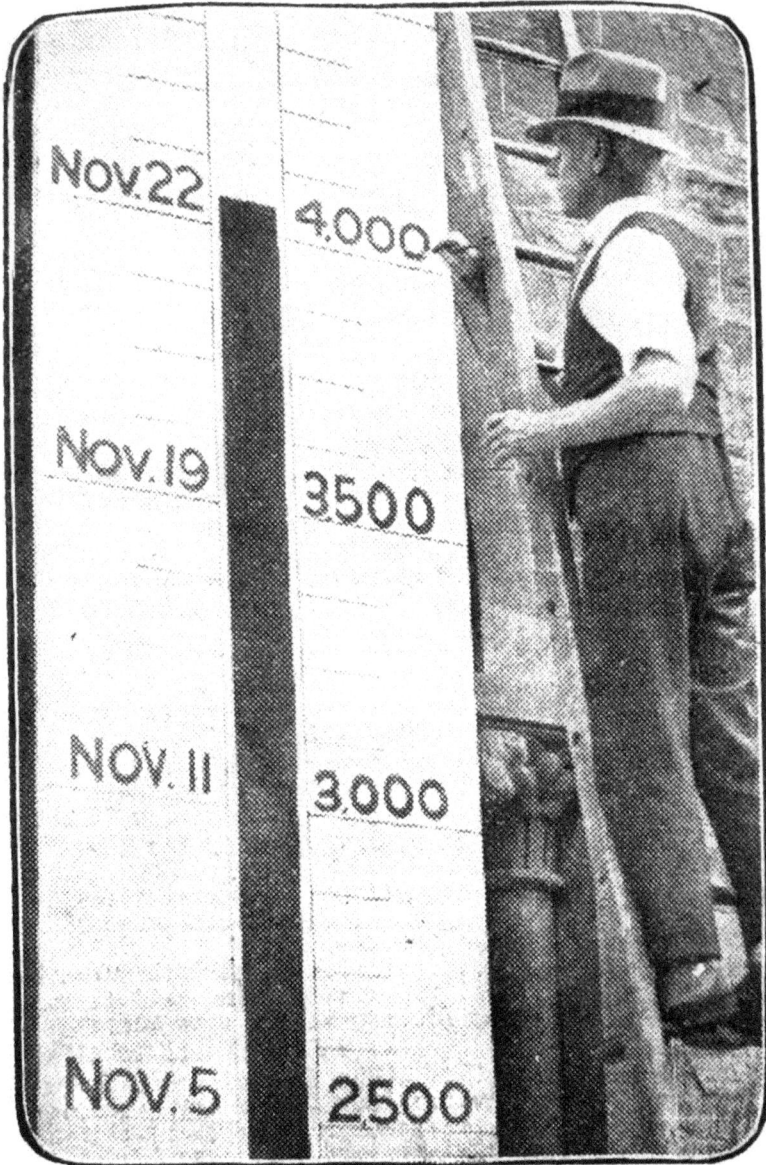

THE THERMOMETER of the Citizens' League reaches the 4,000th figure. A scene outside the league's offices. The membership now totals 4,000.

Plate 4.1 The Citizens' League of South Australia's 'membership thermometer'

Source: *The Register*, [Adelaide], 25 November 1930, 28.

Plate 4.2 Inaugural meeting of the Citizens' League of South Australia at the Adelaide Town Hall

Source: *The Register*, [Adelaide], 16 October 1930, 13.

Plate 4.3 Advertisement for a Citizens' League of South Australia 'monster meeting'

Source: Box 1, item 8, CLSA Papers, NLA.

This reinforced the link between individual action and national wellbeing. Attendees were cast as the pivotal players in ensuring whether government carried out its duties responsibly, but they could only play this role by acting in unison. Mass meetings were typically concluded with a resolution condemning government inaction or calling for greater unity and cooperation between parties, which invariably gathered unanimous support. The text of these resolutions was usually prepared in advance, which made the mass expression of approval by attendees the closing act of a public ceremony rather than democratic participation.[9]

Recruitment methods

One of the crucial ingredients in the success of the citizens' movements was the importance they placed on the attainment of a mass membership. The very legitimacy of their cause depended on the belief that they represented a silent majority of decent, loyal citizens, and that the only path to affecting meaningful change lay in mobilising this silent majority. As a result, the citizens' movement leaders devoted a considerable amount of time to establishing new branches. For months on end, they travelled from town to town, holding meetings and asking attendees to join and form new branches. Between 17 February and 26 March 1933, New Zealand Legion committee members travelled nearly 15,000 kilometres across the country, organising meetings and establishing branches. Begg alone traversed 8,491 kilometres and attended 42 meetings, which led *The Evening Post* to declare that he 'must have some of St. Paul's qualifications as a missionary'.[10] Begg, who was an early proponent of flight, joked that he must have flown in every aircraft in New Zealand at the time to keep up with his punishing schedule of meetings and be back in Wellington in time for his morning hospital shift.[11] Inaugural legion meetings were by invitation only and were closed to the press, which generated an air of mystery about the new movement.[12] The Australian movements were no less energetic; the Citizens' League of South Australia held 221 public meetings between October 1930 and June 1931, which

---

9   Resolution passed at Citizens' Public Meeting in Adelaide Town Hall, 14 October 1930, box 1, item 1, CLSA Papers, NLA.
10   Itinerary in Forming the NZ Legion, file 1, folder 1, NZL Papers, AUL; *The Evening Post*, [Wellington], 6 April 1933, 10.
11   Begg, *The Secret of the Knife*, 84–85.
12   Letter to Y.T. Shand from the Organiser of the inaugural Legion meeting in Christchurch, 17 March 1933, Papers concerning the New Zealand Legion, MS-Papers-0426-086, Field Papers, ATL; Pugh, The New Zealand Legion and conservative protest in the Great Depression, 97–98.

attracted a total attendance of 42,000 people. Bagot, in particular, was praised as the figure to whom 'the success of the League's operations to date has been due in a very large measure'.[13]

The citizens' movements utilised novel enrolment techniques to encourage recruitment. The Citizens' League, for example, awarded gold badges and brooches to individuals who encouraged large numbers of individuals to join.[14] It also created the 'L.G. Abbott Shield', which was awarded each month to the district which recruited the most new members.[15] The All for Australia League and the Australian Citizens' League operated hugely successful enrolment booths in central Sydney and Melbourne. An advertising campaign by the All for Australia League for its first convention in March netted 25,000 new members in one week.[16] In New Zealand, the legion utilised a 'ticket' system of enrolment whereby each new member was requested to recruit five new members. Enrolment booths were planned for several cities, although the only one that appears to have been established was in the square at Palmerston North.[17] Cheap membership fees of 2 shillings or less, which were often waived in cases of financial hardship, further ensured the spread of the movements. The subscription for the Citizens' League was voluntary.[18]

Organisational structure

The organisational structure of the citizens' movements was designed to facilitate participation and encourage leadership at multiple levels. The lowest units of organisation were typically arranged at the level of a town or suburb. These units—known variously as subdivisions, branches, or centres—were supposed to meet frequently and discuss important political and economic questions. They would also review

13 Report of Executive Committee presented at Third Convention of Delegates, 10 June 1931, box 1, item 1, CLSA Papers, NLA.
14 ibid.
15 Report of Executive Committee presented at First Convention of Delegates of Branch Committees of the CLSA, 1 December 1930, box 1, item 1, CLSA Papers, NLA.
16 *Sydney Morning Herald*, 18 March 1931, 9, and 21 March 1931, 1; *The Argus*, [Melbourne], 21 February 1931, 18. Bagot was very impressed with this achievement, and considered opening enrolment booths for the Citizens' League of South Australia in Adelaide; see Letter from Bagot to J. Blitz, 19 March 1931, box 12, item 2, CLSA Papers, NLA.
17 Minutes of Meeting of the Provisional National Council, 4–5 April 1933, file 1, folder 1, NZL Papers, AUL; *National Opinion* [Wellington] 1(5) (5 October 1933): 7.
18 *The Evening Post*, [Wellington], 27 April 1933, 12; *The Argus*, [Melbourne], 2 April 1931, 7; Minutes of Inaugural Meeting, 3 October 1930, box 1, item 1, CLSA Papers, NLA.

policies proposed by the leadership and nominate members to represent them at higher levels of the organisation.[19] The New Zealand Legion was particularly interested in maximising the participation of its members. Frontline 'centres' were supposed to investigate and develop policy ideas that would be submitted to the National Council that met quarterly in Wellington. Ideas considered worthy of pursuing would be circulated to all centres, and those that received the approval of every centre would be adopted as official legion policy. In practice, however, centres typically looked for guidance to the National Executive—a small body appointed by Begg to manage the everyday business of the movement. To assist in the production and dissemination of discussion material, the executive appointed research committees in Wellington to study topics including central government, local government, economics, unemployment, and land.[20]

These organisational techniques helped the citizens' movements to spread rapidly. Within a week of its official launch on 14 October 1930, the Citizens' League of South Australia had 1,500 members.[21] That figure tripled to 4,765 by the end of November, and tripled again to 14,200 by the following March.[22] At its height in August 1932, the league had 21,752 members, or 6.71 per cent of the total registered voters in South Australia.[23] In New South Wales, the All for Australia League amassed a membership of 30,000 by March 1931, with between 400 and 500 new members enrolling every day.[24] A peak figure of 137,000 was reached at the end of June.[25] The Australian Citizens' League in Victoria recruited

---

19   *All for Australia League: Draft Constitution* (Sydney: All for Australia League, 1931); All for Australia League: Locality Layout for Metropolitan Campaign, 3 March 1931, item 70, Mutch Papers, SLNSW; *Constitution of Citizens' League of South Australia* (Adelaide: F. Cockington & Co. Printers, 1931); Constitution and Rules of the New Zealand Legion, No. NZL 15, file 1, folder 1, NZL Papers, AUL; *All for Australia League Shows the Way to Prosperity*, 26.

20   Minutes of Meeting of the Provisional National Council, 4–5 April 1933, file 1, folder 1, and Ref. 6/2/16, 12 May 1933, file 1, folder 2, NZL Papers, AUL; Pugh, The New Zealand Legion and conservative protest in the Great Depression, 92–93.

21   Minutes of Meeting held at Balfour's Café, 21 October 1930, box 1, item 1, CLSA Papers, NLA.

22   Report of Executive Committee presented at First Convention of Delegates of Branch Committees of the CLSA, 1 December 1930; Report of Executive Committee presented at Second Convention of Delegates of Branches of the CLSA, 16 March 1931, box 1, item 1, CLSA Papers, NLA.

23   Report of Executive Committee presented to the First Annual Convention of Branch Delegates, 16 September 1931, box 1, item 2, CLSA Papers, NLA. A slightly higher figure of 23,133 was reported in August 1932; however, it is likely that most members were nominal by this point, as the league had rapidly declined in strength and influence from the end of 1931.

24   *Horsham Times*, 13 March 1931, 2; Matthews, 'The All for Australia League', 139.

25   *Sydney Morning Herald*, 26 June 1931, 16; Committees (handwritten note), undated, item 79, Mutch Papers, SLNSW.

5,691 members by 4 March 1931, when it decided to adopt the name and objects of the All for Australia League.[26] By its first annual meeting on 19 May, its membership was 80,000; two months later, it claimed to have exceeded 100,000 members.[27] Across the Tasman, the New Zealand Legion enrolled 2,000 individuals in its first month and, by July 1933, its membership totalled 15,000 people.[28] At the end of August, it claimed to have in excess of 20,000 members.[29] In total, close to 300,000 Australians and New Zealanders joined one of the four citizens' movements.

Symbolism

A sense of belonging was reinforced by easily recognisable and culturally resonant symbols. This use of symbolism was similar to that identified by Bruce Scates in his study of radical left-wing culture in the 1890s. Scates argued that symbols allowed those who were unfamiliar with the issues under discussion to still feel as though they belonged. They represented broader ideas and forces with which the observer could identify, even if they did not fully understand those ideas and forces.[30] Symbols of Britishness served the same function for the citizens' movements. Mass meetings always began and closed with *God Save the King*, *Rule Britannia*, or other patriotic songs, and the Union Jack was usually hung from the podium where speakers stood. Badges provided a much more potent symbol of the movements themselves; as the quote at the start of this chapter demonstrates, the All for Australia League badge became a regular sight on the streets of Sydney and provided an effective barometer of the movement's growth. So pervasive was the badge that opponents of the league measured its failure by the same standard. In July, *The Worker* proudly proclaimed that '[t]o-day it is difficult to find anyone wearing' the badge, whereas it had once 'decorated every second coat lapel in Sydney'.[31] Public interest pieces in the newspapers further enhanced the

---

26 *Sydney Morning Herald*, 5 March 1931, 10; *The Argus*, [Melbourne], 6 March 1931, 6.

27 *Age*, [Melbourne], 20 May 1931, 8; *Wodonga and Towong Sentinel*, 24 July 1931, 3.

28 No. NZL. 1, 11 March 1933; Circular to all members, 28 July 1933, file 1, folder 2, NZL Papers, AUL.

29 Letter from J.B. Wilson to Hawke's Bay members, 22 August 1933, file 5, folder 1, NZL Papers, AUL. Wilson claimed membership was 'in excess of 20,000 and is increasing daily', but he may have been exaggerating given the purpose of his letter was to remind members to regularly attend meetings and encourage them to enrol more members.

30 Bruce Scates, *A New Australia: Citizenship, Radicalism and the First Republic* (Cambridge, UK: Cambridge University Press, 1997), 30–32.

31 *The Worker*, [Brisbane], 15 July 1931, 13.

badges' recognisability. In March 1931, for example, the *Sydney Morning Herald* claimed that a man wearing a league badge subdued a crowd of unemployed people threatening to riot:

> When it looked as though a procession of unemployed through the city yesterday would culminate in riot near Parliament House, a tactful address by a member of the All for Australia League saved the situation.
>
> … Mr O.W. Lapham, who was wearing the badge of the All for Australia League, scrambled up on to a derrick nearby, and appealed for law and order. To the consternation of the leaders, the majority of the unemployed gathered below to listen to him. The militant element counted him out on several occasions, but he persisted and out-talked them.[32]

While this story was undoubtedly exaggerated—the timely intervention of the Minister for Labour was likely a deciding factor as well—it demonstrates the power that members associated with the badge. It identified the wearer as embodying something greater than themselves. They carried with them the ideals of the movement, and their rational and clear-headed rhetoric could be expected to win through the false and pernicious doctrines of the disloyal minority stirring up the unemployed.

Mass media

The culture of mass conservative mobilisation was further promoted by the extensive use of mass media. In its first year, the Citizens' League of South Australia distributed 222,250 dodgers and dispatched 4,261 letters and 29,605 circulars.[33] The Australian Citizens' League distributed batches of circulars directly to employers across Melbourne so that they might encourage their staff to join en masse.[34] Pamphlets, booklets, and journals allowed the movements to distribute in-depth collections of ideas and policies through popular outlets. The New Zealand Legion's two booklets, *Light on the Legion* and *National Unity in Crisis*, sold well in many bookstores and newsagents, although its journal, *National Opinion*,

---

32 *Sydney Morning Herald*, 7 March 1931, 15.
33 Report of Executive Committee presented to the First Annual Convention of Branch Delegates, 16 September 1931, box 1, item 2, CLSA Papers, NLA.
34 Geoff Hewitt, 'The All for Australia League in Melbourne', *La Trobe Historical Studies* 3 (1972): 5–15, at pp. 5–7.

had a more modest circulation of 2,400 copies.[35] Radio provided a more modern, and potentially far-reaching, distribution medium. Speeches at large meetings of the Citizens' League were broadcast on Adelaide radio station 5AD, and twice-weekly broadcasts commenced in June 1931.[36] The All for Australia League gave broadcasts on Sydney's theosophist radio station, 2GB, three nights a week.[37] The New Zealand Legion discussed the use of radio broadcasts, but it is unclear whether they used them. Given Begg's avid championing of other burgeoning technologies (such as flight), it seems likely they did.[38] As with the movements' organisational techniques, this focus on the mass dissemination of ideas emphasised a conscious focus on scale. The movements were demonstrating their ability to reach far and wide with their mission to educate the masses while reinforcing the belief that they represented a significant body of moderate opinion.

Spreading the faith across Australia

From its inception, the Citizens' League of South Australia was considered by Bagot as the first branch of a nationwide movement. In his speech before the inaugural town hall meeting on 14 October, he called on 'similar minded people in other States to take similar action, so that the voices of the citizens of Australia will be heard as one'.[39] An Australia-wide organisation, he told the league's Executive Committee, could recruit as many as 680,000 individuals, and he offered to visit other states to 'get the movement going there'.[40] This was the impetus that led him to approach the Melbourne Citizens' Committee about forming a Victorian branch, which was discussed in Chapter Two. He also contacted other Constitutional Clubs across the country and discovered that 'similar bodies to the South Australian League' were already taking shape in several

---

35   *Light on the Legion*; Ref. 6/12/17, 15 May 1933, Letter from Begg to all Divisions and Centres, 3 February 1934, file 1, folder 2, Letter from A.S. Tonkin to J.R.V. Sherston, 6 June 1933, file 2, folder 3, NZL Papers, AUL.

36   Report of Executive Committee presented to the First Annual Convention of Branch Delegates, 16 September 1931, box 1, item 2, CLSA Papers, NLA; *The Advertiser*, [Adelaide], 11 February 1931, 8; *Advertiser and Register*, [Adelaide], 17 April 1931, 20.

37   *All for Australia League*, 16.

38   Minutes of Meeting of the Provisional National Council, 4–5 April 1933, file 1, folder 1, NZL Papers, AUL.

39   Address by Bagot at a Citizens' Public Meeting in Adelaide Town Hall, 14 October 1930, box 1, item 1, CLSA Papers, NLA.

40   Minutes of Executive Committee Meeting, 16 October 1930, box 1, item 2, CLSA Papers, NLA.

states: the Vigilance Committee in Brisbane, the Citizens' Federation in Perth, and the 'Who's for Australia?' League in Sydney (also discussed in Chapter Two). Bagot advocated forming an 'interstate organisation' as soon as possible, arguing that the 'moral effect' of holding simultaneous demonstrations across the country 'would be enormous'.[41] Such a massive force of public opinion would either compel the federal government to act or allow its directed voting power to elect a government that would.

Despite Bagot's lofty ambitions, most of the embryonic citizens' movements in other states failed to achieve a mass following. There were several reasons for this, including a lack of political or organisational nous, local infighting, and the inability to tap into conservative discontent with Labor's 'inflationist' and 'repudiationist' policies.

Queensland

The Brisbane organisation named the Vigilants was formed in October 1930 by representatives of several dozen conservative groups, including the Constitutional Club, the Chamber of Commerce, the Taxpayers' Association, and the United Graziers' Association. It initially focused on achieving drastic government economies, including the suspension of industry awards and a reduction in the size of the federal and state governments.[42] However, in mid-November, the Vigilants redirected their efforts towards local government reform in Brisbane, seeking a reduction in the number of aldermen and the abolition of their salaries. A combination of bad publicity and repeated failures to convince the mayor to implement their recommendations led to the sidelining of the Vigilants by a new municipal party, the Civic Reform League.[43] In December, the Secretary of the Citizens' League of South Australia, C.W. Andersen, visiting Brisbane on business, gave a speech before the Constitutional Club and 'several members of the Vigilant Association' in the hopes of establishing the basis of interstate cooperation. Nothing came of the visit, for the Vigilants were largely defunct by this time.[44]

41 Report of Sub-Committee, 21 October 1930, box 1, item 1; Minutes of Executive Committee Meeting, 21 October 1930, box 1, item 2, CLSA Papers, NLA.
42 *Brisbane Courier*, 8 October 1930, 13.
43 Brian Costar, 'Was Queensland Different?', in *The Wasted Years? Australia's Great Depression*, ed. Judy Mackinolty (Sydney: Allen & Unwin, 1981), 170–2.
44 Minutes of Executive Committee Meeting, 15 December 1930, box 1, item 2; Letter from Bagot to Phillip Frankel, 18 February 1931, box 13, item 12, CLSA Papers, NLA.

As the Vigilants had fallen through, Bagot instead attempted to establish a branch of the Citizens' League in Queensland. In January 1931, Philip Frankel, owner of a motor accessories distribution company in Brisbane, wrote a well-publicised open letter calling for the abolition of political parties and replacing state parliaments with regional councils under a uniform central government.[45] Bagot read Frankel's commentary with interest and sent him a copy of the Citizens' League program in the hope he might start a branch in Brisbane. The two entered into correspondence for the next several months, during which time Frankel attempted to establish a Citizens' Federation in Queensland with several members of a non-party electoral organisation, the Grand Council of Progress Associations.[46] At Frankel's request, Bagot forwarded him a copy of the Citizens' League's constitution and several other pamphlets 'as a foundation' for drawing up similar documents in Queensland.[47] Bagot also forwarded copies of this material to W.A. Burns, an associate of Frankel's in Cairns who had intended to establish a local branch of the All for Australia League but decided to work with Frankel on the Citizens' Federation instead.[48] Despite this support, the Queensland Citizens' Federation failed to make headway. Frankel decided in June to join the Queensland Non-Party League—a group formed by the new mayor and Progress Association candidate J.W. Greene.[49] Frankel gave all the material he had received from Bagot to the new group, which established relations with the Citizens' League of South Australia in July 1931.[50] However, like its predecessors, the Non-Party League proved short-lived, accomplishing little beyond a series of public debates with kindred associations such as the League of Women Voters.[51]

---

45 *Brisbane Courier*, 19 January 1931, 13. The same letter was republished in several other papers, including the *Cairns Post*, *The Morning Bulletin* [Rockhampton, Qld], and the *Albany Advertiser*. Frankel wrote a follow-up letter in February advocating the reduction of the franchise to 'those capable of giving an intelligent reflex of the wishes of the people'; see *Brisbane Courier*, 14 February 1931, 15.

46 Letter from Bagot to Frankel, 18 February 1931; Letter from Frankel to Bagot, 28 February 1931; Letter from Bagot to Frankel, 9 March 1931; Letter from Frankel to Bagot, 30 April 1931, box 13, item 12, CLSA Papers, NLA.

47 Letter from Bagot to Frankel, 4 May 1931; Letter from Frankel to Bagot, 12 May 1931; Letter from Bagot to Frankel, 16 May 1931; Letter from Frankel to Bagot, 15 June 1931, box 13, item 12, CLSA Papers, NLA.

48 Letter from W.A. Burns to Bagot, 22 May 1931; Letter from Bagot to W.A. Burns, 2 June 1931, box 12, item 1, CLSA Papers, NLA.

49 Letter from Frankel to Bagot, 25 June 1931, box 13, item 12, CLSA Papers, NLA; *Brisbane Courier*, 10 June 1931, 10.

50 Minutes of Executive Committee Meeting, 7 July 1931, box 1, item 2, CLSA Papers, NLA.

51 *Brisbane Courier*, 30 September 1931, 16. The Non-Party League may also have influenced the formation of the rabidly anti-party Queensland Party in 1932, which ran several independent candidates in the June 1932 state elections. See Box 33, Albert Welsby Papers, UQFL40, University of Queensland Fryer Library, Brisbane.

Why did the various attempts to build a citizens' movement in Queensland fail? One historian has argued that the Vigilants lacked a clear enemy in their state, as the Queensland Government was in conservative hands for most of the Depression.[52] Yet in South Australia, where a centrist and economically orthodox Labor government held power, the Citizens' League was still able to thrive by directing its frustrations against the federal government.[53] It seems more likely that individuals like Frankel simply lacked the organisational and promotional skills of the Citizens' League's leaders, or they did not have the time and energy to devote as much attention as their South Australian contemporaries to building a mass movement.

Western Australia

The Citizens' League of South Australia fared little better with its attempts to cooperate with a group known as the Citizens' Federation of Western Australia. The federation's founder and president, Colin Unwin, subscribed to a very particular and parochial form of anti-partyism, which he termed 'Unism' and had promoted through a variety of short-lived protest movements since before the Great War.[54] Unwin was very protective of his philosophy, which was focused heavily on parliamentary reform and rejected any form of economic policy as potentially divisive. As a result, he was wary of forming an alliance with the other citizens' movements. Despite sharing their distaste for party politics, he feared that any 'broad common policy' would require the federation to adopt 'proposals of an economic or financial character'.[55] As he explained to S.R. Dickinson, editor of the Melbourne *Argus*, in March 1931:

> [W]e cannot trace that any of them [the citizens' movements] are dealing with fundamental electoral and parliamentary reform, but rather do they seem to urge a mixture of principles and political, financial and economic planks all more or less debatable, and thus liable to split any movement at any time, especially as new planks are introduced.[56]

---

52   Costar, 'Was Queensland Different?', 173.
53   James, 'God, Mammon and Mussolini', 31.
54   Colin Unwin, *Unism: The New Constructive Policy* (Fremantle, WA: Porter & Salmon, 1916).
55   *The Abolition of Party Government Depends Upon You* (Perth: Citizens' Federation of Western Australia, 1931), 1.
56   Letter from Unwin to S.R. Dickinson, 6 March 1931, folder 15, Colin Unwin Papers, ACC 6321A [hereinafter Unwin Papers], State Library of Western Australia, Perth [hereinafter SLWA].

Instead of cooperating with the established citizens' movements, Unwin sought to establish branches of his own movement in other states. He wrote to Kingsley Henderson during the formation of the Australian Citizens' League in February 1931, urging them to adopt the federation's platform, and sent a similar letter to Dickinson in the hopes that he would publish it.[57] When Dickinson replied stating he had declined to join the Australian Citizens' League because of its economic policy, Unwin urged him to join the federation and form local 'propaganda groups' in Victoria.[58] He asked Citizens' Federation assistant organiser Mrs C.T. Wright to do the same during her six-week stay in Adelaide in early 1931, even if this 'conflict[ed] with The Citizen's League in Adelaide'.[59] These efforts came to nothing: Wright left Adelaide the following month without forming a local branch of the Citizens' Federation and, if Dickinson complied with Unwin's request, the press took no notice.[60]

The Citizens' Federation failed to achieve the mass mobilisation of its eastern cousins for several reasons. First, by refusing to consider economic policies, it missed the opportunity to tap into the widespread conservative discontent over the policies of Scullin, Theodore, and Lang. The citizens' movements in South Australia, Victoria, and New South Wales were all fluent in the language of conservative grievances, which provided them with a large base of potential members. Second, Unwin was opposed to the idea of holding 'big meetings first', preferring 'study circles' and 'Propaganda Groups ... until we can be sure of reasonable support in the Town or other large halls'.[61] This cautious approach proved to be counterproductive: the federation never held a town hall meeting, which prevented its message from reaching the wide audiences reached by the citizens' movements with their mass rallies. As a result, its propaganda efforts were limited to several letters in the *West Australian* and the occasional small public meeting.[62]

---

57   Telegram from Unwin to Kingsley Henderson, 11 February 1931; Telegram from Unwin to Dickinson, 11 February 1931, folder 15, Unwin Papers, SLWA.

58   Letter from Unwin to Dickinson, 6 March 1931, folder 15, Unwin Papers, SLWA.

59   Letter from Unwin to Mrs C.T. Wright, 6 March 1931, folder 15, Unwin Papers, SLWA.

60   *Advertiser and Register*, [Adelaide], 4 April 1931, 19.

61   Letter from Unwin to S.R. Dickinson, 6 March 1931, folder 15, Unwin Papers, SLWA; *An Australia-Wide Appeal for the Abolition of the Party System of Government* (Perth: Citizens' Federation of Western Australia, 1931), 8.

62   *West Australian*, [Perth], 20 March 1931, 15; 31 March 1931, 8; 27 April 1931, 5.

Third, and more fundamentally, aspiring citizens' movements in Western Australia had to compete with the growing tide of secessionist sentiment in that state, which exploded during the Depression in the form of the Dominion League of Western Australia.[63] R.F. Rushton, a Perth accountant, encountered this problem when he attempted to form a local branch of the Citizens' League of South Australia in 1933:

> The swing towards Secession is most pronounced and the bulk of those sane-minded citizens who could be looked to support our movement are now becoming somewhat active supporters of the Secession movement with the result that much time and much money which could be expected to be given to our movement is being absorbed in other directions.[64]

As a result, the small nucleus of members whom Rushton was able to assemble decided to focus their energies on empire trade, tariff reduction, and the formation of a 'lesser states movement'.[65] Even this failed to make headway, and the September 1933 Annual Convention of the Citizens' League reported: 'The Secession movement in [Western Australia] … was so strong that no close affiliation was possible.'[66] In essence, the Dominion League channelled populist sentiment in Western Australia against the Commonwealth itself rather than against party politicians.[67]

Tasmania

While Bagot never attempted to form a Citizens' League branch in Tasmania, attempts were made to form a local branch of the All for Australia League. However, this was hampered by internal divisions virtually from the outset. It was delayed until May 1931 by bickering among its founders over who would lead the movement and how many labour representatives would be included on its committee. Even after it was founded, the movement was only concerned with holding on to the 'floating vote' that had swung in favour of the conservatives in 1930 rather than actively recruiting a mass membership. As a result, one contemporary noted that the All for Australia League had not found 'any

---

63 Hiller, 'Secession in Western Australia'; Musgrave, 'The Western Australian Secessionist Movement', 103–5.
64 Letter from Rushton to Bagot, 19 January 1933, box 14, item 20, CLSA Papers, NLA.
65 Letter from Rushton to Bagot, 24 January 1933, box 14, item 20, CLSA Papers, NLA.
66 Report of the Executive Committee presented to the Third Annual Convention of Delegates, 12 September 1933, box 1, item 4, CLSA Papers, NLA.
67 Lloyd, The formation and development of the U.A.P., 58–59.

substantial footing in Tasmania'.[68] The Tasmanian All for Australia League also had to compete with a group named the Tasmanian Reform League, which was founded in April 1931 to agitate for a smaller state parliament, a reduction in members' salaries, and the banning of seditious literature.[69] The relatively small population of Tasmania likely further reduced the potential expansion of the league.

Other mass conservative movements

The spread of the citizens' movements in Australia had a more appreciable impact on other forms of mass conservative mobilisation. Eric Campbell, the founder and Chief Commander of the New Guard, attended the inaugural meeting of the All for Australia League and was thoroughly impressed with its anti-party stance.[70] The New Guard subsequently utilised mass rallies and demonstrations in its campaign against communism, and combating 'machine politics' became one of its core aims.[71] Campbell was also friends with All for Australia League executive member Sydney Snow, and the two believed 'the New Guard was the fighting wing and the A.F.A. the political wing of the same brand of thought'.[72] The secessionist Riverina Movement in southern New South Wales also relied on 'monster meetings' and opposition to party politics. Its inaugural open-air rally in Wagga Wagga in February 1931 attracted 10,000 attendees, which was widely touted as the biggest meeting of its kind ever held in rural Australia.[73] The policy and rhetoric of the new movement, which blended anti-partyism with criticisms of city dominance, represented an adaptation of citizens' movement ideology to the rural sector.[74]

---

68 *Mercury*, [Hobart], 21 May 1931, 9; Letter from F. Mary Parker to Latham, 29 May 1931, Letter from Latham to Parker, 11 June 1931, box 89, series 49, folder 2, Sir John Latham Papers, MS 1009 [hereinafter Latham Papers], NLA.
69 *Examiner*, [Launceston, Tas.], 7 May 1931, 6.
70 Campbell, *The Rallying Point*, 42–43.
71 Cunningham, 'Australian Fascism?', 386.
72 Campbell, *The Rallying Point*, 43.
73 *Sydney Morning Herald*, 2 March 1931, 9; *The Argus*, [Melbourne], 7 March 1931, 15.
74 *Townsville Daily Bulletin*, 16 March 1931, 4. Hardy claimed several years later that the two primary objectives of the Riverina Movement had been to combat party politics and to combat city dominance; see Ellis, *A Pen in Politics*, 195.

The geographical distribution of the citizens' movements

While citizens' movements did not arise in every Australian state, they were very successful in attaining mass memberships where they did arise. But did they attract the kind of broad, cross-class support they claimed to? Figures 4.1–4.3 display the locations of known branches, divisions, and subdivisions of the three Australian movements. Unfortunately a complete list of centres for the New Zealand Legion has not survived. Together with an analysis of their internal correspondence, this demonstrates that the citizens' movements fared extremely well in urban areas but had mixed success in rural areas. Their ability to spread into rural areas depended on several factors, including the presence (or absence) of executive members with rural backgrounds and expertise and whether there were other movements competing for members in the area. For example, the initial growth of the Citizens' League of South Australia was restricted to suburban Adelaide, with as many as 130 branches established there by March 1931.[75] Some of these branches evidently failed or were combined with other branches, because in September, it was reported that there were 94 branches in the six urban districts. However, the period from March to June witnessed a dramatic increase in rural branches. This was largely due to the work of the league's country organiser A.L. Langsford, who held 40 country meetings addressing a total audience of 8,150 people.[76] His speech proved so convincing in the town of Moculta that, of a town population of 142, 141 signed membership forms.[77] By September, there were 4,877 country members across 64 branches, or 22.4 per cent of the total membership of the league—an impressive figure given the concentration of the state's population in urban areas.[78] The location of the league's country branches aligned with the distribution of the non-Aboriginal population in South Australia in the 1930s, which reinforces the fact it was successful in appealing to rural citizens.[79]

---

75 Attendance Book for Second Convention, 16 March 1931, box 2, item 20, CLSA Papers, NLA.
76 Report of Executive Committee presented at Third Convention of Delegates of Branches, 10 June 1931, box 1, item 1, CLSA Papers, NLA.
77 Minutes of Executive Committee Meeting, 16 June 1931, box 1, item 2, CLSA Papers, NLA.
78 Report of Executive Committee presented to the First Annual Convention of Branch Delegates, 16 September 1931, box 1, item 2, CLSA Papers, NLA.
79 Graeme Hugo, 'A Century of Population Change in Australia', in *Year Book Australia, 2001*, Cat. no. 1301.0 (Canberra: Australian Bureau of Statistics, 2001), available from: www.abs.gov.au/Ausstats/abs@.nsf/0/0B82C2F2654C3694CA2569DE002139D9?Open.

The Australian Citizens' League enjoyed considerable success in rural Victoria. Of a total of 317 branches and subbranches in May 1931, only 28 were in metropolitan Melbourne.[80] The geographical analysis of those branches suggests a fairly even distribution throughout Victoria. The overall distribution was roughly congruent with the rural population density of Victoria, which was similar in size but broader in spread than New South Wales and greater on both accounts than South Australia.[81] The cause of this dramatic success in rural areas is not clear. The lack of rural protest movements in Victoria, and the dramatic success of the Kyabram Reform Movement 30 years earlier, may have been contributing factors.

In contrast, the All for Australia League fared poorly in rural New South Wales. Its original plan envisaged the creation of 14 country divisions of the league that would share equal representation with their urban counterparts on the State Council. But rural New South Wales was a crowded ideological space in 1931. The league was competing against established bodies such as the Country Party and the Farmers and Settlers' Association, along with new groups such as the Producers' Advisory Council and the new-state movements in New England and the Riverina. The league attempted to overcome this competition by drawing on the tenets of Don Aitkin's 'countrymindedness', or the romanticisation of rural life and the importance of primary production to the nation's welfare.[82] They also played on fears of city dominance:

> The cost of Government has grown like a mushroom, the city has fattened at the expense of the rural districts, and the whole social structure of the community to-day is ill-balanced and conducive to bitter factional animosities.[83]

Their efforts were mostly unsuccessful. The attempt to convince Riverina Movement leader Charles Hardy to unite with the All for Australia League was rebuffed, although Hardy did attend several league meetings and maintained correspondence with its leaders.[84] Other secessionists were less enamoured with the league's perceived interference in country

---

80   *All for Australia League Shows the Way to Prosperity*, 26.
81   Hugo, 'A Century of Population Change in Australia'.
82   Don Aitkin, '"Countrymindedness"', 51.
83   *All for Australia League*, 5.
84   Beveridge, The Riverina Movement and Charles Hardy, 31; Ellis, *The Country Party*, 143–44; Geoffrey Robinson, 'The All for Australia League in New South Wales: A Study in Political Entrepreneurship and Hegemony', *Australian Historical Studies* 39(1) (2008): 36–52, at p. 42; *Sydney Morning Herald*, 30 March 1931, 12; First Meeting of the State Executive, 1 June 1931, item 79, Mutch Papers, SLNSW.

affairs. The western secessionist movement, for example, was 'definite in its opinion that the league should confine its activities to the metropolitan area'.[85] One Country Party stalwart in Griffith responded to a request to form a local league division by telling them to 'confine their operations to the Cities and leave the country districts alone'.[86] In a last-ditch effort to secure a country foothold, the league supported a constitutional convention to consider, among other things, the revision of state boundaries in the interests of creating new states within New South Wales.[87] This, too, failed to build their rural base, and when the new-state movements agreed to form the United Country Movement in August 1931, the league announced it would disband its country organisation.[88]

Nevertheless, the All for Australia League was not entirely limited to metropolitan Sydney. By the end of March, it had 15 subdivisions outside Sydney, compared with 84 in the city.[89] It enjoyed considerable support in suburban Newcastle, where eight subdivisions were created and an official journal titled *The Hunter Statesman* was produced.[90] It is likely the majority of the league's proclaimed '30000 Country + Newcastle badges'—which represented almost 22 per cent of the movement's total membership—came from the greater Hunter area.[91] The few rural subdivisions it established performed relatively well: Broken Hill reported a local membership of 'well over 125', while in Lithgow the number 'exceeded 200' people.[92] The location of these two towns west of Sydney may explain why the western secessionist movement was so opposed to the league's intrusion into its domain. The metropolitan-adjacent country electorates of Macquarie and Werriwa were represented at the September State Council, as was Eden-Monaro in south-eastern New South Wales.[93] The latter is surprising given that Eden-Monaro was also home to a new-state movement, although the fact that it was not launched until April 1931 may have allowed the league time to gather supporters there.[94]

---

85 *Sydney Morning Herald*, 19 June 1931, 10.
86 Letter from W. Moses to Earle Page, 15 May 1931, box 19, folder 76, Ulrich Ellis Papers, MS 1006 [hereinafter Ellis Papers], NLA.
87 *Policy as Adopted by Convention of the League*, 4, 13–15.
88 Circular re: Decision to close down country district organisations, 14 August 1931, item 70, Mutch Papers, SLNSW.
89 *Sydney Morning Herald*, 20 March 1931, 12.
90 There may have been only one volume of this; see *The Hunter Statesman*, [Newcastle, NSW], 2 July 1931, item 68, Mutch Papers, SLNSW.
91 Committees (handwritten note), undated, item 79, Mutch Papers, SLNSW.
92 *Barrier Miner*, [Broken Hill, NSW], 16 June 1931, 2; *Sydney Morning Herald*, 1 June 1931, 10.
93 *Sydney Morning Herald*, 22 September 1931, 8.
94 *Sydney Morning Herald*, 10 April 1931, 10; Monaro–South Coast Movement: Its history summarised, undated, box 19, folder 76, Ellis Papers, NLA.

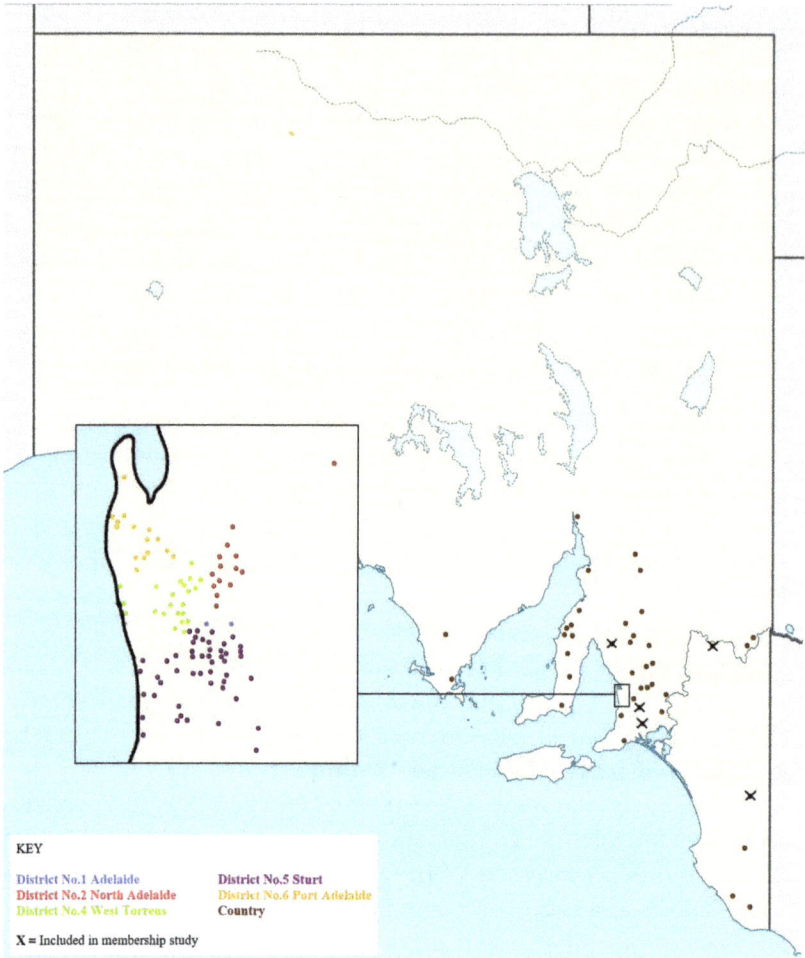

Figure 4.1 Geographical distribution of members, Citizens' League of South Australia

Source: Data drawn from Matthew Cunningham, The reactionary and the radical: A comparative analysis of mass conservative mobilisation in Australia and New Zealand during the Great Depression (PhD diss., Victoria University of Wellington, 2015), Appendix A.

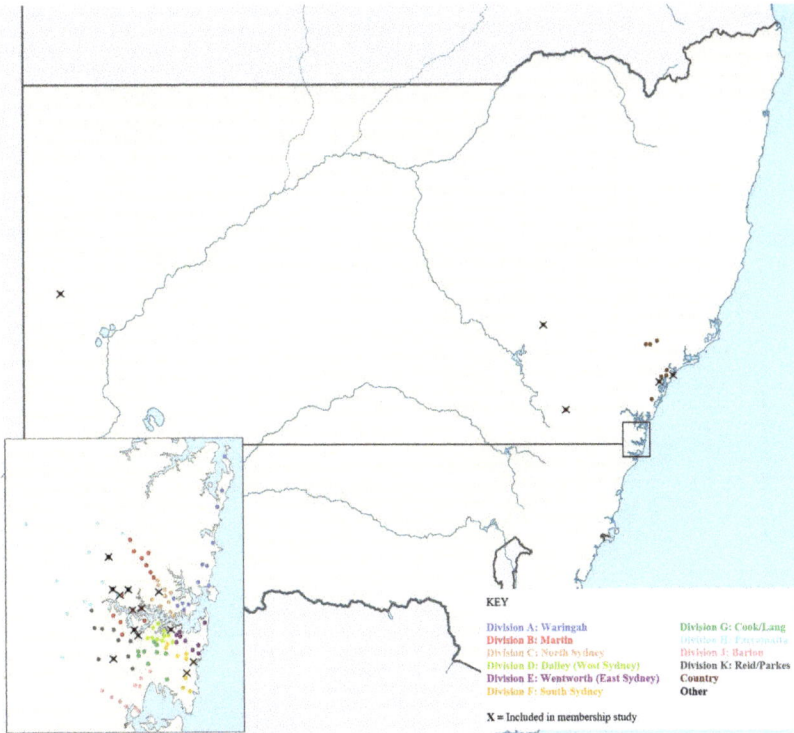

KEY

Division A: Waringah	Division G: Cook/Lang
Division B: Martin	Division H: Warringah
Division C: North Sydney	Division J: Barton
Division D: Dalley (West Sydney)	Division K: Reid/Parkes
Division E: Wentworth (East Sydney)	Country
Division F: South Sydney	Other

X = Included in membership study

Figure 4.2 Geographical distribution of members, All for Australia League, New South Wales

Source: Data drawn from Matthew Cunningham, The reactionary and the radical: A comparative analysis of mass conservative mobilisation in Australia and New Zealand during the Great Depression (PhD diss., Victoria University of Wellington, 2015), Appendix A.

The centres of the New Zealand Legion were more evenly distributed between city and country. While a complete list of centres has not survived, a geographical analysis of the legion in Otago shows a significant rural presence in Central Otago and in the country west of Oamaru.[95] It is difficult to determine whether this equated to an equal distribution of membership between city and country, but the 1,007 members in the rural Hawke's Bay division represented one-twentieth of the legion's total strength—an almost one-to-one ratio with the total number of divisions.[96] This rural spread may have been due to a lack of rural political alternatives in New Zealand. New Zealand's Country Party, which existed from 1928

---

95   Campbell, The New Zealand Legion in Otago, Figure 3.
96   List of members in H.B. Division of N.Z. Legion, undated, file 2, folder 1, NZL Papers, AUL. The tally on the list itself claims a total of 1,011, but four names were repeated twice.

until 1938, was a mere shadow of its Australian counterpart. Its ideology was a mixture of rural activism and social credit, and it only ever managed to secure two seats in parliament. A proposed country protest movement in 1930 named the Political Committee failed to secure widespread support, and the Douglas social credit movement did not begin to make headway in rural areas until mid-1933.[97] The legion's success was also greatest in regions represented by conservative Reform MPs, which, prior to Labour's success in 1935, included most of rural New Zealand.[98]

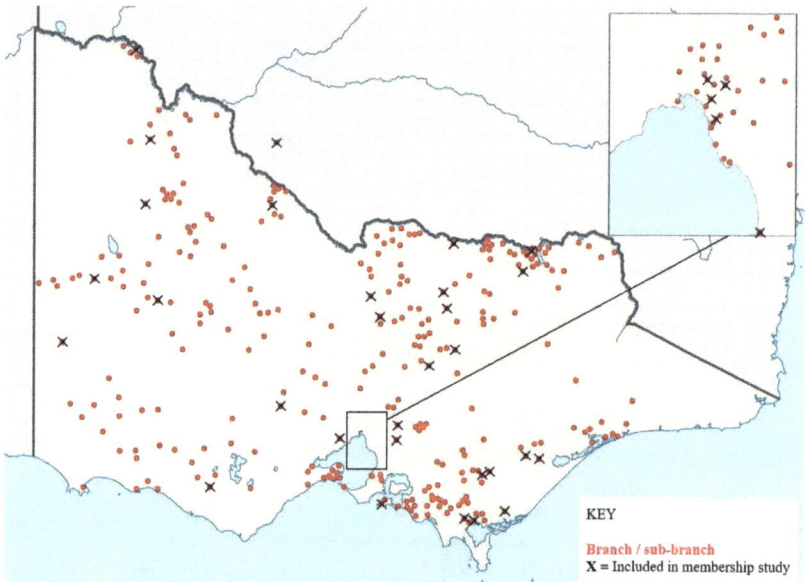

Figure 4.3 Geographical distribution of members, Australian Citizens' League, Victoria and New South Wales
Source: Data drawn from Matthew Cunningham, The reactionary and the radical: A comparative analysis of mass conservative mobilisation in Australia and New Zealand during the Great Depression (PhD diss., Victoria University of Wellington, 2015), Appendix A.

Nevertheless, the bulk of the legion's activity occurred in major cities or urban hubs in rural areas. Previous studies of the legion's activities in Otago and the Manawatu–Wanganui regions paint a picture of highly active city leadership mirrored by moribund rural centres. The Otago leadership

97   Dominion Executive Meeting, 28 January 1931, Dominion Executive—Minutes 1928–1931, New Zealand Farmers' Union Papers, ATL; Clifton, Douglas credit and the Labour Party, 73–76, 128–29.
98   Pugh, The New Zealand Legion and conservative protest in the Great Depression, 98.

was particularly active, producing several reports on local government reform that became official legion policy.[99] And while the Ashburton and Waipukurau centres were more active than most city centres, this was the exception rather than the rule. Waipukurau had the well-respected Sir Andrew Russell as a drawcard for local members, and Ashburton was the third-largest town in Canterbury.[100]

Membership of the citizens' movements

Geographical spread did not automatically imply that the citizens' movements enjoyed the cross-class, urban–rural support they claimed. A thorough analysis of all surviving membership lists, along with a scouring of newspapers for names of members of those movements where membership lists did not survive, reveals that a narrower range of people were drawn to the movements. The average member was white, male, aged in his forties, and more likely than not a professional, semi-professional, or businessperson—what I have termed the professional and business fraction of capital. He was also most likely Protestant (although the source material on this is more anecdotal than quantitative) and had a one in three chance of having served during the Great War.

Leadership

Rather unsurprisingly, there were variances between the movements' leaders and frontline members. Leaders—or those who helped found the movement and/or actively participated by joining committees and attending conventions—were drawn predominantly from the professional and business fraction, making up between 60 and 75.5 per cent of each leadership sample. The All for Australia League also had a significant minority of manufacturers (11.3 per cent), which explains why it was so reluctant to commit to tariff reform, unlike the other citizens' movements.[101] In addition, most of the leaders were over 40 years

99 Campbell, The New Zealand Legion in Otago, 23–31; Elizabeth Ward, The New Zealand Legion in Manawatu–Wanganui, 1933–1935 (BA Hons diss., Massey University, Palmerston North, NZ, 2011), 11–15, 17.
100 Pugh, The New Zealand Legion and conservative protest in the Great Depression, 98.
101 After much obfuscation, the All for Australia League ultimately decided to leave the tariff in the hands of its proposed Economic Advisory Board, which would 'scientifically' determine 'the limits of tariff incidence and the industrial directions in which it should be imposed'. See Policy as Adopted by Convention of the League, 18; All for Australia League, 11.

of age, with the average age for each movement ranging between 44.9 and 45.7 years. The percentage of eligible leaders who served in the Great War was 46 per cent in New Zealand and varied between 25.7 and 32.5 per cent for the Australian movement, which may have been because conscription was introduced in the former but not the latter. More than half of those leaders who served in the military did so at a commissioned or non-commissioned officer level.

Table 4.1 Employment statistics (leadership): All for Australia League

Occupation	No. of members	Percentage
Primary production		
Farmers	2	**2.8 (3)**
Pastoralists	1	
Manufacturing	12	**11.3 (12)**
Professional, business, and commercial		
Professionals	35	**72.7 (77)**
Semi-professionals	9	
Business	19	
Commercial	14	
Working class		
Skilled workers	9	**10.4 (11)**
Unskilled workers and unemployed	2	
Other	3	**2.8 (3)**
Total number for whom occupations were identified	**106**	

Table 4.2 Employment statistics (leadership): Citizens' League of South Australia

Occupation	No. of members	Percentage
Primary production		
Farmers	8	**13.7 (10)**
Pastoralists	2	
Manufacturing	1	**1.4 (1)**
Professional, business, and commercial		
Professionals	20	**65.7 (48)**
Semi-professionals	11	
Business	11	
Commercial	6	

Occupation	No. of members	Percentage
Working class		
Skilled workers	12	**19.2 (14)**
Unskilled workers and unemployed	2	
Other	0	
Total number for whom occupations were identified	**73**	

Table 4.3 Employment statistics (leadership): Australian Citizens' League

Occupation	No. of members	Percentage
Primary production		
Farmers	38	**25.4 (56)**
Pastoralists	18	
Manufacturing	1	**0.5 (1)**
Professional, business, and commercial		
Professionals	54	**60 (132)**
Semi-professionals	25	
Business	26	
Commercial	27	
Working class		
Skilled workers	19	**14.1 (31)**
Unskilled workers and unemployed	12	
Other	0	
Total number for whom occupations were identified	**220**	

Table 4.4 Employment statistics (leadership): New Zealand Legion

Occupation	No. of members	Percentage
Primary production		
Farmers	12	**14.5 (23)**
Pastoralists	11	
Manufacturing	1	**0.6 (1)**
Professional, business, and commercial		
Professionals	68	**75.5 (120)**
Semi-professionals	14	
Business	21	
Commercial	17	

Occupation	No. of members	Percentage
Working class		
Skilled workers	7	**8.8 (14)**
Unskilled workers and unemployed	7	
Other	1	**0.6 (1)**
Total number for whom occupations were identified	**159**	

Frontline members

Only two partial lists of frontline members have survived: the Hawke's Bay division of the New Zealand Legion, and the North Adelaide branch of the Citizens' League of South Australia. Therefore, any conclusions that are drawn from these data may not necessarily be reflective of the broader movements, or indeed of the two other movements for which no frontline membership lists exist. Nevertheless, they indicate that, in those regions at least, the class spread of frontline members was slightly broader than that of their leaders. More than three-quarters of the North Adelaide branch of the Citizens' League of South Australia were professionals and businesspeople, although these figures cannot be taken as representative of the movement as a whole given that North Adelaide was a wholly urban branch. In contrast, the professional and business fraction only constituted 42.6 per cent of the Hawke's Bay division of the New Zealand Legion, while 34.4 per cent of the sample were primary producers. Given the predominantly rural nature of the Hawke's Bay division, this is not unusual; a previous study of legion leadership in the Manawatu–Wanganui found that primary producers constituted a significant fraction in this area as well.[102] However, the fact that almost one in four Hawke's Bay members was working class is surprising—especially since just over half of that number were unskilled workers. Frontline members in Hawke's Bay were slightly younger than the leaders at the average age of 42.9, although unlike the leadership, there was a significant number of members under 35—particularly in the 25–29 bracket. Some 38.4 per cent of eligible frontline legionnaires had served in the Great War—fewer

---

102 Ward, *The New Zealand Legion in Manawatu–Wanganui*, 22.

than the 46 per cent of leaders—however, almost 60 per cent did not progress beyond the rank of private or equivalent. Seven had served in the Boer War, and two members had fought in both wars.

Table 4.5 Employment statistics (frontline membership): Citizens' League of South Australia

Occupation	No. of members	Percentage
Primary production		
Farmers	0	0
Pastoralists	0	
Manufacturing	0	0
Professional, business, and commercial		
Professionals	25	**76.5 (124)**
Semi-professionals	32	
Business	45	
Commercial	22	
Working class		
Skilled workers	14	**14.8 (24)**
Unskilled workers/unemployed	10	
Other	14	8.7 (14)
Total number for whom occupations were identified	162	

Table 4.6 Employment statistics (frontline membership): New Zealand Legion

Occupation	No. of members	Percentage
Primary production		
Farmers	189	**34.4 (257)**
Pastoralists	68	
Manufacturing	4	**0.5 (4)**
Professional, business, and commercial		
Professionals	127	**42.6 (319)**
Semi-professionals	78	
Business	51	
Commercial	63	

Occupation	No. of members	Percentage
Working class		
Skilled workers	82	**22.5 (168)**
Unskilled workers/unemployed	86	
Other	**0**	**0**
Total number for whom occupations were identified	**748**	

It is difficult to determine how many frontline members were actively involved in the movements. In his study of the New Zealand Legion, Michael Pugh claimed that signing a membership form and paying the subscription were the extent of participation for a majority of individuals, and that only one-quarter of the total membership actively participated in the legion.[103] The experience in New South Wales was similar: league members in the Sydney suburb of Fairfield, for example, did not attend any meetings, while another member complained that he had not received any communication after joining the movement.[104] In contrast, branches of the Citizens' League of South Australia appear to have been quite active throughout 1931, and reports of decline did not begin to appear until the beginning of 1932.[105] The fact that the All for Australia League badge adorned so many lapels in Sydney further attests to a level of pride among members, even if this did not equate to regular attendance at meetings.[106] Any attempt to estimate participation without further evidence is problematic and ultimately unnecessary for the purposes of gauging the conservative discontent underlying the citizens' movements. After all, even the act of signing a membership card required some form of commitment.

103 Pugh, The New Zealand Legion and conservative protest in the Great Depression, 97.
104 Letter from R.T. Gillies to Mutch, 13 July 1931, item 70, Mutch Papers, SLNSW; *Sydney Morning Herald*, 18 July 1931, 5.
105 Report of Executive Committee presented to the Second Annual Convention of Branch Delegates, 12 September 1932, box 1, item 9; Country Organisers' Report, 23 July 1932, box 13, item 10; Address to the Executive Committee, 19 December 1933, box 3, item 25A, CLSA Papers, NLA. At least one member of the Citizens' League resigned in 1931 due to a lack of communication from his leaders, although he was also motivated by his belief that it had become a 'class conscious' movement. See Letter from R.B. Petch to Bagot, 2 February 1931, box 12, item 5, CLSA Papers, NLA.
106 *The Argus*, [Melbourne], 16 March 1931, 8.

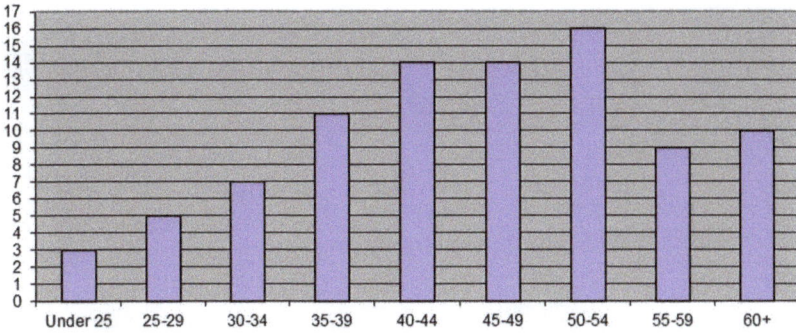

Figure 4.4 Age statistics (leadership): All for Australia League

Note: Average age, 45.7.

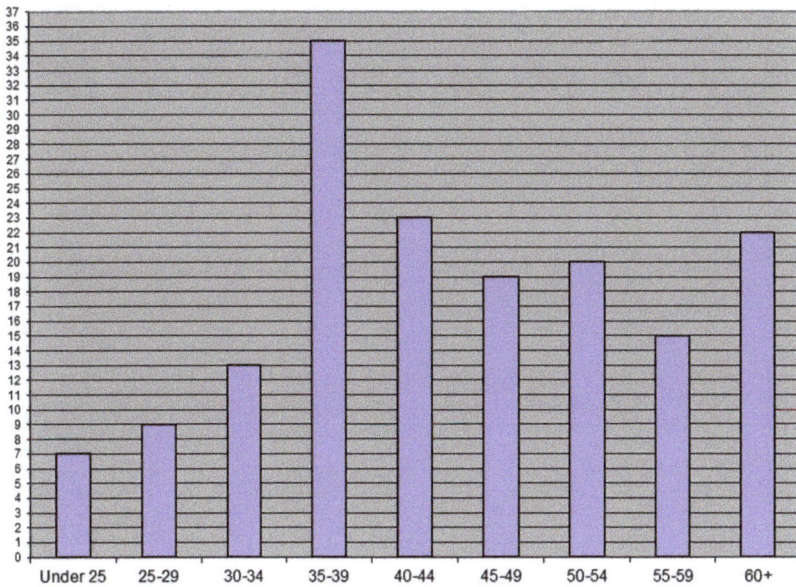

Figure 4.5 Age statistics (leadership): Australian Citizens' League

Note: Average age, 44.9.

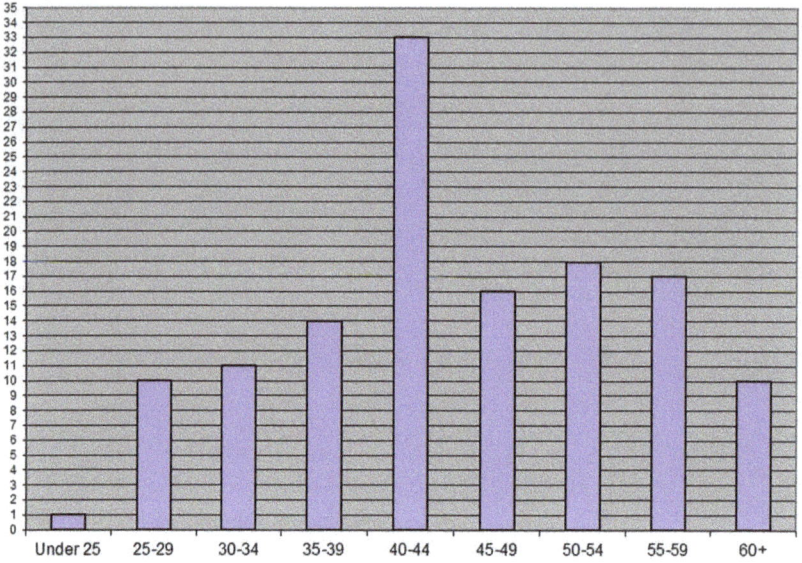

Figure 4.6 Age statistics (leadership): New Zealand Legion
Note: Average age, 45.1.

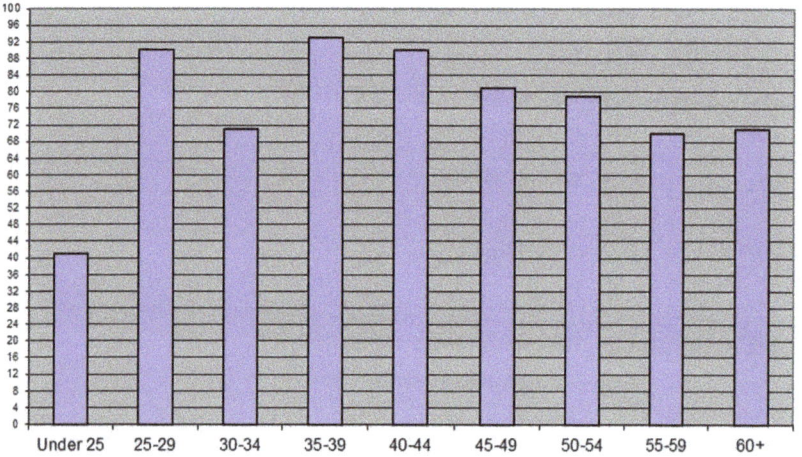

Figure 4.7 Age statistics (frontline membership): New Zealand Legion
Note: Average age, 42.9.

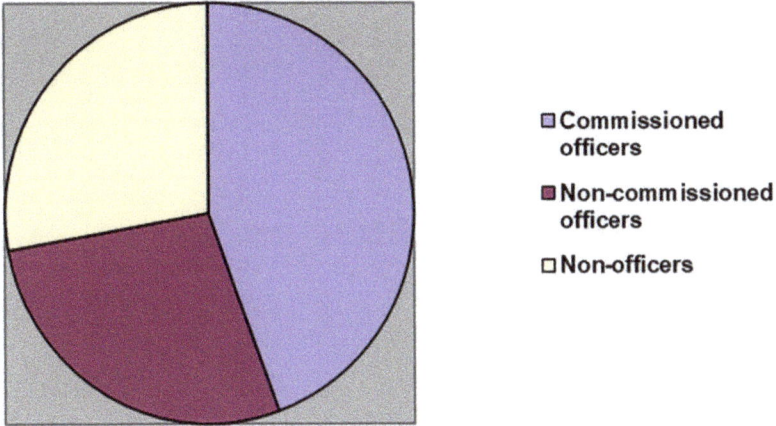

- ▣ Commissioned officers
- ▣ Non-commissioned officers
- ☐ Non-officers

Figure 4.8 Military statistics (leadership): All for Australia League

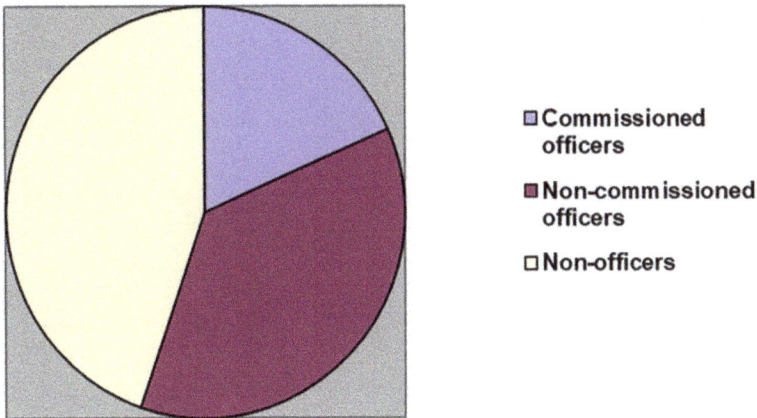

- ▣ Commissioned officers
- ▣ Non-commissioned officers
- ☐ Non-officers

Figure 4.9 Military statistics (leadership): Australian Citizens' League

Note: If the individual was aged 18–47 in 1918, they will be treated as having been eligible to serve in the Australian military: 'In 1914 recruits had to be 18–35 years with a height of 167.6 centimetres and a chest measurement of 86.3 centimetres. In June 1915 the age and height standards were changed to 18–45 years and 157.5 centimetres. The minimum height was lowered again, to 152.4 centimetres, in April 1917. The standard of medical fitness required from recruits was also lowered.' ('Australian Recruitment Statistics for World War I', National Archives of Australia, available from: www.naa.gov.au/learn/learning-resources/learning-resource-themes/ war/world-war-i/australian-recruitment-statistics-world-war-i).

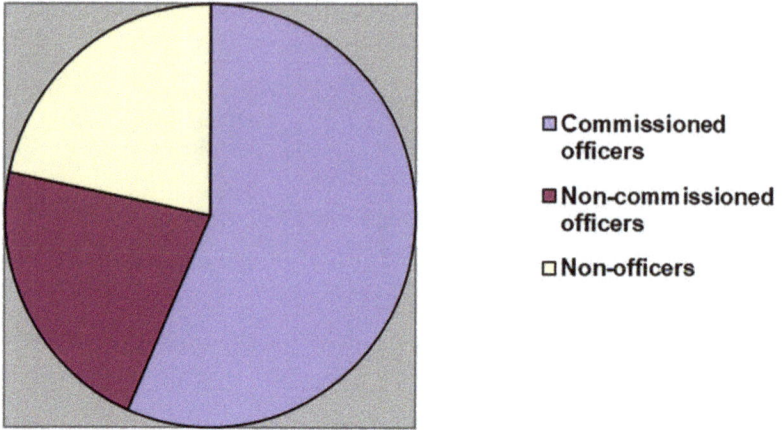

Figure 4.10 Military statistics (leadership): New Zealand Legion

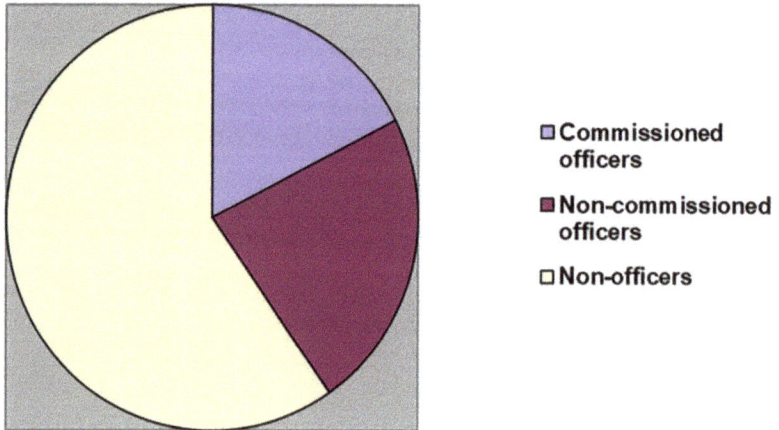

Figure 4.11 Military statistics (frontline membership): New Zealand Legion

Note: If the individual was aged 20–47 in 1918, they will be treated as having been eligible to serve in the New Zealand military, based on the conscription range of 20–45 years that was introduced in 1916. (James Belich, *Paradise Reforged* (Auckland: Penguin Press, 2001): 99.)

Similarities with other conservative mass movements

The citizens' movements appealed to the same middle-class audience as the other conservative mass movements that arose during the Depression, particularly the paramilitary New Guard. Andrew Moore, the leading scholar on paramilitary movements in inter-war Australia, concluded that the New Guard consisted predominantly of 'small capitalists, those reliant on bank credit and subject to the fierce competition of larger and more established business firms', but there was also a 'significant minority' of working-class members.[107] Working-class support for the New Guard's thoroughly anti-working-class platform might seem contradictory, and several scholars concluded that the proletariat must therefore have been sparsely represented in the movement.[108] Yet one unpublished study of the Five Dock locality of the New Guard—one of the few localities for which the membership list has survived—demonstrated that 18 per cent of members were from the working class.[109] Moore wisely advised against extrapolating this figure across the entire movement, given that Five Dock was a predominantly working-class suburb and the New Guard's locality leader was 'unusually attentive to trade union issues'.[110] Nevertheless, the New Guard enjoyed the support of several right-wing trade unions, such as the Railway Service Association, and it managed to make inroads into communities with a strong working-class Returned and Services League presence.[111] This minor working-class presence mirrors what the data suggest about the citizens' movements. The percentage of ex-servicemen in the New Guard was similar to that in the citizens' movements.[112]

---

107 Andrew Moore, 'Workers and the New Guard: Proletarian Fascism in New South Wales, 1931–35', in *Transforming Labour: Work, Workers, Struggle and Change: Proceedings of the 8th National Labour History Conference*, eds B. Bowden and J. Kellett (Brisbane: Brisbane Labour History Association, 2003), 244.

108 Humphrey McQueen, 'The Social Character of the New Guard', *Arena* 40 (1975): 67–86, at pp. 85–86; William Tully, The New Guard of New South Wales, 1931–1932 (BA Hons diss., The Australian National University, Canberra, 1974), 1, 6; Phyllis Mitchell, 'Australian Patriots: A Study of the New Guard', *Australian Economic Historical Review* 9(2) (1969): 156–78, at p. 164.

109 J. O'Mara, Guarding Five Dock: A study of the Five Dock locality of the New Guard, 1931–1935 (BA Hons diss., University of Western Sydney, 1997), 50–52.

110 Andrew Moore, 'The New Guard and the Labour Movement, 1931–1935', *Labour History* 89 (2005): 55–72, at p. 56.

111 ibid., 57; Moore, 'Workers and the New Guard', 242.

112 Amos, *The New Guard Movement*, 7–9; Mitchell, 'Australian Patriots', 163–64; Tully, The New Guard of New South Wales, 3–8; McQueen, 'The Social Character of the New Guard', 68–69.

Motivations for joining the citizens' movements

The dominant position of professionals and businesspeople at a leadership and frontline level suggests the citizens' movements were an important outlet for the frustrations of this fraction of capital. Unlike farmers and manufacturers, who could seek some form of protection from the government for their goods—in the form of a tariff or guaranteed price—the services of the professional and business fraction were relatively intangible. Since government assistance was not an option, the best ideological defence for their trades lay in lower taxes and minimal government interference. The tropes of individualism thus assumed a particular importance for them, unlike manufacturers and farmers, who were able to fall back on the state for assistance. This further reinforces the symbiotic relationship between the citizens' movements and their members. The movements provided a channel for conservative discontent, yet their immense popularity was predicated on their ability to recognise the nature of the discontent expressed by the professional and business fraction and respond using the same individualist language in which their grievances were being expressed.

There are limitations to a purely material analysis of motivation. For example, conservatives and capitalists of all stripes could hardly be considered marginalised or unrepresented; there was a swathe of conservative party options available to them at the time. Some conservatives were likely motivated by the deeply ingrained notion of good citizenship, which extolled individuals to participate in voluntary endeavours to give back to the community. This was almost certainly a factor for the leaders of the citizens' movements, whose middle and upper-class upbringing had afforded them significant opportunities in education, business, politics, and the military. By the time the Great Depression hit, they were well established within their business or professional fields and possessed sufficient means to be able to devote significant time and resources to establishing and running large-scale voluntary endeavours such as the citizens' movements. For example, the Provisional Committee of the Australian Citizens' League included the founders and managers of Nicholas Aspro Pty Ltd and retail chain G.J. Coles & Co., and the State Council of the All for Australia League included the managing directors of James Sandy & Co. Ltd and General Industries Ltd. A significant number of leaders were involved in other voluntary endeavours, including community service organisations and unemployment relief committees. Several were serving or had previously served as mayors, councillors, and aldermen, and others had presided on government commissions.[113]

Conservative notions of 'good citizenship' are less likely to have been a primary motivating factor for frontline members, particularly those from the working class, who possessed far less in the way of disposable time and income for such endeavours. Unfortunately, the views of these members were less often preserved in the historical record. They were not the ones giving speeches or writing pamphlets; nor were they, in their later years, as likely to write memoirs. Nevertheless, a small number of firsthand accounts of what drew individuals to join the citizens' movements have survived. These number little more than a dozen and are primarily the recollections of former members of the New Zealand Legion, which were recorded by Tony Simpson in the 1970s when writing his oral history of the Depression in New Zealand, *The Sugarbag Years*. Nevertheless, some tentative themes emerge from these accounts.

The desire to 'do something'

Many New Zealand Legion members joined out of a pressing desire for urgent action. Shortly after launching the movement's journal, *National Opinion*, the editor wrote that he had received many letters expressing disappointment that it 'did not reflect a bolder note of immediate action—something that would stir and perhaps startle the public'.[114] One letter written under the moniker 'Do Something' noted that the author had 'joined the Legion at its birth [in the] hopes that [it] might do some good', but was bitterly disappointed in its apparent inactivity.[115] L.E. Earle, who wrote several articles for the journal, recalled that he had joined 'because I was out of work and because I thought that things were in an awful mess and here seemed to be someone who was doing something'.[116] Legionnaire W. Bright, who was also president of the local Rotary Club and Unemployment Relief Committee, wrote that he was 'attracted to the Legion ... by the desperate state of the country with its

---

113 Pugh, The New Zealand Legion and conservative protest in the Great Depression, 102, 104; Campbell, The New Zealand Legion in Otago, 41–42; Ward, The New Zealand Legion in Manawatu–Wanganui, 25–26; Matthews, 'The All for Australia League', 138.

114 *National Opinion* [Wellington] 1(2) (24 August 1933): 2.

115 ibid., 2(16) (29 March 1934): 12; 2(23) (5 July 1934): 13.

116 Letter from L.E. Earle, 27 August 1972, Simpson Papers, ATL.

ever increasing numbers of unemployed'.[117] Doing 'something' did not need to be well defined, as one member recalled: 'The man in the street felt doubtful—he could easily be sold a pup with so little support.'[118] This demonstrates the growing sense of desperation and disenchantment with which these members greeted the worsening conditions of the Depression. The citizens' movements appeared to offer a simple yet far-reaching solution—a psychological salve, however nebulous, which swept away doubts with high ideals and platitudes that promised a radical turnaround of the nation's woes.

The desire for action led many members to view the citizens' movements with an almost spiritual reverence. Sir Douglas Robb, who would later have a distinguished career as a surgeon and a reformer of the medical profession, waxed lyrical about the way he and his professional colleagues viewed the birth of the legion:

> I was very unaware of politics—its motives, mechanics etc. We all knew there were parties in Wgn [Wellington], but it was before a serious Labour Party came up ... But we were interested in the depression & the effect on our new-born practices, and on our friends, particularly farmers. There were also street riots to be feared. The Gov[ernmen]t. of the day seemed as confused as we were and we heard the self-appointed saviours professing new economic doctrines, particularly Social Credit & Major Douglas ... When Dr Campbell Begg, a urologist in Wellington—in good professional status—started to raise his voice ... we sniffed a saviour.[119]

A letter published in the *Sydney Morning Herald* in 1931 by an All for Australia League member used similar language:

> Like many other people in those misguided times, I hoped for some relief from Mr. Lang's oppression and looked upon this league as the saviour. I was prepared to help the league in every possible way, and was enthusiastic enough to wear the badge for a time.[120]

---

117 Letter from W. Bright, 26 August 1972, Simpson Papers, ATL.
118 Letter from N. Tilley, 26 August 1972, Simpson Papers, ATL.
119 Letter from Sir Douglas Robb, 29 September 1972, Simpson Papers, ATL.
120 *Sydney Morning Herald*, 18 July 1931, 5.

Given the author wrote this letter out of frustration with the lack of communication he had received after joining, his reverence is likely to have been genuine. The fact that both writers used the word 'saviour' suggests the connection these members felt to the citizens' movements was emotional as well as material. The movements inspired faith that the growing economic turmoil could be addressed and that society could be transformed so that such crises would never occur again. This emotional investment was also driven by a sense of personal threat: while the upper class may have possessed the means to insulate themselves from the Depression, the middle class had no such luxury.

Dislike for party politics

Unsurprisingly, a dislike for party politics was also a strong motivating factor. As Chapter Two argued, anti-partyism was a central component of the conservative radicalisation that occurred during the Depression. According to former legionnaire J.D. Hall:

> I think the main thing which attracted us (certainly the under 30s) was the ideal that it would be possible to elect a governing body, which would recognise no party ties, obey no government whips but vote solely as our consciences dictated. This seems incredible nowadays and probably does to you now—but, I can assure you that to a 30 year old in the thirties, it actually appeared possible.[121]

Such a hope would certainly have seemed possible in the 1930s, given that party politics was a relatively new phenomenon and the nineteenth-century ideal of the independent colonial statesman was within living memory. For many who had witnessed the growth of extra-parliamentary machines and the solidification of the two-party system—in particular, those who recalled the supposed unity of wartime—it was an unwelcome intrusion on the once dignified field of politics. As R.F. Gambrill, author of an unofficial history of the Russell family, put it:

> It was not my experience of the depression which attracted me to the Legion. As a Returned Service Man from World War I, after 4 ½ years of active Service, I was (in 1919) concerned with the state of party politics. No party then seemed to have any policy other than to become the Government … We suffered 'depression'

---

121 Letter from J.D. Hall, 24 August 1972, Simpson Papers, ATL.

in 1920 and other years prior to 1933, but these were more or less local ones. Enough, however, to convince me of the 'rottenness' of party politics.[122]

Given that Hall and Gambrill wrote their recollections in the 1970s, when such rampant anti-partyism was imbued with fascist connotations, it is likely they were telling the truth.

Traditional conservative values

Conservative values played a part in attracting members as well. H.L. Paterson, chairman of the Otago division of the New Zealand Legion, 'understood that the legion was to combat the growing multiplicity of local bodies of all types and the increasing burden of taxation created by these local bodies'.[123] The rationalisation of government also appealed to Wanganui division chairman W.R. Brown, who drew parallels between the legion and the Kyabram Reform Movement that had secured a reduction in the number of members of the Victorian Parliament 30 years earlier:

> [I]nfluence could be attained by securing a predominating portion of voting power, and this the Legion felt hopeful of securing. A similar movement was started in Victoria 30 years ago, and at the following elections the movement was influential in securing the return of 64 members out of 93. The New Zealand Legion aspired to succeed in the same way, so as to be instrumental in effecting a big improvement on the present unsatisfactory state of affairs.[124]

Others joined the legion simply because of their positive impressions of its leaders. One member noted that 'the main advocate in H.B. [Hawke's Bay] was our one-time Div. Com., Sir Andrew Russell, a man for whom I had a great respect'. This led him to assume that Begg must also be 'of Andy Russell's type, one who would automatically receive respect & confidence'.[125]

122 Letter from R.F. Gambrill, 24 August 1972, Simpson Papers, ATL.
123 Letter from H.L. Paterson, 28 August 1972, Simpson Papers, ATL.
124 *Taihape Times*, 2 June 1933, 3.
125 Letter from N. Tilley, 26 August 1972, Simpson Papers, ATL.

Women and the citizens' movements

If the citizens' movements are an understudied aspect of Australasian history, the role of women in the movements is woefully underappreciated. The only work that has included a gender analysis is an unpublished thesis on the New Zealand Legion in the Manawatu–Wanganui, which concluded that 'women were more involved … than previously assumed'.[126] The quantitative data discussed above demonstrate that women were indeed more involved in the citizens' movements than previously assumed, albeit much more so at a frontline than a leadership level. Women only made up between 5.2 and 6.4 per cent of the leadership samples for the four citizens' movements, and only in the case of the Australian Citizens' League had women participated in the founding of a movement.[127] Conversely, women made up 20.3 per cent of the membership of the Hawke's Bay division of the New Zealand Legion. Two of these women were particularly active: Lady Russell, the wife of Sir Andrew Russell, and Dorothy de Castro, who had previously worked for the Conservative and Unionist Party in Britain.[128] Women also made up a startling 54.4 per cent of the frontline membership of the North Adelaide branch of the Citizens' League of South Australia, which may have reflected the ongoing cooperation between the Citizens' League and the South Australian branch of the Women's Non-Party Association. Female leaders tended to be married, while there were roughly equal numbers of married and unmarried women in the frontline membership. Many women appear to have joined alongside their husbands or other family members as part of a wider family unit.

A qualitative analysis provides more information on the role of women in the citizens' movements. Their motivations for joining and participating in the movements may have been influenced by the traditions of 'conservative feminism' and 'female imperialism' discussed in Chapter One. As New Zealand Legion member Edith Willoughby saw it, the citizens' movements were a continuation of this tradition—in particular, of the women's patriotic societies that arose during the Great War:

---

126 Ward, The New Zealand Legion in Manawatu–Wanganui, 21.
127 The female participants on the Australian Citizens' League's provisional committee were L.M. Skene, A.F. Moss, and W. Thomas (who was also a member of the Melbourne Housewives' Association).
128 *National Opinion* [Wellington] 2(24) (19 July 1934): 14.

> Wake up, women citizens! You answered the call for help to the nation in August, 1914. Now, once again, use your powers and do your bit in this August, 1933, to help alleviate the chaos that exists … Let us think more of our sisters' need, and practise daily doing unto others as we would be done by. You can be a magnificent support and help to your people if the right spirit prevails in your doings. Get together! Discuss serious questions of national import. Form your committees and work wholly and solely for the salvation of this beautiful country![129]

The citizens' movements were a valuable arena for women to express themselves politically. By the time the citizens' movements arose in the 1930s, a younger generation of post-suffrage women were beginning to seek avenues for political participation in a society in which female representation in parliament was still very much the exception rather than the norm. The citizens' movements provided one such environment. Not only did they encourage their members to learn about current affairs, but they also provided opportunities to gain leadership and public speaking experience. While this still occurred within the confines of a conservative world view that remained uncomfortable with female political power, it nevertheless provided a level of exposure to matters of national importance that the ballot box alone did not. This suggests the citizens' movements fulfilled a function similar to women's non-party organisations and branches of conservative political organisations such as farmers' unions.[130]

The All for Australia League was the only citizens' movement that took deliberate measures to encourage female representation at all levels of the organisation. Women were entitled to create their own women's divisions and subdivisions to parallel the existing structure of the movement. In addition, five seats were reserved for women on the State Council. Along with this parallel organisation, women were still entitled to join standard subdivisions and run for office.[131] Feminist organisations such as the National Council of Women and the United Associations of Women initially treated the All for Australia League with suspicion, but by July, several of their members, including Mildred Muscio, had joined the State Council.[132] Despite this, women represented only 5.2 per cent

---

129 ibid., 1(3) (7 September 1933): 14.
130 See Fitzherbert, *Liberal Women*; Henderson, *Enid Lyons*; Heather Gunn, '"For the Man on the Land": Issues of Gender and Identity in the Formation of the Victorian Farmers' Union Women's Section, 1918–1922', *Journal of Australian Studies* 18(42) (1994): 32–42.
131 *All for Australia League: Draft Constitution*, 14–15.
132 Robinson, 'The All for Australia League in New South Wales', 48–49.

of the leadership sample of the league—the lowest of the four citizens' movements—and most of these women held the reserved seats on the State Council. This suggests that, despite its progressive intentions, the All for Australia League was still hampered by the cultural barriers against female leadership in the Anglo world.

Populist ideology and populist culture were two ingredients that allowed the four citizens' movements to build mass memberships and rise to national prominence in such a short time. From the start, the movements staked their legitimacy on their ability to harness a large body of popular opinion. This was accomplished through a populist culture of mass conservative mobilisation that was based on certain key strategies: public ceremonies to demonstrate mass appeal, recruitment strategies aimed at rapidly building a large membership, organisational structures that encouraged democratic participation and leadership, culturally resonant symbols, and a variety of mass media such as radio and print culture. Yet despite their claims to represent a broad, cross-class national consensus, the citizens' movements largely represented the frustrations of professionals, semi-professionals, and businesspeople. They were drawn to the citizens' movements for various reasons, including a commitment to conservative values and traditions, a distaste for party politics, and a simple desire to 'do something'. So long as the citizens' movements could avoid exposing those differing—and often competing—motivations, their rise would continue largely unabated. But this could not last forever. The demands of real-world politics, and their members' desire for substance as well as spirit, would expose the inherent contradictions within the movements. The next two chapters explore how these contradictions played out in Australia and New Zealand, respectively. It was a process that would ultimately lead to the movements' demise.

5

Flirting with party politics: The Australian citizens' movements and the United Australia Party

By the beginning of 1931, the Australian Labor Party held power at a federal level as well as in every state except Queensland and Western Australia. In contrast, the Nationalist Party and its supporters were in disarray and had only just begun to rebuild their political brand. Although their majority in the federal Senate allowed them to block many of the government's less orthodox proposals, this was not enough to force the government to adopt a deflationary approach or prevent Lang from repudiating Australia's debt obligations to British bondholders. The Nationalists and their Country Party allies needed to oust Labor at the next federal election to accomplish that. However, at a time when the need for conservative political unity was greater than ever, a powerful backlash of populist conservatism had arisen. This anti-partyism lay the blame for the Depression at the feet of political parties of all persuasions, including the Nationalists, and questioned whether they even had a future. The citizens' movements, which sat at the apex of this backlash, were willing to bypass existing political parties altogether by supporting independent candidates. This threatened to undercut the Nationalists' electoral base by splitting the conservative vote and handing the Labor Party another term at the nation's helm.

The divide between the Nationalists and the citizens' movements was deeply concerning to many conservatives. This was no mere political contest to them; it was a choice between a sane, respectable government that upheld traditional conservative values and a radical rabble that was willing to destroy the currency and repudiate the nation's debts. The very soul of the nation was at stake. Conservatives needed someone who could bridge the gap between the Nationalists and the mass of frustrated people who had thrown their weight behind the citizens' movements. They needed someone palatable to both sides who could unite the forces of conservatism under one platform with a single set of mutually agreed candidates. In sum, conservatives yearned for a leader—one who could navigate the political machinery in Canberra while bringing the citizens' movements back into the fold. Ironically, the citizens' movements were also looking for a leader. The only question, as the citizens' movements themselves came to ask, was 'who is the man?'.[1] The answer was a relative newcomer to federal politics—a man on the right of the Labor Party Cabinet who was often caricatured as a sleepy koala.

The defection of Joseph Lyons

Winning the support of the opposition

When Joseph Lyons resigned from the Labor Cabinet in January 1931 to protest his colleagues' approach to the Depression, a contemporary observer might have thought his days in politics were numbered. As head of a small group of Labor dissidents, the best he might hope for was to win the Labor caucus to his side in the hope that it might sway Cabinet. But Lyons had also spent the second half of 1930 establishing his credentials as a fiscal conservative. As Chapter Two discussed, he had adhered to the conditions of the deflationary Melbourne Agreement reached by state premiers in August. He had also successfully conducted a £28 million loan conversion campaign in the closing months of 1930—despite caucus opposition—thus avoiding the spectre of repudiation that so terrified conservatives. His resignation over Prime Minister Scullin's reappointment of Theodore as treasurer cemented his image among conservatives as an honest man who was willing to defy the directions of his party on matters

---

1   Bagot, 'A Dictator Needed', submitted to the Editor of 'The Advertiser', 5 September 1930, box 3, item 25D, CLSA Papers, NLA.

of principle. As the editors of the *Sydney Morning Herald* put it: 'In these days of political opportunism, it is refreshing to know that there are still a few public leaders who prefer honour to power.'[2]

Lyons was in the perfect position to reinvent his political career—and conservatives were quick to spot the opportunity. Chapter Two noted that a small clique of Melbourne politicians and professionals informally known as 'the Group of Six' had worked with Lyons during the loan conversion campaign. Members of this group were closely associated with the Citizens' Committee—the precursor to the Australian Citizens' League—as well as the chief conservative political fundraising organisation known as the National Union. By the beginning of 1931, the Group of Six came to view Lyons as a potential leader who could unite the various anti-Scullin forces inside and outside parliament. In early February, they encouraged Lyons to cross to the opposition benches and pledged their support to uniting the forces of conservatism behind him. After much soul-searching and a final failed attempt to defeat Theodore's economic proposals in caucus, Lyons and his small group of followers issued a joint vote of censure against the government with the Nationalist Party on 13 March.[3] While the vote failed to achieve a majority, it cemented Lyons' image among conservatives as a principled man who was willing to place the good of the nation above party interests and his own personal ambitions. It also signalled Lyons' final break from the Labor Party; he pledged to form a new centrist party with his small group of followers, which received the tentative support of the opposition parties.

Lyons' supporters in the Group of Six and the National Union were keen for him to assume the leadership of the opposition. Since the end of 1929, the Nationalists had been led by Sir John Latham, a former judge and attorney-general who, while a skilled and intelligent politician, lacked Lyons' popular appeal and accessible speaking style. Faced with the concerted pressure of the Group of Six and the National Union, Latham ultimately agreed in April 1931 to step aside as leader of the opposition and recommend Lyons as his successor. Meanwhile, Lyons and his groups of centrists strengthened their relationship with the Nationalist and Country parties by agreeing on a set of seven common policy points. The wording of these points was ambiguous at best—a mere bandaid over the wounds that divided urban professionals and businesspeople, manufacturers, and

---

2   *Sydney Morning Herald*, 31 January 1931, 12.
3   Hart, 'Lyons', 43–45; Lonie, 'From Liberal to Liberal', 65; Martin, *Robert Menzies*, 86.

farmers—but it signalled Lyons' intention to act as a force of unity rather than division. It promised balanced budgets and the encouragement of 'productive enterprise', while also committing to assist primary producers with 'real money' and ensuring that tariff policy was 'economically sound'. It also promised a 'fair deal' for employers and employees.[4] In short, there were words in there that everyone could support.

The citizens' movements' view of mainstream conservative parties

While Lyons had secured the support of mainstream conservative parties, this was only half the battle. In March 1931, the citizens' movements were on a triumphant upward climb. They had already recruited more than 100,000 members between them—a number that would nearly triple in the coming months. To secure unopposed the leadership of a united conservative opposition, Lyons needed to gain their support as well. But how? Despite the occasionally anti-democratic and proto-corporatist nature of the citizens' movements' economic policies, they shared the same traditional conservative values as the mainstream conservative parties. But anti-partyism complicated this ideological congruence. It was an ideological line in the sand that the movements had drawn, a foundation on which they defined what made them different from 'sectional' party machines. If Lyons became the leader of the opposition, he risked losing much of the non-party credentials he had accrued by resigning from the Labor Party in protest.

The Nationalist (or National) Party, which was the leading conservative political force at the federal level in 1931, was an organisational chimera. Rather than comprising a series of united and hierarchical party divisions, the Nationalist Party was a loose coalition of different state-based conservative organisations, including the National Federation of Victoria, the Nationalist Association of New South Wales, and the Liberal Federation of South Australia. Federal policy was developed through the Australian National Federation, comprising six delegates from each state, although only five interstate conferences were ever convened.[5] It was at the state level where the conservative parties' extra-parliamentary support apparatus was

---

4   The Seven Points: Policy announced by Mr. J.A. Lyons, 26 March 1931, item 101, box 89, series 49, folder 3, Latham Papers, NLA.

5   C.J. Lloyd, 'The Rise and Fall of the United Australia Party', in *Liberalism and the Australian Federation*, ed. J.R. Nethercote (Sydney: The Federation Press, 2001), 157.

most apparent. The state organisations preselected candidates for both state and federal elections and channelled their resources into promoting those candidates. In turn, those candidates agreed to support the policy platform set forth by the party. This made the Nationalist Party and its state arms the targets of fierce and uncompromising criticism from the citizens' movements, which drew no distinction between the Nationalists' methods and those of their Labor opponents. As the All for Australia League put it in one of their pamphlets:

> [T]he Reds dominate the Labour Movement and the Reactionaries have gained control of the Nationalist Party. Controlling these organisations as they do, the extreme sections have forced Parliament to legislate in the interests of their respective factions, regardless of the welfare of the community at large.[6]

This criticism of conservative parties was more than just a half-hearted attempt to win the support of centrist voters by colonising the middle ground. The citizens' movements were squarely set against the methods of party politics irrespective of where on the political spectrum they lay. They viewed party politics of all strands as equally anti-democratic.

The question the citizens' movements inevitably faced was: how could they secure the election of a government committed to the 'national interest' without resorting to party politics themselves? Though this question might seem simple, it raised a host of other questions that required much more specific answers than the high-level platitudes with which the citizens' movements were more comfortable. It was easy to speak of expanding 'until we are such a huge power that our wishes can no longer be ignored'.[7] But who would fulfil those wishes? Would it be acceptable if they were fulfilled by a party government, even if only in the short term? If this was acceptable, did this mean that anti-partyism was less important, and could therefore be temporarily cast aside, to achieve the more pressing goal of a change in government? And finally, if the goal of sound government was so important, was it acceptable for the citizens' movements to cooperate with other conservative organisations—even if only temporarily—to ensure it was realised? These were very important

---

6   The Financial Record of Party Politics, undated, item 68, Mutch Papers, SLNSW.
7   Address by Bagot at a Citizens' Public Meeting in Adelaide Town Hall, 14 October 1930, box 1, item 1, CLSA Papers, NLA.

questions in 1931 in Australia, where the three Labor bogeymen—Scullin, Theodore, and Lang—presented conservatives with a real and immediate threat to everything in which they believed.

As the first of the citizens' movements to be founded, the Citizens' League of South Australia was also the first to grapple with these questions. Its original strategy was to pressure the Scullin Government to enact its desired reforms, by creating an all-party coalition if necessary. However, when Scullin openly sided with Theodore's proposals to expand federal spending, the Citizens' League condemned this as a 'refusal to deal with matters affecting the interests of the citizens on national instead of party lines'.[8] Even if he had declined to support Theodore, Scullin was an ill-suited saviour for the Citizens' League. Apart from being a party politician, his approach to combating the Depression was perceived by the league as hesitant and contradictory. Latham and the Nationalists were a possible alternative, although this would still have required throwing their lot in with party politicians. Bagot even considered asking Sir John Monash to temporarily assume dictatorial control of the nation, as Chapter Three discussed.

What the Citizens' League needed was a leader who could bridge the gap between extra-parliamentary agitation and intra-parliamentary action—someone part of, but not beholden to, the nation's political machinery. Such a leader could, in the league's eyes, effect change from within parliament without being attached to any party, thus preserving the illusion of a national non-party government. Leaders of this calibre would not even be politicians at all, but *statesmen*—an important rhetorical differentiation in the eyes of the Citizens' League:

> Out of this new movement new leaders will be found. Men and women who are prepared to serve for the good of the country as a whole instead of for party. We demand statesmen instead of politicians, that all legislation be reviewed as to whether it is for the good of the people as a whole instead of for a section of them.[9]

This search for a leader who was external to the movement is unusual for populist organisations, which tend to place faith in their own leaders; indeed, the relationship between the leader and 'the people' is

---

8   Letter from Bagot to Scullin, 29 January 1931, box 13, item 11, CLSA Papers, NLA.
9   Address given by Mr. E.D.A. Bagot at public meeting held in the Exhibition Building, 11 December 1930, box 3, item 25D, CLSA Papers, NLA.

a key component of the strategic approach to populism discussed in the Introduction. The Citizens' League, however, was candid in its search for an external leader who could lead the citizenry in their struggle against the political elite.

As the Citizens' League rose to prominence in the closing months of 1930, so, too, did Lyons. His loan conversion campaign utilised many of the same populist tactics as the Citizens' League, including mass rallies, idealistic notions of national honour, and direct appeals to the people against the supposedly apathetic attitudes of those in power. By December, he was a nationally recognised figure and the Citizens' League's leaders were praising him for his 'courage and plain speaking'.[10] A league 'Monster Rally' was held on 11 December 1930 in part to encourage widespread support for Lyons' loan conversion, and a telegram from Lyons addressed to the league was read to the audience.[11] When Scullin failed to enforce deflationary measures during the premiers' conference in February 1931, the Citizens' League called on Lyons to overthrow the government and form a new ministry with the opposition. Bagot offered him the league's unqualified backing and circulated telegrams to MPs in New South Wales and South Australia urging them to support Lyons.[12]

Lyons' view of the citizens' movements

Lyons' stand against his Labor colleagues appeared to provide an avenue for the citizens' movements into parliamentary politics that did not overly stretch their non-party credentials. He was, in essence, a conservative politician without the burden of the conservative party machine. This made him the ideal candidate to lead a group of self-proclaimed non-party movements. However, two things needed to happen for this marriage to be realised: Lyons had to want the job, and all three citizens' movements needed to accept him.

---

10   *The Advertiser*, [Adelaide], 12 December 1930, 19.
11   Telegram from the Hon. J.A. Lyons re: Conversion Loan, 11 December 1930, box 1, item 1, CLSA Papers, NLA.
12   Telegram from Bagot to Scullin, 12 February 1931, box 13, item 11, Telegram from Bagot to Lyons, 20 February 1931, box 13, item 13, Minutes of Executive Committee Meeting, 23 February 1931, box 1, item 2, Letter from Bagot to Lyons, 7 March 1931, box 13, item 13, CLSA Papers, NLA; *The Advertiser*, [Adelaide], 12 February 1931, 7; *Advertiser and Register*, [Adelaide], 21 February 1931, 15.

Lyons' position in February 1931 was complicated by the division between the Nationalist Party (along with its various state arms) and the citizens' movements. If he chose to align himself too closely with political parties, he risked alienating the citizens' movements. Conversely, if he aligned himself too closely with non-party interests, he could lose his chance at leading a united opposition. Consequently, Lyons did not respond to the Citizens' League's overtures to overthrow the Scullin Government until 13 March, when he announced his intention to form 'a new party which would place the country before party'. His brief response said the following, in the usual clipped telegram prose: 'Letters received … speech today shows my position … Glad [to] do anything [to] help Australia.'[13]

Lyons' noncommittal response is an important indicator of his thinking at the time, both for what it says and for what it does not say. He knew how fragile and fractious the opposition parties were at that time, and he had no wish to damage his chances of becoming opposition leader by taking up the mantle of leader of the citizens' movements. However, he also realised the electoral boon such a large mass of supporters could bring to a united opposition. When cautioned privately by the editor of *The Argus* a few days later that he should 'check the growth of sectional mushroom movements that may be a menace to unity later', Lyons replied that he did not wish to alienate these movements.[14] He knew the force of public opinion that the citizens' movements could bring to bear and he did not want to reject the tentative support they had offered him.

Uniting the citizens' movements behind Lyons

Disagreement between the citizens' movements

While all the Australian citizens' movements generally supported Lyons, there was considerable disagreement between the Citizens' League of South Australia and the two eastern movements on what a united non-party front should look like. The Citizens' League viewed Lyons' desertion from Labor as a chance for all the forces opposed to Labor—including

---

13   *Advertiser and Register*, [Adelaide], 13 March 1931, 15; Telegram from Lyons to Bagot, 13 March 1931, box 13, item 13, CLSA Papers, NLA.
14   Hart, 'Lyons', 46.

mainstream conservative parties, the citizens' movements and other non-party organisations, and the forces of 'sane labour'—to unite behind him under one non-party banner. While each organisation would retain its own separate identity under this new united front, the Citizens' League believed the large membership of the citizens' movements would form its backbone. Bagot boasted that Lyons would inherit 'an Australia-wide organisation with an immediate membership of 200,000' should he choose to accept it.[15] The notion that such a political force could really be non-party in nature may seem farcical today; however, it must be remembered that in March 1931 Lyons was, for all intents and purposes, a free political agent. He had resigned from the Labor Party on principle, he had yet to succeed Latham as leader of the opposition, and he had only just announced his intention to form a new minority party. With the citizens' movements enjoying a spectacular rise and the Nationalists in disarray, it was easy for individuals like Bagot to imagine that a new political order free from party domination was being forged.

In contrast, the All for Australia League saw no place for the mainstream conservative parties in a united non-party movement. Instead, it argued that all true conservatives should disavow their existing allegiances, dissolve their separate parties and organisations, and unite under the banner of 'All for Australia'. A Citizens' League delegate to a meeting of the two eastern state leagues in March 1931 reported that the All for Australia League was unwilling to discuss a common policy and refused to support Lyons as federal leader.[16] The reason for their reluctance became clear when, at the first All for Australia League of New South Wales state convention on 28 March, delegates voted by 598 to 40 to launch a new political movement that would support its own candidates at state and federal elections. Delegates stressed that their members, who supposedly came from both sides of the political spectrum, were looking to the All for Australia League for leadership and action and would not countenance supporting either Labor or Nationalist candidates. Their object, one of the founding members explained bluntly, was 'to save Australia and not to save the National party'.[17] When confronted by Latham about the need for unity to defeat Scullin, All for Australia League President Alex J. Gibson replied that he was '[v]ery friendly' towards the federal opposition forces

15 *Mail*, [Adelaide], 21 March 1931, 1.
16 Minutes of Executive Committee Meeting, 23 March 1931, box 1, item 2, CLSA Papers, NLA.
17 *Sydney Morning Herald*, 30 March 1931, 12.

but not to the Nationalist Party in general. The solution to the 'federal problem', he explained, was for Lyons and the leaders of the Nationalist and Country parties to join the All for Australia League.[18]

These differing visions of a united non-party movement were partially influenced by lingering mistrust between the Citizens' League and its counterparts in the eastern states. As was discussed in Chapter Two, the Australian Citizens' League's upper-class leadership was wary of Bagot's middle-class origins and fiery rhetoric, which they considered a potential liability. The Australian Citizens' League found the leadership of the All for Australia League—which included several prominent businessmen and manufacturers—much less objectionable at first, which explains their decision to adopt the latter's name and objects in March 1931. The placatory excuse they offered the Citizens' League of South Australia for their name change was that 'the name "citizen" to the country dweller connoted too much of city interests'.[19]

A heated struggle occurred throughout March 1931 for control of the direction of the citizens' movements. Both eastern state leagues pressured the Citizens' League of South Australia to fall into line with them in a wider movement under the title of All for Australia. The South Australian Citizens' League refused to amalgamate 'on the ground[s] of dominance from New South Wales and Victoria', and Bagot called the Australian Citizens' League 'selfish' for affiliating with the All for Australia League.[20] In truth, the leaders of the Australian Citizens' League were far less enamoured with their alliance than they appeared. At the beginning of March, the All for Australia League was a dynamic and rapidly expanding force whose only tangible targets were the forces of inflation and repudiation. By the end of the month, however, its opposition to cooperation with the Nationalists on all fronts was becoming increasingly apparent. This placed the leadership of the Australian Citizens' League in an increasingly uncomfortable position given their work with Lyons on the loan conversion campaign. Indeed, while the All for Australia League was railing against the Nationalists, the Australian Citizens' League leaders who were associated with the National Union and the Group of Six were manoeuvring for Lyons to assume the leadership of the opposition.

---

18 Notes made on 6 April 1931, item 106, box 89, series 49, folder 3, Latham Papers, NLA.
19 Letter from Bagot to W.A. Burns, 2 June 1931, box 12, item 1, CLSA Papers, NLA.
20 Minutes of Executive Committee Meeting, 9 March 1931; Minutes of Executive Committee Meeting, 23 March 1931, box 1, item 2; Letter from Bagot to Sir William Sowden, 23 March 1931, box 13, item 11, CLSA Papers, NLA.

The day after the All for Australia League of New South Wales launched itself as an independent political movement, the Australian Citizens' League leadership met with Latham to reassure him of their support. They also expressed their concern over the hostility from the All for Australia League and suggested it would be difficult to convince them to support the Nationalists.[21] This may explain Bagot's cryptic statement to a South Australian journalist that the Australian Citizens' League had come to regret changing their name. The reason Bagot cited for the league's regret—that the badge of the newly formed Australian Labor Army bore a startling resemblance to that of the All for Australia League—is humorous but unconvincing.[22]

The April 1931 conference

The competing visions of the Citizens' League and the All for Australia League came to a head at a conference of non-party organisations at Balfour's Café in Adelaide on 9–10 April 1931. The purpose of the conference, which was arranged by the Citizens' League, was 'to secure co-ordination of effort, and enunciate common principles, aiming mainly at support of Mr. Lyons'.[23] It is hardly likely the All for Australia League of New South Wales shared this vision, given it had recently decided to field its own candidates. The conference must therefore be seen as an attempt by the Citizens' League to regain control of the citizens' movement phenomenon by securing widespread support for its vision of a united coalition of conservative organisations under Lyons. The number of groups invited to attend may have been part of this strategy. Apart from the three citizens' movements, delegates were invited from the Sane Democracy League, the Empire Party, the Citizens' Federation of Western Australia, the Tasmanian Producers' Advisory Council, the Emergency Committee of South Australia, the South Australian Proportional Representation Group, the South Australian Women's Non-Party Association, the Producers' and Business Men's Political League, and a revived Kyabram Reform Movement.[24] The majority of these movements supported forming a united front under Lyons to avoid splitting the conservative

---

21   Notes made on 6 April 1931, item 106, box 89, series 49, folder 3, Latham Papers, NLA.
22   Letter from Bagot to Sir William Sowden, 23 March 1931, box 13, item 11, CLSA Papers, NLA.
23   Minutes of Executive Committee meeting, 8 April 1931, box 1, item 2, CLSA Papers, NLA.
24   Minutes of Executive Committee Meeting, 23 March 1931, Minutes of Executive Committee Meeting, 7 April 1931, Minutes of Executive Committee Meeting, 8 April 1931, box 1, item 2, CLSA Papers, NLA; *Advertiser and Register*, [Adelaide], 9 April 1931, 9.

vote. The fact that their combined membership did not even come close to the ever-growing number of All for Australia League members did not matter; at the conference, the All for Australia League delegates would be in the minority.

Lyons accepted an invitation from the Citizens' League to address the conference. He also decided to make the occasion the inaugural event of a broader speaking tour across Australia.[25] His campaigning zeal, which had been honed by the loan conversion campaign the previous December and influenced by the populist style of the citizens' movements, was on full display. He and his wife, Enid, were greeted at Adelaide train station by an adoring crowd of supporters and the press, to whom he gave an ostensibly impromptu address in which he uttered his famous line that together they would 'strike a match to-night which will start a blaze throughout Australia'.[26] That evening, he gave a speech to a mass rally in the Exhibition Hall that was broadcast live on 5AD and relayed to several other radio stations in Sydney, Melbourne, and Brisbane. Attendance was so large that he repeated his address later that night to overflow crowds at the Garden Theatre and Palais Royal.[27] His speech skilfully blended the populist rhetoric of the citizens' movements with the orthodox economic rhetoric that had won him acclaim among conservatives:

> The first problem facing us is to restore the confidence of overseas people in Australia. In that objective there should be no party, no sectional, and no State antagonisms ... let us unite on certain leading questions and then leave our representatives freedom of action in order that we might have true representative government.[28]

However, Lyons' schedule for most of his time in Adelaide was booked solid with meetings and luncheons with conservative organisations and businessmen's groups.[29] This demonstrated that he was cognisant of the political power held by the citizens' movements and mainstream conservatives and was keen to maintain support from both.

---

25 Minutes of Executive Committee Meeting, 16 March 1931, box 1, item 2, CLSA Papers, NLA; *Advertiser and Register*, [Adelaide], 19 March 1931, 9.
26 *Advertiser and Register*, [Adelaide], 10 April 1931, 21.
27 ibid., 9 April 1931, 9.
28 ibid., 10 April 1931, 19–20.
29 ibid., 19, 21; 11 April 1931, 17.

The citizens' movement conference opened on 9 April 1931. Despite the importance of the occasion, no agreed minutes appear to have survived. The Adelaide *News* captured Bagot's opening address to the conference, but little else:

> We are all only too well aware that Australia is facing a crisis. It is our duty as citizens to think nationally instead of individually, to sink petty jealousies, subordinate party politics to national needs, and to unite in a common cause of loyalty and service as the price of our citizenship.
>
> … To preserve as wide a field as possible for our deliberations we submit on the conference agenda one item only—to discuss means by which coordination of action throughout Australia on matters of general importance can best be secured. Briefly, our problem is to find a common equation as a solution of our difficulties.[30]

The notes and reports of those who attended the conference capture some of the flavour that is missing from the rather bland newspaper coverage. These private recordings detail the heated debate that occurred between the All for Australia League and the various other movements that opposed its vision of unifying all conservative forces under the 'All for Australia' banner. The delegates from the Emergency Committee provided the following report to their colleagues:

> Sydney A.F.A. [All for Australia League] people came down to get certain things from Citizens' League e.g. change of name, and formation of new party. Owing to Mr. Bagot's clever tactics they were brought round from their plan of united party to Adelaide plan of cooperating parties. Things very bad in Sydney … Many of us also tried to impress on them the danger of a split vote. This is very real danger. If A.F.A. hangs out from other parties in Sydney, Senate may feel that an election is too risky, and may pass Theodore legislation rather than face loss of our last bulwark. Admitted AFA have only ⅓ of vote. Good hopes that all may go on lines of Adelaide Plan.[31]

---

30   *News*, [Adelaide], 9 April 1931, 8.
31   Minutes of meeting of Emergency Committee Executive, 12 April 1931, series 4, item 1, Price Papers, SLSA.

The minutes of the Citizens' League Executive Committee meeting on 12 April support this account. They praised the league's delegates for withstanding the efforts of the All for Australia League to 'swamp' them, and for 'persuading them that the South Australia scheme of uniting the parties was the best'.[32]

So, what caused the All for Australia League delegates to lose heart? Was it really Bagot's 'clever tactics', as the reports of the Emergency Committee and the Citizens' League suggested? Both groups shared the goal of uniting behind Lyons, so their reports may be tinged with triumphalism. It is equally likely that Lyons' speech to the conference on the morning of 10 April managed to persuade the recalcitrant delegates from New South Wales to toe the line. Parts of his speech were preserved by the *Advertiser and Register*:

> You know what is needed to set Australia right and bring back prosperity, probably better than any politician does.
>
> … You can accomplish nothing unless you are united. In my discussions with members of various parties, I have found a little hesitation on the part of some persons to forgo their party labels. As one who has given up his party label, I can assure you that it is essential to have one united party. Do not let mere labels stand in the way![33]

Lyons' words were carefully chosen. He was aware of the dissenting view of the All for Australia League in New South Wales and how important it was that the opposition forces were united in the most populated Australian state.

Whatever the cause, the outcome was that the conference delegates agreed to unite behind Lyons. But what exactly did that unity involve? Only two resolutions were passed at the conference. The first was that, due to the crisis of the Depression, the movements represented at the conference agreed to cooperate to 'maintain the principles of national integrity and sound finance, and to oppose inflation, repudiation, and financial drift'. This was hardly controversial; it essentially repeated what each group had already committed to independently. The second resolution contained the more substantial commitment to unify under Lyons:

---

32 Minutes of Executive Committee Meeting, 13 April 1931, box 1, item 2, CLSA Papers, NLA.
33 *Advertiser and Register*, [Adelaide], 10 April 1931, 21.

This conference confirms the desirability of unity being achieved on non-party lines under a policy of broad principles submitted by the Hon. J.A. Lyons amongst all political groups opposed to Scullin, Theodore, Beasley policies. If this unity is achieved the conference recommends wholehearted support of the new united movement. As negotiations between Latham, Page, Lyons groups are proceeding, the furtherance of same be left in the hands of the Citizens' League of South Australia, and the All for Australia Leagues of New South Wales and Victoria, with power to add to their number.[34]

The first two sentences of this resolution suggested that, should a new united movement be formed under Lyons with an agreed set of broad principles, the citizens' movements would support it. However, the third sentence indicated that, as Lyons and the leaders of the Nationalist and Country parties had yet to form a united movement, it was up to the citizens' movements to do so instead, and leave the door open for other groups to join the movement later. This was also reflected in the joint telegram that was sent to Lyons on 11 April by the three citizens' movement leaders:

Pending the time when all the existing political organizations in Australia that stand for the principles enunciated by you shall have united to form one great non-partisan organization under a common name, as outlined in our telegraphic invitation to you it is obvious that you, Mr. Lyons, and the small group of legislators you directly lead should not be handicapped by the lack of an organization in the constituencies, wholly devoted to the task of securing the return to Parliament of all candidates who are prepared to subscribe to the policy indicated in terms of the above-mentioned telegram. We are in a position to supply you with that service, and we have the honor now to place at your disposal the whole force of the All for Australia movement of New South Wales and Victoria, and of the Citizens' League of South Australia, and we invite you to become our leader.[35]

This carefully worded telegram was essentially offering Lyons the leadership and dedicated service of the citizens' movements, given that he and his group of centrists did not yet have an extensive political

34   Minutes of Executive Committee Meeting, 13 April 1931, box 1, item 2, CLSA Papers, NLA.
35   Letter from Gibson, Turnbull, and Bagot to Lyons, 11 April 1931, box 1, folder 8, Joseph Aloysius Lyons Papers, MS 4851 [hereinafter Lyons Papers], NLA.

apparatus themselves. In other words, the citizens' movements were offering themselves as the foundation for a new political organisation led by Lyons—a party in all but name. Bagot and his colleagues interpreted this as a victory over the All for Australia League. But the wording of the conference resolutions and the telegram to Lyons were undoubtedly seen as a victory by the All for Australia League delegates, too. If Lyons accepted their offer, the citizens' movements would hold a powerful position over the Nationalist and Country parties. If these mainstream parties wanted to join in a united front, they would have to do so at the mercy and whim of the citizens' movements, of which the All for Australia League remained the largest by a wide margin. Furthermore, the united front would have a 'common name', and no doubt the All for Australia League delegates envisioned that it would be theirs.

Despite the glowing press accounts, then, the conference of 9–10 April achieved little. The only agreement reached was that the citizens' movements would support a united non-party movement led by Lyons. There was still no agreement on what shape that movement would take or how it would iron out the disagreements between the citizens' movements and the mainstream conservative parties. In addition, Lyons' small group of Labor defectors lacked the political support apparatus enjoyed by the other parties in parliament—a gap the citizens' movements had enthusiastically offered to fill.

The murky birth of the United Australia Party

Lyons followed up on the conference by arranging a meeting in Melbourne on 19 April with delegates from the Nationalist Party and the three citizens' movements. The purpose of the meeting was to agree on the name and shape of the 'new united movement' the citizens' movements had endorsed at the conference. If Lyons was to lead a successful coalition of conservative forces to victory in the next federal election, he needed the attendees to agree on two things. First, he needed the citizens' movements and the mainstream conservative parties to agree on a common list of candidates who supported the broad principles set out in his seven-point policy. Second, he needed them to apply their members and their resources to promoting those candidates.

The delegates supported Lyons' proposal that the new movement be called the United Australia Movement. However, as at the conference at the beginning of April, the wording of subsequent resolutions was murkier. The organisations represented at the conference were 'urged' to appoint central committees in each state to 'secure the return [of] United Australia candidates'. If this could not be accomplished before the next federal election, the central committees were to 'secure united action in the electorates'. There was no clear commitment to a single agreed list of candidates—in fact, the resolutions specifically noted that 'no section shall preselect a candidate'—and the number of candidates in each electorate would only be limited 'in necessary and appropriate cases'.[36] In other words, the United Australia Movement seemed to offer something for everyone. For the Citizens' League of South Australia and the Australian Citizens' League, it provided the promised united non-party front for which they had asked. For the All for Australia League, it allowed them the freedom to continue to field their own candidates whenever and wherever they deemed it necessary. And for the Nationalist Party and Lyons' small parliamentary faction, it provided a new party banner under which they could unite. On 7 May, Lyons and his fellow Labor defectors along with the sitting Nationalist Party MPs rebranded themselves as the United Australia Party. Lyons was elected leader of the opposition to the uproarious support of the House of Representatives.[37]

Coopting the Citizens' League of South Australia and the Australian Citizens' League

The Emergency Committee of South Australia

With a loose commitment to unity achieved, the conservative parties in each state set about coopting the populist enthusiasm of the citizens' movements. The conference of 19 April had established a mechanism for doing so in the form of the proposed central committees in each state. This was likely modelled on a template that had been established in South Australia several weeks earlier. With tensions running high between the Citizens' League and the South Australian Liberal Federation in the first few months of 1931, leading Liberals W.G. Duncan and Charles Hawker

36 Minutes of a Conference held in Melbourne, 19 April 1931, box 1, item 2, CLSA Papers, NLA.
37 Hart, 'Lyons', 51. They were also joined by W.M. Hughes's Australian Party, comprising himself and three other MPs who had defected from the Nationalists in 1930.

had begun to consider how best to rein in the fiery and unpredictable Bagot. Since he seemed implacably opposed to the Liberals' party structure, they formed the Emergency Committee of South Australia to provide a neutral front under which the Liberal Federation, the Country Party, and the various non-party groups in South Australia could field agreed candidates to contest the next federal election. To be credible, it needed fresh, nonpartisan leadership. Duncan and Hawker approached A.G. Price, author of the highly influential and widely distributed pamphlet *The Menace of Inflation*, to lead the new movement. Invitations were sent to five organisations to attend the inaugural meeting of the committee on 1 April 1931: the Liberal Federation, the Country Party, the Citizens' League, the Political Reform League (whose founder, Keith Wilson, participated in the formation of the Citizens' League), and the Producers' and Business Men's Association.[38]

An analysis of Price's world view reveals the similarities and differences between mainstream conservatism and the citizens' movement ideology. Price was a typical conservative: British in his loyalties, staunch in his defence of orthodox economics, yet relatively ambivalent about the conservative party apparatus. He believed deflation and balanced budgets were natural—and therefore apolitical—tools of economic management, whereas the methods pursued by Labor were 'absolutely wrong'. Those who supported a sane economy were 'good men' who 'refused to be bound', whereas Scullin led 'a Government of wobblers, and financial extremists' who had 'temporarily sapped the foundations of individualism' with arbitration, pensions, and 'a dozen [other] socialistic policies'. Nevertheless, Price was deeply concerned by Bagot's uncompromising anti-partyism. He agreed to lead the Emergency Committee not because of any strong sympathy for the Liberals, but to prevent the Citizens' League from splitting the vote and 'letting in the extremists again'. This was a fear shared by Duncan and Hawker, who believed the league represented an 'immediate danger' and hoped to keep it under control until it ran out of money or momentum.[39] When interviewed many years later about the impetus for the formation of the Emergency Committee, Price's response was blunt: '[W]e started the Emergency Committee to control Bagot.'[40]

---

38   Price, 'The Emergency Committee of South Australia and the Origin of the Premiers' Plan', 11–13; Circular sent by Price, 29 March 1931, series 4, item 1, Price Papers, SLSA.
39   Price, 'The Emergency Committee of South Australia and the Origin of the Premiers' Plan', 5–6, 11, 13–14, 40.
40   Quoted in Lonie, Conservatism and class in South Australia during the Depression years, 248.

Bagot approached the inaugural meeting of the Emergency Committee with considerable bluster. Before the meeting, he told the Citizens' League president and fellow delegate William Queale that he intended to 'let the bastards show themselves and then shoot them'. However, while Bagot proclaimed that he was 'dead against cooperation' with the Liberal Federation, the more moderate Queale was won over by Price's appeals for electoral unity and convinced Bagot to change his mind.[41] The fear of splitting the conservative vote was likely a powerful influence on Bagot's change of heart. He knew that if the Citizens' League fielded its own candidates, there was a strong possibility Labor would emerge triumphant at the next election.

Having agreed to field a single list of candidates, the Emergency Committee then expanded Lyons' seven-point policy into a 12-point policy it would require its candidates to uphold. Two of these additional policies demonstrated the willingness of mainstream conservatives to graft aspects of the citizens' movement ideology on to an orthodox core. Candidates would be required to support the freedom of MPs from party or caucus control and a truce on contentious party issues for the duration of the next parliament.[42] While this may have been little more than a token appeasement of the Citizens' League, it was enough to satisfy Bagot that he could support the Emergency Committee without compromising his anti-party stance. This was aided by Emergency Committee members such as Price making use of the kind of non-party language for which the citizens' movement was renowned:

> [The Emergency Committee] is not really a political movement. It is an effort on the part of disinterested volunteers who have left their work and business simply to help the old parties co-operate, simply to aid them in one essential task of putting the country straight.[43]

41   Price, 'The Emergency Committee of South Australia and the Origin of the Premiers' Plan', 14–15; Minutes of meeting of representatives to the Emergency Committee, 1 April 1931, series 4, item 1, Price Papers, SLSA.
42   Report of subcommittee to the Emergency Committee, 7 April 1931, series 4, item 1, Price Papers, SLSA.
43   Speech by Price to the Emergency Committee, 18 May 1931, series 4, item 1, Price Papers, SLSA.

"THE LION'S SHARE"

A striking pictorial poster issued b y the All-For-Australia League. The
title given to it is "This is our Ly ons.   See that he gets the lion's
share.

Plate 5.1 Australian Citizens' League cartoon in support of Joseph Lyons
Source: *News*, [Adelaide], 17 December 1931, 11.

Nevertheless, Price strongly disapproved of the Citizens' League's
continuing 'desire to run stunts' and he chided Bagot on many occasions
for making 'overstrong statements' about the Liberal Federation.[44] Price's
loyalty lay with the existing party system and the parliamentary process,
even if he was not connected to any party.

---

44   Price, 'The Emergency Committee of South Australia and the Origin of the Premiers' Plan',
19–20.

Plates 5.2, 5.3, 5.4 Australian Citizens' League billboards in support of Joseph Lyons (after the movement adopted the 'All for Australia League' brand)
Source: Turnbull Papers, NLA.

While Price had not completely ironed out the differences between the Liberal Federation and the Citizens' League, he had managed to secure their cooperation in selecting and supporting pro-Lyons candidates for the next federal election. If the United Australia Party was to successfully oust Scullin at the election and avoid splitting the vote, a similar unity would need to be achieved in the other states. The ties of the Australian Citizens' League to the conservative political establishment in Victoria ensured the central committee established in that state was successful. So confident was Lyons of their support that he decided to publicly announce the launch of the United Australia Movement at a conference of conservative parties and non-party movements in Melbourne on 5 May. The conference agreed to form a central committee to ensure the cooperation of the various Victorian groups in fielding candidates at the next federal election without sacrificing their individual identity.[45] As with the Citizens' League of South Australia, the fear of splitting the vote overcame any scruples regarding preselection:

---

45   *The Argus*, [Melbourne], 6 May 1931, 9; Conference of delegates, 5 May 1931, Ernest Turnbull Papers, MS 1942/2 [hereinafter Turnbull Papers], NLA.

> One of the chief aims of the council will be to prevent three-cornered contests between two non-Labour and one Labour candidate at the polls, with consequent division of non-Labour votes and advantage to the Labour candidate. The object will be to ensure the complete cooperation of the various parties in supporting one candidate in each electorate[.][46]

Unlike the Citizens' League of South Australia, however, the Australian Citizens' League delegates expressed few qualms about surrendering anti-partyism in the name of political expediency. The political ties of its leaders were simply too strong. This was demonstrated by the election of two founding members of the Group of Six and the Australian Citizens' League to the positions of temporary secretary and chairman of the new central committee. The strongest opponent of unity in Victoria was the Country Party; its delegates soon abandoned the unity movement, and the remaining groups agreed the central committee should consist of five representatives each from the Australian Citizens' League, the National Federation, and the Young Nationalist Organisation.[47] The Australian Citizens' League subsequently spent considerable time and money campaigning for Lyons, particularly in the industrial constituencies of Yarra, Batman, Bourke, and Maribyrnong. It erected 8,000 billboards and posters, issued newspaper advertisements, and gave daily radio talks.[48] Two league members were even selected as United Australia Party candidates.[49]

Justifying the alliance with political parties

The Citizens' League of South Australia and the Australian Citizens' League portrayed their support of the United Australia Movement as the logical progression of their anti-party spirit to the political arena. Nationalism was a tarnished brand, inescapably bound to the tired system of machine politics. 'United Australia', as its name implied, was a new and invigorated political force that represented unity along national rather than party lines. Having Lyons at the helm made it easier to preserve this veneer of non-partyism. But moderate or not, Lyons was still a politician engaged in

---

46 *The Argus*, [Melbourne], 6 May 1931, 9.
47 Meeting of the United Australia Movement, 27 May 1931; Speech made by Ernest Turnbull to the State Council, 20 January 1932, 3–4, Turnbull Papers, NLA.
48 Speech made by Ernest Turnbull to the State Council, 20 January 1932, Turnbull Papers, NLA.
49 Hewitt, 'The All for Australia League in Melbourne', 12–13.

the political process, and the citizens' movements needed to account for this if they were to justify supporting him. They did this by arguing that the principles they shared with Lyons transcended party politics:

> Just as we are not 'pro' any party, so we are not 'anti' any party, Labour or other. The best proof of our non-party character is that we have given our support to Mr. Lyons, both before and since he left the Labour Party. In supporting Mr. Lyons we are supporting our own principles, and if we declined to support Mr. Lyons we would be false to our principles, irrespective of the party in which he may belong.[50]

This stance, argued the Australian Citizens' League, was 'political' but not 'party' because United Australia 'was not a political party in the [traditional] sense'.[51]

Working with political machines via the emergency and central committees—even if theoretically on an even footing—meant inevitably having to agree on a candidate list. Since the citizens' movements were opposed to preselection, this posed a dilemma: how to agree on a single candidate for each electorate without opening themselves to the charge of hypocrisy? The solution required a certain amount of rhetorical gymnastics. The citizens' movements had always maintained that they were willing to support any candidate, whether a card-carrying party member or an independent, provided they met their strict self-sacrificing and apolitical criteria. Since the candidate lists produced by the emergency and central committees included Nationalists, Liberals, Country Party members, and ex-Laborites, the Citizens' League of South Australia and the Australian Citizens' League could nominally claim that they were merely being consistent in agreeing to them.[52] This was not preselection, the Australian Citizens' League argued, but merely 'endorsement'—a subtle distinction, noted the *Age* with mirth, that 'the managers of other political parties must be sorry they never before thought of'.[53]

---

50 *All for Australia League Shows the Way to Prosperity*, 23–24.

51 ibid., 24; First Meeting of the Council under the new Constitution of the All for Australia League, 9 July 1931, Turnbull Papers, NLA.

52 Minutes of Executive Committee Meeting, 2 June 1931, box 1, item 2; Minutes of Executive Committee Meeting, 29 September 1931, box 1, item 3; OPP Minutes, 13 October 1931, box 1, item 3, CLSA Papers, NLA.

53 *Age*, [Melbourne], 20 May 1931, 8.

Rhetorical gymnastics or not, the Citizens' League of South Australia and the Australian Citizens' League had stretched the definition of 'non-party' to the breaking point. Their leaders justified their actions in several ways. Bagot argued that the imperative of defeating Scullin outweighed any small loss of independence the Citizens' League might incur:

> [T]he position in Federal politics is so critical that even at a temporary sacrifice of some degree of independence, we [are] acting in the best interests of the country and citizens by co-operating with other political bodies to ensure the return to Parliament ... of representatives who will stand for the broad principles of national integrity and sound finance.[54]

Likewise, the Australian Citizens' League's 'immediate object' was securing the election of 'all who stand on the common ground of opposition to the dishonest policies of repudiation and inflation' to whom 'we can quite safely leave the details of ... policy'.[55]

The citizens' movements also argued that cooperation would allow them to further their goal of curbing the excesses of party politics. Australian Citizens' League President Ernest Turnbull warned members not to 'delude' themselves into thinking that, by participating in the political process, they were 'altering the party system'. The league might be able to counter 'some of its worst faults' by cooperating with United Australia, but its main purpose was longer term:

> The true function of this organisation in the future is to be not a political party, with a policy of a hundred and one planks, but a watch dog, an overseer on behalf of the people to supervise the work of the political parties. Only in some such way can we prevent the parties in the future, as in the past, from sacrificing national to party interests.[56]

Likewise, the Citizens' League of South Australia claimed that its participation in the Emergency Committee would 'break down the control of political parties over candidates' by ensuring they would not 'be tied in any way to any particular political party'. To prove this claim, Bagot pointed to the two 'non-party' planks the league had secured in the Emergency Committee's 12-point policy.[57]

---

54 Letter from Bagot to Whiteman, 1 June 1931, box 13, item 10, CLSA Papers, NLA.
55 *The Argus*, [Melbourne], 7 May 1931, 3.
56 *All for Australia League Shows the Way to Prosperity*, 27.
57 Report of Executive Committee presented at Third Convention of Delegates, 10 June 1931, box 1, item 1, CLSA Papers, NLA.

The movements also stressed that their cooperation with mainstream conservative parties would only last until Scullin was defeated. The Australian Citizens' League admitted that there was 'no satisfactory substitute' for the party system of government and it was likely to be 'the prevailing system for a long time to come'.[58] Nevertheless, it stressed that its participation in the central committee was for 'a specific purpose' and, once that purpose had been achieved, it would 'consider whether there is any reason for continuing [it]'. This would avoid committing it 'to policies and to parties with which it has only some things in common'.[59] Similarly, the Citizens' League of South Australia stated that its role on the Emergency Committee would last 'only until the next Federal election has been completed' and would not affect its 'permanent aims and objects and ideals'.[60] Apart from establishing a fixed time frame for cooperation, this was also aimed at reassuring members that cooperation would not derail the fundamental purpose of the movements.

Exposing the inherent contradictions

The decision of the Citizens' League of South Australia and the Australian Citizens' League to cooperate with mainstream conservative parties raised valid questions among their memberships. Despite their protestations to the contrary, the movements' leaders had implicitly acknowledged that anti-partyism was less important than the more immediate goal of securing the election of a conservative government. This exposed a contradiction between those members who agreed with this hierarchy of values and those who had joined primarily out of the anti-party fervour that had arisen in Australia during the Depression. Complaints were raised hard and fast. One concerned member of the Citizens' League of South Australia wrote to Bagot that the movement was in danger of being 'swallowed up by the Liberal Federation', while another thought the Emergency Committee was really 'one big party' in disguise.[61] This sense of shock and betrayal was summarised by Miss L. Rudkin in her letter of resignation:

58　*All for Australia League Shows the Way to Prosperity*, 27.
59　Speech made by Ernest Turnbull, 20 January 1932, Turnbull Papers, NLA.
60　Report of Executive Committee presented at Third Convention of Delegates of Branches of the CLSA, 10 June 1931, box 1, item 1, CLSA Papers, NLA.
61　Letter to Bagot, 3 May 1931; Letter from A. Whiteman to Bagot, 20 May 1931, box 13, item 10, CLSA Papers.

> It seems a pity that a movement with such a fine organization behind it should not undertake educational propaganda instead of tampering with politics. The public it seems need education in Citizenship more than anything. We need to develop a Public Conscience and to understand what true Citizenship means.[62]

Her choice of words demonstrates the central legitimating role that anti-partyism played for some members. The citizens' movements were supposed to be a force that transcended politics entirely in their quest for spiritual and moral renewal. 'Tampering' with party politics shattered this illusion, stripping away the veneer of nonpartisanship and revealing the movements as simply conservative political vehicles of a more populist bent. While those who supported cooperation may have been able to justify this ideological compromise, it was clearly an uncomfortable move for others.

Cooperation with mainstream conservative parties seriously impacted on the fortunes of the two citizens' movements. Enrolment of new members dropped rapidly; attempts to form four new branches of the Australian Citizens' League in June 1931 failed.[63] The Citizens' League of South Australia noted that metropolitan subscriptions fell dramatically after it decided to align with the Emergency Committee. Bagot would later conclude that this was the point at which 'public support fell away to an alarming degree' and 'the League lost initiative and popular support'.[64] Existing members from both the leadership and the front line also responded with protest, dissension, and resignation. Australian Citizens' League Provisional Committee member Alexander Dowsley resigned, claiming the movement's choice would merely reinforce 'the present unsound system of party politics'.[65] The Echuca district council resolved that its members should ignore the endorsed candidate list circulated by the Australian Citizens' League leadership and follow the original policy of voting for any candidate who was prepared to abide by the movement's ideals.[66] The Preston branch condemned the leadership for kowtowing to the Nationalists and called on them to resign:

---

62 Letter from Miss L. Rudkin to Bagot, 12 February 1932, box 13, item 10, CLSA Papers, NLA.
63 Hewitt, 'The All for Australia League in Melbourne', 11–12.
64 Report to Chairman, Finance Committee, from Bagot, 15 March 1932, box 1, item 3, CLSA Papers, NLA.
65 *Age*, [Melbourne], 6 May 1931, 5.
66 *The Argus*, [Melbourne], 20 October 1931, 9.

That owing to the All for Australia League becoming swallowed up by a Nationalist organisation, and thus losing its identity and departing from its original ideals of non-party politics and opposition to pre-selection, the All for Australia League has failed in its duty to its members[.][67]

The use of the word 'identity' reinforces the importance of anti-partyism to some members. It suggests that it was a core component of how they perceived the citizens' movements, and by extension their participation in them. Sacrificing this ideal, even if supposedly on a short-term basis, transformed the movements into something unrecognisable and therefore unworthy of their continued support.

The last hold-out: The All for Australia League

Failed attempts at unity

The All for Australia League was much more torn than the other citizens' movements over the question of whether to collaborate with the Nationalist Party. Their dissident position before the citizens' movements conference on 9–10 April certainly contributed to this. The league's leaders also genuinely believed the situation in New South Wales was different to that in other states. Given that the Nationalist Association of New South Wales was the most organised of the conservative political machines in Australia in 1931, this belief was not entirely without merit. The fact that chief conservative bogeyman Jack Lang was Premier of New South Wales at the time further contributed to this perception. '[T]he problem in this State is different to the problems in the other States or in the Federal arena', explained one of the league's founders in a letter to Lyons: '[It] calls for different handling and [a] different solution.'[68]

The question of ideological purity or political expediency plagued the All for Australia League virtually from the outset. Its leadership was split over this question at the state convention on 28 March 1931, when the resolution to field its own candidates was raised. Two founding figures in particular, O.D.A. Oberg from the Sane Democracy League and

---

67   ibid., 1 December 1931, 8.
68   Letter from Norman Keysor to Lyons, 23 May 1931, box 1, folder 8, Lyons Papers, NLA.

A.E. Heath from the Constitutional Association, tried to dissuade the league from launching itself as an independent political force. Oberg warned that such a move would split the movement and 'relegate us to the limbo of disunity in which more than one political party finds itself to-day'.[69] Their appeal was unsuccessful; as noted earlier in this chapter, the convention overwhelmingly voted in favour of the resolution. The citizens' movement conference in Adelaide on 9–10 April, and the formation of the United Australia Movement in Melbourne on 19 April, did little to mollify their position. Gibson continued to publicly advise Nationalist candidates to 'efface themselves' and join the All for Australia League if they hoped to be re-elected.[70] League pamphlets proclaimed that it stood 'just as staunchly against the reactionary forces who have gained control of Nationalism' as it did against 'Mr. Lang and his Communist friends who preach the class war'.[71] Price, the leader of the Emergency Committee of South Australia, repeatedly described the All for Australia League as 'dangerous' in his private correspondence; he later recalled that 'the A.F.A. in N.S.W. seemed to dislike the Nationalists even more than they did the Lang crowd'.[72]

The Sane Democracy League convened a series of unity conferences between the All for Australia League and the Nationalist Association in the hope that the gap could be bridged. The first of these conferences was held on 25 April. The Nationalist delegates suggested that both organisations should be asked to endorse the formation of a central committee to support the United Australia Movement at the next federal election, as was being done in the other states. Gibson flatly replied that the All for Australia League had decided it would have no association with the Nationalist Party unless it dissolved itself and its members joined the league. After some cajoling, however, he reluctantly agreed to put a heavily caveated resolution to the league's Executive Committee supporting the formation of a central committee, provided there would be 'no preselection of candidates'. Instead, the committee would be responsible for deciding whether to endorse 'one or more' of the candidates put forward by its constituent organisations. The committee would have sole

---

69 *Sydney Morning Herald*, 30 March 1931, 12.
70 *Sydney Morning Herald*, 17 April 1931, 12; *The Canberra Times*, 21 April 1931, 1.
71 Socialisation of Industry, undated, item 70, Mutch Papers, SLNSW.
72 Minutes of citizens' movement conference, 9–10 April 1931, series 4, item 1, Minutes of meeting of Emergency Committee Executive, 12 April 1931, series 4, item 1, Price Papers, SLSA; Price, 'The Emergency Committee of South Australia and the Origin of the Premiers' Plan', 18.

control over the electoral campaign, and it would be housed in its own premises. Finally, representation on the committee would be based on 'financial membership' of these organisations and would not include any parliamentary representatives.[73]

While this resolution did not call for the dissolution of the Nationalist Party, it would certainly have denuded it of many of its limbs. However, it proved successful as a lever to get the All for Australia League to commit to further unity conferences—which may have been the intention of the Nationalist delegates. At a further conference on 29 April, the delegates agreed to recommend the following revised resolution to their two organisations:

> That this conference decides to recommend to the National Association of New South Wales and the All for Australia League the appointment of an Emergency Committee, consisting of five representatives of the National Association and five representatives of the All for Australia League, to control all matters connected with the United Australia Movement at the next Federal elections in this State. Mr Lyons and Mr Latham are to nominate an independent chairman and secretary of the committee. This committee is to function on behalf of the United Australia Movement, led by Mr Lyons in the Federal Parliament.[74]

Gibson's proposal that membership of the central or 'emergency' committee be proportional based on the respective memberships of the two organisations had been stripped from this watered-down resolution. This was a victory for the Nationalists, given that the league's membership vastly outnumbered theirs. In addition, the Country Party delegates who attended the conference agreed to ask their organisation to associate itself with the United Australia Movement, at which time they would be granted representation on the Emergency Committee.

What followed over the next month was a confusing, and occasionally contradictory, set of resolutions and counter-resolutions by the nascent Emergency Committee and its constituent organisations. While the delegates from the All for Australia League and the Nationalist and Country parties were cautiously willing to try working together, their respective leadership bodies were wary of the wording of the resolution

73 Conference at Sydney, 25 April 1931, item 130, box 89, series 49, folder 2, Latham Papers, NLA.
74 *Sydney Morning Herald*, 26 May 1931, 9.

adopted by their delegates on 29 April. The Nationalists were reluctant to surrender all control of electoral activities to the committee. The Country Party wanted to partner with the United Australia Movement rather than be one of three organisations participating in it. The All for Australia League continued to issue public statements that it only intended to cooperate with the Nationalists in the federal sphere, as there were matters of principle at the state level over which the two organisations did not see eye to eye. The representatives on the Emergency Committee modified their resolutions to try to address some of these concerns, but with limited success. Furthermore, as their deliberations were occurring largely behind closed doors, the newspapers, the members of the three organisations, and the general public drew their own conclusions about what was going on.[75] Oberg and Heath resigned from the All for Australia League in disgust, and Heath publicly denounced its leadership in the *Sydney Morning Herald* for not agreeing to work with the Nationalists at the state level.[76] Conversely, the 16 Newcastle and Hunter subdivisions of the All for Australia League jointly objected to the Executive Committee's decision to take part in the Emergency Committee, which they feared would 'submerge AFA [All for Australia League] entirely' and undermine the league's 'principle of complete political independence'.[77] The league's Executive Committee tried to reassure these disaffected divisions that their arrangement with the Emergency Committee 'is confined entirely to the Federal sphere', where they had accepted Lyons as their leader on the basis that he had 'thrown off the shackles of machine control and set out as a leader of the moderate section of the community'.[78] Latham wondered privately whether the only solution was for both the league and the Nationalists to surrender their separate identities and merge into a single United Australia Party.[79]

The straw that broke the camel's back in late May 1931 was a minor procedural matter. With the Country Party still unclear on whether it intended to nominate delegates for the Emergency Committee, the All for Australia League wanted to proceed with a 10-person committee comprising five league and five Nationalist members, with the door left open to amend the committee later should the Country Party decide to

---

75 *Sydney Morning Herald*, 5 May 1931, 9; 13 May 1931, 11; 15 May 1931, 12; 20 May 1931, 11.

76 ibid., 15 May 1931, 12; 20 May 1931, 11.

77 Letter from Norman Keysor to Lyons, 23 May 1931, box 1, folder 8, Lyons Papers, NLA.

78 ibid.

79 Letter from Latham to Bavin, 5 May 1931, item 5e, box 89, series 49, folder 2, Latham Papers, NLA.

join. The Nationalists were adamant that the committee should have 15 members, leaving it to the Country Party to determine the conditions on which it would join. As neither side had a mandate from their organisation to agree to the other's proposal, the meeting was adjourned. Two days later, the newly elected State Council of the All for Australia League resolved that it would 'discharge its electoral responsibilities as a separate entity in both Federal and State spheres'. The All for Australia League and the Nationalist Party issued public statements soon thereafter blaming each other for the collapse of the unity negotiations.[80]

Why had things fallen apart over such a minor matter? For one thing, the All for Australia League had been lukewarm about collaborating with other mainstream conservative parties from its inception. As a result, the heavily caveated resolutions that the embryonic Emergency Committee was able to pass were never likely to satisfy the Nationalist or Country party delegates. But perhaps more telling is that the decision to withdraw from the unity negotiations was the first resolution of the All for Australia League's newly elected State Council. Prior to that, the league had been led by an Executive Committee comprising the movement's founders. While most of the State Council members had previously served on the Executive Committee, they now had a fresh mandate to deliver on their members' wishes. The fact that the Newcastle and Hunter divisions— comprising nearly one-quarter of the active subdivisions of the whole movement—had been in open revolt only days before the election likely confirmed in their minds what that mandate was. With Oberg and Heath having resigned from the executive around the same time, there was no longer a strong contrary view to forging a separate path from the Nationalists. The league would field its own candidates, as it had already avowed to do at the state convention two months previously.

Exposing the inherent contradictions

Unlike the Citizens' League of South Australia and the Australian Citizens' League, the All for Australia League in New South Wales had refused to work with the conservative parties. In effect, it had performed the same prioritisation of values as the other two movements, but in the opposite order. It had elevated its anti-party purity above pragmatic concerns about achieving conservative unity to oust Scullin. This had the same

---

80   *Sydney Morning Herald*, 26 May 1931, 9; 27 May 1931, 12.

effect of exposing the contradictions between the two values and led to heated criticism from many of its members. After the collapse of the unity negotiations in May, letters from disgruntled members began pouring in to the *Sydney Morning Herald*. The letter writers argued that the decision not to cooperate with the Nationalist Association had been made in an undemocratic fashion by the leadership and was distracting the league from its true enemies in Scullin and Lang. As one disgruntled member put it:

> As an original member of the A.F.A., I have for some time resented the tactics employed by its spokesmen in directing their attacks on National representatives instead of attacking the real evils of Socialism and Communism, the growth of which threatens the country like a malignant cancer.
>
> Had the A.F.A. leaders (so far as they are purely self-appointed leaders) devoted one half of their time and energy to opposing the repudiation policy of Mr. Lang, instead of attacking the National party, this State might not now be in its present parlous plight. Then again, there is an element of gross inconsistency in the professed desire of the A.F.A. to co-operate with the National and Country parties in the Federal campaign, while continuing to hamstring them in the State sphere.[81]

A less scathing but no less condemnatory assessment was submitted by the aged and respected diplomat and businessman Sir Henry Braddon, who had recently resigned from the league's executive:

> Coming into existence almost solely to bring about unity, the A.F.A. so far, in State matters, appears to me to have achieved its opposite. Their attitude towards prominent Nationalists seems to me both ungenerous and unjust, and their attitude on the tariff creates difficulties with the country interests.[82]

Wholesale branch resignations followed in North Ryde, Manly, and Blackheath. The chairman of the North Ryde branch explained their action by arguing that the 'only object the people of the State should have in mind to-day was to get rid of the present Government', while the Manly branch resolved to form a new citizens' committee with the local branch of the Nationalists.[83] The Nationalist Association was not slow in

---

81   ibid., 26 May 1931, 6.
82   ibid.
83   ibid., 4 July 1931, 13; 21 August 1931, 9; 25 September 1931, 10.

making use of the opportunity this presented; their leader, Thomas Bavin, proclaimed that the league had abandoned its high ideals, with its main object now being to 'destroy the Nationalist party'.[84]

Little Tommy Bavin finds his new Billygoat rather obstreperous.

Plate 5.5 Cartoon lampooning NSW Nationalist Party leader Thomas Bavin's rocky relationship with the All for Australia League
Source: *The Australian Worker*, [Sydney], 27 May 1931, 3.

Decline

By mid-1931, the three Australian citizens' movements had made a decision regarding their relationship with mainstream conservative parties. While the Citizens' League of South Australia and the Australian Citizens' League had agreed to cooperate through front groups to avoid vote-splitting, the All for Australia League had declared its opposition to any such cooperation. Regardless of their respective choices, each movement

---

84 *Barrier Miner*, [Broken Hill, NSW], 6 June 1931, 1.

had made a decision that exposed one of the crucial contradictions between the radical and the reactionary elements of their ideology: the preservation of anti-party purity to destroy the much-hated political machines versus the need to cooperate with the forces of mainstream conservatism to oust the Labor government. With their cohesion shattered by the exposure of this contradiction, the Australian citizens' movements entered a terminal decline well before the United Australia Party's victory in the December 1931 federal election. Their populist-centred ideology had failed to stand up to the realities of mainstream politics. As a result, their membership rapidly dropped away and their sources of finance—which were never particularly strong—began to dry up. The All for Australia League was so starved of funds and members by October that it did a complete about-face and agreed to cooperate with the Nationalist Association after all.[85]

By the beginning of 1932, the Australian citizens' movements were largely a spent force, devoid of the enthusiastic momentum and mass membership that characterised their heyday. Neither the All for Australia League nor the Australian Citizens' League survived for long after the election. In a stinging blow from the political mainstream in January 1932, branches of the Nationalist Association throughout New South Wales unilaterally renamed themselves United Australia Party branches and cordially invited members of the All for Australia League to join them—despite an agreement the previous November that the two organisations would work together to build the new party's structure.[86] The league's executive voted unanimously to sever its ties with the Nationalists in February, although some branches sought to work with them.[87] There was a slight increase in league activity during the NSW state elections in mid-1932, but—with the exception of a few enthusiastic branches—the league essentially ceased functioning after the election. The Australian Citizens' League resolved to enter hibernation in January 1932, although its State Council asked that its members continue to keep a 'watchful eye' for when it might be needed again.[88] The National Federation of Victoria interpreted this as a decision to disband and decided to follow the example of its northern sibling by

---

85   *Sydney Morning Herald*, 15 October 1931, 9. Trevor Matthews argued that the members of the league executive were gifted £1,000 to pay off their debts in exchange for cooperating with the Nationalists; see Matthews, 'The All for Australia League', 145.

86   Letter from Sydney Snow to Lyons, 29 January 1932, Alex J. Gibson Papers, privately held.

87   *Newcastle Morning Herald and Miners' Advocate*, 5 February 1932, 10; *Sydney Morning Herald*, 3 February 1932, 3.

88   Speech made by Ernest Turnbull to the State Council, 20 January 1932; Minutes of the State Council meeting, 20 January 1932, Turnbull Papers, NLA.

renaming itself the United Australia Organisation. The league issued a public statement criticising the federation for failing to consult with them and stressing that it would not accede to becoming a 'party hack'.[89] It was a parting blow from a movement that never again awoke from its slumber.

Only the Citizens' League of South Australia, the first of the citizens' movements, survived the United Australia Party's victory in any meaningful form. Several branches amalgamated in early 1932 due to a drop-off in branch activity, which helped to temporarily stave off the movement's decline. It ostensibly increased its total membership despite the increase in resignations, reaching a peak of 23,133 in August—or 7.11 per cent of the total state electorate—although it is likely many of these members were nominal by this point. With Scullin defeated, the league focused its attention on reducing government expenditure, abolishing the tariff, increasing empire trade, combating communism, and reducing unemployment. League President W.M. Queale was appointed as a member of the Unemployment Relief Council.[90] The league considered forming a new political party in 1933 to combat its declining membership and revenue, but ultimately decided against it.[91] Under Bagot's tireless guidance, it managed to limp on until December 1934 in a severely restricted capacity before resolving to enter into voluntary liquidation.[92] In what probably amounted to the closest admission of their own partisan stance ever made by a citizens' movement, the Citizens' League noted in its death throes that the majority of its members in its heyday had been 'Liberals who had [since] returned to the party ranks'.[93]

The crisis had passed, and the swathes of disenchanted conservatives who had flocked to the citizens' movements returned to the fold. The mainstream conservative parties bent instead of breaking. Lyons had coopted the populist style of the citizens' movements just enough to wrap them into a new centre-right political framework with the Nationalists. The risk of vote-splitting was overcome, just as European fascist movements were 'smash[ing] the electoral base of the mainstream liberal

---

89 *The Argus*, [Melbourne], 24 February 1932, 8.

90 Report of Executive Committee presented to the Second Annual Convention of Branch Delegates, 12 September 1932, box 1, item 9, CLSA Papers, NLA.

91 Minutes of Special Convention of Delegates of Branches, 3 October 1933, box 1, item 9, CLSA Papers, NLA.

92 Minutes of Special Meeting of Executive Committee and General Council, 17 December 1934, box 1, item 4, CLSA Papers, NLA.

93 Minutes of Special Meeting of enrolled members of the Citizens' League, 4 October 1934, box 1, item 2, CLSA Papers, NLA.

and conservative parties'. The conservative establishment stayed solid and the elites in finance and industry were never forced to turn to a more extreme alternative to defend their interests, unlike their contemporaries in Germany. Rather than breaking the control of the political machines, the citizens' movements ultimately helped to reinforce them.

Arise Sir U.A.P.!

Although the All For Australia League, which provided much of the driving force of the United Australia Organisation at the last Federal election, has not been consulted, the President of the Nationalist Federation (Mr R. G. Menzies) has announced that the National Federation will in future be known as the United Australia Organisation.

Plate 5.6 Robert Menzies, president of the National Federation of Victoria, is anointed leader of the United Australia Organisation after failing to consult with the Australian Citizens' League about the change

Source: *The Herald*, [Melbourne], 24 February 1932, 3.

6

'New deals' and 'funny money': The New Zealand Legion and monetary reform

In December 1933, the editor of the New Zealand Legion's official journal, *National Opinion*, reflected on the year of 'rapid change' that had passed. All over the world, it seemed, people were setting aside their faith in the free market in favour of government-directed economic recovery. President Franklin D. Roosevelt had upturned the status quo in the United States of America with his widescale public spending program dubbed the 'New Deal'. In Germany, the Nazis were driving the nation towards economic self-sufficiency while investing heavily in public infrastructure and the military. The British, too, were also being increasingly drawn to 'economic nationalism' through tariffs to protect their native industries. And Douglas social credit—once merely 'the plaything of a few cranks'— now counted its supporters in the hundreds of thousands. The editor believed the legion was the vehicle for bringing similarly rapid change to New Zealand and stressed that these changes '*must* come quickly'.[1]

The editor of *National Opinion* had neatly summed up the unique political landscape with which the legion had to grapple in 1933. In addition to the dramatic changes occurring overseas, New Zealand's domestic environment differed in many ways from that of Australia

---

1   *National Opinion* [Wellington] 1(10) (14 December 1933): 1, 3.

in 1931. Most importantly, New Zealand was governed almost entirely by centre-right political parties throughout the Depression. When the legion was founded in February 1933, power was held by a coalition of the two leading conservative parties, United and Reform. There was no socialist bogeyman for conservatives to direct their frustration at, save the fear that the Labour Party might trump the Coalition at the next election. However, as Chapter Two discussed, the Coalition's attempts to balance traditional deflationary methods with a more interventionist stance on issues such as unemployment and insolvency had proven increasingly unpopular among conservatives. Its decision to devalue the currency in January 1933 was the final straw and caused a populist revolt against the political establishment. But without a socialist counterpoint in a position of power, there was no unified drive among legionnaires to restore a government committed to free-market principles. One was already in power, even if its record was not completely satisfactory. Instead, many legionnaires had to look elsewhere for political inspiration. They found it in the broad church of 'unorthodox' economics.

The appeal of 'unorthodox' economics

The changes on the global stage observed by the editor of *National Opinion* were paralleled by changes in the domestic political environment. As Chapter Two showed, the Depression had given rise to a variety of unorthodox economic ideas and theories in New Zealand. These ranged from revolutionary socialism to a desire to simply 'finetune' the capitalist economic system to address its perceived failings. The common theme uniting these myriad—and often contradictory—theories was the belief that the Depression had caused, or exposed, a crisis of consumption. While goods were still being produced in vast quantities, consumers lacked the money to purchase them. The proponents of unorthodox economics agreed that the solution to 'overproduction' and 'underconsumption' required some form of wealth redistribution, but they differed widely on how that might be achieved. Some favoured borrowing or printing money to stimulate demand, whereas others sought to nationalise the banking system so the state could exert greater control over monetary policy.

WILL IT RISE AGAIN?

Plate 6.1 New Zealand Legion cartoon criticising the control of British financiers over the New Zealand economy

Source: *National Opinion* [Wellington], 1(1) (10 August 1933): 4.

New Zealand: "Give them work and they will buy your products!"
(In normal times 60% of New Zealand's products are used in New Zealand.)

Plate 6.2 Cartoon calling for farmers to employ more men so that they can buy farming produce

Source: *National Opinion* [Wellington], 1(2) (24 August 1933): 3.

The New Zealand Legion was influenced by two broad schools of unorthodox economic thought. The first was the growing global trend of greater economic intervention and planning, which in 1933 had yet to fully mature into the Keynesian consensus that would eventually become the new orthodoxy across the Western world after World War Two. The chief proponent of this school of thought in New Zealand was the Labour Party, which promoted the nationalisation of key industries, large public works programs, increased wages, and guaranteed prices for certain primary exports. The second was monetary reformism—in particular, Douglas social credit—whose adherents sought to finetune the capitalist economic system. According to Douglas's theory, there was an inherent flaw in capitalism that meant consumers could never receive enough money in wages to buy the amount of goods being produced. This was given just enough pseudo-scientific gloss in the form of the 'A + B' theorem as to seem plausible. Social creditors' principal strategy for rectifying this imbalance involved nationalising the banking system and issuing some form of credit scrip or 'dividend' to embattled consumers to bring consumption power in line with production. Yet beneath this degree of plausibility, many social creditors—and monetary reformists more generally—believed the Depression crisis had been engineered by a secret cabal of international financiers and bankers who sought to control the world economy.

The tensions between these two schools of thought and orthodox economics originally played out among the legion's leadership in Wellington. While legion policy was supposed to be proposed by frontline members, in practice, the 'centres' typically looked for guidance to the National Executive—a small body appointed by Robert Campbell Begg to manage the everyday business of the movement. To assist in the production and dissemination of discussion material, the executive appointed research committees in Wellington to study topics such as central government, local government, economics, unemployment, and land. The Economic Research Committee was by far the most prolific; its members published several pamphlets, wrote extensive articles in *National Opinion*, and circulated dozens of articles and reading lists on economics to frontline members. Wellington-based, they were also able to directly influence the executive and the quarterly meetings of the National Council that were attended by delegates from across the country. This influence over individuals and printed material allowed the Economic Research Committee to frame the debate between the competing schools of thought.

Economic planning

The leading proponent of the economic planning school was the Chairman of the Economic Research Committee, Evan Sydney Parry. Parry was the son of the renowned electoral engineer of the same name and a partner in the law firm Buddle, Anderson, Kirdcaldie and Parry.[2] He was very much a man of his time. Aged just 32 in 1933, he was more than 10 years younger than the average legionnaire. He was also thoroughly disappointed with the economic orthodoxy of his elders and had become enamoured with Roosevelt's New Deal as an alternative. This led him to believe that the only answer to the Depression was for New Zealand to reject free markets in favour of an 'adapted Roosevelt plan':

> There are still quite a number of well-meaning people who go about their daily business, if any, in the comfortable belief that in some miraculous manner the world depression will right itself … the public should face the truth and recognise the fact that the trade depression cannot and will not right itself upon the old basis, and that the only hope of a return to prosperity lies in a consciously-planned economic system.[3]

Drawing on this proto-Keynesian discourse, Parry claimed the crisis was caused by 'over-production and under-consumption', and that governments should focus on increasing the purchasing power of consumers at home before expanding their export markets or investing funds overseas.[4] To accomplish this, the state needed to enact a deliberate plan for economic rehabilitation that involved increased wages, shorter working hours, and job creation for the unemployed.[5] It was only through such planning that the existing economic system could survive:

> The existing economic system, if it is to survive at all, can do so only as the result of strict and intelligent control, involving the carrying into effect of an organised plan of rehabilitation … We must reconstruct the existing system and embark upon a plan of increasing consuming power, limiting the accumulation of money for investment and organising industry, or we must scrap the existing system in favour of something else.[6]

These measures were essential not only to recovery, but also to long-term peace and stability; the alternative, Parry believed, was revolution or war.[7]

---

2   *The Evening Post*, [Wellington], 29 July 1944, 8. Little could be found on Parry's background and upbringing; however, his first task on joining the firm in 1926 appears to have been compiling a law guide to workers' compensation in New Zealand with C.A.L. Treadwell; see *Workers' Compensation in New Zealand* (Wellington: Whitcombe & Tombs, 1927). This suggests he was somewhat left-leaning.
3   *National Opinion* [Wellington] 1(2) (24 August 1933): 5.
4   ibid.; 1(4) (21 September 1933): 5; 1(6) (19 October 1933): 5.
5   ibid., 1(5) (5 October 1933): 5.
6   ibid.
7   ibid., 1(3) (7 September 1933): 5.

Parry's position within the legion's leadership allowed him to disseminate material on economic planning across the movement. The reading list he compiled for the Economic Research Committee included works by Keynes, Fabian socialists Sir William Beveridge and G.D.H. Cole, and the Australian social creditor Arthur E. Powell.[8] This list was also circulated to centres as recommended economic study material, along with a reprint from the *British Fortnightly Review* that praised the 'sane planning or State collectivism' of Fascist Italy and called for 'the overthrow of laisser-faire'.[9] Parry also had a hand in developing the legion's constitution and was part of the committee that established its journal, which subsequently published several of his articles on economic planning.[10]

Parry's ideas proved persuasive among the legion's leadership, due perhaps in part to his legal background, and he was able to wield considerable influence over the movement's policy. When the legion released a 'Statement of Principles' in June 1933, it included an entire section on 'political economy' that called for a 'bold reorganisation of our economic life' along the lines advocated by Parry:

> [T]he basic idea directing such reorganisation must be that all industry should be the servant of the consumer, and that production, distribution and finance are simply means to an end … economic recovery will not be automatic and cannot be looked for solely as the result of occurrences overseas.[11]

Planned economics soon spread to almost every aspect of the legion's policy. Begg himself even supported it on occasion, calling on the nation to 'throw off … the laissez faire of the past and deal boldly with the reconstruction of New Zealand'.[12] To facilitate domestic consumption, the legion proposed putting the unemployed to work on extensive public works programs at full wages. For those who still could not find work, new employment bureaus would be established to connect them with employers 'willing to give employment at adequate wages'.[13] Begg also developed an ambitious proposal to absorb one million of Britain's unemployed in exchange for

---

8 Ref. 6/2/32, 5 June 1933, file 1, folder 2, NZL Papers, AUL.
9 ibid.; Ref. 6/2/63, 8 August 1933, file 1, folder 2, NZL Papers, AUL.
10 Minutes of Meeting of the Provisional National Council, 4–5 April 1933, file 1, folder 1, Ref. 6/2/41, 26 June 1933, file 1, folder 2, NZL Papers, AUL; *National Opinion* [Wellington] 1(2) (24 August 1933): 5, 1(3) (7 September 1933): 5, 1(4) (21 September 1933): 5, 1(5) (5 October 1933): 5, 1(6) (19 October 1933): 5, 1(8) (16 November 1933): 5, 11.
11 Ref. 6/2/34, 6 June 1933, file 1, folder 2, NZL Papers, AUL.
12 Ref. 6/2/75, 16 October 1933, file 1, folder 2, NZL Papers, AUL.
13 *National Opinion* [Wellington] 2(14) (1 March 1934): 5.

the British Government taking over New Zealand's foreign debt. The new arrivals would be put to work on the land, thus creating 'an economic internal market for the products of land and industry'.[14] The legion even toyed with proto-corporatist reforms, including one suggestion that local body government should be reconstituted on a vocational rather than geographical franchise.[15] The culmination of this new direction was the legion's proposal for an economic advisory council comprising representatives from various business organisations and trade unions that would be responsible for issuing policy recommendations on all economic and industrial matters.[16] This was very similar to the boards proposed by the All for Australia League and the Citizens' League of South Australia.

The legion also drew some inspiration from a London-based group called the New Britain Movement, which sought to reinvent the British Empire along corporatist lines. The legion published several reprints from the movement's journal, *New Britain*, including its platform calling for the replacement of the existing British political machinery with political, cultural, and economic parliaments.[17] This was the extent of the connection between the two movements; neither sought to establish formal ties with the other, and the legion provided no analysis or commentary on the material it reproduced. The legion appeared even less in the British movement's rhetoric and was not acknowledged at all in *New Britain* despite the journal's repeated references to continental European allies such as the French L'Ordre Nouveau. Indeed, the legion appears to have been a mere passing curiosity to the provincial wing of the New Britain Movement, and its claim that the legion's principles were 'exactly in line with our own' was clearly an exaggeration.[18]

Monetary reformism

The second school of thought that influenced legion policy was monetary reform. As Chapter Two discussed, monetary reformism—in particular, Douglas social credit—had attracted significant public attention in New

---

14 This was (rather unoriginally) termed the 'Begg Plan'. See *National Opinion* [Wellington] 1(5) (5 October 1933): 1–3; 1(6) (19 October 1933): 2–3; 2(14) (1 March 1934): 1.
15 *National Opinion* [Wellington] 1(7) (2 November 1933): 8. The proposal envisioned a 'Regional Council composed of one representative of each of the following interests:—Agriculture, Manufacturing, Commerce, Transport, Medical, Finance (Banking, Insurance or Accountancy), Engineering, Women'.
16 *National Opinion* [Wellington] 2(14) (1 March 1934): 1, 5, 7.
17 ibid., 2(11) (18 January 1934): 7; 2(12) (1 February 1934): 7; 2(15) (15 March 1934): 3–4; 2(18) (26 April 1934): 8.
18 *New England* 1(1) (29 December 1933): 4. *New England* was the journal of the provincial wing of the New Britain Movement.

Zealand by mid-1933. Many committed monetary reformers joined the New Zealand Legion in the hope it could be used to achieve their goals. For instance, while the Douglas social credit movement was generally hostile to the legion, several members of the Wellington branch joined so they might 'influence it towards Douglasism'. They also claimed that one of their members served on 'the Central Executive of the Legion', but it is not clear whether this was the case.[19] One such monetary reformer within the legion was C.R.C. Robieson, who had previously been involved with minor conspiratorial and millenarian groups such as the New Economic Research Association and the British–Israel League.[20] Robieson wrote several articles for *National Opinion*, including one in response to a proposed Reserve Bank Bill, which he claimed was the work of a small clique of international financiers seeking to control the nation's economy:

> Currency and credit are the vehicles of production, distribution and exchange, and whoever controls those controls the very basis of a nation's existence. There was a time when an attempt made to deprive a people of their sovereign rights would have been regarded as high treason; but to-day the sovereign rights of a people are sought to be made the playthings of the international financiers.[21]

This conspiratorial talk became popular among some of the legion's leaders, some of whom drew on it to try to resolve the uncomfortable contradiction between imperial patriotism and dissatisfaction with the colonial financial system. New Zealand, like Australia, had been largely dependent on British loans to finance economic growth in the 1920s. Conservatives who were disgruntled at having to service this public debt needed a way to channel that resentment without it clashing with their patriotic loyalty to Britain. Their target was 'Tooley Street' in London, the funnel through which Antipodean dairy produce and British capital flowed. Tooley Street had attracted similar criticism from elements of the rural community in the 1920s in response to its perceived role in the torpedoing of the Dairy Board's attempts to establish guaranteed prices for its exports. It represented the anxieties of New Zealand's primary producers over the financial power that Tooley Street wielded over empire suppliers. However, rather than being imbued with anti-Semitism, the financier the legion caricatured was more reminiscent of John Bull than Shylock (see Plate 6.1). This allowed

---

19   *Farming First*, [Auckland], 10 April 1933, 18–19; Wellington Douglas Social Credit Association, 8th Newsletter, 15 April 1933, Inward correspondence, 1930–1958, Hansen Papers, ATL.
20   *The Evening Post*, [Wellington], 16 July 1931, 8, 20 October 1932, 20; *Auckland Star*, 6 September 1932, 3.
21   *National Opinion* [Wellington] 1(3) (7 September 1933): 2.

some legionnaires to lay the blame for the crisis on a small band of British financiers rather than the broader imperial system or the dependence of the colonies on Britain for capital investment. The legion could thus aspire to forge a closer relationship with the 'mother country' while arguing that this would require New Zealand to shed its reliance on British financiers.[22] By separating the negative elements of the metropole–colony relationship from the broader community of empire, the legion was thus able to preserve its sense of imperial patriotism.

The economic aspects of monetary reformism had less impact on legion policy. A 'stamped scrip' scheme produced by the Economic Research Committee in 1933 was vaguely reminiscent of social credit ideals; however, its main inspiration was a similar policy employed in several American cities rather than Major Douglas's 'National Dividend'.[23] Furthermore, its author, A.W. Free, was more inclined to favour economic orthodoxy, and one of the circulars he distributed explicitly rejected the social credit explanation of the causes of the Depression.[24] It was not until Major Douglas's visit to New Zealand in early 1934 that the legion began to cautiously consider the economic aspects of monetary reformism. Begg met with Douglas twice during his time in New Zealand and attended a speech he gave in Wellington.[25] He was supportive of but noncommittal on the major's message:

> With the knowledge that Lister, Simpson and Pasteur in my own profession were opposed as cranks by the orthodox school, I am willing to believe that the same error may be made in the sacred realms of economics ... That Douglas is opposed by the so-called orthodox school makes the pleasure of listening to him more attractive.[26]

The legion subsequently adopted a commitment to state control of currency, although this was influenced more by proto-Keynesianism than by social credit. Begg, for instance, claimed that his inspiration came from 'Roosevelt's dictum of the inherent right of the government to issue currency'.[27] The legion maintained that it held 'deep suspicions

---

22 ibid., 1(5) (5 October 1933): 2.
23 Ref. 6/2/70, 12 September 1933, file 1, folder 2, NZL Papers, AUL; *The Evening Post*, [Wellington], 5 May 1933, 7.
24 Circular No. 1, 2 August 1933, file 1, folder 4, NZL Papers, AUL.
25 Pugh, The New Zealand Legion and conservative protest in the Great Depression, 128–29; Clifton, Douglas credit and the Labour Party, 91.
26 *National Opinion* [Wellington] 2(13) (15 February 1934): 15.
27 ibid., 14.

of the A+B theorem' and when one member expressed concern that the movement was adopting Major Douglas's proposals, its response was blunt: 'Of course the Legion does not advocate Douglas Credit.'[28] It was also critical of Douglas's submission to the Coalition Government's 1934 Monetary Commission, claiming that he had 'sidestepped and twisted and bluffed' and ultimately 'crashed'.[29]

Single-tax theory

The legion was influenced to a much smaller extent by single-tax theory, which was developed by an American political economist named Henry George in the nineteenth century. Proponents of single-taxism considered land to be the fundamental resource on which all economic activity was based and argued that the entire tax system should be scrapped in favour of a single tax on the unimproved value of land to ensure its maximum utility. The leading single-tax supporter within the legion was E.W. Nicolaus. In 1931, Nicolaus had founded a group named the Citizens' National Movement with several other Henry George supporters and single-tax veterans to contest the Wellington Central electorate. When this proved unsuccessful, the group briefly reformed itself as a local branch of the Commonwealth Land Party—a single-tax party in Britain.[30]

Nicolaus joined the legion in the first half of 1933 and became a member of the Economic Research Committee, where he was able to disseminate ideas on single-tax theory to frontline members. However, his ideas did not gather the same level of support as those on economic planning or monetary reformism. About the closest single tax came to influencing the legion's policy was their commitment in early 1934 to effect 'the maximum development and settlement of land'.[31] This was hardly a radical position, however; closer settlement of land had attracted bipartisan support since the heyday of the Liberal Party in the 1890s. Nevertheless, Nicolaus's position on the Economic Research Council allowed him to export his ideas to a wider milieu, adding further to the confused mix of different economic ideas being espoused within legion publications and circulars.

---

28   ibid., 2(12) (1 February 1934): 3; 2(20) (24 May 1934): 12.
29   ibid., 2(24) (19 July 1934): 7, 15.
30   *Manifesto of the Citizens' National Movement to the Coalition Government* (Wellington: Citizens' National Movement, 1932); *The Evening Post*, [Wellington], 16 December 1932, 13; Letter from R.A. Gosse, 20 December 1932, series 2, item 157, Sir George Fowlds Papers, A-17, AUL.
31   1934 Circular No. 2, 8 February 1934, file 1, folder 4, NZL Papers, AUL.

Exposing the inherent contradictions

Committing the legion to economic planning

The fractures between these various schools of thought manifested clearly when the Economic Research Council presented a plan for economic recovery to the legion's National Council in July 1933. The difficulty in reconciling the radical economic ideas of Parry and Nicolaus with the more orthodox ideas of other committee members was hinted at by Parry when he presented the plan to the council:

> [Parry] made it clear that the scheme endeavoured to reach a compromise which would meet the conflicting views of those comprising the Committee. The main difficulty they had encountered was that of overcoming the various lines of conflicting thought and opinion and moulding them into a common plan.[32]

As a result, the plan was a hodgepodge of different economic principles and policies. It began in a rather orthodox fashion by referring to the intolerable burden of debt and interest that previous governments had amassed by excessive borrowing. However, it then argued that the Depression had been worsened by banks whose interests in preserving their stakeholders' profit margins were incompatible with the national interest. The solution to this problem, according to the plan, was for the state to assume control over currency by establishing a state credit board that would stimulate the economy through interest-free loans to public and private enterprise. The board would also be granted sole control over importing and exporting to maintain a stable internal price level independent of fluctuations in the global market. The plan also referred to land as the 'foundation of the nation's economic life' and it recommended the Crown 'reassert sovereignty over land' by taxing its unimproved value to prevent speculation.[33] This demonstrated a mix of economic planning and single-tax theory with language that was reminiscent of the anti-banking conspiracy favoured by monetary reformers.

---

32   Minutes of Meeting of National Council of the New Zealand Legion, 19–21 July 1933, file 1, folder 1, NZL Papers, AUL.
33   *The Evening Post*, [Wellington], 24 July 1933, 8.

Plate 6.3 'Caesar's Dilemma': The divisive effect of the New Zealand Legion's policies
Source: *Auckland Star*, 22 September 1934, 10. Courtesy of Stuff Limited.

Parry was doubtful the National Council would approve the ambitious economic plan; he simply asked that it be circulated to the various centres for discussion. What he got was much more. While the council did not agree with the specifics of the report, it nevertheless resolved that 'the Legion is convinced that a planned economic system is necessary for the purpose of co-ordinating consumption and production, with a view to increasing consumption'.[34] For a conservative movement based on a general commitment to the free market, this was a radical stance—especially given the fact that policy was supposed to be vetted by all centres before being adopted. The minutes of the National Council meeting do not reveal why the legion's leadership took such a dramatic step, but it is possible the apparent failure of New Zealand's mainstream conservative parties to deal with the Depression made the legionnaires more willing to consider drastic alternatives. The Depression had entered its fourth year in 1933, and discontented conservatives in New Zealand did not have a Labour bogeyman in power against whom they could direct their frustrations. Conversely, Australia in 1931 was dominated by the Labor Party, which meant there was less need for discontented conservatives to

---

34 Minutes of Meeting of National Council of the New Zealand Legion, 19–21 July 1933, file 1, folder 1, NZL Papers, AUL; *The Evening Post*, [Wellington], 24 July 1933, 6.

experiment with alternative economic remedies. In addition, the vaguely worded resolution could easily be interpreted by moderate conservatives as compatible with their world view. Increased state control may have been anathema to free markets, but the relatively pragmatic boundaries of Australasian conservatism readily encouraged such interventions when they were seen as serving the national interest. So, while it was a radical new direction, it was still nominally within the boundaries of the nineteenth-century developmentalist tradition.

LEGION LEADER ARRIVES IN AUCKLAND

Dr. Campbell Begg (right), president of the New Zealand Legion, photographed when he arrived yesterday morning. Mr. A. St. Clair Brown, chairman of the Auckland division, is in the centre, and Mr. L. F. Rudd is on the left.

Plate 6.4 Robert Campbell Begg arrives in Auckland for a New Zealand Legion meeting

Source: *New Zealand Herald*, [Auckland], 24 August 1933, 6.

This confused mix of different economic ideas was repeated in the legion's 12-point policy in March 1934. On the one hand, it recommended a reduction in the size and cost of parliament and the decentralisation of power to semi-autonomous 'shire councils'; on the other, it called for the establishment of new government departments such as the economic advisory council and the creation of a 'unity government' to carry out aspects of economic planning such as public works, vocational training, and employment bureaus for the unemployed. A separate plank for the state control of currency was reminiscent of monetary reformism, while a commitment to closer land settlement and the prevention of speculation may have partially appeased the single-taxers.[35] In effect, the 12-point policy represented an attempt to corral a series of contradictory ideas into a single platform.

Conflict with the reactionary backbone

The expression of such divergent schools of thought within legion policy exposed the inherent contradictions within the movement. The chief division lay between the proponents of the new radical alternatives and the supporters of the economic status quo, who formed the backbone of the movement. One of the places where this contradiction was most evident were the letters' pages of *National Opinion*, where members expressed their frustrations with the different ideas being floated by the legion's leadership. In the very first volume, one member wrote a letter protesting Nicolaus's proposal regarding Crown ownership of all land; in a following volume, two replies were published defending Nicolaus.[36] This set off a debate that spanned several issues in 1933 between Nicolaus himself and A.W. Free, a more orthodox member of the Economic Research Committee.[37] As Free put it:

> Mr. Nicolaus's views on Credit and Currency prove again that shoemakers should stick to their lasts ... Practical observation by a layman would lead to the conclusion that the sun moves around the earth. I rely upon the authorities who assure me that the reverse is true. So with money—the analyses of the experts are more important than the conclusions of the amateur observer.[38]

---

35   *National Opinion* [Wellington] 2(14) (1 March 1934): 1, 5.
36   ibid., 1(1) (10 August 1933): 4; 1(3) (7 September 1933): 4.
37   ibid., 1(4) (21 September 1933): 4; 1(5) (5 October 1933): 4; 1(6) (19 October 1933): 4; 1(7) (2 November 1933): 4; 1(8) (16 November 1933): 9; 1(9) (30 November 1933): 7; 1(10) (14 December 1933): 8.
38   ibid., 1(5) (5 October 1933): 4; 1(7) (2 November 1933): 4.

Similarly, Parry's articles on planned economics attracted letters in support and opposition. One member praised his attempt to 'evolve a system of finance whereby consumption can be made to equate with production', while another believed that all other options needed to be exhausted before resorting to 'the desperation of "planning"'.[39]

The legion's flirtation with monetary reformism provoked the most significant debates in *National Opinion*. One orthodox member criticised Robieson's conspiratorial approach to the Reserve Bank Bill as 'heavy-handed', while another outright condemned the Economic Research Council's stamped scrip plan.[40] As the doctrine of social credit became more prominent in 1934, so, too, did the letters for and against it. A lengthy debate between the poet and dedicated social creditor A.R.D. Fairburn and a supporter of orthodox economics named E. Keating spanned several months, with many other legion members contributing to each side. The closest the debate came to a conclusion was Fairburn's insinuation that Keating was secretly an economist or a banker in disguise.[41] Other members disagreed over whether the legion had adopted too much, or not enough, social credit doctrine. E. Manoy argued that social credit had been 'proved a fallacy by leading economic authorities throughout the world' and hoped the legion was not 'advocating such a disastrous proposal'.[42] In contrast, a 'Disgusted Subscriber' lamented that the legion was spending too much time talking about reducing government expenditure and not enough on monetary reform.[43] Another member, E.F. Rothwell, argued that state control of currency should be given central importance rather than being 'relegated to a position among the "odds and bits"' of the 12-point platform.[44]

Once the inherent contradictions between reactionary and radical economic ideas had been exposed, widespread resignations soon followed. The majority of those who resigned were supporters of traditional conservative values who believed the legion had betrayed its founding principles by veering towards unorthodox economics. One subscriber to

---

39   ibid., 1(5) (5 October 1933): 4; 2(12) (1 February 1934): 12.
40   ibid., 1(5) (5 October 1933): 4; 1(6) (19 October 1933): 4.
41   ibid., 2(11) (18 January 1934): 11–12; 2(12) (1 February 1934): 12; 2(14) (1 March 1934): 12; 2(16) (29 March 1934): 12; 2(21) (7 June 1934): 12; 2(22) (21 June 1934): 13; 2(23) (5 July 1934): 13; 2(25) (2 August 1934): 12–13; 2(26) (1 September 1934): 15–16.
42   ibid., 2(20) (24 May 1934): 12.
43   ibid., 2(25) (2 August 1934): 12–13.
44   *Legion* [Wellington] 1(3) (29 November 1934): 4.

National Opinion wrote that the legion's refusal to believe that Britain's orthodox economic policies were causing a recovery was 'criminal' because it was 'kill[ing] the spirit of confidence'.[45] The secretary of the Christchurch centre resigned 'when it became apparent control had passed in Wellington to an extreme Left Wing group whose aims were directly contrary to our own', and even took the extreme measure of destroying the centre's membership lists out of fear they would be misused.[46] The chairman of the Hastings centre provided a long list of grievances that had led him to quit the movement:

> [T]he movement has not come up to my expectations, that I do not agree with the system of local organisation that has been adopted, that I cannot see any hope of success on present lines and that I believe I can make better use of myself in the ordinary political sphere as we know it.[47]

That the chairman had been driven back into the fold of mainstream conservatism further demonstrates that it was the reactionary wing of the legion that was most alienated by its policies. They had joined out of a growing perception of crisis and a desire to do something about it, but their sense of civic duty did not extend to abandoning their faith in limited government, free markets, and individual self-reliance. While the legion's leadership appeared to be obsessively looking forward to new and modern ideas about how to combat the Depression, they preferred to look backwards to the tried and tested methods of their forefathers in the nineteenth century.

Those supporters of orthodox economics who remained in the movement advised the leadership to distance itself from its radical policies. The secretary of the Otane centre suggested they avoid expressing any 'ambitious & rather vague (to the rank and file) views' that might 'frighten some members away'.[48] The Wilder centre proposed the legion focus on the reform of parliament rather than the more contentious question of economics:

---

45   *National Opinion* [Wellington] 1(10) (14 December 1933): 8–9.
46   Letter from J.D. Hall, 24 August 1972, Simpson Papers, ATL.
47   Letter from Ald. Harrison to Tonkin, 5 September 1933, file 5, folder 1, NZL Papers, AUL.
48   Letter from J.A.S. Logan to the General Secretary, 6 January 1934, file 2, folder 3, NZL Papers, AUL.

[T]here exists an urgent need, in order to attract to the Legion a greater and wider measure of public support, to delete, for the time being at least, from the Legion's published programme all controversial matters such as managed currency, the question of community created values etc., and to place before the public with more prospect of endorsement, a short and simply worded programme with reform of the Parliamentary system as the Prime objective.[49]

To these members, parliamentary reform met the definition of nonpartisanship whereas 'managed currency' did not. This demonstrated their perception of conservative values as being natural and therefore nonpartisan. Parliamentary reform, in their world view, meant the rationalisation and standardisation of the government to rid the public sector of services deemed frivolous or unnecessary. Economics of this sort was a natural, and therefore uncontroversial, policy, whereas ideas such as a 'managed currency' were seen as partisan and controversial.

The legion decides to field its own candidates

The fractures were further exposed during the July 1934 National Council when the legion resolved to field its own candidates for the next election. The move was partially a response to the criticisms of the legion's confusing and contradictory economic policies. To overcome this criticism, the council resolved that candidates would only be required to support the reform of local and central government and the establishment of an economic advisory council, rather than the more controversial elements of its 12-point policy.[50] However, this decision alienated legion members who wanted the movement to maintain its non-party purity. Several division and centre executives resigned in protest, including the one in Dunedin:

[T]he sole aim of the Legion was the securing of more efficient government, central and local, and government based on national and not sectional interests … it had become evident that the aims of the Legion had departed from this interpretation, and that the Legion was prepared to enter the field as a political party. In view of this, the executive felt that it would not, in fairness to the members who had been induced to join the Legion on the old understanding, remain in office.[51]

---

49   Remit from Wilder Branch N.Z. Legion, undated, file 1, folder 5, NZL Papers, AUL.
50   *National Opinion* [Wellington] 2(25) (2 August 1934): 5.
51   *The Evening Post*, [Wellington], 20 September 1934, 12.

This reiterated the central importance that moderate members placed on parliamentary reform as the core business of the legion. The decision to support its own candidates, which effectively meant rebranding itself as a political party, contradicted the nonpartisan ideals on which these members believed the movement had been founded. Even worse, it raised the spectre of vote-splitting at a time when the New Zealand Labour Party was in the ascendant and the conservatives needed to retain every vote. The legion countered that it was more likely to split the Labour or 'progressive' vote, but this was a hollow defence given the overwhelmingly conservative nature of its membership.[52]

By the time the legion had decided to launch itself as a new political party, it was already largely irrelevant. The inherent contradictions exposed by the adoption of controversial economic policies had begun to weaken the legion from the second half of 1933 and, by October, the leadership reported that only seven of the 18 divisions were fully operational. The other 11 were still nominally operating under their original provisional committees, although none of their centres was active.[53] In the Hawke's Bay division, only two of six centres were functioning satisfactorily, and of the outlying centres it was reported that 'complete silence reigns'.[54] By the end of 1933, the legion was haemorrhaging money and members. The lofty aspiration to run its own candidates never materialised due to a lack of funds and manpower, although a particularly active branch in the Hutt Valley managed to get several of its members elected to local government bodies in 1935. J.W. Andrews and E.W. Wise were elected unopposed as mayors of Lower Hutt and Eastbourne, respectively.[55] In May 1935, Begg resigned as the legion's president in favour of Clarence Meachen, a fellow medical professional and a pioneer in blood transfusion.[56] The movement disappeared after putting out a list of endorsed candidates for the general election in November 1935, although a few centres in the Hastings division survived into 1936.[57] In what might be claimed as one of its few lasting successes, eight former members of the legion were selected as National Party candidates in 1938—one of whom, Sidney Holland, would later become prime minister.[58]

---

52   *National Opinion* [Wellington] 2(20) (24 May 1934): 1–2.
53   Ref. 6/2/75, 16 October 1933, file 1, folder 2, NZL Papers, AUL.
54   Letter from R.B.G. Chadwick to J. Stewart, 21 October 1933, file 2, folder 3, NZL Papers, AUL.
55   *The Evening Post*, [Wellington], 27 April 1935, 13.
56   ibid., 15 May 1935, 12.
57   Section labelled 'New Zealand Legion', 1–3, The Russell Saga Vol. 4, qMS-0823, ATL.
58   Pugh, The New Zealand Legion and conservative protest in the Great Depression, 195–99.

Conclusion

> Talking of large families, the Lyons' visiting card is popular in England. Destiny plays her cards in a very peculiar way. Little did Mr. Bagot, of the Citizens' League (now faded into the background), dream that through his sponsorship it was made possible for Mr. Lyons to go before the public in the Adelaide Exhibition Building. 'Lyons hysteria' followed, and the other States fell into step at once. All parties then sank their differences, the emergency committee was formed, and now Mr. Lyons is the constant guest of the King! So far, Mr. Bagot has been unable to secure a seat even in Parliament. The public soon forgets.[1]

As the citizens' movements faded from the political scene, so, too, did they fade from the public consciousness. By 1936, the only time they were mentioned in the press was in the obituaries pages, where the families of former members dutifully recognised the deceased's service with the citizens' movements well down their long lists of personal achievements. This rather ironic form of remembrance—or lack thereof—may partially explain why the citizens' movements have attracted so little scholarly attention. This book has aspired to fill that gap. It implicitly argues not only that the citizens' movements are worthy of study, but also that they were an important social and political force that contributed more to Australasian history than a mere blip on the radar. They were an important part of the history of Australian and New Zealand conservatism and economic liberalism, particularly the emergence of consolidated centre-right parties in each country in the 1930s and 1940s. The fact they arose contemporaneously with a wave of fascist movements and regimes internationally also begs comparison. Finally, and to return to a point raised in the Introduction, the citizens' movements bear many similarities to the rise of right-wing populism in the late twentieth and early twenty-

---

1   *Recorder*, [Port Pirie, SA], 10 April 1935, 3. Bagot would eventually be elected to the South Australian Legislative Council in 1938.

first centuries. Before positioning the movements within these broader historical trends, however, let us refresh some of the key themes explored in this book and investigate what the comparative approach tells us about the different experiences on either side of the Tasman.

The reactionary and the radical

In the Introduction, I suggested that viewing the citizens' movements as a contradictory blend of reactionary and radical tendencies provides a useful framework for understanding them. This pattern of looking both forwards and backwards for political inspiration is evident throughout their history. Chapter One analysed the origins of the movements in the long tradition of Australasian conservatism, which had three key components: a strong patriotic and economic orientation towards Britain, a general commitment to free-market capitalism, and staunch opposition to communism and socialism. This world view evolved through both the official centre-right party organs in each country and a diverse array of conservative pressure groups, educational associations, and protest movements that arose across the Tasman, British, and Anglo worlds from the late nineteenth century. This wider conservative milieu utilised language to build a broader, more inclusive vision of what it meant to be a conservative. Two of the key tropes in this language were the notion of what it meant to be a citizen and the claim that conservative values were 'non-party', akin to natural laws that transcended politics; they represented the national interest. This tradition became radicalised during the Depression as some conservatives began to seek alternative political and economic solutions to the crisis. As Chapter Two demonstrated, the main component of this radicalisation was a form of 'anti-political political thought' that laid the blame for the crisis on political parties and their supposedly self-serving and parochial party politicians. Non-party metastasised into anti-party, in short. In New Zealand, where the government remained in the hands of conservative parties throughout the Depression, discontented conservatives also turned to radical economic theories such as Douglas social credit, which suggested simple 'tweaks' to the capitalist system that would supposedly return prosperity.

The citizens' movements sat at the peak of this process of conservative radicalisation. Their ideology was centred on a populist struggle between the average citizens and the party politicians, along with the political 'machines' that supported them. As Chapter Three showed, this contradiction between looking backward to a mythical pioneering past and looking forward to new and modern ways of reshaping the nation's political machinery was temporarily obscured by high-level ideals that supposedly transcended the political process entirely. Their aim, the movements stressed, was nothing less than the transformation of the nation's political system and the reinvigoration of an apathetic electorate. Chapter Four demonstrated that the founders envisioned their new creed as nationwide forms of mass protest that would force their governments to act. They promoted a populist culture that was designed to build enthusiastic and committed mass followings. Through semi-ritualistic mass meetings and the shrewd use of traditional and modern media, the movements' leaders deliberately, and successfully, connected with a wide audience and cultivated an image of sheer size. While their membership was drawn primarily from the professional and business fraction, it included significant farming and working-class minorities. This adroit mixture of ideology and method was what led the citizens' movements to attract such a vast membership, and achieve national significance, in such a short period. Their leaders were able to tap into long-held public sentiments and prejudices that had been heightened by the Depression and channel them through a skilful blend of organisational and promotional techniques. I have described this as a 'populist culture' of mass conservative mobilisation.

While previous conservative non-party organisations may have occasionally questioned the merits of machine politics, the citizens' movements transformed this into a large-scale challenge against the political status quo. Despite their ideological affinity with mainstream conservatives, their populist opposition to party politics was so deeply ingrained in their world view that they were compelled to reject political parties on both sides of the spectrum with equal fervour. As a result, they directly challenged the electoral base of these parties by promoting independent candidates of all shades who were willing to pledge themselves to upholding the movements' broad ideals. This challenge was particularly strong in Australia, where mainstream conservatives went to great lengths to contain it. Chapter Five discussed the attempts of Joseph Lyons and the Nationalists to rein in the citizens' movements and the tortured ideological explanations the movements developed to justify their cooperation with mainstream conservative parties. While the New Zealand Legion did not pose a similar degree of threat to the United and Reform parties, it was affected by a contradiction between the traditional economic views of many of its members and the desire of others to experiment with unorthodox ideas such as economic planning and monetary reform. The result was the same: once the citizens' movements attempted to transform their ideals into formal policy, they exposed the inherent contradictions that had previously been concealed. The ruptures that followed ultimately caused their downfall.

There were, of course, other contributing factors to the movements' decline. In Australia, Lyons' appropriation of populist rhetoric and his success at bringing the citizens' movement under the aegis of the United Australia Party effectively undercut the reason for the movements' existence, especially after his victory in the December 1931 federal election. Similarly, the New Zealand Legion's confused mix of unorthodox economic ideas could never compete with the clearly enunciated reformist program of the New Zealand Labour Party. As Labour grew in strength and its policies became more popular, the legion's lofty ideas appeared increasingly hollow by comparison. A lack of finance was also a common hindrance for the movements. However, these issues were secondary, and often arose after the movements had decided on policies that exposed their inherent contradictions. As this book has shown, exposing these contradictions caused a chain reaction of protests and resignations that weakened the movements to the point that they struggled to remain in existence. This explains why, in Australia, the citizens' movements lost their momentum several months before Lyons' electoral victory in December 1931.

The reactionary/radical framework may have wider applicability within studies of Australasian conservatism. Like most ideologies, conservatism is a broad school of thought containing many inherent contradictions. Some contradictions, like those of the citizens' movements, lay between the reactionary and the radical fringes of conservative opinion; others, however, are structural in nature, such as those that divide the interests of farmers, manufacturers, and professionals and businesspeople. The constant splits and consolidations of the non-labour parties in Australia and New Zealand during the first half of the twentieth century demonstrate how divisive these contradictions could be. This book has suggested that, rather than ironing out these contradictions in the interests of narrative consistency, they must be embraced if a deeper historical understanding is to be achieved. Contradictions can reveal how alliances are forged and broken, how consensus is built around common issues without causing splits on more divisive ones, and how ideas and movements rise and fall by their ability to achieve this consensus. By exploring the antithesis—and occasionally the synthesis—of inherent contradictions, a fuller understanding of Australasian conservatism might be achieved.

What a comparative approach tells us

This book has approached the four citizens' movements from a comparative, and occasionally a cross-national, perspective. The trans-Tasman similarities this has revealed are self-evident. Both Australia and New Zealand witnessed the rise of populist conservative movements during the Depression, which challenged the legitimacy of the party system. These movements were influenced by the same international network of conservative political parties, pressure groups, educational associations, and protest movements that arose across the British and Anglo worlds from the late nineteenth century, which became radicalised during the Depression. They all concealed within them inherent contradictions, which, when exposed, ultimately led to their downfall.

Arguably, however, the power of comparative and cross-national history is in its ability to identify and explain differences rather than similarities. This book suggests that three key factors contributed to when, and how, everyday conservatives in Australia and New Zealand became radicalised by the Depression: the speed at which the effects of the Depression were felt in each country, whether conservative or labour governments were in power when it hit, and the measures these governments adopted in response. In Australia, the crisis hit early and hard, peaking in the first half of 1932. A federal Labor government was in power until December 1931, and Labor parties controlled every state except Queensland and Western Australia. The perceived shortcomings of Scullin's federal government, combined with the unorthodox economic proposals of Theodore and Lang in early 1931, played a major role in generating widespread conservative mobilisation, including the citizens' movements. Anti-party sentiment therefore arose early, and fiercely, in Australia. In New Zealand, the Depression did not hit hardest until 1933. The liberal United Party held power from 1928 to 1931 with the support of Labour, and a United–Reform coalition government reigned from 1931 until 1935. Economic orthodoxy generally ruled the day, although the two governments did introduce some novel interventions to counter growing unemployment and insolvency. It would take a highly controversial act by the Coalition in January 1933—the devaluing of the currency—for anti-party sentiment to fully take hold in New Zealand.

These differences in national context explain the different trajectories of the Australian and New Zealand citizens' movements. The Australian movements—like the paramilitary, new-state, and secessionist movements that arose alongside them—were staunchly in favour of classical liberalism. Their militant individualism was a more extreme version of mainstream conservatives' horror at the dual spectres of inflation and repudiation. Beyond party politicians, their enemies were clear: a federal Labor government which they believed was incapable of implementing the necessary measures to combat the Depression, along with the Lang Government in New South Wales, which they feared would besmirch the nation's financial honour. Combined with varying degrees of conspiratorial rhetoric about communism, the Australian movements had no need to seriously investigate economic alternatives to classical liberalism; their enemies were already doing that. In New Zealand, however, there was no labour bogeyman to generate a similarly united front against unorthodox economics. Conservatives held the balance of power throughout the Depression and had done a generally satisfactory job in conservatives' eyes of deflating the economy, reducing public spending, and responding swiftly and harshly to episodes of civil unrest in April–May 1932. Lacking a left-wing enemy against which to direct their frustrations, many legionnaires looked to unorthodox economic alternatives, particularly the growing international trends of economic planning and monetary reform. In this, they were joined by many other New Zealanders of all political persuasions who were drawn to monetary reform (particularly Douglas social credit) and the Labour Party's more interventionist platform. The timing of the New Zealand Legion's arrival on the political scene also enabled it to learn from the mistakes the Australian New Guard had made, leading it to consciously disavow any paramilitary activity.

The differences between the Australian and New Zealand citizens' movements are closely tied to the broader political trajectories of both countries. In Australia, the movements ultimately contributed to—and, in some cases, were wholly subsumed within—a renewed conservative political party that remained in power at a federal level until 1941. The United Australia Party was not the first example of political conservatives reinventing themselves by absorbing labour splinter groups and non-party conservative movements, nor would it be the last.

In contrast, the New Zealand Legion was one manifestation of a broader crisis within conservative politics, combined with a growing disaffection with economic orthodoxy. Unlike in Australia, where conservatives were brought together under the United Australia Party, the political right in New Zealand continued to splinter until the November 1935 election. In addition to the United Party and the legion, the other main splinter group was the Democrat Party, a laissez-faire group formed in 1934 by the well-known political campaigner Albert Davy. While the Democrats did not win any seats in 1935, they received around 7.8 per cent of the total votes cast. This vote-splitting appears to have been a factor in at least eight of the seats won by Labour.[2] A further 10.5 per cent of the vote was received by independent candidates. In a sense, then, the legion went down with the ship of a divided right wing, although by the 1935 election, it was already largely defunct. Conservatives subsequently regrouped behind the enduring banner of the National Party in 1936, but it did not achieve power again until 1949.

A link in the chain of the Australasian centre-right

While the citizens' movements soon faded into the obituary pages, their novel methods of political mobilisation and ideological expression played a role in the long-term trends and processes of Australasian conservative thought. Their most direct contribution was in the way that centre-right parties in Australia and New Zealand reinvented themselves in subsequent decades as representatives of a silent middle class. This may have been influenced by former members of the citizens' movements who subsequently went on to have political careers within the mainstream conservative establishment—in particular, those from the Australian Citizens' League and the New Zealand Legion. Much like the individuals of the pre-Depression conservative non-party organisations, these former members of the citizens' movements brought their ideological baggage with them, which in turn shaped the ways in which they interacted with, and influenced, mainstream conservatism.

2   Michael C. Pugh, 'Doctrinaires on the Right: The Democrats and Anti-Socialism, 1933–36', *New Zealand Journal of History* 17(2) (October 1983): 103–19, at p. 115.

A transnational parallel can be drawn between the two biggest success stories of the citizens' movements, Robert Menzies in Australia and Sid Holland in New Zealand. The latter was an enthusiastic member of the Christchurch centre of the New Zealand Legion, while the former had worked closely with the Australian Citizens' League through his involvement with the Victorian Young Nationalists Organisation and the Group of Six. Both subsequently became leading figures in the consolidation of mainstream conservatism in Australia and New Zealand. They oversaw, to varying degrees, the creation of the Liberal and National parties and their transformation into mass organisations based on permanent hierarchical branch structures similar to their labour opponents. As the vanguard of a younger generation of conservative politicians, they also oversaw a shift away from the tempered, patrician rhetoric of their predecessors to a more populist style aimed at colonising the electoral middle ground. They sought to turn their new political organisations away from elite financial backers towards the middle class, which they portrayed as the backbone of the nation's economic prosperity and social stability. Menzies' new approach was summed up in his 1942 radio address to 'the forgotten people', who formed this middle class, while Holland's came a year later in his pamphlet titled 'Passwords to Progress'.[3] This suggests that, despite their failure, the citizens' movements had a lasting impact through the new, populist style of conservative politics pioneered by their former members. However, the extent to which the experiences of Menzies and Holland with the citizens' movements influenced their long-term political outlook must remain a subject for further study.

The citizens' movements also demonstrated the persistence of classical liberalism in Australasia during the twentieth century. This tradition was explored in the Australian context by Frank Bongiorno, who argued that the claim that free trade was banished to the political wilderness after the 'Australian Settlement'—as is so often asserted by neoliberals—is an oversimplification:

---

3   Sid Holland, *Passwords to Progress: A Plan for Post-War Security, Freedom and Prosperity* (Christchurch, NZ: Whitcombe & Tombs, 1943). For a thorough analysis of Menzies' appeal to the middle class (including a copy of the 'forgotten people' speech itself), see Judith Brett, *Robert Menzies' Forgotten People* (Sydney: Pan Macmillan, 1992).

[A]ny suggestion that Free Trade liberalism was eclipsed between Federation and the 1980s requires some qualification, for there are some obvious continuities in ideology and rhetoric between the Free Traders of the Federation era, and non-Labor political discourse of the middle decades of the twentieth century.[4]

One minor caveat to Bongiorno's approach is that, if Australasian conservatism is viewed within the framework of the nineteenth-century developmentalist ethos, the progression from free trade to neoliberalism, along with the intervening period of the Australian Settlement, was merely part of a continuum of greater or lesser state economic activity. Nevertheless, there is clearly an ideological 'low point' for classical liberalism during the middle of the twentieth century, which was marked especially in Australia and New Zealand by the advent of the Keynesian consensus in the postwar period. The citizens' movements are a clear example of how the ideology and rhetoric of classical liberalism persisted during those years. It was particularly relevant to their largely professional, semi-professional, and business membership base, for whom the temptations of protection and price guarantees were largely irrelevant.

An Antipodean fascism?

The phenomenon of mass conservative mobilisation was by far the largest and most significant right-wing reaction in the Antipodes during the Depression. Disconcerted conservatives rose in considerable numbers to join the citizens' movements, the paramilitary New Guard and its more secretive counterparts, the regional new-state sentiments in the Riverina and New England, and the secessionist Dominion League of Western Australia. This phenomenon inevitably lends itself to a comparison with the rise of fascist movements and regimes internationally during the inter-war years, which accelerated during the Depression. This is not an easy task, given the lack of consensus around a concise definition of fascism. As I noted in the Introduction, fascism is typically approached by scholars in two ways: ideologically (What does fascist ideology look like? Is there a 'minimum' set of ideological characteristics that must be met for the definition to apply?) and materially (How do fascist movements

4   Frank Bongiorno, 'Whatever Happened to Free Trade Liberalism?', in *Confusion: The Making of the Australian Two-Party System*, eds Paul Strangio and Nick Dyrenfurth (Melbourne: Melbourne University Press, 2009), 250.

arise? What conditions are required for them to gain strength and legitimacy?). These approaches are not mutually exclusive; indeed, they are complementary.

So, were the citizens' movements fascist? The conditions that gave birth to the movements were similar to those that nurtured fascism. Both were born of, or given added impetus by, crises within the economic system coupled with the disarray or disunity of mainstream conservative parliamentary forces. As centre-right parties struggled to cope with the Depression, disaffected conservatives turned to political alternatives in the hopes of a dramatic turnaround in their fortunes. Both were also buoyed by the rise of communism, socialism, and organised labour, although the Australasian communist parties were far smaller than their European counterparts. However, the ideological backgrounds of fascism and the citizens' movements were vastly different. Where fascists drew on forms of organic nationalism and anti-rationalist socialism, the citizens' movements emerged from a wholly conservative tradition.[5] Fascism also typically attracted broad, cross-class support, whereas the citizens' movements drew most of their support from the professional, business, and commercial fraction of the capitalist class.[6]

There are elements of the citizens' movements' ideology that are reminiscent of fascism. While idealism is a component of most political ideologies, the elevation of idealism to the position of a driving transformative force and the relegation of policy to a minor secondary role were similar to fascism's vitalist and anti-rationalist spirit. In other words, fascists, too, were renowned for promoting spirit over substance. Fascists were also known for their appeals to national unity, self-sacrifice, and demonisation of the 'other', although the fascist 'other' was more often a dynamic mix of Jews, communists, and other perceived enemies than party politicians. The citizens' movements also experimented to varying degrees with corporatist economic ideas, although never to the same extent as fascist movements elsewhere in the British Empire such as the British Union of Fascists.[7]

---

5   Sternhell, *The Birth of Fascist Ideology*.

6   For a good overview of the membership of various fascist movements, see Stein Ugelvik Larsen, Bernt Hagtvet, and Jan Petter Myklebust, eds, *Who Were the Fascists? Social Roots of European Fascism* (Oslo: Universitetsforlaget, 1980).

7   For a recent study of the British Union of Fascism's most renowned corporatist thinker, Alexander Raven Thomson, see Matthew McMurray, 'Alexander Raven Thomson, Philosopher of the British Union of Fascists', *The European Legacy: Toward New Paradigms* 17(1) (2012): 33–59.

Despite their belief in cooperation and the subsuming of difference, the citizens' movements could hardly be considered totalitarian or authoritarian in nature. Their professed goal was a more democratic society, albeit within the bounds of conservative tradition, and while they shared a belief in the necessity for new and charismatic leadership, this was almost always within the confines of the existing democratic structure. Only the Citizens' League of South Australia was openly willing to countenance more extreme measures, such as a dictatorship or the employment of force by extra-parliamentary means. Some of the citizens' movements' ideas on governmental reform were reminiscent of fascist policies of class collaboration and corporatism, although they were far less developed and far more wedded to the economic status quo. Only the New Zealand Legion seriously considered radical alternatives to the existing economic system. The reactionary component of the citizens' movement ideology had far more in common with traditional Australasian conservatism than it did with fascism. While the nostalgia of the citizens' movements for a mythical nineteenth-century utopia was reminiscent of fascism's desire for a national rebirth, their reliance on the pillars of conservatism was the opposite of fascism's anti-liberal and anti-conservative attitudes. Even their anti-communism was more in line with the attitudes of mainstream conservatives than it was with fascism. In fact, had it not been for their populism and their penchant for developing radical policies, there would have been little to distinguish the ideas of the citizens' movements from those of their mainstream conservative counterparts. The paramilitary New Guard had far more in common with fascism than the citizens' movements, although the extent to which it can be classified as fascist has generated some debate.[8]

Comparisons with the postwar far right

In the first few decades after World War Two, the Australasian far right developed along vastly different lines to the citizens' movements. Paul Spoonley described the far right in New Zealand in the 1970s and 1980s as a monist style of politics centred on conspiracy theory, distrust of democracy, sexism, nationalism, and racism.[9] Moore suggested a similar set of ideological characteristics in his study of Australian right-wing

8   Cunningham, 'Australian Fascism?'.
9   Spoonley, *The Politics of Nostalgia*, 29–44.

politics. He noted that the Australian far right was typically a more extreme version of mainstream conservatism, which embraced conspiracy theory 'as a central organising concept', encompassed an exclusionary form of nationalism, and expressed suspicion or outright contempt for liberal parliamentary democracy.[10] Virtually none of these was a central preoccupation of the citizens' movements. While it is true that many of the far right's views were relatively mainstream prior to World War Two—particularly those on race—it is also true that the citizens' movements' positions on race and gender were more of an implicit assumption than an explicit element of their ideology. The only movement that explicitly sought to promote female representation at all levels of its organisation was the All for Australia League, although its attempts were largely unsuccessful. And while the movements did not openly discuss race, it is likely their assumptions of what constituted 'whiteness' differed from that of the postwar far right. My recent edited collection on the radical right in New Zealand suggests that prewar conceptions of 'whiteness' were heavily intertwined with 'Britishness', whereas white nationalists in the postwar period have increasingly drawn on a pan-European definition of whiteness that incorporates Eastern and Southern European cultures that were once viewed as 'others' by mainstream New Zealand.[11] These are tentative conclusions that beg further research.

The postwar far right drew more inspiration from the conspiratorial and anti-establishment circles of monetary reform and social credit that arose in the 1930s than the citizens' movements. Apart from the New Zealand Legion, these groups had little involvement with the citizens' movements, and were often critical of them. There are many instances where prominent monetary reformists from this period went on to lead, or strongly influence, the ideas of the postwar far right, including Eric Butler and Arthur Nelson Field. The Social Credit Association of New Zealand also provided a vehicle through which prewar prejudices were carried across into the postwar period, although there was a sharp tension after the war between the old guard and a more pragmatic, tolerant new guard within the association.[12] This tension exemplifies the ideological retreat in the postwar period that contributed to the rise of the far right. As society partially withdrew from overly racist and bigoted ideas in the

---

10   Moore, *The Right Road*, 2–4.
11   Matthew Cunningham, Marinus La Rooij, and Paul Spoonley, eds, *Histories of Hate: The Radical Right in Aotearoa/New Zealand* (Dunedin, NZ: Otago University Press, forthcoming), Introduction.
12   Spoonley, *The Politics of Nostalgia*, 59–61.

postwar period, the far right arose to fill the ideological vacuum left behind. The recoil effect of the Holocaust, coupled with the centre-right's failure to respond to crises in the way the adherents of the far right wanted, provided a space where opponents of greater pluralism, multiculturalism, civil rights, and gender and sexual liberation could fester in a stew of intolerance.

Despite their ideological differences, the citizens' movements' specific focus on the nation foreshadowed the far right's shift away from Britain towards the nation-state, which Moore described as a change from imperial patriotism to nationalist chauvinism.[13] While the citizens' movements remained loyal to Britain, their focus on national issues and their lack of international connections distinguished them from the multitude of conservative non-party organisations that preceded them. They arose in response to specific national manifestations of an international crisis. Their enemies were largely nationally based, with the exception of international communism. The nation was also the rhetorical unit for recovery, inasmuch as recovery required national unity and self-sacrifice in the service of the national interest. Eschewing strong international ties was therefore one way for the citizens' movements to reinforce their exclusively 'national' credentials, despite the imperial focus of their patriotism. This partly reflected the complementary national and imperial patriotisms felt by many Australians and New Zealanders by the early twentieth century.[14] However, it also presaged the changing priorities of the far right in the postwar era. An ambitious argument might therefore be made that the citizens' movements sat at the crossroads of prewar and postwar right-wing nationalist loyalties in Australasia. While some postwar far-right movements remained loyal to the British Empire, the direction of travel was towards a distinctly national sense of patriotism. Many postwar stalwarts of the far right, for example, drew much more inspiration from Jack Lang's defiance of British bondholders than from the anti-communist antics of the New Guard.[15] This is not to say that Lang was on the far right, but merely that the priorities of those on the radical fringes of the right have changed.

---

13   Moore, *The Right Road*, 2–4.

14   Douglas Cole, 'The Problem of "Nationalism" and "Imperialism" in British Settlement Colonies', *Journal of British Studies* 10(2) (1970): 160–82; Russel Ward, 'Two Kinds of Australian Patriotism', *Victorian Historical Magazine* 41(1) (1970): 225–43; W. David McIntyre, 'Imperialism and Nationalism', in *The Oxford History of New Zealand*, ed. Geoffrey Rice (Auckland: Oxford University Press, 1992).

15   James Saleam, The other radicalism: An inquiry into contemporary Australian extreme right ideology, politics and organization 1975–1995 (PhD diss., University of Sydney, 1999), 44–49.

The citizens' movements have much more in common with Mudde's fourth wave of the far right, which he described as the 'populist radical right'.[16] According to Mudde, a significant wave of far-right politics arose in Western Europe in the 1980s and 1990s driven by unemployment and mass immigration. By the turn of the century, the populist radical right dominated this European far-right tradition and had even begun making headway in national and European parliaments. A series of crises in the early twenty-first century—the September 2001 terrorist attacks, the Global Financial Crisis of 2008, and the refugee crisis of 2015—buoyed the populist radical right even further and saw its ideas and strategies increasingly adopted by mainstream parties. It also spread beyond Europe to the United States, Latin America, and Asia, and achieved electoral success in countries that had previously resisted penetration by the far right (such as Germany and Sweden). The populist radical right has also grown beyond party politics to include broad social movements and subcultures such as identitarianism and the alt-right. Mudde identified four themes shared by this 'fourth wave': a fear that mass immigration presents 'an existential threat' to the nation and the state, a heightened focus on security and law and order, a populist belief that 'the elite' in politics and business are corrupting the nation with 'postmodernist' and 'cultural Marxist' ideas, and an obsession with the supposed threat of internationalism or cosmopolitanism. It has responded to this with a mixture of nativism (a belief that nations should be inhabited exclusively by members of the native group), populism, authoritarianism, Islamophobia, a distrust of political 'elites' (especially those associated with transnational entities such as the European Union and the United Nations), and an opposition to 'political correctness' and 'do-goodism'.

Much of the populist radical right's ideological content is specific to the issues of our time, but there is some similarity with the citizens' movements' populist revolt against the political establishment. Those drawn to the populist radical right and the citizens' movements also shared a belief that traditional political parties did not represent, or no longer represented, their interests and values. The citizens' movements believed that political parties had stepped away from the hardy, individualist ethos of their nineteenth-century forebears to become enslaved to sectional interests and their demands on the public purse. They sought a return to an imagined past where citizens had not depended on the patronage of

---

16   Mudde, *The Far Right Today*, 1.

the state and politicians were free to vote according to their conscience. The contemporary populist radical right, however, is partially the result of a process of political de-alignment as voters have begun stepping away from traditional class-based party allegiances towards a politics based on values, identity, and culture.[17] It is this sense of politics-in-transformation that led Enzo Traverso to describe the populist radical right as 'post-fascism', in that it represents both continuity and change from inter-war fascism and the neofascist groups of the postwar period: 'a phenomenon in transition, a movement that is still in transformation and has not yet crystallised'.[18] At a time when free-market capitalism has become the ideological default, the radical right has provided a surrogate for the lack of utopian alternatives since the end of the Cold War.[19]

The comparison becomes much more apt when examining manifestations of the populist radical right at home. The dramatic rise of One Nation in rural Queensland and New South Wales in the 1990s, for example, is reminiscent of the citizens' movements' revolt against mainstream conservative parties. Similar to the citizens' movements, One Nation's ideology consists of a struggle between the ordinary people and a new class elite seeking to destroy traditional values.[20] As Andy Fleming and Aurelian Mondon recently noted, One Nation disrupted the bipartisan consensus that had emerged in the 1970s and 1980s in Australia regarding multiculturalism. Echoing the United Australia Party's successful cooption of the citizens' movements, the Liberal Party normalised and entrenched One Nation's policies in the late 1990s to such an extent that it undercut One Nation's support base. Several groups emerged to fill the void opened by the near collapse of One Nation, including the Australia First Party and the United Patriots Front, although they struggled to attract

---

17   Jens Rydgren, 'The Radical Right: An Introduction', in *The Oxford Handbook of the Radical Right*, ed. Jens Rydgren (New York: Oxford University Press, 2018).

18   Enzo Traverso, *The New Faces of Fascism: Populism and the Far Right*, trans. David Broder (London: Verso, 2019), 6.

19   ibid., 184. Traverso sees Islamic extremism as filling the same utopian need.

20   Gregory Melleuish, 'Populism and Conservatism in Australian Political Thought', in *The Politics of Australian Society: Political Issues for the New Century*, eds Paul Boreham, Geoffrey Stokes, and Richard Hall (Sydney: Longman, 2000), 51–64; Geoffrey Stokes, 'One Nation and Australian Populism', in *The Rise and Fall of One Nation*, eds Michael Leach, Geoff Stokes, and Ian M. Ward (Brisbane: University of Queensland Press, 2000), 23–41; Bligh Grant, Tod Moore, and Tony Lynch, eds, *The Rise of Right-Populism: Pauline Hanson's One Nation and Australian Politics* (Singapore: Springer, 2019); Anna Broinowski, *Please Explain: The Rise, Fall and Rise Again of Pauline Hanson* (Sydney: Penguin Random House, 2017); Murray Goot, 'Pauline Hanson's One Nation: Extreme Right, Centre Party or Extreme Left?', *Labour History* 89 (2005): 101–19.

even a fraction of One Nation's support.[21] The New Zealand First Party represents a similar conservative backlash in New Zealand, albeit one that has proven much more successful electorally.[22] Moffitt argued that New Zealand First's political agenda extends beyond the usual anxieties of the radical right, which has complicated attempts to define where it sits on the ideological spectrum.[23] Yet the conservatism of One Nation and New Zealand First lies predominantly in the sociocultural sphere, seeking to question progressive values on gender, race relations, indigenous liberation, and immigration. Their economic policies are much more centrist, and—in many cases—somewhat left-leaning. The citizens' movements were much more concerned with economics than sociocultural matters, and of the four citizens' movements, only the New Zealand Legion was willing to abandon its commitment to laissez-faire economics.

The closest political analogue to the citizens' movements in recent years was the Tea Party movement in the United States. Born in early 2009 amid the economic and political uncertainty of the Global Financial Crisis, it represented a coalescing of libertarian and conservative discontent against the Obama administration's policies. Unlike the citizens' movements, the Tea Party movement comprised hundreds of different organisations, although umbrella groups like the Tea Party Patriots and Americans for Prosperity provided some national order and direction. Nevertheless, these various groups were united in their calls for limited government, a reduction in taxation, and decreased government spending to balance the federal budget and reduce national debt. Their members have endorsed candidates who support these goals, regardless of which party they belong to—although, in practice, they tend to be conservatives. In many cases, Tea Party members and organisations have supported candidates who

---

21   Andy Fleming and Aurelian Mondon, 'The Radical Right in Australia', in in *The Oxford Handbook of the Radical Right*, ed. Jens Rydgren (New York: Oxford University Press, 2018), 650–62.
22   Ben Thomas McLachlan, In search of a New Zealand populism: Heresthetics, character and populist political leadership (MA diss., Victoria University of Wellington, 2013); Benjamin Moffitt, 'Populism in Australia and New Zealand', in *The Oxford Handbook of Populism*, eds Rovira Kaltwasser, Paul Taggart, Paulina Ochoa Espejo, and Pierre Ostiguy (London: Oxford University Press, 2017), 121–39; Jack H. Nagel, 'Populism, Heresthetics and Political Stability: Richard Seddon and the Art of Majority Rule', *British Journal of Political Science* 23(2) (1993): 139–74; Hans-Georg Betz, 'New Zealand First', in *The New Politics of the Right: Neo-Populist Parties and Movements in Established Democracies*, eds Hans-Georg Betz and Stefan Immerfall (New York: St Martin's Press, 1998); Claire Haeg, *The Cross of Gold Revisited: Neo-Populist Party Emergence in Australia, Canada, and New Zealand* (Berlin: VDM Verlag, 2009); Barry Gustafson, 'Populist Roots of Political Leadership in New Zealand', in *Political Leadership in New Zealand*, eds Raymond Miller and Michael Mintrom (Auckland: Auckland University Press, 2006), 51–69.
23   Moffitt, 'Populism in Australia and New Zealand'.

ran against 'establishment' Republican nominees.[24] However, opposing
the 'establishment' appears to have been less of a concern for Tea Party
advocates than it was for the citizens' movements, for whom opposing
party politicians and their political 'machines' was a fundamental priority.
Arguably, Tea Party supporters seek only to transform the Republican
Party rather than destroy political parties entirely.

The Trump presidency, in some ways, represented the success the citizens'
movements never achieved. While the Australian citizens' movements
were coopted by the mainstream, the mainstream was coopted by Trump.
His popularity, his ability to connect with alienated voters, and his
diehard support base enabled him to push the Republican Party's style
of politics away from Reagan and Bush-era neoconservatism towards a
more isolationist, protectionist, and populist style of politics. Had Joseph
Lyons been a politician similar in style to Trump, the United Australia
Party may have adopted a more overtly populist stance. But Lyons was
not a political novice seeking to shake up the political order; he was
a sober and considered politician, a Labor man with a conservative's heart.
The similarities between Trump and the citizens' movements grow even
thinner when comparing their beliefs. The citizens' movements did not
share Trump's sociocultural preoccupations and, while they would have
found little to complain about in his tax cuts and slashing of regulations,
they would have frowned on his increased federal spending and the
swelling national debt. Even their populism sought different ends. Trump's
goal was never to eliminate political parties, but to transform one of them
from within. Perhaps, then, this helps to explain his success: he never had
to grapple with the inherent contradiction between anti-party purity and
political expediency that split the Australian citizens' movements.

Final thoughts

There is a common truism that states that those who do not learn from
history are doomed to repeat it. Whenever I hear this phrase, I—like
most historians, I suspect—cringe a little. It is not because I believe

---

24   See Jill Lepore, *The Whites of Their Eyes: The Tea Party's Revolution and the Battle over American History* (Princeton, NJ: Princeton University Press, 2010); Theda Skocpol and Vanessa Williamson, *The Tea Party and the Remaking of Republican Conservatism* (Oxford, UK: Oxford University Press, 2012); Nella Van Dyke and David S. Meyer, *Understanding the Tea Party Movement* (New York: Routledge, 2014); Michael Leahy, *Covenant of Liberty: The Ideological Origins of the Tea Party Movement* (New York: HarperCollins Publishers, 2012).

history cannot teach us anything, or that I am a purist who only values studying history for history's sake. History does have lessons; they are simply replete with caveats. There are certainly many similarities between the populist conservatism of the citizens' movements and the rise of the 'populist radical right' in recent years. Like the citizens' movements, leaders of the modern populist right have skilfully used crises to tap into long-held public sentiments and prejudices that, in ordinary times, do not animate people to the same extent. However, in many cases, they have successfully transformed that discontent into electoral victories without alienating their followers by participating in an allegedly corrupt political system—perhaps because, to borrow from Donald Trump's vocabulary, they have promised to 'drain the swamp'.[25] The citizens' movements never managed to do this.

The key lesson of this book is simply this: understanding the past helps us to understand the present. Having a sense of how the right has responded previously in times of crisis makes the contemporary rise of right-wing populism seem less bewildering. This does not require one to forgive the atrocities perpetrated by violent white nationalists, who sit at the sharp end of the contemporary far right. But it can provide the tools to unpick—and, depending on one's political persuasion, to unravel—the broad tapestry of ideas that is constantly being woven and rewoven on the fringes.

---

25   Although Trump cannot claim inspiration for this quote; it has been increasingly used by politicians on both sides of the spectrum since the 1980s.

Bibliography

Primary sources

Unpublished papers

Archives New Zealand, Wellington

Rifle Clubs—Christchurch Citizens Defence Corps, 1914–1919, AAYS 8638 AD1/1035.

Alexander Turnbull Library, Wellington

Arthur Nelson Field Papers, MS-Group-1534.

New Zealand Employers' Federation Papers, 2001-129-01/3.

New Zealand Farmers' Union Papers, MS-Papers-1159.

Raymond Ernest Hansen Papers, 84-204-74.

Sir John Hall Papers, MS-Papers-1784-183.

The Russell Saga Vol. 4, qMS-0823.

Transcripts of taped interviews with various people for Tony Simpson, 'The Sugar Bag Years', MS-Papers-9902.

Wellington Chamber of Commerce Papers, MS-Group-0018.

Wellington Civic League Papers, MS-Papers-0158-300D.

Wellington Rotary Club Papers, MS-Group-0286.

Will Lawson Papers, MS-Papers-1679-5.

Auckland University Library

Hawke's Bay Division of the New Zealand Legion Papers, A38.

Sir George Fowlds Papers, A-17.

Australian War Memorial, Canberra

Australian National Defence League, NSW Division Papers, 1905–38, 2DRL/1098.

Macmillan Brown Library, Christchurch, NZ

Victoria League of New Zealand Canterbury Branch Records, 1919–1993, Accession No. 367.

National Archives of Australia, Canberra

Commonwealth Investigation Branch Correspondence Files, A369.

National Library of Australia, Canberra

Citizens' League of South Australia Papers, MS 1186.

Directorate of War Propaganda Papers, MS 897.

Ernest Turnbull Papers, MS 1942/2.

Herbert and Ivy Brookes Papers, MS 1924.

Hilda and C.L.A. Abbott Papers, MS 4744.

H.M. Storey Papers, MS 8539.

Joseph Aloysius Lyons Papers, MS 4851.

New Zealand Welfare League, Interim Report for Period Ending 31 May 1921, MHE 14:114.

Sir John Latham Papers, MS 1009.

Ulrich Ellis Papers, MS 1006.

State Library of New South Wales, Sydney

British Empire Union in Australia Records, MLMSS 1532.

Constitutional Association of New South Wales Papers, 1925–61, MLMSS 7646C.

Francis Edward de Groot Papers, volume 4 (CY3091) and volume 5 (CY3092).

George Waite Papers, MLMSS 208.

Thomas D. Mutch Papers, MLMSS 426.

Will Lawson Papers, MLMSS 356 and MLMSS 3129.

State Library of South Australia, Adelaide

Archibald Grenfell Price Papers, PRG7.

Interview with Sir Keith Wilson, SRG 660/1/147.

State Library of Victoria, Melbourne
A.&K. Henderson Records, MS9317.

State Library of Western Australia, Perth
Colin Unwin Papers, ACC 6321A.

University of Queensland Fryer Library, Brisbane
Albert Welsby Papers, UQFL40.

Unpublished papers (privately held)
Alex J. Gibson Papers.

Aubrey Colville Henri de Rune Barclay Papers.

Eric Campbell Memoirs.

James Begg Papers.

New Zealand Section of the Theosophical Society Papers.

Ormond Family Papers.

Published primary sources

A Collection of Policy Statements and Speeches of the League. Sydney: League of Good Citizenship, 1919.

All for Australia League. Sydney: All for Australia League, 1931.

All for Australia League: Draft Constitution. Sydney: All for Australia League, 1931.

All for Australia League: Draft Policy. Sydney: All for Australia League, 1931.

All for Australia League: Its Real Significance. Sydney: All for Australia League, 1931.

All for Australia League Shows the Way to Prosperity. Melbourne: All for Australia League, 1931.

An Australia-Wide Appeal for the Abolition of the Party System of Government. Perth: Citizens' Federation of Western Australia, 1931.

Annual Report of the Executive Committee of the Australian National Defence League, N.S.W. Division. Sydney: Australian National Defence League, 1911.

Annual Report of the Executive Committee of the Australian National Defence League, N.S.W. Division. Sydney: Australian National Defence League, 1912.

Annual Report of the Executive Committee of the Australian National Defence League, N.S.W. Division. Sydney: Australian National Defence League, 1913.

A Recipe for Revolution. Sydney: Constitutional Association of New South Wales, 1932.

Begg, Robert Campbell. *The Secret of the Knife.* Norwich, UK: Jarrold & Sons, 1966.

Campbell, Eric. *The Rallying Point: My Story of the New Guard.* Melbourne: Melbourne University Press, 1965.

Campbell, G.R. *Summary of Swiss Military System, and Suggestions as to How a Similar System Might be Applied in Australia.* Sydney: Australian National Defence League, 1905.

Campbell, G.R. *The Swiss Military System Including Proposed Changes.* Sydney: Australian National Defence League, 1907.

Citizens' League: Its Formation, Aims, and Objects. Adelaide: Citizens' League of South Australia, 1931.

Constitution of Citizens' League of South Australia. Adelaide: F. Cockington & Co. Printers, 1931.

Exhibition of all Australian Manufactures at Drummoyne. Sydney: 'Who's for Australia?' League, 1930.

Harper, Arthur P. *The Revolutionary Campaign: Facts Which Everyone Should Know.* Wellington: New Zealand Welfare League, 1921.

Industrial Sectarianism Versus Industrial Democracy. Melbourne: The Loyalist League of Victoria, 1920.

Interim Report for Period Ending May 31st, 1921. Wellington: New Zealand Welfare League, 1921.

Lang, Lunacy, Loot. Sydney: Constitutional Association of New South Wales, 1931.

Lee Neil, E. *Why We Need a Citizens' League.* Melbourne: Australian Citizens' League, 1931.

Light on the Legion. Wellington: Commercial Printing Company Ltd, 1933.

Manifesto of the Citizens' National Movement to the Coalition Government. Wellington: Citizens' National Movement, 1932.

Manifesto of Provisional Committee of the Australian Citizens' League. Melbourne: Australian Citizens' League, 1931.

Meeson, John. *The Proper Functions of Government and the Evils that Arise from Overstepping Them: A Paper Read before the Nelson Philosophical Society on Monday, 14th Sept., 1885.* Nelson, NZ: R. Lucas & Son, 1885.

National Unity in Crisis: The Story of the N.Z. Legion. Wellington: New Zealand Legion, 1933.

Objects, League of Good Citizenship: A Collection of Policy Statements and Speeches of the League. Sydney: League of Good Citizenship, 1919.

Parliament vs Soviet; To Working Men and Women, League of Good Citizenship: A Collection of Policy Statements and Speeches of the League. Sydney: League of Good Citizenship, 1919.

Parry, Evan and C.A.L. Treadwell. *Workers' Compensation in New Zealand.* Wellington: Whitcombe & Tombs, 1927.

Policy and Aims of [Political Reform] League. Adelaide: Commercial Printing House, 1930.

Policy as Adopted by Convention of the League. Sydney: All for Australia League, 1931.

Price, A.G. *The Menace of Inflation.* Adelaide: F.W. Preece & Sons, 1931.

Primary Producers' Problems: The Way Out. Sydney: Land Newspaper Ltd, 1931.

Report of the Fifth Annual Meeting of the Liberty and Property Defence League. London: Liberty and Property Defence League, 1887.

Reports of Inaugural Meetings. Sydney: King and Empire Alliance, 1920.

Revolution or Evolution? Melbourne: The Loyalist League of Victoria, 1919.

Ruth, T.E. *Australia at the Crossroads.* Sydney: Robert Dey & Co., 1931.

Sane Democracy: Some Radio Lectures on 2KY. Sydney: Sane Democracy League, 1926.

Sinn Fein and Germany. Melbourne: The Loyalist League of Victoria, 1919.

The Abolition of Party Government Depends Upon You. Perth: Citizens' Federation of Western Australia, 1931.

The Australasian Naval and Military Annual, 1911–1912. Sydney: Angus & Robertson, 1912.

The Australasian Naval and Military Annual, 1912–1913. Sydney: Angus & Robertson, 1913.

The Constitutional Association of New South Wales. Sydney: W.C. Penfold & Co., March 1931.

The Election Issue, from the Viewpoint of the N.S.W. Constitutional Association. Sydney: Constitutional Association of New South Wales, 1929.

The Menace of an Irish Republic. Melbourne: The Loyalist League of Victoria, 1920.

The True Story of Sinn Fein. Melbourne: The Loyalist League of Victoria, 1919.

Unwin, Colin. *Unism: The New Constructive Policy.* Fremantle, WA: Porter & Salmon, 1916.

Who's for Australia? Four Songs in Her Praise. Sydney: 'Who's for Australia?' League, 1930.

Who's for Australia? League. Sydney: 'Who's for Australia?' League, 1929.

Newspapers and periodicals

Advance! Australia [Sydney]

Advertiser and Register [Adelaide]

Age [Melbourne]

Akaroa Mail and Banks Peninsula Advertiser

Albany Advertiser

Alexandra and Yea Standard and Yarck, Gobur, Thornton and Acheron Express

Argonaut [Perth]

Auckland Star

Australian Quarterly [Sydney]

Australian Theosophist [Sydney]

Australian Town and Country Journal [Sydney]

Barrier Miner [Broken Hill, NSW]

Blackshirt [London]

Brisbane Courier

Burra Record

Cairns Post

Camperdown Chronicle

Daily Telegraph [Sydney]

Essendon Gazette and Keilor, Bulla and Broadmeadows Reporter

Examiner [Launceston, Tas.]

Farming First [Auckland]

Frankston & Somerville Standard

Freedom [Wellington]

Gippsland Times [Sale, Vic.]

Horsham Times

King and Empire

Laura Standard and Crystal Brook Courier

Legion [Wellington]

LIFE [New York]

Mail [Adelaide]

Manawatu Standard

Marlborough Express [Blenheim, NZ]

Mercury [Hobart]

Morwell Advertiser

National Opinion [Wellington]

New Economics [Melbourne]

New England [Rugby, NSW]

New Zealand Financial Times [Wellington]

New Zealand Herald [Auckland]

New Zealand Observer [Auckland]

New Zealand Truth [Wellington]

News [Adelaide]

North Eastern Ensign [Benalla, Vic.]

North Western Advocate and the Emu Bay Times [Burnie, Tas.]

Northern Advocate [Whangarei]

Otago Daily Times [Dunedin]

Progress

Recorder [Port Pirie, SA]

Register News-Pictorial [Adelaide]

Sane Democracy [Sydney]

Singleton Argus

Smith's Weekly [Sydney]

Sydney Morning Herald

Taihape Times

Telegraph [Brisbane]

The Advertiser [Adelaide]

The Argus [Melbourne]

The Australian Worker [Sydney]

The Canberra Times

The Colonist [Sydney]

The Dominion [Wellington]

The Evening Post [Wellington]

The Herald [Melbourne]

The Hunter Statesman [Newcastle, NSW]

The Morning Bulletin [Rockhampton, Qld]

The Press [Christchurch]

The Register [Adelaide]

The Worker [Brisbane]

Townsville Daily Bulletin

Traralgon Record

Wanganui Chronicle

Werribee Shire Banner

West Australian [Perth]

Western Argus [Kalgoorlie, WA]

Western Mail [Perth]

Who's for Australia? [Sydney]

Wodonga and Towong Sentinel

World Theosophy

Secondary sources

Books

Aitkin, Don. *The Country Party in New South Wales: A Study of Organisation and Survival*. Canberra: Australian National University Press, 1972.

Amos, Keith. *The New Guard Movement, 1931–1935*. Melbourne: Melbourne University Press, 1976.

Anderson, Don. *The Kyabram Reform Movement of 1902*. Kyabram, Vic.: Kyabram Free Press, 1989.

Argersinger, Peter H. *Populism and Politics: William Alfred Peffer and the People's Party*. Lexington, KY: University Press of Kentucky, 2015.

Ballantyne, Tony. *Webs of Empire: Locating New Zealand's Colonial Past*. Wellington: Bridget Williams Books, 2012. doi.org/10.7810/9781927131435.

Bassett, Michael. *Three Party Politics in New Zealand, 1911–1931*. Auckland: Historical Publications, 1982.

Bassett, Michael. *Coates of Kaipara*. Auckland: Auckland University Press, 1995.

Bassett, Michael. *The State in New Zealand*. Auckland: Auckland University Press, 1998.

Bayley, William A. *History of the Farmers and Settlers' Association of N.S.W.* Sydney: Farmers and Settlers' Association, 1957.

Bayly, C.A. *Empire and Information: Intelligence Gathering and Social Communication in India, 1780–1870*. Cambridge, UK: Cambridge University Press, 1996. doi.org/10.1017/CBO9780511583285.

Belich, James. *Making Peoples: A History of the New Zealanders from Polynesian Settlement to the End of the Nineteenth Century*. Auckland: Penguin Press, 1996.

Belich, James. *Paradise Reforged: A History of the New Zealanders from the 1880s to the Year 2000*. Auckland: Penguin Press, 2001.

Bennett, James. *'Rats and Revolutionaries': The Labour Movement in Australia and New Zealand 1890–1940*. Dunedin, NZ: Otago University Press, 2004.

Bird, David. *Nazi Dreamtime: Australian Enthusiasts for Hitler's Germany*. Melbourne: Australian Scholarly Publishing, 2012.

Bolton, Geoffrey. *A Fine Country to Starve In*. Perth: University of Western Australia Press, 1994.

Bongiorno, Frank. *The People's Party: Victorian Labor and the Radical Tradition, 1875–1915*. Melbourne: Melbourne University Press, 1996.

Bossence, William Henry. *Kyabram*. Melbourne: Hawthorn Press, 1963.

Brett, Judith. *Robert Menzies' Forgotten People*. Sydney: Pan Macmillan, 1992.

Brett, Judith. *Australian Liberals and the Moral Middle Class*. Cambridge, UK: Cambridge University Press, 2003. doi.org/10.1017/CBO9780511481642.

Broinowski, Anna. *Please Explain: The Rise, Fall and Rise Again of Pauline Hanson*. Sydney: Penguin Random House, 2017.

Brooking, Tom. *The History of New Zealand*. Westport, CT: Greenwood Press, 2004.

Bush, Julia. *Edwardian Ladies and Imperial Power*. London: Leicester University Press, 2000.

Butlin, Noel G. *Investment in Australian Economic Development, 1861–1900*. London: Cambridge University Press, 1964. doi.org/10.1017/CBO978131 6530160.

Cain, Frank. *The Origins of Political Surveillance in Australia*. Melbourne: Angus & Robertson, 1983.

Capling, Ann and Brian Galligan. *Beyond the Protective State: The Political Economy of Australia's Manufacturing Industry Policy*. Cambridge, UK: Cambridge University Press, 1992.

Cathcart, Michael. *Defending the National Tuckshop: Australia's Secret Army Intrigue of 1931*. Melbourne: McPhee Gribble, 1988.

Cohen, Deborah and Maura O'Connor. *Comparison and History: Europe in Cross-National Perspective*. New York: Routledge, 2004. doi.org/10.4324/9780203312346.

Condliffe, J.B. *New Zealand in the Making: A Study of Economic and Social Development*. London: Allen & Unwin, 1936.

Cowen, Zelman. *Sir John Latham and Other Papers*. Sydney: Halstead Press, 1965.

Cresciani, Gianfranco. *Fascism, Anti-Fascism and Italians in Australia, 1922–1945*. Canberra: Australian National University Press, 1980.

Cunningham, Matthew, Marinus La Rooij, and Paul Spoonley, eds. *Histories of Hate: The Radical Right in Aotearoa/New Zealand*. Dunedin, NZ: Otago University Press, forthcoming.

Davidson, Alexander. *Two Models of Welfare: The Origins and Development of the Welfare State in Sweden and New Zealand, 1888–1988*. Uppsala: Acta Universitatis Upsaliensis, 1989.

Dunsdorfs, Edgars. *The Australian Wheat-Growing Industry, 1788–1948*. Melbourne: Melbourne University Press, 1956.

Durden, Robert Franklin. *The Climax of Populism: The Election of 1896*. Lexington, KY: University Press of Kentucky, 2015.

Eccleshall, Robert. *English Conservatism Since the Restoration: An Introduction and Anthology*. London: Unwin Hyman, 1990.

Elenio, Paul. *'Alla Fine Del Mondo': To the Ends of the Earth*. Wellington: Petone Settlers Museum & the Club Garibaldi, 1995.

Ellis, Ulrich. *The Country Party: A Political and Social History of the Party in New South Wales*. Melbourne: F.W. Cheshire, 1958.

Ellis, Ulrich. *A History of the Australian Country Party*. Melbourne: Melbourne University Press, 1963.

Ellis, Ulrich. *A Pen in Politics (Finished and published by Max Ellis)*. Canberra: Ginninderra Press, 2007.

Evans, Raymond. *The Red Flag Riots: A Study of Intolerance*. Brisbane: University of Queensland Press, 1988.

Fitzgerald, Ross. *'Red Ted': The Life of E.G. Theodore*. Brisbane: University of Queensland Press, 1994.

Fitzherbert, Margaret. *Liberal Women: Federation to 1949*. Sydney: The Federation Press, 2004.

Freeden, Michael. *Ideology: A Very Short Introduction*. New York: Oxford University Press, 2003. doi.org/10.1093/actrade/9780192802811.001.0001.

Gentry, Kynan. *Raising the Capital: An Illustrated History of 100 Years of the Wellington Regional Chambers of Commerce*. Wellington: Raupo Publishing, 2006.

Glezer, Leon. *Tariff Politics: Australian Policy-Making 1960–1980*. Melbourne: Melbourne University Press, 1982.

Goodman, David. *Gold Seeking: Victoria and California in the 1850s*. Stanford, CA: Stanford University Press, 1994.

Gourevitch, Peter. *Politics in Hard Times: Comparative Responses to International Economic Crises*. Ithaca, NY: Cornell University Press, 1986.

Graham, B.D. *The Formation of the Australian Country Parties*. Canberra: Australian National University Press, 1966.

Grant, Bligh, Tod Moore, and Tony Lynch, eds. *The Rise of Right-Populism: Pauline Hanson's One Nation and Australian Politics*. Singapore: Springer, 2019. doi.org/10.1007/978-981-13-2670-7.

Griffin, Roger. *The Nature of Fascism*. London: Routledge, 1993.

Grimshaw, Patricia. *Women's Suffrage in New Zealand*. Auckland: Auckland University Press, 1988.

Haeg, Claire. *The Cross of Gold Revisited: Neo-Populist Party Emergence in Australia, Canada, and New Zealand*. Berlin: VDM Verlag, 2009.

Hamer, David. *The New Zealand Liberals: The Years of Power, 1891–1912.* Auckland: Auckland University Press, 1988.

Hawke, Gary. *The Making of New Zealand: An Economic History.* Cambridge, UK: Cambridge University Press, 1985.

Hempenstall, Peter, ed. *Remaking the Tasman World.* Christchurch, NZ: Canterbury University Press, 2008.

Henderson, Anne. *Enid Lyons: Leading Lady to a Nation.* Melbourne: Pluto Press, 2008.

Henderson, Anne. *Joseph Lyons: The People's Prime Minister.* Sydney: UNSW Press, 2012.

Hild, Matthew. *Greenbackers, Knights of Labor, and Populists: Farmer–Labor Insurgency in the Late-Nineteenth-Century South.* Athens, GA: University of Georgia Press, 2007.

Holland, Sid. *Passwords to Progress: A Plan for Post-War Security, Freedom and Prosperity.* Christchurch, NZ: Whitcombe & Tombs, 1943.

Hollingsworth, Mark and Charles Tremayne. *The Economic League: The Silent McCarthyism.* London: National Council for Civil Liberties, 1989.

Howard, Frederick. *Kent Hughes: A Biography of Colonel the Hon. Sir Wilfred Kent Hughes.* Melbourne: Macmillan, 1972.

Hughes, Mike. *Spies at Work.* Bradford, UK: 1 in 12 Publications, 1994.

Kealey, Gregory S. and Greg Patmore, eds. *Canadian and Australian Labour History: Towards a Comparative Perspective.* Sydney: Australian Society for the Study of Labour History, 1990.

Kelly, Paul. *The End of Certainty: Power, Politics, and Business in Australia.* Sydney: Allen & Unwin, 1994.

Laidlaw, Zoë. *Colonial Connections, 1815–45: Patronage, the Information Revolution and Colonial Government.* Manchester, UK: Manchester University Press, 2005.

Larsen, Stein Ugelvik, Bernt Hagtvet, and Jan Petter Myklebust, eds. *Who Were the Fascists? Social Roots of European Fascism.* Oslo: Universitetsforlaget, 1980.

Leahy, Michael. *Covenant of Liberty: The Ideological Origins of the Tea Party Movement.* New York: HarperCollins Publishers, 2012.

Lepore, Jill. *The Whites of Their Eyes: The Tea Party's Revolution and the Battle over American History*. Princeton, NJ: Princeton University Press, 2010. doi.org/ 10.1515/9781400839810.

Lester, Alan. *Imperial Networks: Creating Identities in Nineteenth-Century South Africa and Britain*. London: Routledge, 2001. doi.org/10.4324/97802 03995723.

Liebich, Susann. *The Transported Imagination: Australian Interwar Magazines and the Geographical Imaginaries of Colonial Modernity*. New York: Cambria Press, 2018.

Love, Peter. *Labour and the Money Power: Australian Labour Populism, 1890–1950*. Melbourne: Melbourne University Press, 1984.

Macintyre, Stuart. *A Colonial Liberalism: The Lost World of Three Victorian Visionaries*. Melbourne: Oxford University Press, 1991.

Macintyre, Stuart. *A Concise History of Australia*. Melbourne: Cambridge University Press, 2004.

Mackenzie, John. *Propaganda and Empire: The Manipulation of British Public Opinion, 1880–1960*. Manchester, UK: Manchester University Press, 1984.

Mannheim, Karl. *Ideology and Utopia: An Introduction to the Sociology of Knowledge*. New York: Harcourt, 1946.

Mannheim, Karl. *Conservatism: A Contribution to the Sociology of Knowledge*. London: Routledge & Kegan Paul, 1986.

Martin, A.W. *Robert Menzies: A Life. Volume 1, 1894–1943*. Melbourne: Melbourne University Press, 1993.

McAloon, Jim. *No Idle Rich: The Wealthy in Canterbury and Otago, 1840–1914*. Dunedin, NZ: Otago University Press, 2002.

McFarlane, Bruce. *Professor Irvine's Economics in Australian Labour History: 1913– 1933*. Canberra: Australian Society for the Study of Labour History, 1966.

McKenna, Mark. *The Captive Republic: A History of Republicanism in Australia 1788–1996*. Melbourne: Cambridge University Press, 1996.

McKenzie, Kirsten. *Scandal in the Colonies: Sydney and Cape Town, 1820–1850*. Melbourne: Melbourne University Publishing, 2004.

McKinnon, Malcolm. *The Broken Decade: Prosperity, Depression and Recovery in New Zealand, 1928–39*. Dunedin, NZ: Otago University Press, 2016.

Mein Smith, Philippa. *A Concise History of New Zealand.* New York: Cambridge University Press, 2005.

Mein Smith, Philippa, Donald Denoon, and Marivic Wyndham. *A History of Australia, New Zealand and the Pacific: The Formation of Identities.* Oxford, UK: Blackwell Publishers, 2000.

Melleuish, Gregory. *Cultural Liberalism in Australia.* Cambridge, UK: Cambridge University Press, 1995.

Melleuish, Gregory. *A Short History of Australian Liberalism.* Sydney: Centre for Independent Studies, 2001.

Meredith, David and Barrie Dyster. *Australia in the Global Economy: Continuity and Change.* Cambridge, UK: Cambridge University Press, 1999.

Millar, J.H. *The Merchants Paved the Way: The First Hundred Years of the Wellington Chamber of Commerce.* Wellington: Reed, 1956.

Millmow, Alex. *The Power of Economic Ideas: The Origins of Keynesian Macroeconomic Management in Interwar Australia 1929–39.* Canberra: ANU E Press, 2010. doi.org/10.22459/PEI.05.2010.

Moffitt, Benjamin. *The Global Rise of Populism: Performance, Political Style, and Representation.* Palo Alto, CA: Stanford University Press, 2017. doi.org/ 10.1515/9780804799331.

Moffitt, Benjamin. *Populism: Key Concepts in Political Theory.* Oxford, UK: Polity Press, 2020.

Moore, Andrew. *The Secret Army and the Premier: Conservative Paramilitary Organisations in New South Wales, 1930–32.* Sydney: UNSW Press, 1989.

Moore, Andrew. *The Right Road: A History of Right-Wing Politics in Australia.* Melbourne: Oxford University Press, 1995.

Moore, Andrew. *Francis de Groot: Irish Fascist, Australian Legend.* Sydney: The Federation Press, 2005.

Morris, Sherry. *Wagga Wagga: A History.* Wagga Wagga, NSW: Council of the City of Wagga Wagga, 1999.

Mudde, Cas. *The Far Right Today.* Cambridge, UK: Polity Press, 2019.

Muirden, Bruce. *The Puzzled Patriots: The Story of the Australia First Movement.* Melbourne: Melbourne University Press, 1968.

Nairn, Bede. *The 'Big Fella': Jack Lang and the Australian Labor Party, 1891–1949.* Melbourne: Melbourne University Press, 1986.

Nethercote, J.R., ed. *Liberalism and the Australian Federation.* Sydney: The Federation Press, 2001.

Nolan, Melanie, ed. *Revolution: The 1913 Great Strike in New Zealand.* Christchurch, NZ: Canterbury University Press, 2005.

Oldfield, Audrey. *Woman Suffrage in Australia: A Gift or a Struggle?* Cambridge, UK: Cambridge University Press, 1993.

Olssen, Erik. *The Red Feds: Revolutionary Industrial Unionism and the New Zealand Federation of Labour, 1908–14.* New York: Oxford University Press, 1988.

Panizza, Francisco. *Populism and the Mirror of Democracy.* London: Verso, 2005.

Parker, Selwyn. *Wealthmakers: A History of the Northern Employers' and Manufacturers' Associations.* Auckland: Employers' & Manufacturers' Association (Northern) Inc., 2005.

Payne, Stanley G. *A History of Fascism 1914–1945.* Madison: University of Wisconsin Press, 1995.

Pickles, Katie. *Female Imperialism and National Identity: Imperial Order Daughters of the Empire.* Manchester, UK: Manchester University Press, 2002. doi.org/10.7228/manchester/9780719063909.001.0001.

Potter, Simon J. *News and the British World: The Emergence of an Imperial Press System, 1876–1922.* Oxford, UK: Clarendon Press, 2003. doi.org/10.1093/acprof:oso/9780199265121.001.0001.

Potts, Eli Daniel and Annette Potts. *Young America and Australian Gold: Americans and the Gold Rush of the 1850s.* Brisbane: University of Queensland Press, 1974.

Poulantzas, Nicos. *Fascism and Dictatorship: The Third International and the Problem of Fascism.* London: NLB, 1974.

Pugh, Martin. *The Tories and the People, 1880–1935.* Oxford, UK: Basil Blackwell Publishing, 1985.

Ransom, Josephine. *A Short History of the Theosophical Society.* Madras: Vasanta Press, 1938.

Rasmussen, Carolyn. *The Lesser Evil? Opposition to War and Fascism in Australia 1920–1941.* Melbourne: Melbourne University Press, 1992.

Reitsma, A.J. *Trade Protection in Australia*. Brisbane: University of Queensland Press, 1960.

Renton, David. *Fascism: Theory and Practice*. London: Pluto Press, 1999.

Rickard, John. *Class and Politics: New South Wales, Victoria and the Early Commonwealth, 1890–1910*. Canberra: Australian National University Press, 1976.

Rivett, Rohan. *Australian Citizen: Herbert Brookes, 1867–1963*. Melbourne: Melbourne University Press, 1965.

Roe, Jill. *Beyond Belief: Theosophy in Australia 1879–1939*. Sydney: UNSW Press, 1986.

Rowse, Tim. *Australian Liberalism and National Character*. Melbourne: Kibble Books, 1978.

Rydgren, Jens, ed. *The Oxford Handbook of the Radical Right*. New York: Oxford University Press, 2018. doi.org/10.1093/oxfordhb/9780190274559.001.0001.

Sawer, Marian. *The Ethical State? Social Liberalism in Australia*. Melbourne: Melbourne University Press, 2003.

Scates, Bruce. *A New Australia: Citizenship, Radicalism and the First Republic*. Cambridge, UK: Cambridge University Press, 1997.

Schedvin, C.B. *Australia and the Great Depression: A Study of Economic Development and Policy in the 1920s and 1930s*. Sydney: Sydney University Press, 1970.

Simpson, Tony. *The Sugarbag Years: An Oral History of the 1930s Depression in New Zealand*. Auckland: Hodder & Stoughton, 1984.

Simpson, Tony. *The Slump: The Thirties Depression, Its Origins and Aftermath*. Auckland: Penguin Books, 1990.

Sinclair, Keith. *A History of New Zealand*. Harmondsworth, UK: Penguin Books, 1969.

Sinclair, Keith, ed. *Tasman Relations: New Zealand and Australia, 1788–1988*. Auckland: Auckland University Press, 1987.

Sinclair, W.A. *The Process of Economic Development in Australia*. Melbourne: Cheshire Publishing, 1976.

Skocpol, Theda and Vanessa Williamson. *The Tea Party and the Remaking of Republican Conservatism*. Oxford, UK: Oxford University Press, 2012. doi.org/10.1093/acprof:osobl/9780199832637.001.0001.

Smith, Rodney K. *Against the Machines: Minor Parties and Independents in New South Wales, 1910–2006*. Sydney: The Federation Press, 2006.

Spoonley, Paul. *The Politics of Nostalgia: Racism and the Extreme Right in New Zealand*. Palmerston North, NZ: Dunmore Press, 1987.

Sternhell, Zeev. *The Birth of Fascist Ideology*. Princeton, NJ: Princeton University Press, 1994. doi.org/10.2307/20046694.

Taggart, Paul. *Populism*. Buckingham, UK: Open University Press, 2000.

Tait, P.S. *In the Chair: The Public Life of Sir John Ormond*. Waipukurau, NZ: CHB Print, 1989.

Teich, Mikuláš and Roy Porter, eds. *Fin de Siècle and its Legacy*. Cambridge, UK: Cambridge University Press, 1990.

Traverso, Enzo. *The New Faces of Fascism: Populism and the Far Right*. Translated by David Broder. London: Verso, 2019.

Tripp, L.O.H. *The War Effort of New Zealand*. Auckland: Whitcombe & Tombs, 1923.

Van Dyke, Nella and David S. Meyer. *Understanding the Tea Party Movement*. New York: Routledge, 2014.

Vennell, Jock. *The Forgotten General: New Zealand's World War I Commander Major-General Sir Andrew Russell*. Auckland: Allen & Unwin, 2011.

Venturi, Franco. *Roots of Revolution: A History of the Populist and Socialist Movements in 19th Century Russia*. New York: Phoenix Press, 2001.

Weedon, Alexis. *Victorian Publishing: The Economics of Book Production for a Mass Market, 1836–1916*. Aldershot, UK: Ashgate, 2003.

White, Hayden. *Metahistory: The Historical Imagination in Nineteenth-Century Europe*. Baltimore: Johns Hopkins University Press, 1973.

Williams, John R. *John Latham and the Conservative Recovery from Defeat, 1929–1931*. Sydney: Australian Political Studies Association, 1969.

Winter, Barbara. *The Australia-First Movement: Dreaming of a National Socialist Australia*. Brisbane: Interactive Publications, 2005.

Wood, Jeanne. *A Challenge Not a Truce: A History of the New Zealand Women's Christian Temperance Union, 1885–1985.* Nelson, NZ: New Zealand Women's Christian Temperance Union Inc., 1985.

Woodley, Daniel. *Fascism and Political Theory: Critical Perspectives on Fascist Ideology.* New York: Routledge, 2010.

Year Book Australia. Canberra: Australian Bureau of Statistics, 2001.

Book chapters

Aitkin, Don. '"Countrymindedness": The Spread of an Idea.' In *Australian Cultural History*, edited by S.L. Goldberg and F.B. Smith, 50–57. Melbourne: Cambridge University Press, 1988.

Albertazzi, Daniele and Duncan McDonnell. 'Introduction: The Sceptre and the Spectre.' In *Twenty-First Century Populism: The Spectre of Western European Democracy*, edited by Daniele Albertazzi and Duncan McDonnell, 1–11. New York: Palgrave Macmillan, 2008. doi.org/10.1057/9780230592100_1.

Arnold, John. 'Newspapers and Daily Reading.' In *A History of the Book in Australia, 1891–1945*, edited by Martyn Lyons and John Arnold, 255–68. Brisbane: University of Queensland Press, 2001.

Betz, Hans-Georg. 'New Zealand First.' In *The New Politics of the Right: Neo-Populist Parties and Movements in Established Democracies*, edited by Hans-Georg Betz and Stefan Immerfall. New York: St Martin's Press, 1998.

Bongiorno, Frank. 'Whatever Happened to Free Trade Liberalism?' In *Confusion: The Making of the Australian Two-Party System*, edited by Paul Strangio and Nick Dyrenfurth, 249–74. Melbourne: Melbourne University Press, 2009.

Brett, Judith. '"The Fortunes of My Own Little Band": The Dilemma of Deakin and the Liberal Protectionists.' In *Confusion: The Making of the Australian Two-Party System*, edited by Paul Strangio and Nick Dyrenfurth, 23–44. Melbourne: Melbourne University Press, 2009.

Breward, Ian. 'Protestantism in Australia, New Zealand and Oceania to the Present Day.' In *The Blackwell Companion to Protestantism*, edited by A.E. McGrath and D.C. Marks, 232–38. Malden, MA: Blackwell Publishing, 2007. doi.org/10.1002/9780470999196.ch24.

Buckley, Ken. 'Primary Accumulation: The Genesis of Australian Capitalism.' In *Essays in the Political Economy of Australian Capitalism*, edited by E.L. Wheelwright and Ken Buckley, 12–32. 2 vols. Sydney: Australia & New Zealand Book Company, 1975.

Butlin, Noel G. 'Colonial Socialism in Australia, 1860–1900.' In *The State and Economic Growth*, edited by Hugh Aitken, 26–78. New York: Social Science Research Council, 1959.

Chapman, Robert. 'The Decline of the Liberals.' In *Ends and Means in New Zealand Politics*, edited by Robert Chapman, 18–24. Auckland: Dobbie Press, 1961.

Costar, Brian. 'Was Queensland Different?' In *The Wasted Years? Australia's Great Depression*, edited by Judy Mackinolty, 159–74. Sydney: Allen & Unwin, 1981.

Crawford, John. 'A Tale of Two Cities: Military Involvement in the 1913 Strike.' In *Revolution: The 1913 Great Strike in New Zealand*, edited by Melanie Nolan, 122–41. Christchurch, NZ: Canterbury University Press, 2005.

Cunningham, Matthew, 'Massey's Cossacks Reborn? Public and Private Counterrevolutionary Preparations in New Zealand, 1920–1921' (currently seeking publication).

Fairburn, Miles. 'Is There a Good Case for New Zealand Exceptionalism?' In *Disputed Histories: Imagining New Zealand's Pasts*, edited by Tony Ballantyne and Brian Moloughney, 143–68. Dunedin, NZ: Otago University Press, 2006.

Fitzherbert, Margaret. 'Alfred Deakin and the Australian Women's National League.' In *Liberalism and the Australian Federation*, edited by J.R. Nethercote, 98–112. Sydney: The Federation Press, 2001.

Fleming, Andy and Aurelian Mondon. 'The Radical Right in Australia.' In *The Oxford Handbook of the Radical Right*, edited by Jens Rydgren, 650–62. New York: Oxford University Press, 2018. doi.org/10.1093/oxfordhb/978019 0274559.013.32.

Gardner, W.J. 'The Reform Party.' In *Ends and Means in New Zealand Politics*, edited by Robert Chapman, 25–33. Auckland: Dobbie Press, 1961.

Gibbons, P.J. 'The Climate of Opinion.' In *The Oxford History of New Zealand*, edited by Geoffrey W. Rice, 308–36. Auckland: Oxford University Press, 1992.

Gordon, Amanda. 'The Conservative Press and the Russian Revolution.' In *Australian Conservatism: Essays in Twentieth Century Political History*, edited by Cameron Hazlehurst, 29–50. Canberra: Australian National University Press, 1979.

Graham, B.D. 'The Country Party Idea in New Zealand Politics, 1901–1935.' In *Studies of a Small Democracy*, edited by Robert Chapman and Keith Sinclair. Auckland: Auckland University Press, 1963.

Gustafson, Barry. 'Populist Roots of Political Leadership in New Zealand.' In *Political Leadership in New Zealand*, edited by Raymond Miller and Michael Mintrom, 51–69. Auckland: Auckland University Press, 2006.

Hart, Philip. 'The Piper and the Tune.' In *Australian Conservatism: Essays in Twentieth Century Political History*, edited by Cameron Hazlehurst, 111–48. Canberra: Australian National University Press, 1979.

Harvey, Ross. 'Newspapers.' In *Book and Print in New Zealand: A Guide to Print Culture in Aotearoa*, edited by Penny Griffith, Ross Harvey, and Keith Maslen, 128–35. Wellington: Victoria University Press, 1997.

Hawke, Gary. 'Australian and New Zealand Economic Development from about 1890 to 1940.' In *Tasman Relations: New Zealand and Australia, 1788–1988*, edited by Keith Sinclair, 104–23. Auckland: Auckland University Press, 1987.

Kaltwasser, Rovira, Paul Taggart, Paulina Ochoa Espejo, and Pierre Ostiguy. 'Populism: An Overview of the Concept and the State of the Art.' In *The Oxford Handbook of Populism*, edited by Rovira Kaltwasser, Paul Taggart, Paulina Ochoa Espejo, and Pierre Ostiguy, 10–29. New York: Oxford University Press, 2017. doi.org/10.1093/oxfordhb/9780198803560.001.0001.

Lloyd, C.J. 'The Rise and Fall of the United Australia Party.' In *Liberalism and the Australian Federation*, edited by J.R. Nethercote, 134–62. Sydney: The Federation Press, 2001.

Lloyd, P.J. 'Australia–New Zealand Trade Relations: NAFTA to CER.' In *Tasman Relations: New Zealand and Australia, 1788–1988*, edited by Keith Sinclair, 142–63. Auckland: Auckland University Press, 1987.

Lonie, John. 'From Liberal to Liberal: The Emergence of the Liberal Party and Australian Capitalism, 1900–45.' In *Critical Essays in Australian Politics*, edited by Graeme Duncan, 47–76. Melbourne: Edward Arnold Ltd, 1978.

Loveday, Peter. 'The Federal Parties.' In *The Emergence of the Australian Party System*, edited by Peter Loveday, A.W. Martin, and R.S. Parker, 383–452. Sydney: Hale & Iremonger, 1977.

Loveday, Peter. 'Emergence: Realignment and Consolidation.' In *The Emergence of the Australian Party System*, edited by Peter Loveday, A.W. Martin, and R.S. Parker, 453–87. Sydney: Hale & Iremonger, 1977.

Loveday, Peter. 'The Liberals' Image of their Party.' In *Australian Conservatism: Essays in Twentieth Century Political History*, edited by Cameron Hazlehurst, 239–62. Canberra: Australian National University Press, 1979.

Lyons, Martyn. 'Britain's Largest Export Market.' In *A History of the Book in Australia, 1891–1945*, edited by Martyn Lyons and John Arnold, 19–26. Brisbane: University of Queensland Press, 2001.

Marsh, Ian. 'The Federation Decade.' In *Liberalism and the Australian Federation*, edited by J.R. Nethercote, 69–97. Sydney: The Federation Press, 2001.

Martin, John. 'Development from Above: God Made the Country and Man the Town.' In *Development Tracks: The Theory and Practice of Community Development*, edited by Ian Shirley, 90–116. Palmerston North, NZ: Dunmore Press, 1982.

Martin, John. 'Blueprint for the Future? "National Efficiency" and the First World War.' In *New Zealand's Great War: New Zealand, the Allies and the First World War*, edited by John Crawford and Ian McGibbon, 516–33. Auckland: Exisle Publishing, 2007.

Matthews, Trevor. 'The All for Australia League.' In *The Great Depression in Australia*, edited by Robert Cooksey, 136–47. Canberra: Australian Society for the Study of Labour History, 1970. doi.org/10.2307/27507959.

McAloon, Jim. 'The Making of the New Zealand Ruling Class.' In *Revolution: The 1913 Great Strike in New Zealand*, edited by Melanie Nolan, 217–36. Christchurch, NZ: Canterbury University Press, 2005.

McClelland, Keith and Sonya Rose. 'Citizenship and Empire, 1867–1928.' In *At Home with the Empire: Metropolitan Culture and the Imperial World*, edited by Catherine Hall and Sonya Rose, 275–97. Cambridge, UK: Cambridge University Press, 2006. doi.org/10.1017/CBO9780511802263.013.

McGibbon, Ian. 'Australia–New Zealand Defence Relations to 1939.' In *Tasman Relations: New Zealand and Australia, 1788–1988*, edited by Keith Sinclair, 164–82. Auckland: Auckland University Press, 1987.

McIntyre, W. David. 'Imperialism and Nationalism.' In *The Oxford History of New Zealand*, edited by Geoffrey Rice, 338–47. Auckland: Oxford University Press, 1992.

McQueen, Humphrey. 'Shoot the Bolshevik! Hang the Profiteer! Reconstructing Australian Capitalism 1918–1921.' In *Essays in the Political Economy of Australian Capitalism*, edited by E.L. Wheelwright and Ken Buckley, 185–206. Sydney: ANZ Book Company, 1978.

Mein Smith, Philippa. 'The Tasman World.' In *The New Oxford History of New Zealand*, edited by Giselle Byrnes, 297–319. Melbourne: Oxford University Press, 2009.

Melleuish, Gregory. 'Populism and Conservatism in Australian Political Thought.' In *The Politics of Australian Society: Political Issues for the New Century*, edited by Paul Boreham, Geoffrey Stokes, and Richard Hall, 51–64. Sydney: Longman, 2000.

Melleuish, Gregory. 'Australian Liberalism.' In *Liberalism and the Australian Federation*, edited by J.R. Nethercote, 28–41. Sydney: The Federation Press, 2001.

Miller, Michael. 'Comparative and Cross-National History: Approaches, Differences, Problems.' In *Comparison and History: Europe in Cross-National Perspective*, edited by Deborah Cohen and Maura O'Connor, 115–32. New York: Routledge, 2004. doi.org/10.4324/9780203312346_chapter_8.

Moffitt, Benjamin. 'Populism in Australia and New Zealand.' In *The Oxford Handbook of Populism*, edited by Rovira Kaltwasser, Paul Taggart, Paulina Ochoa Espejo, and Pierre Ostiguy, 121–39. London: Oxford University Press, 2017. doi.org/10.1093/oxfordhb/9780198803560.013.5.

Moore, Andrew. 'Workers and the New Guard: Proletarian Fascism in New South Wales, 1931–35.' In *Transforming Labour: Work, Workers, Struggle and Change—Proceedings of the 8th National Labour History Conference*, edited by B. Bowden and J. Kellett, 239–46. Brisbane: Brisbane Labour History Association, 2003.

Moore, Andrew. 'The Nazification of the New Guard: Colonel Campbell's Fascist Odyssey, 1933–1938.' In *National Socialism in Australia: A Critical Evaluation of its Effect and Aftermath*, edited by Emily Turner-Graham and Christine Winter, 97–114. Germanica Pacifica Vol. 4. Berlin: Peter Lang Publishers, 2010.

Oakeshott, Michael. 'On Being Conservative.' In *Rationalism in Politics, and Other Essays*, edited by Michael Oakeshott, 168–96. London: Methuen, 1962.

Panayi, Panikos. 'The British Empire Union in the First World War.' In *The Politics of Marginality*, edited by Tony Kushner and Kenneth Lunn, 113–19. London: Frank Cass, 1990.

Patterson, Brad. '"We Stand for the Protestant religion, the (Protestant) King and the Empire": The Rise of the Protestant Political Association in World War One.' In *New Zealand Society at War 1914–1918*, edited by Steven Loveridge. Wellington: Victoria University Press, 2016.

Perkins, John and Andrew Moore. 'Fascism in Interwar Australia.' In *Fascism Outside Europe: The European Impulse against Domestic Conditions in the Diffusion of Global Fascism*, edited by Stein Ugelvik Larsen, 269–86. New York: Columbia University Press, 2001.

Richardson, Len. 'Parties and Political Change.' In *The Oxford History of New Zealand*, edited by Geoffrey W. Rice, 201–29. Auckland: Oxford University Press, 1992.

Rydgren, Jens. 'The Radical Right: An Introduction.' In *The Oxford Handbook of the Radical Right*, edited by Jens Rydgren, 7–10. New York: Oxford University Press, 2018. doi.org/10.1093/oxfordhb/9780190274559.013.1.

Sinclair, Keith. 'The Legislation of the Liberal Party, 1891–1898.' In *Ends and Means in New Zealand Politics*, edited by Robert Chapman, 11–17. Auckland: Dobbie Press, 1961.

Sinclair, Keith. 'The Great Anzac Plant War: Australia–New Zealand Trade Relations, 1919–39.' In *Tasman Relations: New Zealand and Australia, 1788–1988*, edited by Keith Sinclair, 124–41. Auckland: Auckland University Press, 1987.

Soldon, Norbert. '*Laissez-Faire* as Dogma: The Liberty and Property Defence League, 1882–1914.' In *Essays in Anti-Labour History: Responses to the Rise of Labour in Britain*, edited by K.D. Brown, 208–33. London: Macmillan, 1974. doi.org/10.1007/978-1-349-02039-3_9.

Stokes, Geoffrey. 'One Nation and Australian Populism.' In *The Rise and Fall of One Nation*, edited by Michael Leach, Geoff Stokes, and Ian M. Ward, 23–41. Brisbane: University of Queensland Press, 2000.

Strangio, Paul. 'Introduction: From Confusion to Stability.' In *Confusion: The Making of the Australian Two-Party System*, edited by Paul Strangio and Nick Dyrenfurth, 1–19. Melbourne: Melbourne University Press, 2009.

Summers, Anne. 'The Character of Edwardian Nationalism: Three Popular Leagues.' In *Nationalist and Racialist Movements in Britain and Germany before 1914*, edited by Paul Kennedy and Anthony Nicholls, 68–87. London: Macmillan, 1981. doi.org/10.1007/978-1-349-04958-5_4.

Ward, Damen. 'Colonial Communication: Creating Settler Public Opinion in Crown Colony South Australia and New Zealand.' In *Imperial Communication: Australia, Britain, and the British Empire c. 1830–50*, edited by Simon J. Potter, 7–46. London: Menzies Centre for Australian Studies, 2004.

Watson, Lex. 'The United Australia Party and its Sponsors.' In *Australian Conservatism: Essays in Twentieth Century Political History*, edited by Cameron Hazlehurst, 71–109. Canberra: Australian National University Press, 1979.

Articles

Alder, Baron. 'The Ideology of the New Guard Movement.' *Journal of the Royal Australian Historical Society* 82(2) (1996): 192–209.

Alexander, Malcolm. 'Conservatism, Counterrevolution, and Semiperipheral Politics: Australia and Argentina in the Interwar Period.' *Review (Fernand Braudel Center)* 12(2) (1989): 299–333.

Allcock, J.B. 'Populism: A Brief Biography.' *Sociology* 5(3) (1971): 371–87. doi. org/10.1177/003803857100500305.

Arundale, G.S. 'The Australian Experiment.' *World Theosophy* (February 1931): 103–6.

Bagot, E.D.A. 'Principles in Politic: What the Citizens' League Hopes to Achieve.' *Progress* (31 October 1930): 11.

Bassett, Judith. 'Sir Harry Atkinson and the Conservative Faction in New Zealand Politics, 1879–1890.' *New Zealand Journal of History* 2(2) (1968): 130–47.

Beasley, F.R. 'The Secession Movement in Western Australia.' *Australian Quarterly* [Sydney] 8 (1936): 31–36. doi.org/10.2307/20629298.

Berzins, Baiba. 'Douglas Credit and the A.L.P.' *Labour History* 17 (1969): 148–60. doi.org/10.2307/27507960.

Besant, Christopher. 'Two Nations, Two Destinies: A Reflection on the Significance of the Western Australian Secessionist Movement to Australia, Canada and the British Empire.' *University of Western Australia Law Review* 20 (1990): 209–310.

Blacklow, Nancy. '"Riverina Roused": Representative Support for the Riverina New State Movements of the 1920s and 1930s.' *Journal of the Royal Australian Historical Society: Special Riverina Issue* 80(3–4) (1994): 176–94.

Brett, Judith. 'Retrieving the Partisan History of Australian Citizenship.' *Australian Journal of Political Science* 36(3) (2001): 423–37. doi.org/10.1080/10361140120100631.

Brett, Judith. 'Class, Party and the Foundations of the Australian Party System: A Revisionist Interpretation.' *Australian Journal of Political Science* 37(1) (2002): 39–56. doi.org/10.1080/13603100220119010.

Bristow, Edward. 'The Liberty and Property Defence League and Individualism.' *The Historical Journal* 18(4) (1975): 761–89. doi.org/10.1017/S0018246X 00008888.

Broomhill, Ray. 'Political Consciousness and Dissent: The Unemployed in Adelaide during the Depression.' *Labour History* 34 (1978): 58–67. doi.org/10.2307/27508309.

Brown, M. Craig and Charles N. Halaby. 'Machine Politics in America, 1870–1945.' *Journal of Interdisciplinary History* 17(3) (1987): 587–612. doi.org/10.2307/204612.

Cain, Frank. 'Some Aspects of Australian–Soviet Relations from 1800 to 1960.' *Journal of Communist Studies* 7(4) (1991): 501–21. doi.org/10.1080/13523279108415113.

Canovan, Margaret. 'Trust the People! Populism and the Two Faces of Democracy.' *Political Studies* 47(1) (1999): 2–16. doi.org/10.1111/1467-9248.00184.

Clarke, F.G. 'The Argonauts Civic and Political Club: An Early Attempt at Industrial Group Organisation in Western Australia, 1925–1930.' *Labour History* 18 (1970): 32–39. doi.org/10.2307/27507969.

Cole, Douglas. 'The Problem of "Nationalism" and "Imperialism" in British Settlement Colonies.' *Journal of British Studies* 10(2) (1970): 160–82. doi.org/10.1086/385614.

Colebatch, Hal. 'Inflation, Deflation, or Common Sense.' *Australian Quarterly* [Sydney] 2(4) (December 1930): 31–43.

Cooper, Roslyn Pesman. '"We Want a Mussolini": Views of Fascist Italy in Australia.' *Australian Journal of Politics and History* 39(3) (1993): 348–66. doi.org/10.1111/j.1467-8497.1993.tb00073.x.

Cowper, Norman. 'Reform of the Upper House of New South Wales.' *Australian Quarterly* [Sydney] 1(4) (December 1929): 107–18.

Cunningham, Matthew. 'Conservative Protest or Conservative Radicalism? The New Zealand Legion in a Comparative Context, 1930–1935.' *Journal of New Zealand Studies* 10 (2011): 139–58. doi.org/10.26686/jnzs.v0i10.157.

Cunningham, Matthew. 'Australian Fascism? A Revisionist Analysis of the Ideology of the New Guard.' *Politics, Religion & Ideology* 13(3) (2012): 375–93. doi.org/10.1080/21567689.2012.701188.

Denoon, Donald. 'Re-Membering Australasia: A Repressed Memory.' *Australian Historical Studies* 34(122) (2003): 290–304. doi.org/10.1080/10314610308596256.

Eldred-Grigg, Steven. 'Whatever Happened to the Gentry? The Large Landowners of Ashburton County, 1890–1896.' *New Zealand Journal of History* 11(1) (1977): 3–27.

Evans, Ray. '"Some Furious Outbursts of Riot": Returned Soldiers and Queensland's "Red Flag" Disturbances, 1918–1919.' *War and Society* 3(2) (1985): 75–98. doi.org/10.1179/106980485790303953.

Evans, Richard. '"A Menace to this Realm": The New Guard and the New South Wales Police, 1931–32.' *History Australia* 5(3) (2008): 76.1–76.20. doi.org/10.2104/ha080076.

Fischer, Nick. 'An Inspiration Misunderstood: Australian Anti-Communists and the Lure of the U.S., 1917–1935.' *Eras* 5 (2003): 1–19.

Fischer, Nick. 'The Australian Right, the American Right and the Threat of the Left, 1917–35.' *Labour History* 89 (2005): 17–36. doi.org/10.2307/27516073.

French, Maurice. '"One People, One Destiny": A Question of Loyalty—The Origins of Empire Day in New South Wales, 1900–1905.' *Journal of the Royal Australian Historical Society* 61(4) (1975): 236–48.

Funke, Manuel, Moritz Schularick, and Christoph Trebesch. 'Going to Extremes: Politics after Financial Crises, 1870–2014.' *European Economic Review* 88 (2016): 227–60. doi.org/10.1016/j.euroecorev.2016.03.006.

Gollan, Robin. 'American Populism and Australian Utopianism.' *Labour History* 9 (1965): 15–21. doi.org/10.2307/27507798.

Goot, Murray. 'Pauline Hanson's One Nation: Extreme Right, Centre Party or Extreme Left?' *Labour History* 89 (2005): 101–19. doi.org/10.2307/27516078.

Griffiths, John. 'Were there Municipal Networks in the British World c. 1890–1939?' *Journal of Imperial and Commonwealth History* 37(4) (2009): 575–97. doi.org/10.1080/03086530903327085.

Gunn, Heather. '"For the Man on the Land": Issues of Gender and Identity in the Formation of the Victorian Farmers' Union Women's Section, 1918–1922.' *Journal of Australian Studies* 18(42) (1994): 32–42. doi.org/10.1080/14443059409387184.

Hall, Richard. 'The Secret Army.' *National Times* (23–28 January 1978): 12–13.

Hamilton, W. Mark. 'The "New Navalism" and the British Navy League, 1895–1914.' *The Mariner's Mirror* 64(1) (1978): 37–44. doi.org/10.1080/00253359.1978.10659063.

Harford, Shelley. 'A Trans-Tasman Union Community: Growing Global Solidarity.' *Labour History* 95 (2008): 133–49. doi.org/10.2307/27516313.

Harman, Grant. 'New State Agitation in Northern New South Wales, 1920–1929.' *Journal of the Royal Australian Historical Society* 63(1) (1977): 26–39.

Hart, P.R. 'Lyons: Labor Minister—Leader of the U.A.P.' *Labour History* (17) (1969): 37–51. doi.org/10.2307/27507952.

Henderson, Gerard. 'All Quiet on the Civil War Front.' *Sydney Institute Quarterly* 31 (2007): 6–12.

Hendley, Matthew. 'Constructing the Citizen: The Primrose League and the Definition of Citizenship in the Age of Mass Democracy in Britain, 1918–1928.' *Journal of the Canadian Historical Association* 7(1) (1996): 3–297. doi.org/10.7202/031105ar.

Hewitt, Geoff. 'The All for Australia League in Melbourne.' *La Trobe Historical Studies* 3 (1972): 5–15.

Hiller, Harry H. 'Secession in Western Australia: A Continuing Phenomenon?' *Australian Quarterly* [Sydney] 59(2) (1987): 222–33. doi.org/10.2307/20635434.

Hunter, T.A. 'Some Aspects of Depression Psychology in New Zealand.' *Economic Record* 10(1) (1934): 31–45. doi.org/10.1111/j.1475-4932.1935.tb02764.x.

James, Paul. 'Armies of the Right: In Defence of Empire and Nation.' *Melbourne Journal of Politics* 16 (1984–85): 78–101.

James, Stephen A. 'God, Mammon and Mussolini: The Ideology and Policy of the Citizens' League of South Australia, 1930–1934.' *Australian Journal of Politics and History* 37(1) (1991): 39–60. doi.org/10.1111/j.1467-8497.1991.tb00024.x.

Johnson, Matthew. 'The Liberal Party and the Navy League in Britain before the Great War.' *Twentieth Century British History* 22(2) (2011): 137–63. doi.org/10.1093/tcbh/hwq055.

Kenderdine, R.W. 'The Demand for Honest Government.' *Life* (1 May 1931): 400.

Kirk, Neville. '"Australians for Australia": The Right, the Labor Party and Contested Loyalties to Nation and Empire in Australia, 1917 to the Early 1930s.' *Labour History* 91 (2006): 95–111. doi.org/10.2307/27516154.

La Rooij, Marinus. 'From Colonial Conservative to International Antisemite: The Life and Work of Arthur Nelson Field.' *Journal of Contemporary History* 37(2) (2002): 223–39. doi.org/10.1177/00220094020370020401.

La Rooij, Marinus. 'Arthur Nelson Field: Kiwi Theoretician of the Australian Radical Right.' *Labour History* 89 (2005): 37–54. doi.org/10.2307/27516074.

Leigh, Andrew. 'Trade Liberalisation and the Australian Labor Party.' *Australian Journal of Politics and History* 48(4) (2002): 487–508. doi.org/10.1111/1467-8497.00272.

Logan, James. 'Re-Examining Senator Charles Hardy's Role in Coordinating the Country Protest Movements in NSW in the 1930s.' *The Page Review* 1(2) (2005): 19–27.

Lonie, John. '"Good Labor Men" and "Non-Labor" during the Great Depression in South Australia.' *Journal of the Historical Society of South Australia* 2(1) (1976): 30–45.

Loveday, Peter. 'Anti-Political Political Thought.' *Labour History* 17 (1969): 121–35. doi.org/10.2307/27507958.

Markey, Ray and Kerry Taylor. 'Trans-Tasman Labour History: Introduction.' *Labour History* 95 (2008): 1–2. doi.org/10.2307/27516306.

McCarthy, John. '"All for Australia": Some Right Wing Responses to the Depression in New South Wales, 1929–1932.' *Journal of the Royal Australian Historical Society* 57(2) (1971): 160–71.

McCarthy, John. 'A "Law and Order" Election: New South Wales, June 1932.' *Journal of the Royal Australian Historical Society* 60(2) (1974): 105–16.

McIvor, Arthur. '"A Crusade for Capitalism": The Economic League, 1919–1939.' *Journal of Contemporary History* 23(4) (1988): 631–55. doi.org/10.1177/002200948802300407.

McKenna, Mark. 'A History for Our Time? The Idea of the People in Australian Democracy.' *History Compass* 1(1) (2003): 1–15. doi.org/10.1111/1478-0542.030.

McMurray, Matthew. 'Alexander Raven Thomson, Philosopher of the British Union of Fascists.' *The European Legacy: Toward New Paradigms* 17(1) (2012): 33–59. doi.org/10.1080/10848770.2011.640191.

McQueen, Humphrey. 'The Social Character of the New Guard.' *Arena* 40 (1975): 67–86.

Mein Smith, Philippa and Peter Hempenstall. 'Australia and New Zealand: Turning Shared Pasts into a Shared History.' *History Compass* 1(1) (2003): 1–8. doi.org/10.1111/1478-0542.031.

Melville, L.G. 'The Australian Tariff: A Review on the Report of the Committee Appointed by the Prime Minister.' *Australian Quarterly* [Sydney] 1(3) (September 1929): 54–63.

Mitchell, Phyllis. 'Australian Patriots: A Study of the New Guard.' *Australian Economic Historical Review* 9(2) (1969): 156–78. doi.org/10.1111/aehr.92004.

Moore, Andrew. 'The Old Guard and "Countrymindedness" during the Great Depression.' *Journal of Australian Studies* 27 (1990): 52–64. doi.org/10.1080/14443059009387033.

Moore, Andrew. 'Another Wild Colonial Boy? Francis de Groot and the Harbour Bridge.' *Australian Journal of Irish Studies* 2 (2002): 135–48.

Moore, Andrew. 'The New Guard and the Labour Movement, 1931–1935.' *Labour History* 89 (2005): 55–72. doi.org/10.2307/27516075.

Moore, Andrew. 'Superintendent Mackay and the Curious Case of the Vanishing Secret Army: A Response to Richard Evans.' *History Australia* 6(3) (2009): 72.1–72.18. doi.org/10.2104/ha090072.

Moore, Andrew. 'Discredited Fascism: The New Guard after 1932.' *Australian Journal of Politics and History* 57(2) (2011): 188–206. doi.org/10.1111/j.1467-8497.2011.01591.x.

Moore, William Harrison. 'Experts in Government.' *Australian Quarterly* [Sydney] 2(4) (December 1930): 29–30.

Muscio, Mildred. 'Reflections on Party Politics.' *Australian Quarterly* [Sydney] 1(3) (September 1929): 91.

Musgrave, Thomas. 'The Western Australian Secessionist Movement.' *Macquarie Law Journal* 3 (2003): 98–129.

Nagel, Jack H. 'Populism, Heresthetics and Political Stability: Richard Seddon and the Art of Majority Rule.' *British Journal of Political Science* 23(2) (1993): 139–74. doi.org/10.1017/s0007123400009716.

Neale, R.G. 'New States Movement.' *Australian Quarterly* [Sydney] 22(3) (1950): 9–23. doi.org/10.2307/20633275.

Nicholls, David. 'Positive Liberty, 1880–1914.' *The American Political Science Review* 56(1) (1962): 114–28. doi.org/10.2307/1953101.

Nicholls, Roberta. 'The Collapse of the Early National Council of the Women of New Zealand, 1896–1906.' *New Zealand Journal of History* 27(2) (1993): 157–72.

Nolan, Melanie. 'Personalizing Class Conflict across the Tasman: The New Zealand Great Strike and Trans-Tasman Biography.' *Journal of New Zealand Studies* 10 (2014): 118–36. doi.org/10.26686/jnzs.v0i18.2185.

Noonan, M.A. 'The Aims of the New Zealand Welfare League, 1919–1922.' *Historical Society Annual* (1969): 28–46.

O'Connor, P.S. 'Mr Massey and the PPA: A Suspicion Confirmed.' *New Zealand Journal of Public Administration* 28(2) (March 1966): 69–74.

O'Connor, P.S. 'Sectarian Conflict in New Zealand, 1911–1920.' *Political Science* 19(1) (July 1967): 3–16. doi.org/10.1177/003231876701900101.

O'Connor, P.S. 'Storm Over the Clergy: New Zealand 1917.' *Journal of Religious History* 4(2) (1966–67): 129–48. doi.org/10.1111/j.1467-9809.1966.tb00492.x.

Olssen, Erik and Bruce Scates. 'Class Formation and Political Change: A Trans-Tasman Dialogue.' *Labour History* 95 (2008): 3–24. doi.org/10.2307/27516307.

Parkin, Frank. 'Working-Class Conservatives: A Theory of Political Deviance.' *The British Journal of Sociology* 18 (1967): 278–90. doi.org/10.2307/588640.

Perkins, John. 'The Swastika Down Under: Nazi Activities in Australia, 1933–39.' *Journal of Contemporary History* 26(1) (1991): 111–29. doi.org/10.1177/002200949102600106.

Pickles, Katie. 'A Link in "the Great Chain of Empire Friendship": The Victoria League in New Zealand.' *Journal of Imperial and Commonwealth History* 33(1) (2005): 29–50. doi.org/10.1080/0308653042000329003.

Price, Archibald G. 'The Emergency Committee of South Australia and the Origin of the Premiers' Plan, 1931–2.' *South Australiana* 17(1) (1978): 5–55.

Pugh, Martin. 'Popular Conservatism in Britain: Continuity and Change, 1880–1987.' *Journal of British Studies* 27(3) (1988): 254–82. doi.org/10.1086/385913.

Pugh, Michael C. 'The New Zealand Legion, 1932–1935.' *New Zealand Journal of History* 5(1) (1971): 49–69. doi.org/10.1080/00779962.1971.9722955.

Pugh, Michael C. 'Doctrinaires on the Right: The Democrats and Anti-Socialism, 1933–36.' *New Zealand Journal of History* 17(2) (October 1983): 103–19.

Quartly, Marian. 'Defending "the Purity of Home Life" against Socialism: The Founding Years of the Australian Women's National League.' *Australian Journal of Politics and History* 50(2) (2004): 178–93. doi.org/10.1111/j.1467-8497.2004.00331.x.

Richmond, Keith. 'Response to the Threat of Communism: The Sane Democracy League and the People's Union of New South Wales.' *Journal of Australian Studies* 1 (1977): 70–84. doi.org/10.1080/14443057709386765.

Richmond, Keith. 'Reaction to Radicalism: Non-Labour Movements, 1920–9.' *Journal of Australian Studies* 5 (1979): 50–63. doi.org/10.1080/144430579 09386799.

Richmond, Keith. 'The New Road to Salvation: Eric Campbell and the Centre Party.' *Journal of the Royal Australian Historical Society* 66(3) (1980): 184–98.

Riedi, Eliza. 'Women, Gender, and the Promotion of Empire: The Victoria League, 1901–1914.' *The Historical Journal* 45(3) (2002): 569–99. doi.org/ 10.1017/s0018246x02002558.

Robinson, Geoffrey. 'The All for Australia League in New South Wales: A Study in Political Entrepreneurship and Hegemony.' *Australian Historical Studies* 39(1) (2008): 36–52. doi.org/10.1080/10314610701837227.

Russell, F.A.A. 'Should Industrial Arbitration Go? The Evolution of Industrial Arbitration.' *Australian Quarterly* [Sydney] 1(2) (June 1929): 38–49.

Simms, Marian. 'Conservative Feminism in Australia: A Case Study of Feminist Ideology.' *Women's Studies International Quarterly* 2(3) (1979): 305–18. doi.org/10.1016/s0148-0685(79)91516-1.

Smart, Judith. '"Principles Do Not Alter, but the Means by Which We Attain Them Change": The Australian Women's National League and Political Citizenship, 1921–1945.' *Women's History Review* 15(1) (2006): 51–68. doi.org/10.1080/09612020500440879.

Spenceley, Geoff. '"The Minister for Starvation": Wilfrid Kent Hughes, Fascism and the Unemployment Relief (Administration) Act of 1933.' *Labour History* 81 (2001): 135–54. doi.org/10.2307/27516808.

Stevens, B.S.B. 'Financial and Economical Outlook.' *Australian Quarterly* [Sydney] 2(1) (March 1930): 16–27.

Trapeznik, Alexander. 'New Zealand's Perceptions of the Russian Revolution of 1917.' *Revolutionary Russia* 19(1) (2006): 63–77. doi.org/10.1080/0954654 0600670142.

Turner, J.A. 'The British Commonwealth Union and the General Election of 1918.' *English Historical Review* 93(368) (1978): 528–59. doi.org/10.1093/ehr/XCIII.CCCLXVIII.528.

van Heyningen, Elizabeth and Pat Merrett. '"The Healing Touch": The Guild of Loyal Women of South Africa 1900–1912.' *South African Historical Journal* 47(1) (2003): 24–50. doi.org/10.1080/02582470208671433.

Ward, Russel. 'Two Kinds of Australian Patriotism.' *Victorian Historical Magazine* 41(1) (1970): 225–43.

Watt, Edward. 'Secession in Western Australia.' *University Studies in Western Australian History* 3 (1958): 43–86.

Williams, J.R. 'Financing Conservative Parties in Australia.' *Australian Quarterly* [Sydney] 43(1) (1971): 7–19. doi.org/10.2307/20634415.

Unpublished theses and conference papers

Allington, Adam. Gold-shirts in God's own? The extreme right in New Zealand during the 1930s Depression. BA Hons diss., Victoria University of Wellington, 2009.

Berzins, Baiba. The social credit movement in Australia to 1940. MA diss., University of New South Wales, Sydney, 1967.

Beveridge, W.A. The Riverina Movement and Charles Hardy. BA Hons diss., University of Sydney, 1954.

Blacklow, Nancy. Regional support for Riverina new state movements in the 1920s and 1930s. BA Hons diss., Charles Sturt University, Wagga Wagga, NSW, 1992.

Bollard, Robert. 'The active chorus': The mass strike of 1917 in eastern Australia. PhD thesis, Victoria University, Melbourne, 2007.

Brockett, Richard. Douglas social credit in Queensland 1929–1939. BA Hons thesis, University of Queensland, Brisbane, 1993. doi.org/10.14264/uql. 2020.341.

Campbell, Gerard. The New Zealand Legion in Otago, 1933–1935. BA Hons diss., University of Otago, Dunedin, NZ, 1987.

Cathcart, Michael. The white army of 1931: Origins and legitimations— The League of National Security in Victoria in 1931 and the means by which it was legitimated. PhD thesis, The Australian National University, Canberra, 1985.

Clifton, Robin. Douglas credit and the Labour Party, 1930–1935. MA diss., Victoria University of Wellington, 1961.

Coward, Dan. The impact of war on New South Wales: Some aspects of social and political history, 1914–1917. PhD diss., The Australian National University, Canberra, 1974.

Cunningham, Matthew. The reactionary and the radical: A comparative analysis of mass conservative mobilisation in Australia and New Zealand during the Great Depression. PhD diss., Victoria University of Wellington, 2015.

Dalton, Sarah. The pure in heart: The New Zealand Women's Christian Temperance Union and social purity, 1885–1930. MA diss., Victoria University of Wellington, 1993.

Darlington, Robert. Was there a significant working class element in the New Guard? Paper presented at the Armies of the Night, Armies of the Right Conference, Macquarie University, Sydney, 25 August 1979.

Dowling, Sarah. Female imperialism: The Victoria League in Canterbury, New Zealand, 1910–2003. MA diss., University of Canterbury, Christchurch, NZ, 2004.

Evans, Richard. William John Mackay and the New South Wales Police Force, 1910–1948: A study of police power. PhD diss., Monash University, Melbourne, 2006.

Francis, Andrew. 'To be truly British we must be anti-German': Patriotism, citizenship and anti-alienism in New Zealand during the Great War. PhD diss., Victoria University of Wellington, 2009.

Hughes, V. Massey's Cossacks: The farmers and the 1913 strike. MA diss., University of Auckland, 1977.

James, Paul. Militarism and loyalty: Civilian paramilitary movements in Melbourne during the interwar period. BA Hons diss., University of Melbourne, 1980.

James, Stephen A. 'The big hand of service': The Citizens' League of South Australia, 1930–1934—Origins, ideology and policy. BA Hons diss., University of Melbourne, 1986.

La Rooij, Marinus. Political antisemitism in New Zealand during the Great Depression: A case study in the myth of the Jewish world conspiracy. MA diss., Victoria University of Wellington, 1998.

Littlewood, David. 'Should he serve?' The Military Service Boards' operations in the Wellington Provincial District, 1916–1918. MA diss., Massey University, Palmerston North, NZ, 2010.

Lloyd, C.J. The formation and development of the U.A.P., 1929–1937. PhD diss., The Australian National University, Canberra, 1984.

Lonie, John. Conservatism and class in South Australia during the Depression years, 1929–34. MA diss., University of Adelaide, 1973.

McAloon, Jim. Militarist campaigns in New Zealand c. 1899–1914: Trade and imperialism. Paper presented at the New Zealand Historical Association Conference, Wellington, 1996.

McKinnon, Malcolm. Funny about money? Paper presented at the Reserve Bank of New Zealand Museum, Wellington, 24 July 2012.

McLachlan, Ben Thomas. In search of a New Zealand populism: Heresthetics, character and populist political leadership. MA diss., Victoria University of Wellington, 2013.

Milnes, Dickon John. The church militant: Dunedin churches and society during WWI. PhD diss., University of Otago, Dunedin, NZ, 2015.

Moore, Andrew. 'Send lawyers, guns and money': A study of conservative paramilitary organisations in New South Wales, 1930–1932—Background and sequel, 1917–1952. PhD diss., La Trobe University, Melbourne, 1982.

Moores, Harold. The rise of the Protestant Political Association: Sectarianism in New Zealand during World War I. MA diss., University of Auckland, 1966.

O'Mara, J. Guarding Five Dock: A study of the Five Dock locality of the New Guard, 1931–1935. BA Hons diss., University of Western Sydney, 1997.

Orwin, David. Conservatism in New Zealand. PhD diss., University of Auckland, 1999.

Penati, Beatrice. Anticommunism and empire in China (1924–1939): A transnational network among Shanghailanders and Russian emigres. Final research note, research internship, Hokkaido University, Sapporo, 2008.

Peter, Phyllis. Social aspects of the Depression in New South Wales, 1930–1934. PhD diss., The Australian National University, Canberra, 1964.

Piesse, Sarah Jane. Patriotic welfare in Otago: A history of the Otago Patriotic and General Welfare Association 1914–1950 and the Otago Provincial Patriotic Council 1939–. MA diss., University of Otago, Dunedin, NZ, 1981.

Priday, Chris. Sane Democracy in New South Wales 1920–1940. BA Hons diss., Macquarie University, Sydney, 1975.

Pugh, Michael C. The New Zealand Legion and conservative protest in the Great Depression. MA diss., University of Auckland, 1969.

Reid, Stephen. The New Guard in decline: Eric Campbell and the Centre Party, 1933–1935. BA Hons diss., Macquarie University, Sydney, 1980.

Saleam, James. The other radicalism: An inquiry into contemporary Australian extreme right ideology, politics and organization 1975–1995. PhD diss., University of Sydney, 1999.

Satchell, Max. Pulpit politics: The Protestant Political Association in Dunedin from 1917 to 1922. BA Hons diss., University of Otago, Dunedin, NZ, 1983.

Schauble, John. Right-wing militancy in Australia: The rise of the League of National Security. BA Hons diss., University of Melbourne, 1979.

Sweetman, Rory M. New Zealand Catholicism, war, politics and the Irish issue 1912–1922. PhD diss., University of Cambridge, 1990.

Thomas, Ian. Confronting the challenge of socialism: The British Empire Union and the National Citizens' Union, 1917–1927. MA diss., University of Wolverhampton, 2010.

Thompson, Michael J. Government and depression in South Australia, 1927 to 1934. MEc diss., Flinders University, Adelaide, 1972.

Tully, William. The New Guard of New South Wales, 1931–1932. BA Hons diss., The Australian National University, Canberra, 1974.

Tuziak, Peter. Riverina awake! A history of the Riverina Movement. BA Hons diss., University of Sydney, 1990.

van der Krogt, Christopher John. More a part than apart: The Catholic community in New Zealand society, 1918–1940. PhD diss., Massey University, Palmerston North, NZ, 1994.

Wait, R.N. Reactions to demonstrations and riots in Adelaide 1928–1932. MA diss., University of Adelaide, 1973.

Ward, Elizabeth. The New Zealand Legion in Manawatu–Wanganui, 1933–1935. BA Hons diss., Massey University, Palmerston North, NZ, 2011.

Ward, Liz. 'For light and liberty': The origins and early development of the Reform Party, 1887–1915. PhD diss., Massey University, Palmerston North, NZ, 2018.

Watson, James. Crisis and change: Economic crisis and technological change between the World Wars, with special reference to Christchurch, 1926–36. PhD diss., University of Canterbury, Christchurch, NZ, 1984.

Watt, Edward. Western separation: The history of the secession movement in Western Australia, 1918–1935. MA diss., University of Western Australia, Perth, 1957.

Webb, L.C. Rise of the Reform Party: A history of party politics in New Zealand between 1910 and 1920. MA diss., Victoria University of Wellington, 1928.

Woolmington, E.R. The geographical scope of support for the new state movement in northern N.S.W. PhD diss., University of New England, Armidale, NSW, 1963.

Electronic resources

Antill, J.M. 'Gibson, Alexander James (1876–1960).' *Australian Dictionary of Biography*, National Centre of Biography, The Australian National University, first published in hardcopy 1981. Available from: adb.anu.edu.au/biography/gibson-alexander-james-6306.

Balderstone, Susan M. 'Henderson, Kingsley Anketell (1883–1942).' *Australian Dictionary of Biography*, National Centre of Biography, The Australian National University, published first in hardcopy 1983. Available from: adb.anu.edu.au/biography/henderson-kingsley-anketell-6634.

Barrett, John. 'Campbell, Gerald Ross (1858–1942).' *Australian Dictionary of Biography*, National Centre of Biography, The Australian National University, published first in hardcopy 1979. Available from: adb.anu.edu.au/biography/campbell-gerald-ross-5489.

Bassett, Michael. 'Ward, Joseph George.' *Dictionary of New Zealand Biography*, first published in 1993. *Te Ara: The Encyclopedia of New Zealand*. Available from: www.teara.govt.nz/en/biographies/2w9/1.

Bassett, Michael. 'Coates, Joseph Gordon.' *Dictionary of New Zealand Biography*, first published in 1996. *Te Ara: The Encyclopedia of New Zealand*. Available from: www.teara.govt.nz/en/biographies/3c24/1.

Blavatsky, H.P. *The Key to Theosophy*. Pasadena, CA: Theosophical University Press Online Edition. Available from: www.theosociety.org/pasadena/key/key-3.htm.

Borchardt, D.H. 'Knox, Sir Robert Wilson (1890–1973).' *Australian Dictionary of Biography*, National Centre of Biography, The Australian National University, published first in hardcopy 1983. Available from: adb.anu.edu.au/biography/knox-sir-robert-wilson-6993.

Cain, Neville. 'Theodore, Edward Granville (1884–1950).' *Australian Dictionary of Biography*, National Centre of Biography, The Australian National University, published first in hardcopy 1990. Available from: adb.anu.edu.au/biography/theodore-edward-granville-8776.

Cook, B. 'Dixson, Sir Hugh (1841–1926).' *Australian Dictionary of Biography*, National Centre of Biography, The Australian National University, published first in hardcopy 1981. Available from: adb.anu.edu.au/biography/dixson-sir-hugh-5983.

Easton, Brian. 'Economy: Agricultural Production.' *Te Ara: The Encyclopedia of New Zealand*, updated 16 September 2016. Available from: www.TeAra.govt.nz/en/diagram/4236/percentage-of-employment-in-different-sectors-1841-2001.

Gardner, W.J. 'Forbes, George William.' *Dictionary of New Zealand Biography*, first published in 1996. *Te Ara: The Encyclopedia of New Zealand*. Available from: www.teara.govt.nz/en/biographies/3f9/1.

Geeves, Philip. 'Bennett, Alfred Edward (1889–1963).' *Australian Dictionary of Biography*, National Centre of Biography, The Australian National University, published first in hardcopy 1979. Available from: adb.anu.edu.au/biography/bennett-alfred-edward-5207.

Goldstone, Paul. 'Lane, William.' *New Zealand Dictionary of Biography*, first published in 1996. *Te Ara: The Encyclopedia of New Zealand*. Available from: www.teara.govt.nz/en/biographies/3l3/1.

Hart, P.R. and C.J. Lloyd. 'Lyons, Joseph Aloysius (Joe) (1879–1939).' *Australian Dictionary of Biography*, National Centre of Biography, The Australian National University, published first in hardcopy 1986. Available from: adb.anu.edu.au/biography/lyons-joseph-aloysius-joe-7278.

Hugo, Graeme. 'A Century of Population Change in Australia.' *Year Book Australia, 2001*. Cat. no. 1301.0. Canberra: Australian Bureau of Statistics, 2001. Available from: www.abs.gov.au/Ausstats/abs@.nsf/0/0B82C2F2654C3694CA2569DE002139D9?Open.

Jones, Helen. 'Rees George, Madeline (1851–1931).' *Australian Dictionary of Biography*, National Centre of Biography, The Australian National University, published first in hardcopy 1981. Available from: adb.anu.edu.au/biography/george-madeline-rees-6296.

Lonie, John. 'Bagot, Edward Daniel (1893–1968).' *Australian Dictionary of Biography*, National Centre of Biography, The Australian National University, published first in hardcopy 1979. Available from: adb.anu.edu.au/biography/bagot-edward-daniel-5091.

Nairn, Bede. 'Robertson, Sir John (1816–1891).' *Australian Dictionary of Biography*, National Centre of Biography, The Australian National University, published first in hardcopy 1976. Available from: adb.anu.edu.au/biography/robertson-sir-john-4490.

National Archives of Australia. 'James Scullin.' *Australia's Prime Ministers*. Canberra: National Archives of Australia. Available from: www.naa.gov.au/explore-collection/australias-prime-ministers/james-scullin.

National Archives of Australia. 'Joseph Lyons.' *Australia's Prime Ministers*. Canberra: National Archives of Australia. Available from: www.naa.gov.au/explore-collection/australias-prime-ministers/joseph-lyons.

National Library of Australia. 'Australian Recruitment Statistics for World War I.' *Learning Resources*. Canberra: National Library of Australia. Available from: www.naa.gov.au/learn/learning-resources/learning-resource-themes/war/world-war-i/australian-recruitment-statistics-world-war-i.

National Museum of Australia. 'James Scullin.' *Prime Ministers of Australia*. Canberra: National Museum of Australia. Available from: www.nma.gov.au/primeministers/james_scullin.

Norris, R. 'Deakin, Alfred (1856–1919).' *Australian Dictionary of Biography*, National Centre of Biography, The Australian National University, published first in hardcopy 1981. Available from: adb.anu.edu.au/biography/deakin-alfred-5927

Olssen, Erik. 'Paul, John Thomas.' *Dictionary of New Zealand Biography*, first published in 1996. *Te Ara: The Encyclopedia of New Zealand*. Available from: www.teara.govt.nz/en/biographies/3p16/1.

Patrick, Alison. 'Brookes, Herbert Robinson (1867–1963).' *Australian Dictionary of Biography*, National Centre of Biography, The Australian National University, published first in hardcopy 1979. Available from: adb.anu.edu.au/biography/brookes-herbert-robinson-5372.

Smart, Judith. 'Women's Non-Party Political Organisations.' *The Encyclopedia of Women and Leadership in Twentieth-Century Australia*. Australian Women's Archives Project, 2014. Available from: www.womenaustralia.info/leaders/biogs/WLE0693b.htm.

Stace, F. Nigel. 'Ferguson, William.' *Dictionary of New Zealand Biography*, first published in 1996. *Te Ara: The Encyclopedia of New Zealand.* Available from: www.teara.govt.nz/en/biographies/3f4/1.

Strahan, Frank. 'Ricketson, Staniforth (1891–1967).' *Australian Dictionary of Biography*, National Centre of Biography, The Australian National University, published first in hardcopy 2002. Available from: adb.anu.edu.au/biography/ricketson-staniforth-11521.

Taylor, Kerry. 'McLaren, David.' *Dictionary of New Zealand Biography*, first published in 1996. *Te Ara: The Encyclopedia of New Zealand.* Available from: www.teara.govt.nz/en/biographies/3m22/1.

'The Depression Riots, 1932.' *An Encyclopedia of New Zealand*, edited by A.H. McLintock, originally published in 1966. *Te Ara: The Encyclopedia of New Zealand.* Available from: www.teara.govt.nz/en/1966/riots/6.

The Theosophical Society in Australia. 'Theosophy in New Zealand, 1908–2006.' Last modified on 16 March 2012. Available from: www.austheos.org.au/indices/TINNZ_.HTM.

Webby, Elizabeth. 'Lawson, William (Will) (1876–1957).' *Australian Dictionary of Biography*, National Centre of Biography, The Australian National University, published first in hardcopy 1986. Available from: adb.anu.edu.au/biography/lawson-william-will-7122.

'Women and the Vote: The National Council of Women.' *New Zealand History.* Wellington: Ministry for Culture and Heritage, updated 13 March 2018. Available from: www.nzhistory.net.nz/politics/womens-suffrage/national-council-of-women.

'Women Fundraising for Belgium, First World War.' *New Zealand History.* Wellington: Ministry for Culture and Heritage, updated 17 May 2017. Available from: www.nzhistory.net.nz/media/photo/womens-fundraising.

Wright, Susan. *A Short Electoral History of the Sydney City Council, 1842–1992.* Sydney: City of Sydney. Accessed from: www.cityofsydney.nsw.gov.au/__data/assets/pdf_file/0011/65549/hs_chos_electoral_history.pdf [page discontinued].

www.ingramcontent.com/pod-product-compliance
Lightning Source LLC
Chambersburg PA
CBHW040154270326
41929CB00041B/3399